Family Experiments

Middle-class, professional families in
Australia and New Zealand c. 1880–1920

Family Experiments

Middle-class, professional families in
Australia and New Zealand c. 1880–1920

SHELLEY RICHARDSON

Australian
National
University

PRESS

Published by ANU Press
The Australian National University
Acton ACT 2601, Australia
Email: anupress@anu.edu.au
This title is also available online at press.anu.edu.au

National Library of Australia Cataloguing-in-Publication entry

Creator: Richardson, Shelley, author.

Title: Family experiments : middle-class, professional families in
                     Australia and New Zealand c 1880–1920 /
                     Shelley Richardson.

ISBN: 9781760460587 (paperback) 9781760460594 (ebook)

Series: ANU lives series in biography.

Subjects: Middle class families--Australia--Biography.
                     Middle class families--New Zealand--Biography.
                     Immigrant families--Australia--Biography.
                     Immigrant families--New Zealand--Biography.

Dewey Number: 306.85092

The ANU.Lives Series in Biography is an initiative of the National Centre of Biography at The Australian National University, ncb.anu.edu.au.

Cover design and layout by ANU Press. Photograph adapted from: flic.kr/p/fkMKbm by Blue Mountains Local Studies.

Contents

List of Illustrations

List of Abbreviations

ADB	*The Australian Dictionary of Biography*
AFW	Anthony Wilding
AFWLED	Life Events Diary of Anthony Wilding
ALP	Alexander Leeper Papers
CMDRC	Canterbury Museum Documentary Research Centre
CWLED	Life Events Diary of Cora Wilding
DNZB	*The Dictionary of New Zealand Biography*
DOMFP	David Orme Masson Family Papers
GW	Gladys Wilding
GWLED	Life Events Diary of Gladys Wilding
HBHP	Henry Bournes Higgins Papers
HT	*The Hereford Times*
HWRO	Hereford and Worcester Country Record Office
JMBP	John Macmillan Brown Papers
JW	Julia Wilding
JWED	Julia Wilding's Events Diary/Diaries
JWHD	Julia Wilding's Household Diary/Diaries
LED	Life Event Diary/Diaries
NLA	National Library of Australia
NZJH	*The New Zealand Journal of History*
WFP	Wilding Family Papers

Acknowledgements

I have many people to thank for their help and support over the course of researching and writing this book. Firstly, I am extremely grateful to Trinity College, University of Melbourne, for allowing me access to the Alexander Leeper Papers, and their archivists and Leeper librarians, past and present, who facilitated my research so readily: Gail Watt, Kitty Vroomen, Hazel Nsair, Nina Waters and Ben Thomas. My thanks go also to the staff of the University of Melbourne Archives; the Stonnington History Centre, Malvern; the National Library of Australia manuscripts department, Canberra; the Macmillan Brown Library at the University of Canterbury, Christchurch and the Canterbury Museum Documentary Research Centre, Christchurch. All provided me with friendly and knowledgeable assistance. John Poynter, Marion Poynter, James Grant and Richard Selleck also steered me in the right direction as I began my research into the Leeper and Masson families.

This book began life as a PhD thesis carried out at The Australian National University's School of History. In this regard I am extremely grateful to my former supervisors, Professors Melanie Nolan, Nicholas Brown and Stuart Macintyre, for their generous and expert guidance. My thanks also go to everyone at the National Centre of Biography, where I was based while a student, for their support, encouragement and friendship. Karen Smith also provided me with a great deal of assistance.

It is frequently said that historians stand on the shoulders of those who have gone before them. In particular, I gratefully acknowledge biographers John Poynter, Marion Poynter, John Rickard, Len Weickhardt and Margaret Lovell-Smith, whose works provided a starting point for my own. Historian Jim Gardner did not live to see this book published but he was there at the start of the project injecting it with his typical enthusiasm. Hopefully he would have approved of the end result. His ideas have certainly influenced my own.

Special thanks are due also to Chris Connolly, Luke Trainor and Graeme Dunstall, who have always shown an interest in my work since my earliest student days at the University of Canterbury, and have assisted me in various ways with this book.

Many thanks to ANU Press for agreeing to publish my work and to the publishing team who saw it through to fruition. Thank you also to the ANU Publication Subsidy Committee for their generosity in providing me with a grant to assist with copy editing costs. I gratefully acknowledge the assistance of Malcolm Allbrook, who guided me through the early stages of the publishing process, and Geoff Hunt's patient and thorough copyediting. Any mistakes are, of course, my own. Every effort has been made to locate copyright owners where appropriate.

Finally, I owe my deepest gratitude to my family, who have encouraged and supported me through earthquakes and more minor crises, to complete this book. I could not have done it without them.

Introduction

In 1978, when Erik Olssen wrote the essay 'Towards a History of the European Family in New Zealand', he did so believing 'that the history of the family provides the missing link ... between the study of culture and the study of social structure, production and power'.[1] Some 20 years later he observed that 'gender' and 'gendering' had, in the intervening years, 'increasingly supplanted "women" and "family" on the research agenda'.[2] One aspect of this recent trend towards a gendered approach to history is a focus on masculinity and femininity as relational constructs. It is therefore something of a paradox that, even though the family has been recognised 'as a primary site where gender is constructed', it has not attracted 'greater interest' in New Zealand and, by extension, Australia.[3] British historian John Tosh observed that 'once the focus shifted to the structure of gender relations, rather than the experience of one sex, the family could be analysed comprehensively as a system, embracing all levels of power, dependence and intimacy'.[4] Leonore Davidoff and Catherine Hall produced such a work, *Family Fortunes: Men and Women of the English Middle Class, 1780–1850*, in 1987.[5] Historians of Australia and New Zealand have been slow to follow the British historians' lead; the family as a social dynamic has been squeezed to

---

1   Erik Olssen, 'Families and the Gendering of European New Zealand in the Colonial Period, 1840–80', in Caroline Daley and Deborah Montgomerie (eds), *The Gendered Kiwi*, Auckland University Press, Auckland, 1999, p. 37; Erik Olssen and Andrée Lévesque, 'Towards a History of the European Family in New Zealand', in Peggy G. Koopman-Boyden (ed.), *Families in New Zealand Society*, Methuen, Wellington, 1978, pp. 1–25.
2   Olssen, 'Families and the Gendering of European New Zealand', p. 37.
3   Olssen, 'Families and the Gendering of European New Zealand', p. 37.
4   John Tosh, *A Man's Place: Masculinity and the Middle-Class Home in Victorian England* [1999], 2nd edn, Yale University Press, New Haven and London, 2007, p. 2.
5   Leonore Davidoff and Catherine Hall, *Family Fortunes: Men and Women of the English Middle Class, 1780–1850*, Hutchinson, London, 1987.

the margins of historical concern. Even less interest has been shown in the role of the elite middle-class family in shaping Australasian society.

This book sets out to explore middle-class family life in two Australasian cities in the late nineteenth and early twentieth centuries. It does so through the experience of five families constructed in the 1880s and 1890s, within the marriages of male British migrants in professional occupations. It seeks to uncover the understandings and expectations of family that they brought with them from the old world as individuals, and to trace the evolution of these ideas as they endeavoured to turn ideals into reality. The close textual analysis necessary to reveal how family life was envisaged and experienced requires strong archival records and dictates a small sample. Christchurch and Melbourne provide significant sets of family archives that allow such close historical interrogation from within a similar occupational band (lawyers and academics), whose members saw themselves, and were seen by others, as part of the colonial intellectual community.

Put simply, and to prefigure an argument throughout the book, for this generation of professional newcomers, the migrant/colonial experience was empowering. The timeliness of their arrival and the generally favourable economic circumstances of their establishment years brought public prominence and bred confidence. They secured a level of financial security that allowed for a comfortable, though not luxurious lifestyle, supported by a small domestic staff. Success fanned the hopes of starting anew that had accompanied the migration and encouraged a sense of cautious social experiment within their attempts to build a colonial family. Nowhere more apparent than in the education of their children, this desire for change, prefigured within the family, is a central concern of this work. Through a close study of a small slice of professional middle-class experience, it throws light on the range of meanings that were invested in family life in late nineteenth- and early twentieth-century Australasia.

* * *

A feature of the emergent middle class in the latter part of the nineteenth century was its rapidly expanding professional segment. This expansion rested upon migrant families from provincial British towns and cities, attracted by what they saw as the more congenial nature of Australasia's urban frontier. Economic and urban historians have noted that new world cities developed a distinctive suburban character.[6] 'Commercial' cities rather than industrial ones, they typically exhibited a low population density that was widely dispersed and permitted the existence of big homes of a semirural character. Such cities appealed to a segment of provincial middle-class professionals who valued retaining something of the rural lifestyle becoming increasingly difficult to preserve in the old world. No Australasian city matched Melbourne in attractiveness to middle-class families seeking the amenities of the city in a context that had not extinguished the virtues of suburbia. The conduit for British investment in pastoralism, manufacturing and mining in Victoria and beyond, Melbourne became the destination of most of a wave of British migrants, which deposited 40,000 newcomers in the city in 1888 alone.[7]

While 'Marvellous Melbourne' grew too quickly and was already exhibiting many of the evils associated with older British cities in the 1880s, it was still able to satisfy the middle-class suburban dream.[8] In New Zealand, such families were drawn in large numbers to the Wakefieldian cities, and especially to Christchurch and Dunedin. Whatever the failings of the systematic colonisers, it was the Wakefieldian ideal, with its stress upon concentrated settlement, as much as any compelling economic consideration, that determined the location and the suburban nature of the city of Christchurch as it emerged in the second half of the nineteenth century. The Wakefieldian influence may have been less pronounced in Dunedin, but, as Olssen comments, it shared with 'Marvellous Melbourne' a slower 'transition from pre-industrial community to modern city' that proved fertile ground for the suburban ideal.[9]

---

6   Lionel Frost, *The New Urban Frontier: Urbanisation and City Building in Australasia and the American West*, New South Wales University Press, Kensington, 1991; Trevor Burnard, 'An Artisanal Town: The Economic Sinews of Christchurch', in John Cookson and Graeme Dunstall (eds), *Southern Capital Christchurch: Towards a City Biography 1850–2000*, Canterbury University Press, Christchurch, 2000, pp. 115–37.

7   Stuart Macintyre, *A Colonial Liberalism: The Lost World of Three Visionaries*, Oxford University Press, Melbourne, 1991, p. 170.

8   See Graeme Davison, *The Rise and Fall of Marvellous Melbourne* [1978], 3rd edn, Melbourne University Press, Melbourne, 1981; Bernard Barrett, *The Inner Suburbs: The Evolution of an Industrial Area*, Melbourne, 1971; Sean Glynn, *Urbanisation in Australian History, 1788–1900*, Nelson, Melbourne, 1970.

9   Erik Olssen, *A History of Otago*, John McIndoe, Dunedin, 1984, p. 102.

The Australasian 'commercial city' was not only born suburban, it was born and remained, in the nineteenth and early twentieth centuries, a British city.[10] Christchurch can be seen as something of an exemplar. The Wakefieldian settlement had never been heavily masculine in the manner commonly associated with new world pioneering communities. By 1881 its population of 30,000 was demographically mature and ethnically homogeneous. A city of families, 40 per cent of the residents were native born, 63.5 per cent of its 'foreign' component was English born, and more than three-quarters came from England, Scotland or Wales. Moreover, as was typical of the commercial city, Christchurch managed to submerge social tensions in the mutual interdependence of its professional and artisanal elements. The middle-class suburban dream rested upon the existence of a stable and well-paid body of craftsmen able to realise a level of home ownership and independence that allowed them to share in the ideal they helped build. In social terms, this was to produce a city housing landscape with a low level of segregation and thus an environment that satisfied the desire of many of the professional middle class to contain, if not obliterate, the social evils and degradation that marred the cities of the old world.[11]

Historians on both sides of the Tasman acknowledge the relative ease with which British middle-class professional families, arriving in the third quarter of the nineteenth century, found a niche among the colonial elite. Stuart Macintyre has suggested that in Australian cities, while it was becoming increasingly difficult to enter the 'moneyed circle', wealth was still able to command entry.[12] The professions, as he points out, offered an 'alternative' pathway: doctors and lawyers, followed by architects and engineers, were able to meld readily into the ranks of the elite.[13] Indeed, 'in a society with little regard for inherited privilege or prestige', such professions 'enjoyed an exaggerated influence'. It was an influence, moreover, that extended

10   Nicholas Brown, 'Born Modern: Antipodean Variations on a Theme', *The Historical Journal*, vol. 48, part 4, 2005, pp. 1139–54.

11   See W. David McIntyre, 'Outwards and Upwards: Building the City', in Cookson and Dunstall (eds), *Southern Capital*, pp. 85–114; Jim McAloon, 'Radical Christchurch', in *Southern Capital*, pp. 162–92; Jim McAloon, 'The Christchurch Elite', in *Southern Capital*, pp. 193–221; Burnard, 'Artisanal Town', in *Southern Capital*, pp. 115–37.

12   Stuart Macintyre, *The Oxford History of Australia, Volume 4, 1901–1942: The Succeeding Age*, Oxford University Press, Melbourne, p. 51.

13   Macintyre, *Oxford History of Australia, Volume 4*, pp. 51–53.

to the political arena. When the first Federal Parliament assembled in Australia in 1901, a quarter of its members were lawyers, and its first cabinet drew two-thirds of its members from the legal fraternity.[14]

The political involvement of the legal fraternity and urban professionals was not as obvious in New Zealand. As W. J. Gardner has put it, the years between 1890 and the mid-1920s constitute the 'classic period of small-farmer predominance' in politics.[15] By his estimate, small-farmer representation stood at 25 per cent in 1893 and reached about 35 per cent in the 1922–5 parliament. If farming was the most common occupation of the parliamentarians, the Liberal Party that controlled the government benches was essentially, as David Hamer described it, 'the party of the towns and especially of the urban frontier'.[16] For newspaper editors and proprietors, businessmen and land agents, all of them joined in town-boosting, politics was an extension of the business of a town; they loomed large in party ranks and played the critical role in the articulation of party policy. City support for their policies was grounded in consensus around the need for closer settlement of country areas as a means of halting the drift of the population to the cities and averting old world evils such as unemployment, destitution and congestion. The search for social harmony held particular appeal for the middle-class professional families in their suburban enclaves, who formed the basis of the Liberal Party's alliance with urban labour.[17] Between 1896 and 1914, the presence of lawyers and solicitors in the House of Representatives had increased markedly from 5 to 13 of its 76 members. At the outbreak of war they were the second largest occupational group and constituted 17 per cent of the New Zealand Parliament.[18]

If the New Zealand political environment did not give lawyers quite the parliamentary presence they attained in Australia at the outset of the twentieth century, its ethos was a broadly congenial one. Jim McAloon's definitive study of the wealthy in the Wakefieldian South Island settlements of Canterbury and Otago provides an

---

14 Macintyre, *Oxford History of Australia, Volume 4*, p. 52.
15 W. J. Gardner, *The Farmer Politician in New Zealand History*, Massey Memorial Lecture 1970, Massey University Occasional Publication No. 3, Palmerston North, 1970, pp. 3–4.
16 David Hamer, *The New Zealand Liberals: The Years of Power, 1891–1912*, Auckland University Press, Auckland, 1988, p. 150.
17 Hamer, *The New Zealand Liberals*, pp. 150–94.
18 *New Zealand Official Year Book*, 1915, pp. 343–44.

illustration of the status the middle-class professional family was able to attain in nineteenth-century New Zealand.[19] As he sees it, the original intentions of the systematic colonisers were 'explicitly elitist'. Their ideal male colonists were to be 'English, Anglican, educated at Oxford or Cambridge'.[20] In the new world they expected to be accorded a status similar to that which they enjoyed at 'Home'. Such exclusivity was unable to be maintained in the face of colonial realities that demanded different attributes and greater versatility. At first the crucial division in society was that between 'land purchasers', designated as 'colonists', and 'labouring emigrants'.[21] As a category, 'colonist' was flexible enough to encompass newcomers but, in McAloon's view, they and their families provided until 1914, and perhaps until the 1940s, the core of the Canterbury and Otago elites.

Around this landowning circle clustered the professionals, who, in one way or another, were essential to the servicing of a pastoral economy. Its more prominent members were bankers, land agents, financiers and lawyers. Within the city their residences defined 'enclaves' that tended to maintain exclusiveness.[22] The men who dominated the membership of the city's most exclusive club were prominent among provincial and then colonial politics, were the gatekeepers of the city's educational institutions and the powerful voices behind the local press. Some indication of the collective social influence of the group is captured in McAloon's characterisation of the typical male member of the elite: 'a lawyer, merchant, bank manager, large-scale farmer or manufacturer, a member of the Christchurch Club, the Provincial Council, the House of Representatives and the A & P Association, a Governor of Canterbury College and a Fellow of Christ's College—and therefore Anglican'.[23] Like all typologies, McAloon acknowledges a degree of fluidity, a capacity to remake itself as changing social circumstances demanded and, above all, an ability to accommodate those who might not satisfy all requirements.[24]

---

19   Jim McAloon, *No Idle Rich: The Wealthy in Canterbury and Otago 1840–1914*, University of Otago Press, Dunedin, 2002.
20   McAloon, 'The Christchurch Elite', p. 194.
21   McAloon, 'The Christchurch Elite', p. 195.
22   McAloon, 'The Christchurch Elite', p. 205.
23   McAloon, 'The Christchurch Elite', p. 197.
24   The same fluidity is noted by Erik Olssen and Clyde Griffen with Frank Jones, *An Accidental Utopia? Social Mobility and the Foundations of an Egalitarian Society, 1880–1940*, Otago University Press, Dunedin, 2011, especially pp. 181–82, 192–94.

The extent to which the consolidation of this colonial elite gave birth to a distinctive class structure has been the subject of considerable recent historical debate. While only its broadest outline is relevant here, it is a debate that is critical to the understanding of the elite family, whether rural or urban. It is a debate, moreover, grounded in a historiographical context in which the layering of colonial society was rarely couched in class terms. The dominant view was that the early achievement of male suffrage, a high degree of social mobility and relatively unrestricted access to land produced something very close to an open society. Similarly, relations between capital and labour were moderated by the peculiarities of a colonial environment characterised by a relatively scattered and transient workforce and the small scale of its enterprises that readily allowed workmen to become 'little masters'.[25]

Miles Fairburn's influential *The Ideal Society and its Enemies* (1989) provides an interpretation of the foundation of modern New Zealand society from 1850 to 1890, in which class all but disappears as a feature of colonial life.[26] By his account, in the second half of the nineteenth century, New Zealand spawned a distinctive colonial ideology that enshrined bourgeois individualism.[27] At its core was an 'assumption' that independence could be achieved 'outside a social framework' and 'did not depend on collaboration, mutuality [or] collective arrangements'.[28] Significantly, the only exception Fairburn allows to this charter of self-reliance is the family.[29] It is a critical exception and one that has drawn comment. The family, as McAloon writes, 'was absolutely crucial to bourgeois identity and economic mobilisation'.[30] The espousal by self-reliant individuals of their professed ideal, the classless society, did not so much provide evidence of its achievement, argues McAloon, as illustrate 'the class consciousness' of colonial capitalism.[31] The effective neglect of the colonial professional elite is more pronounced in the New Zealand historical literature than in

---

25   Jim McAloon, 'Class in Colonial New Zealand: Towards a Historiographical Rehabilitation', *New Zealand Journal of History (NZJH)*, vol. 38, no. 1, 2004, pp. 3–21.
26   Miles Fairburn, *The Ideal Society and its Enemies: The Foundations of Modern New Zealand Society 1850–1900*, Auckland University Press, Auckland, 1989.
27   Fairburn, *The Ideal Society*, pp. 50–52.
28   Fairburn, *The Ideal Society*, pp. 50–51.
29   Fairburn, *The Ideal Society*, pp. 51, 56–57, 111–12, 163, 198–200.
30   McAloon, 'Class in Colonial New Zealand', p. 13.
31   McAloon, 'Class in Colonial New Zealand', p. 14.

its Australian counterpart.[32] Nevertheless, there is no comprehensive history of this group in either New Zealand or Australia, let alone the Australasian region. This study of middle-class urban professional families in New Zealand and Australia between 1880 and 1920 is a small step in the process of filling this gap.

That the debate about the role of class in New Zealand history should turn, in part, on the role of the bourgeois family also underlines the need for deeper analysis of such families in their own right and as a social entity. McAloon's study of the wealthy in Canterbury and Otago provides a starting point and demonstrates the making of a distinct colonial middle class of considerable coherence and longevity. As a group the emergent colonial elites of Otago and Canterbury, McAloon suggests, remained relatively open to newcomers. He presents a range of social markers likely to provide admission to its ranks. Being British mattered; arriving with some capital helped; a professional occupation was useful, as was Anglicanism. Neither individually nor collectively, however, did these attributes guarantee acceptance. Closer exploration of the nature of middle-class family life and the social relationships that developed between elite and would-be elite families offers a perhaps more nuanced way of understanding how this accommodation between newcomers and the colonial establishment was negotiated.[33]

It is still possible to write a general history of New Zealand without direct reference to the family as an institution.[34] Its discussion tends to be subsumed under feminism, the suffrage campaigns and the demographic and racial concerns that underlay colonial definitions of motherhood. Such an emphasis tells us much about the perceptions of the family in settler societies. To a degree, it is grounded in the separate 'spheres ideology' with its rigidly defined public and private worlds. In heavily male-dominated colonial societies, the boundary between these two worlds readily became, as Macintyre has pointed

32   For example, John Higley, Desley Deacon and Don Smart, with the collaboration of Robert G. Cushing, Gwen Moore and Jan Pakulski, *Elites in Australia*, Routledge and K. Paul, London and Boston, 1979; Desley Deacon, *Managing Gender: The State, the New Middle Class and Women Workers 1830–1930*, Oxford University Press, Melbourne, 1989; John Hirst, *Sense and Nonsense in Australian History*, Black Inc. Agenda, Melbourne, 2005, pp. 149–73; Paul de Serville, *Pounds and Pedigrees: The Upper Class in Victoria*, Oxford University Press, Melbourne, 1991.
33   McAloon, *No Idle Rich*; McAloon, 'The Christchurch Elite'.
34   Philippa Mein Smith, *A Concise History of New Zealand*, Cambridge University Press, Cambridge and New York, 2005.

out, a gender boundary.[35] So pervasive were the evils of the new world male frontiers that women, it was argued, needed to be protected from them and this was best achieved within the private sphere, where they could cultivate the 'higher morality of their sex'.[36] Colonial feminists of the late nineteenth century generally chose to build their suffrage campaigns around this assertion of difference. This 'private sphere feminism' accepted, for the most part, the segregation of the sexes and sought to raise the status and authority of women within the family. From this base, they were able to set their sights upon the public sphere. If this involved a conscious strategy, then historians of women's suffrage acknowledge a correlation between women's mobilisation as moral reformers and the achievement of the vote.[37]

Historians of women's suffrage in Australasia have stressed—and perhaps exaggerated—the middle-class nature of first-wave feminism.[38] Its leading advocates are frequently presented as part 'new woman' and part 'colonial helpmeet', thus exhibiting both public and private

---

35   Macintyre, *A Colonial Liberalism*, p. 203.
36   Macintyre, *A Colonial Liberalism*, p. 203–4.
37   Raewyn Dalziel, 'The Colonial Helpmeet: Women's Role and the Vote in Nineteenth-Century New Zealand', *NZJH*, vol. 11, no. 2, October 1977, pp. 112–23; Phillida Bunkle, 'The Origins of the Woman's Movement in New Zealand: The Women's Christian Temperance Union 1885–1895', in Phillida Bunkle and Beryl Hughes (eds), *Women in New Zealand Society*, George Allen & Unwin, Sydney, 1980, pp. 52–76; Patricia Grimshaw, *Women's Suffrage in New Zealand Society*, Auckland University Press, Auckland, 1972; Mein Smith, *A Concise History of New Zealand*, pp. 102–5; Audrey Oldfield, *Woman Suffrage in Australia: A Gift or a Struggle?*, Cambridge University Press, Cambridge and Melbourne, 1992; Judith A. Allen, *Rose Scott: Vision and Revision in Feminism*, Oxford University Press, Melbourne, 1994; Susan Magarey, *Unbridling the Tongues of Women: A Biography of Catherine Helen Spence*, Hale & Iremonger, Sydney, 1985; Marilyn Lake, 'The Politics of Respectability: Identifying the Masculinist Context', in Susan Magarey, Sue Rowley and Susan Sheridan (eds), *Debutante Nations: Feminism Contests the Nineties*, Allen & Unwin, Sydney, 1993, pp. 1–15; Katie Spearitt, 'New Dawns: First Wave Feminism 1880–1914', in Kay Saunders and Raymond Evans (eds), *Gender Relations in Australia: Domination and Negotiation*, Harcourt Brace Jovanich, Sydney, 1992, pp. 325–49.
38   Melanie Nolan and Caroline Daley, 'International Feminist Perspectives on Suffrage: An Introduction'; Patricia Grimshaw, 'Women's Suffrage in New Zealand Revisited: Writing from the Margins'; Susan Magarey, 'Why Didn't They Want to Be Members of Parliament? Suffragists in South Australia'; Nancy F. Cott, 'Early Twentieth-Century Feminism in Political Context: A Comparative Look at Germany and the United States'; Ellen Carol DuBois, 'Woman Suffrage Around the World: Three Phases of Suffrage Internationalism', all in Caroline Daley and Melanie Nolan (eds), *Suffrage and Beyond: International Feminist Perspectives*, Auckland University Press, Auckland, and Pluto Press, Annandale, 1994, pp. 7, 30–33, 72, 236–38, 260–65; Eric Olssen, 'Working Gender, Gendering Work', in Barbara Brookes, Annabel Cooper and Robin Law (eds), *Sites of Gender: Women, Men and Modernity in Southern Dunedin, 1890–1939*, Auckland University Press, Auckland, pp. 44–49.

sphere feminism.[39] Such a depiction draws attention to the role of the middle-class urban family as arguably the crucible in which 'women's rights' were redefined in 'men's countries'.[40] The achievement of women's suffrage becomes less a by-product of colonial politics, in which the votes of women provided a conservative bulwark against the encroachment of class and party, and rather more a creative achievement of 'colonial liberalism'. Macintyre's *A Colonial Liberalism* provides an interpretation of the phenomenon, in its Australian context, that moves beyond the dismissive implications of 'colonial'— 'derivative, imitative and deficient'—and suggests that new world circumstances proved liberating.[41] European liberalism defined itself against the past. By contrast, in the colonies of settlement, 'where there were few traditional forms and no established ruling class', liberalism 'was deprived of its natural enemy … shed its oppositional connotations and became a constructive endeavour'.[42] This more dynamic interpretation, with its stress upon a more open future, reinforces the need to observe more closely the constructions that the swelling ranks of the urban middle-class families put upon that future. And, by 1894, with the enfranchisement of women in New Zealand and in some Australian states, that future came to encompass an increased emphasis upon family.

* * *

Thus the broad historical framework within which the Australian and New Zealand historiography has been constructed has neglected the role of family in general, and particularly, in the case of New Zealand, the growing significance of an emergent professional elite between 1880 and 1920. In the absence of such research, to date the Australasian colonial middle-class family has largely been seen as a derivative of its British parent. The dominant characteristics of the British upper middle-class family, as set out by historians, may be summarised briefly: a patriarchal institution presided over by a 'remote' father and 'decorous' mother, mimicking, as much as it was financially able, the lifestyle of the aristocracy. Its day-to-day functioning relied upon the labour of servants. Children were very largely left in the care of others

---

39   Donald Denoon and Philippa Mein Smith with Marivic Wyndham, *A History of Australia, New Zealand and the Pacific*, Blackwell, Oxford, 2000, pp. 204–8.
40   Denoon et al., *A History of Australia*, p. 204.
41   Macintyre, *A Colonial Liberalism*, p. 11.
42   Macintyre, *A Colonial Liberalism*, p. 12.

and such closer association between mother and child as occurred flowed from the belief that the family stood apart from the real world, and that the nurturing of children involved necessarily a degree of feminisation of the household. It was to remove young boys from the feminising influence of the family that their sons were sent to public schools. Indeed, the expansion of this aristocratic institution and the spread of its ideals in mid-nineteenth-century Britain rested upon the endorsement of an aspirant middle class increasingly keen to secure the prospects of their sons. Whatever the motivation, the popularity of the public school amongst the middle classes became an entrenched feature of family life, at least for boys.[43]

British historians have suggested that this characterisation of the stereotypical middle-class family is both too one-dimensional and unduly influenced by what has been called the 'misery memoir'.[44] Unhappy childhoods, recalled by a few prominent and atypical members of this upper middle class, have come to stand for a majority experience. The reality was more varied and the product of deeper historical forces than mere imitation. Viewed in the broadest of historical senses, the family has been seen as undergoing something of a transformation throughout the nineteenth century as factory and city began to replace farm and countryside as the mainspring of economic life. The separation of work and home that followed recast family dynamics. The father-dominated functional family gave way to a mother-dominated sentimental family. Thus were the seeds of the cult of domesticity sown. Its elaboration marked a retreat from the productive and public sphere to the personal and private. The family thus becomes a sanctuary from the amoral world of men and action.

---

43   M. Jeanne Peterson, *Family Love and Work in the Lives of Victorian Gentlewomen*, Indiana University Press, Bloomington and Indianapolis, 1989, pp. ix–x, 33; John Chandos, *Boys Together: English Public Schools 1800–1964*, Hutchinson, London, 1984; J. R. de Symons Honey, *Tom Brown's Universe: The Development of the Victorian Public School*, Millington, London, 1977; Jonathan Gathorne-Hardy, *The Public School Phenomenon 597–1977*, Hodder and Stoughton, London, 1977; Jonathan Gathorne-Hardy, *The Rise and Fall of the British Nanny*, Hodder and Stoughton, London, 1972.

44   The 'misery memoir' is a relatively recent term for a biographical genre that recounts childhood trauma. Examples from the Victorian period include Samuel Butler's posthumously published *The Way of All Flesh*, Grant Richards, London, 1903; James Anthony Froude's autobiographical fragment reproduced in W. H. Dunn, *James Anthony Froude: A Biography, vol. 1: 1818–1856*, Clarendon Press, Oxford, 1961; John Stuart Mill, *Autobiography* [1873], Currin V. Shields (ed.), Liberal Arts Press, 1957; and Virginia Woolf's autobiographical writings. See also Peterson, *Family, Love and Work*, p. 33, for a discussion of this trend.

It was a sanctuary, moreover, in which the mother assumed the mantle of moral guardian charged with realising the reformation of the public sphere through her children.

Leonore Davidoff and Catherine Hall's seminal work, *Family Fortunes: Men and Women of the English Middle Class, 1780–1850* (1987), provides the fullest elaboration of this transformation of family life.[45] Their thesis is essentially that late eighteenth-century England witnessed a 'historic break' in the evolution of the family: 'something significant changed ... and a realigned gender order emerged, more characteristic of modern times, associated with the development of modern capitalism and urbanisation'.[46] By their account 'separate spheres' became 'the common-sense' response of the middle class as they negotiated the circumstances of time and place.[47] The narrative may be read, as Davidoff and Hall note, as tracing the 'triumph of "separate spheres", the confinement of women to the domestic sphere and their exclusion from the public world'.[48] They reject such a reading and describe *Family Fortunes* as being shaped by a 'multifaceted notion of causation and change' that balances the role of the ideological and material change.[49] Between 1780 and 1850, they suggest 'enterprise, family, home, masculinity and femininity were re-drawn, negotiated, reformed and reinstalled' in ways that 'transform[ed] patterns of life in families and households amongst the "middling sorts"'.[50]

The separation of home and work, whose origins and significance Davidoff has probed, was a process that was nearing its full flowering just as Australasian cities were beginning to take shape. Historians of colonial Australia and New Zealand have seen the new world middle-class family essentially as a version of its old world parent.[51] At first the colonial experience delayed the separation of home and work. The high cost of manufactured imports meant the middle-class family shed its productive function more slowly than it did its British

---

45   Leonore Davidoff and Catherine Hall, *Family Fortunes: Men and Women of the English Middle Class, 1780–1850* [1987], revised edn, Routledge, London, 2002.
46   Davidoff and Hall, *Family Fortunes* [2002 edn], p. xvi.
47   Davidoff and Hall, *Family Fortunes* [2002 edn], p. xvi.
48   Davidoff and Hall, *Family Fortunes* [2002 edn], p. xvi.
49   Davidoff and Hall, *Family Fortunes* [2002 edn], p. xvi.
50   Davidoff and Hall, *Family Fortunes* [2002 edn], p. xvi.
51   Jock Phillips, *A Man's Country? The Image of the Pakeha Male: A History*, Penguin, Auckland, 1987, pp. 51, 221–22; Olssen, 'Families and the Gendering of European New Zealand', pp. 37–62.

parent. In New Zealand the spread of the small-scale dairy farm, after the advent of refrigeration in the late nineteenth century, brought a reliance upon the unpaid labour of a wife and children and thus gave rise to a sharp and enduring difference in the dynamics of urban and rural families. But between 1880 and 1920, the centre of gravity of the colonial population was shifting towards the town and city.[52] It was there that the bourgeois family and its associated cult of domesticity took shape. Its elaboration took its cue from Britain, was influenced by British books and magazines and reinforced by the preferences of successive waves of middle-class British migrants.[53] Historians have demonstrated how a range of social concerns about racial purity, a falling birth rate and drunkenness, grounded in the preoccupations of the urban middle class, enhanced the place of the family in colonial society throughout Australasia.[54]

The growing significance of the middle-class, professional, urban family within Australasia in the late nineteenth and early twentieth centuries has been linked also to a strengthening of the imperial connection. James Belich has argued that in New Zealand the process produced a 'recolonisation' of society.[55] With the advent of refrigeration of meat, butter and cheese, New Zealand became a 'wet dairy frontier' rather than a 'dry' pastoral one.[56] As a virtual British cow-yard, New Zealand was tied 'to London, the centre of the British Empire, as effectively as [by] a bridge'.[57] It made the most of the tightening economic ties by projecting itself as reproducing only 'best British'. Such an environment was a congenial if not a privileged one for middle-class newcomers from Britain. Their arrival, in increasing numbers and with a preference for the city, has encouraged historians to depict them as active agents in the process of 'recolonisation' in social, cultural and political terms. In filling such a role, they confirmed their decision to leave an 'impaired' Britain and embraced their new home as a 'better Britain'.

52   Mein Smith, *A Concise History of New Zealand*, pp. 97–102; Phillips, *A Man's Country?*, pp. 221–22.
53   Phillips, *A Man's Country?*, pp. 221–22.
54   Mein Smith, *A Concise History of New Zealand*, pp. 89–90, 93–95, 99–108, 119–22.
55   James Belich, *Paradise Reforged: A History of the New Zealanders from the 1880s to the Year 2000*, Allen Lane, Auckland, 2001, pp. 11–12, 29–31.
56   Denoon et al., *A History of Australia*, p. 227.
57   Mein Smith, *A Concise History of New Zealand*, pp. 96–97.

Belich's 'recolonisation' thesis carries with it an implied loosening of the Australasian connection. New Zealand is seen as seeking to be not only a 'better Britain', but also 'more' British than Australia.[58] Such an implication draws some of its weight from the stronger radical-nationalist upsurge in Australia, especially evident in literature and art, but also associated with the precocious development of the labour movement and the emergence of labour parties. Whatever the comparative merit of the 'recolonisation' thesis and its implications, our understanding of the attitudes taken by middle-class, professional families to imperial concerns has largely been deduced from political narratives, the activities of influential interest groups, and the biographies and memoirs of male notables. There remain few detailed family studies that might allow us to explore more fully the attitudes, interests and preoccupations of a segment of society whose dynamics are only now beginning to be understood, despite being afforded greater historical acknowledgement.

Recent critiques of the 'recolonisation' theory offer alternative ways of reading the role played by the middle-class professional family. Philippa Mein Smith has suggested that the development of closer economic links with Britain in the late nineteenth and early twentieth centuries need not be seen as some sort of retreat from progressive and less dependent colonialism back into the shelter of the imperial cocoon. She rejects the primacy 'recolonisation' gives 'to Britain and British ties', and presents economic change—the transition from 'dry' pastoral economy to a 'wet' dairying one—as deliberative and underpinned by ideas and policies that were Australasian in origin.[59] In her view, the shift was consistent with a commitment to state development that was distinctively Australasian, grounded in nineteenth-century colonial experience and evident in the twentieth century.[60] Such an interpretation, with its stress on continuity and persistence, allows for a more nuanced interpretation of where newcomers of middle-class, British background fitted into a society in transition. The question now becomes not whether such families were, wittingly or unwittingly, agents of an intensifying imperialism, but where they stood on a continuum in which nationalism and imperialism were not necessarily antithetical but sometimes complementary viewpoints that

58 Belich, *Paradise Reforged*, pp. 46–52; Mein Smith, *A Concise History of New Zealand*, p. 97.
59 Mein Smith, *A Concise History of New Zealand*, pp. 96–98.
60 Mein Smith, *A Concise History of New Zealand*, p.97.

straddled the native born–migrant divide. Such a focus emphasises the commonalities between the Australian and New Zealand experiences rather than the differences.

Mein Smith's argument, which draws upon Paul Kelly's contested notion of a 'settlement', has implications for interpretations of the middle-class professional family.[61] Designed to mediate the effects of shifts in the world economy, the shared features of the compact—white Australasia, arbitration, protection, 'state paternalism' and 'imperial benevolence'—constituted, Mein Smith suggests, the basic ingredients of a peculiarly antipodean democratic citizenship.[62] The elaboration of this social contract was carried out against a background of social unrest, seen by many contemporaries as a contest between labour and capital that endangered the 'better Britain' central to the middle-class ideal. How recently arrived British migrants, in the midst of establishing their families in the suburban fringes of cities as different as Melbourne and Christchurch, viewed these accommodations and what, if any, role they played in the elaboration of them remains to be established. What does seem clear, however, is that the process was a defining one in the history of Australasian liberalism and, as such, provides a window on the social and political aspirations of the antipodean middle classes.

That the argument supporting the Australasian character of the 'social compacts' negotiated on both sides of the Tasman derives much of its impetus from the New Zealand experience is unsurprising. It has a rich historiographical pedigree that can be traced back to William Pember Reeves. One of the political victors in the 1890 New Zealand general election, Reeves had described the verdict of the electors as the triumph of the 'masses' over the 'classes' and a prelude to dramatic change. Within little more than a decade he had produced two historical works—*The Long White Cloud* (1898) and the two volumes of *State Experiments in Australia and New Zealand* (1902)—

---

61   Paul Kelly, in *The End of Certainty: Power, Politics and Business in Australia*, argues that from 1908 until the 1980s, Australian politics was dominated by an agreement or 'settlement' that included White Australia, Industry Protection, Wage Arbitration, State Paternalism and Imperial Benevolence. Critiques have challenged the degree to which this settlement was unchanging and pointed to the renovation of the settlement in the 1940s. See Tim Rowse, *Nugget Coombs: A Reforming Life* [2002], 2nd edn, Cambridge University Press, Melbourne, 2005, pp. 357–61; Paul Kelly, *The End of Certainty: Power, Politics and Business in Australia* [1992], revised edn, Allen & Unwin, St Leonards, NSW, 1994.

62   Mein Smith, *A Concise History of New Zealand*, p. 95.

that cast a long historical shadow. The first laid the foundation for a nationalist and radical interpretation of nineteenth-century New Zealand political history and anticipated what has come to be called the 'born modern' thesis. The second brought together the core Australasian legislative changes that formed the basis of what is now described as a 'social compact'. Both books were written in London while Reeves was Agent-General and are presented by Mein Smith as playing a part in persuading British investors to accept the continuing imperial relationship that was necessary to underwrite the economic transformation and its associated social and political accommodations.[63]

A consistent thread throughout this discussion has been the attractiveness of Australasian cities to the middle-class British family. They came to be seen as constituting something of a social laboratory, in which the family and the role of women within it might be allowed to develop in ways that were less hindered by custom and tradition. As newcomers, their arrival in the new world has been lightly explored. As emigrants, their departure from Britain has begun to attract the attention of feminist historians. Looking, as it were, from the other end of the telescope, they have asked whether the imperial expansion that made migration possible also opened up an 'opportunity for women to experience adventure, employment, status and influence'.[64] Was it the case that the suburban cities 'on the margins of Empire' were liberating for women? Such research rejects the stereotype of middle-class bourgeois womanhood held to prevail from the mid-nineteenth century until the 1950s as being at odds with the reality of most urban 'middling sort of women' in both the new world and the old. Moreover, in a variety of new world settings, the suburban cities have been judged more flexible for women both inside and outside the family than those of the old world.[65]

Nonetheless, it remains true that the balance of the argument for flexibility is tilted very much on the side of women outside of the family. 'The public', as Leonore Davidoff and Catherine Hall have

---

63   Mein Smith, *A Concise History of New Zealand*, pp. 95–97.
64   Stephanie Jessica Wyse, 'Gender, Wealth and Margins of Empire: Women's Economic Opportunity in New Zealand Cities, c.1890–1950', PhD thesis, King's College London, University of London, 2008, p. 13.
65   Wyse, 'Gender, Wealth and Margins of Empire', pp. 11–20, 21–64.

written, 'was not really public and private not really private'.[66] Both were 'constructs with specific meaning' that needed to 'be understood as products of a particular historical time'.[67] The particularities of married women in middle-class, migrant professional families in Australasian cities of the late nineteenth and early twentieth centuries remain less than fully revealed. To some extent, the economic activities of some professional households—most notably those of doctors and lawyers—may be seen as constituting a family 'enterprise', in which 'public' and 'private' sometimes overlapped. Significantly, it was from within the middle-class enclaves that the suffrage movement gathered momentum in the late 1880s. The philanthropic and charitable groups that grew alongside the franchise organisations and exhibited a high degree of shared membership with them similarly offered married middle-class women a greater public presence.

These tendencies within the middle-class suburbs of the new world were scarcely foreign to the middle-class migrant women arriving in the new world in the 1880s. Indeed, the possibility that the colonies might offer greater opportunity for their fuller development serves to underline the degree to which the 'family' envisaged by migrant couples may be seen as an extension of old world families they were leaving behind. The precise role and meaning of 'family' in the establishment of its colonial branch needs elaboration in 'old world' and 'new world' terms. Similarly, despite the element of distancing implicit in the act of migration, the evidence of a persistent British connection remains visible in the life of the colonial family. The persistence of this influence, and whether it was exerted or sought, requires placing in the particular and changing circumstances of family in both the old and new worlds.

The 'family connection' could take a variety of forms and was, as likely as not, to link the new world couple more closely to the family of the wife as the husband. The most obvious was money. As a marriage gift, continuing remittance or inheritance, British capital helped sustain colonial middle-class families and secure a place in their new society. Just as common as direct financial contribution was the dispatch of manufactured goods, objects not available in the colonies, such as musical instruments (most notably the piano), furniture, artworks,

---

66   Davidoff and Hall, *Family Fortunes* [2002 edn], p. 33.
67   Davidoff and Hall, *Family Fortunes* [2002 edn], p. 33.

or more practical household and sporting goods. Assistance from 'Home' might also take the form of advice and counsel, whether proffered or sought. The education of children—especially that of boys—was frequently the subject of correspondence with family members in the old world. Would a colonial education suffice? If it was judged inferior and a son despatched 'Home' to attend public school or university, it was 'family' in Britain that made it possible by providing a home away from home during holidays. Moreover, family provided the network of households that made the trip 'Home' by the new world couple and their children more realisable.

Standing somewhere on the colonial–transnational continuum, such relationships are rooted in the conundrum in which the act of migration is typically wrapped. The precise mix of 'push' and 'pull' factors that exercised the minds of any professional, married couple contemplating migration can only be known at the individual level. Of few middle-class professionals, however, could it be suggested that lack of economic opportunity was itself a sufficient explanation for the decision to migrate.[68] Neither are there many instances where the decision to marry and leave for the new world is accompanied by an elaborated appraisal of the society being left behind and the one about to be embraced. Something of these private musings make their way into personal diaries (mostly the record of women). Such public airings as they receive tend to be the work of men and are most commonly part of farewell speeches given by departing, newly-wed husbands. Encased in the conventions of the day they reveal little. On occasions, however, the considered views of a couple on the eve of migration are given public expression in forms that confront directly the meanings that infuse their conception of 'family', and indicate its importance to their decision to marry and move to the edge of the Empire.[69]

Historians have frequently described British nineteenth-century middle-class migrants as constituting an 'uneasy' segment of society. The uneasiness is said to come in a variety of forms and reflects a variety of concerns, many of them deeply religious or moral in nature. Davidoff and Hall present a picture of an 'intensely religious

68   See Eric Richards, *Britannia's Children: Emigration from England, Scotland, Wales and Ireland since 1600*, Hambledon, London, 2004, ch. 9.
69   Alison Drummond (ed.), *Married and Gone to New Zealand: Being Extracts From the Writings of Women Pioneers*, Paul's Book Arcade and Oxford University Press, Hamilton and London, 1960.

provincial middle class', whose men and women 'placed themselves in opposition to an indolent and dissolute aristocracy, and a potentially subversive working class'.[70] They endorse E. P. Thompson's notion of classes defining themselves in their expressed antagonism for other classes and present a gendered concept of class.[71] As they see it, 'One of the most compelling strands ... of this middle class was the commitment to an imperative moral code within a revised domestic world, a precursor to the Heavenly Home'.[72] In this way, they argue, 'the religious idiom' became a middle class 'cultural norm'.[73] The home and family became the critical site for the construction of redefined concepts of 'manliness' and 'femininity', which became 'key categories' in a new moral order.

Davidoff and Hall see these developments as providing a bridge to the domestic or familial feminism of the second half of the twentieth century: 'The mid-century common-sense division into a public world of politics and market activity assigned to men and the private sphere now contained in the suburban villa set the framework for the feminism of John Stuart Mill.'[74] To the extent that the middle-class professional families who made their way to the suburban cities of the new world in the 1880s were influenced by these changing currents of opinion, they may be seen as carrying its essence in their ideological and cultural baggage. Historians of the suffrage campaigns in both Australia and New Zealand have analysed the public manifestations of these ideas in the debates that preceded the enfranchisement of women and in the social movements that were associated with it. What is less well known is whether these ideas survived the journey to the new world. What role, if any, did the feminism of John Stuart Mill play in the decision to marry and go to the antipodes? To what degree and in what ways can these ideas be shown to influence the construction of the colonial middle-class family?

* * *

---

70 Davidoff and Hall, *Family Fortunes* [2002 edn], p. xviii.
71 E. P. Thompson, *The Making of the English Working Class*, Penguin, Harmondsworth, 1968.
72 Davidoff and Hall, *Family Fortunes* [2002 edn], p. xviii.
73 Davidoff and Hall, *Family Fortunes* [2002 edn], p. xviii.
74 Davidoff and Hall, *Family Fortunes* [2002 edn], p. 454.

In its exploration of how the Australasian fragment of the British professional middle class adapted to its colonial framework, this book stands on the shoulders of an emergent literature about the late nineteenth-century family. It is a literature which, as we have seen, builds upon the path-breaking and closely textured work of Davidoff and Hall's *Family Fortunes*. They demonstrated how the notion of the privatised family developed within the domestic sphere where, as wives and mothers, women came to assume an idealised status. By showing how this gendered ideal was shaped as much by women as by men, they describe the ways in which men and women negotiated the circumstances of their changing environment. In particular, they argue that the middle-class conception of the home as a retreat from the evils of industrial society was grounded in the two major intellectual influences—the Protestant Reformation and the Enlightenment. In apparently contradictory but often complementary ways, the religiosity and emphasis upon the Bible of the Reformation and the rationality of the Enlightenment informed middle-class views of the family. Above all else, Davidoff and Hall demonstrated that the family was a social construct that was being constantly made and remade, as class and gender both accommodated and fashioned the world that men, women and children occupied.

Davidoff and Hall's pioneering work drew upon and has been extended by demographic research that points to significant changes in family size throughout the nineteenth century.[75] Such studies characterise the nineteenth century as one which witnessed the death of the 'long family' and the shrinking of the interlocking web of 'cousinage' that had previously enabled individuals to live out their lives almost completely within the confines of family. The middle class, it has been demonstrated, led the shift towards the smaller family and their pre-eminence has been described as the rational response to a changing society. As part of an emergent meritocracy, their family fortunes

---

75   Simon Szreter, *Fertility, Class and Gender in Britain 1860–1940*, Cambridge University Press, Cambridge, 1996; Angelique Janssens (ed.), *Gendering the Fertility Decline in the Western World*, Peter Lang, Bern, 2007; Mark Rothery, 'The Reproductive Behaviour of the English Landed Gentry in the Nineteenth and Early Twentieth Century', *Journal of British Studies*, vol. 8, no. 3, 2009, pp. 674–94; Eilidh Garrett, Alice Reid, Kevin Schurer and Simon Szreter, *Changing Family Size in England and Wales: Place, Class and Demography 1891–1911*, Cambridge University Press, Cambridge, 2001; Michael Anderson, 'The Social Implications of Demographic Change', in F. M. L. Thompson (ed.), *The Cambridge Social History of Britain 1750–1950*, vol. 2, Cambridge University Press, Cambridge, 1990, pp. 1–70; Wally Seccombe, 'Starting to Stop: Working-Class Fertility Decline in Britain', *Past and Present*, no. 126, 1990, pp. 151–88.

depended upon an ability to provide children with the educational opportunities that would enable them to assume a place within it. It was a response that provided the framework for the emergence of the privatised family held to be the ideal of the nineteenth-century British bourgeoisie.

Whatever the rationality of its origins, it is only in recent years that the dynamics of the middle-class family that took shape in the second half of the nineteenth century have been subjected to closer analysis. By showing that the making of this family was as much the work of women as men, Davidoff and Hall opened the way for closer scrutiny of how in practice 'separate spheres' operated. Historians have identified how, to the extent they relied upon their intellectual labour rather than inherited wealth or family patronage to sustain their place in society, middle-class professionals were obliged by economic reality to see marriage and career as a form of family enterprise. Studies of politicians, academics, members of diplomatic service, and the Protestant ministry have revealed what Hanna Papanek has called 'two-person single career' marriages, in which the wife is expected to participate in her husband's career without direct acknowledgement or remuneration.[76] Such arrangements were often based upon an understanding that fulfilling these functions helped 'to oil the social machinery', and in this sense they merged with whatever wider sense of partnership or family enterprise that existed within individual marriages.[77]

If Davidoff and Hall's *Family Fortunes* placed the family on the historical agenda, the more recent emergence of studies of masculinities has put the middle-class father back in the family.[78] The most influential of the theoretical approaches sustaining such studies has been the notion

---

76   Hanna Papanek, 'Men, Women and Work: Reflections on the Two-Person Career', *American Journal of Sociology*, vol. 78, part 4, 1973, pp. 852–72; Deacon, *Managing Gender*, pp. 13–14.
77   Deacon, *Managing Gender*, p. 13.
78   For examples see John Tosh, *Manliness and Masculinities in Nineteenth-Century Britain: Essays on Gender, Family and Empire*, Person Longman, London, 2005; Phillips, *A Man's Country?*; Megan Doolittle, '"Missing Fathers": Assembling a History of Fatherhood in Mid-Nineteenth Century England', PhD thesis, University of Essex, 1996; Claudia Nelson, *Invisible Men: Fatherhood in Victorian Periodicals, 1850–1910*, University of Georgia Press, Athens, GA, 1995; Shawn Johansen, *Family Men: Middle-Class Fatherhood in Early Industrialising America*, Routledge, New York, 2001.

of 'hegemonic masculinity'.[79] The term has been used in a variety of ways: as a convenient shorthand for the male attributes that were most widely approved within a given society; to suggest that what is being described is the masculinity of a ruling or dominant class and the gendered face of class; to encompass notions of social control and suggest that the rationale of hegemonic masculinity is the maintenance of male authority over women. In this latter sense, it influenced the history of gender and sustained the notion of the patriarchal family, in which male authority was not necessarily accompanied by minimal involvement in family life beyond that directly related to its material well-being.

Moreover, in his recent study of the concepts of masculinity that prevailed within the English middle class of the nineteenth century, John Tosh has demonstrated that commitment to family and positive engagement with developing the potential of children was central to community understandings of manly behaviour and essential to the maintenance of gentlemanly status. Critical to these assessments was a judgement of a father's success in preparing his children to fill a useful role within society. The education of sons was examined more rigorously, but the neglect of a daughter's education might also diminish a man's standing. Thus, Tosh's exploration of the shifts that occurred in nineteenth-century definitions of masculinity suggests that separate spheres were not so separate and that the private and public worlds of the middle class were in constant dialogue. His findings underline the need for a more textured approach to the role of the father within the family and have implications for the persistence of patriarchy as a useful theoretical category in the discussion of the middle-class family. His work strengthens what individual case studies have suggested: namely that middle-class fathers came in a variety of forms, from the stereotypical remote patriarch to the involved parent. Indeed, he makes a compelling case for a need to see middle-class fathers of the late nineteenth century as the first generation of males to grapple with a new social order that cast them in the role of sole breadwinner and also required them to be attentive to the individual needs of family.[80]

---

79 Martin Crotty, *Making the Australian Male: Middle-Class Masculinity 1870–1920*, Melbourne University Press, Carlton South, Victoria, 2001, pp. 4–8; R. W. Connell, *Gender and Power: Society, the Person, and Sexual Politics*, Stanford University Press, Stanford, 1987, p. 183; R. W. Connell, *Masculinities*, Allen & Unwin, Sydney, 1995, p. 77.
80 Tosh, *A Man's Place*, passim.

Such, then, is the broad historiographical context in which the mid-Victorian middle-class professional family has been placed. Somewhat less attention has been given to the decision of members of this segment of British society to migrate. Studies of the rise of the professional class have charted its numerical growth, noted fluctuations in demand for particular professions, observed that the Empire and particularly its settler societies proved increasingly attractive as they matured beyond the pioneering phase and attempted to assess whether those who migrated were the misfits or failures of the old world, or its most adventurous, ambitious or alienated fragment. Such macro studies provide a broad contextual explanation, but do not provide the level of particularity necessary to link migration to developing concepts of the family, apart from the general observation that migration offered better prospects for the professional classes during a time when industrial expansion allowed something like a British world economy to develop.[81]

While migration histories concentrate in the main upon the more numerous urban working class, rural labourers or artisans, they provide a range of perspectives on the role played by family in the migratory process that has general relevance. Family is commonly portrayed as the 'lynchpin' of migration, providing the personal links that encourage and reinforce the decision to migrate. It is sometimes the setting in which utopian notions envisaging migration as transformative, in personal or collective terms, take root. The family is also characterised as a foundational form of migrant identity and in this sense has been portrayed as constituting a form of networking. To historians attempting to see the expansion of the British Empire as a form of globalisation, the middle-class family becomes a part of the 'software of empire', agents of 'Britishness' and part of a global chain of kith and kin that generated within and between colonies personal friendships and professional connections. Historians have come to

81   Daniel Duman, *The English and Colonial Bars in the Nineteenth Century*, Croom Helm, London, 1983; K. Theodore Hoppen, *The Mid-Victorian Generation 1846–1886*, Clarendon Press, Oxford, 1998; W. J. Reader, *Professional Men: The Rise of the Professional Classes in Nineteenth-Century England*, Weidenfield and Nicolson, London, 1966; Patrick O'Farrell, *The Irish in Australia 1788 to the Present*, University of New South Wales Press, Sydney, 2000; Eric Richards, *Britannia's Children*.

see these linkages as enlarging 'Britishness' in a web-like fashion that adds a dimension to the previous conceptions that saw it as being defined along a core–periphery axis.[82]

The act of migration impacted in a variety of ways upon the dynamics of family life. If the death of the 'long family' in nineteenth-century Britain eroded the possibility of a life lived entirely within the extended family, migration threw individual families back on their own devices. Historians have identified two compensatory and complementary responses, greater reliance upon each other and an increased willingness to reach out in search of kindred spirits. Such engagements outside the personal domestic environment, whether between families in the private sphere, or more publicly within ethnic enclaves or professional associations, inside religious congregations, cultural organisations or sporting groups, underline the sense of isolation that enveloped migrant families and the importance of developing networks and friendships. 'Bowling alone', to borrow Robert Putnam's title, offered a fraught pathway to acceptance in a new society, one more likely to ensnare couples who were not natural joiners and women confined by the demands of childrearing to the domestic sphere.[83]

---

82 Gary Magee and Andrew S. Thompson, *Empire and Globalisation: Networks of People and Capital in the British World, c 1850–1914*, Cambridge University Press, Cambridge, 2010, p. 106; Belich, *Paradise Reforged;* W. D. Borrie, *The European Peopling of Australasia: A Demographic History 1788–1988*, Demography Program, Research School of Social Sciences, The Australian National University, Canberra, 1994; Louis Hartz, *The Founding of New Societies,* Harcourt, Brace & World, New York, 1964; Hoppen, *The Mid-Victorian Generation;* James Jupp, *The English in Australia*, Cambridge University Press, Cambridge, 2004; O'Farrell, *The Irish in Australia;* Brad Patterson (ed.), *The Irish in New Zealand: Historical Contexts & Perspectives*, Stout Research Centre for New Zealand Studies, Victoria University of Wellington, Wellington, 2002; Brad Patterson (ed.), *Ulster-New Zealand Migration and Cultural Transfers*, Four Courts Press, Dublin and Portland, 2006; Lyndon Fraser, *Castles of Gold: A History of New Zealand's West Coast Irish*, Otago University Press, Otago, 2007; Lyndon Fraser, *A Distant Shore: Irish Migration and New Zealand Settlement*, University of Otago Press, Dunedin, 2000; Lyndon Fraser and Katie Pickles (eds), *Shifting Centres: Women and Migration in New Zealand History*, University of Otago Press, Dunedin, 2002; Donald Harman Akenson, *Half the World from Home: Perspectives on the Irish in New Zealand 1860–1950,* Victoria University Press, Wellington, 1990; Jim Hewitson, *Far Off in Sunlight Places: Sites of the Scots in Australia and New Zealand*, Melbourne University Press, Carlton, Victoria, and Canongate, Edinburgh, 1998; David Fitzpatrick, *Oceans of Consolation: Personal Accounts of Irish Migration to Australia*, Melbourne University Press, Carlton, Victoria, 1995; Angela McCarthy (ed.), *A Global Clan: Scottish Migrant Networks and Identities since the Eighteenth Century*, Tauris Academic Studies, London and New York, 2006; Jock Phillips and Terry Hearn, *Settlers: New Zealand Immigrants from England, Ireland and Scotland 1800–1945*, Auckland University Press, Auckland, 2008.
83 Robert D. Putnam, *Bowling Alone: The Collapse and Revival of American Community*, Simon & Schuster, New York and London, 2000.

The interaction of ideas and material change fundamental to the reconstruction of the family in the nineteenth century has been given further impetus by classical scholars. They have shown how understandings of antiquity shaped the world view of the educated classes and provided a frame of reference that was instantly recognisable amongst the generations of British professionals who established themselves and their families in the maturing settler societies. Amongst the more influential precepts to be absorbed from the ancients was the notion that the educated classes were morally obliged to cultivate the whole person—mind as well as body—in a quest for excellence that would benefit the civic community. It was but a short step, and one that the writings of John Stuart Mill helped many of the educated middle class to take, to attach this obligation to the family and harness it to the quest for social progress.[84]

This high-minded conception of the family as an instrument of social change flourished alongside the evolution of girls' education and the emergence of the women's movement. The middle-class family was at the forefront of these developments and early historical accounts of their role stress radical intent and feminist purpose.[85] Historians now find ambiguity of purpose and a sometimes hesitant commitment to change expressed in a school curriculum that yielded its old forms only slowly and a cautious attitude to the careers of their daughters.[86]

Alongside these trends there have been a number of significant shifts in the way historians look at the relational aspects of family life. These shifts are neither linear in their development nor strongly present

84   Leigh Dale, *The English Men: Professing Literature in Australian Universities*, Association for the Study of Australian Literature, Canberra, 1997; Frank M. Turner, *The Greek Heritage in Victorian Britain*, Yale University Press, New Haven and Connecticut, 1981; Eugenio F. Biagini, 'Introduction: Citizenship, Liberty and Community', in Eugenio F. Biagini (ed.), *Citizenship and Community: Liberals, Radicals and Collective Identities in the British Isles, 1865–1931*, Cambridge University Press, Cambridge, 1996, pp. 6–9; Biagini, 'Liberalism and Direct Democracy: John Stuart Mill and the Model of Ancient Athens', in Biagini (ed.), *Citizenship and Community*, pp. 23–44.

85   For example, Edith Searle Grossmann, *Life of Helen Macmillan Brown: The First Woman to Graduate with Honours in a British University*, Whitcombe and Tombs, Christchurch, 1905.

86   Marjorie Theobald, *Knowing Women: Origins of Women's Education in Nineteenth-Century Australia*, Cambridge University Press, Cambridge and Melbourne, 1996, pp. 6, 64–90, 94–95, 126–29, 190–93, 210–13; Alison McKinnon, *The New Women: Adelaide's Early Women Graduates*, Wakefield Press, Adelaide, 1986, pp. 15–16; Dorothy Page, 'The First Lady Graduates: Women with Degrees from Otago University, 1885–1900', in Barbara Brookes, Charlotte Macdonald and Margaret Tennant, (eds), *Women in History 2: Essays on Women in New Zealand*, Bridget Williams Books, Wellington, 1992, pp. 98–128.

in their Australasian setting. It is possible to identify two broad and often overlapping approaches: studies of women's lives within notable families and studies that employ the techniques of collective history to explore a single theme or themes within one family or across a range of families.[87] The former has produced a range of popular narratives that focus upon the individual lives of women within prominent families.[88] They add to our knowledge of how these families work, and women's roles within them, but the exploration of the relational aspect of family life is a secondary concern. Typically, within the more themed exploration of women's lives amongst the middle class, the dynamics of family life have assumed greater prominence. Both approaches build their studies upon the close examination of the literary remains of individual lives.

These trends are more weakly present in published historical writing about the middle-class family in Australasia. In both Australia and New Zealand the narrative story of pioneer families dominates the early biographical landscape.[89] The lives of urban middle-class families of the late nineteenth and early twentieth centuries, unless glimpsed fleetingly in the pages of biographies of male politicians, remain largely hidden from view. Something of the newer approaches is present in studies of Australian artistic and literary families such as Brenda Niall's *The Boyds: A Family Biography*, Joanna Mendelssohn's *Letters and Liars: Norman Lindsay and the Lindsay Family* and *Lionel*

---

87 Barbara Caine, *Destined to be Wives: The Sisters of Beatrice Webb*, Clarendon Press, Oxford and New York, 1986; Peterson, *Family, Love and Work*; Judith Flanders, *A Circle of Sisters: Alice Kipling, Georgiana Burne-Jones, Agnes Poynter and Louisa Baldwin*, Viking, London, 2001; Barbara Caine, *Bombay to Bloomsbury: A Biography of the Strachey Family*, Oxford University Press, Oxford, 2005; Martin Pugh, *The Pankhursts: The History of One Radical Family*, Allen Lane, London, 2001; Sheila Fletcher, *Victorian Girls: Lord Lyttelton's Daughters*, Hambledon Press, London, 1997.

88 For example, Mary S. Lovell, *The Mitford Girls: The Biography of an Extraordinary Family*, Little, Brown and Company, London, 2001; Anne de Courcy, *The Viceroy's Daughters: The Lives of the Curzon Sisters*, Wiedenfield & Nicolson, London, 2000; James Fox, *Five Sisters: The Langhornes of Virginia*, Simon & Schuster, New York, 2000; Jeremy Lewis, *Shades of Greene: One Generation of an English Family*, Jonathan Cape, London, 2010.

89 For examples see, John Deans, *Pioneers on Port Cooper Plains: The Deans Family of Riccarton and Homebush*, Simpson and Williams, Christchurch, 1964; Martha Murdoch, *They Built for Tomorrow: The Story of the Blair Family*, Otago Daily Times Ltd, Dunedin, 1970; Janet Holm, *Nothing but Grass and Wind: The Rutherfords of Canterbury*, Hazard Press, Christchurch, 1992; Gordon Ogilvie, *Pioneers of the Plains: The Deans of Canterbury*, Shoal Bay Press, Christchurch, 1996; Marnie Bassett, *The Hentys: An Australian Colonial Tapestry*, Oxford University Press, London, 1954; Mary Durack, *Kings in Grass Castles*, Lloyd O'Neil, Melbourne, 1974; Margaret Kerr, *Colonial Dynasty: The Chambers Family of South Australia*, Rigby, Adelaide, 1980.

Lindsay: An Artist and his Family, and John Rickard's avowedly experimental study of the Deakin family.[90] In *Maud and Amber*, Ruth Fry traces two generations of feminism through the lives of the wife and daughter of the Liberal politician and historian, William Pember Reeves. Paradoxically, we know more of the workings of the New Zealand artisan family than we do of the middle-class professional one. Margaret Lovell-Smith's *Plain Living High Thinking* is an intimate account of the inner dynamics of a Christchurch family's life that traces the relationships within it and explores the prominent role its women (and men) played in the wider suffrage campaigns. Melanie Nolan uses the techniques of collective biography to explore the range of life experiences within a single Christchurch railway family.[91]

The application of these new trends is perhaps more explicitly present in several recent doctoral studies. In her work on English immigrants to eastern Australia in the first half of the nineteenth century, Janet Doust made extensive use of the papers of a single family (supplemented by several other less comprehensive family records) to build up analytical case studies of the motives that prompted family migration.[92] Helen Pfeil's study mined similar sources to construct a broad analysis of parent–child relationships—from birth to adolescence—within the upper middle-class family of eastern Australia between 1840 and 1900.[93] Both studies use the individual case study within the framework of a collective biography as the most effective way of uncovering the relationships, attitudes and values that form the private basis of family life.

90   Brenda Niall, *The Boyds: A Family Biography*, Miegunyah Press, Melbourne, 2002; Joanna Mendelssohn, *Lionel Lindsay: An Artist and His Family*, Chatto and Windus, London, 1988; Joanna Mendelssohn, *Letters and Liars: Norman Lindsay and the Lindsay Family*, Angus and Robertson, Pymble, 1996; John Rickard, *A Family Romance: The Deakins at Home*, Melbourne University Press, Carlton South, Victoria, 1996.

91   Ruth Fry, *Maud and Amber: A New Zealand Mother and Daughter and the Women's Cause, 1865–1981*, Canterbury University Press, Christchurch, 1992; Margaret Lovell-Smith, *Plain Living High Thinking: The Family Story of Jennie and Will Lovell-Smith*, Pedmore Press, Christchurch, 1994; Melanie Nolan, *Kin: A Collective Biography of a Working-Class New Zealand Family*, Canterbury University Press, Christchurch, 2005.

92   Janet Doust, 'English Migrants to Eastern Australia 1815–1860', PhD thesis, The Australian National University, 2004.

93   Helen Pfeil, 'Raising Colonial Families: The Upper-Middle-Class in Eastern Australia, 1840–1900', PhD thesis, The Australian National University, 2009.

The field of family history is 'vast and porous' and the boundaries between it and other forms of history necessarily blurred.[94] Historian Cynthia Comacchio sees this 'messiness' as a reflection of the messiness of family life itself and the fact that 'family reaches into virtually every corner of human existence'.[95] *Family Experiments* demonstrates the broad reach of what might be termed the history of the family, in its thematic focus upon gender, education, migration and social reform. It endeavours to draw attention to the role of the professional middle-class family in the evolution from the 1890s of a relatively comprehensive state welfare system that placed the family at its centre. It suggests that the professional middle class played an instrumental role in defining and initiating the relationship between the family and the particular form of colonial liberalism that nurtured these developments. As a collective biography based on personal papers, diaries and correspondence, *Family Experiments* might be considered a history 'from within' that traces the threads that link—at some times more strongly than others—the private world of the family with the remaking of Australasian society at a time of significant transformation.[96] Comacchio has argued that 'families make history at least as much as the inverse is true'.[97] It is the central contention of *Family Experiments* that the peculiar circumstances of antipodean society of the late nineteenth century enhanced the role of the middle-class professional family as agents of social change.

*   *   *

Within this framework, *Family Experiments* explores the nature of the family, in the late nineteenth century and early twentieth century, amongst an Australasian urban professional class in which first generation British migrants are a dominant force. It takes the form of a thematic, collective biography to reveal the experience of five families. Its central concerns are: to discover the understandings of family that such migrants possessed on the eve of their departure for

---

94   Esme Cleall, Laura Ishiguru and Emily J. Manktelow, 'Imperial Relations: Histories of Family in the British Empire', *Journal of Colonialism and Colonial History*, vol. 14, no. 1, Spring 2013.

95   Cynthia Comacchio, '"The History of Us": Social Science, History, and the Relations of Family in Canada', *Labour/ Le Travail: Journal of Canadian Labour Studies*, vol. 46, Fall 2000, p. 170.

96   Deborah Cohen, *Family Secrets: Shame and Privacy in Modern Britain*, Oxford University Press, New York, 2013, p. 5; Alison Light, *Common People: The History of an English Family*, Penguin Random House, UK, 2015.

97   Comacchio, '"The History of Us"', p. 213.

the new world; to explore what role, if any, these understandings played in their decision to leave Britain; to trace the process by which they established their families within the emergent professional class of the new world cities of Melbourne and Christchurch; to explore the nature of the individual marriages that lay at the centre of these newly constituted colonial families; to examine how, as parents, they constructed the childhoods of their sons and daughters and what expectations they had of them; and, finally, to assess what influence, if any, such families exerted in shaping community attitudes towards the family.

Responses to these questions have, to some degree, been structured around the family that provides the most explicit statement of intent, and has left the most comprehensive record of its life—the Wildings. For Julia Anthony, the daughter of a Manchester textile manufacturer turned Hereford newspaper proprietor, councillor and long-serving mayor, and Frederick Wilding, lawyer, son of a surgeon, prominent athlete and active member of the local Liberal Association, the decision to marry and go to New Zealand in 1879 came after extensive deliberation. Central to their thinking was a well-articulated conception of the family spelt out by Julia in a series of articles she contributed to the *Hereford Times*. In essence, she presents to her readers the family as the crucible in which all future social progress would be achieved. The family possessed the potential to liberate both men and women. Its goal for both sexes should be the encouragement of 'useful citizenship' in which the choice for women to enter the public sphere should be freely available. Hers was, as Davidoff and Hall might put it, the feminism of John Stuart Mill, though she did not share his belief 'in a natural division of labour and of spheres'.[98] Thus Julia Wilding's familial feminism set itself apart from the genteel femininity that Penny Russell has analysed in a finely textured study of women's lives within the colonial gentry. If a 'wish of distinction' produced 'genteel performance', the quest for usefulness produced vigorous engagement.[99] Julia's efforts to put precept into practice, faithfully if not exhaustively recorded from within a familial framework, offer a vantage point from which to construct a composite picture of middle-class professional family life that is more complex and varied.

98   Davidoff and Hall, *Family Fortunes* [2002 edn], p. 454.
99   Penny Russell, *'A Wish of Distinction': Colonial Gentility and Femininity*, Melbourne University Press, Carlton, Victoria, 1994.

In selecting the families for this study an attempt has been made to confront questions of typicality and representativeness. As the table following this introduction makes clear, all five families have a British migrant as their male head of household; two came from Scotland, two from Ireland and one from England. In two cases marriage preceded migration and the two decisions formed part of a considered appraisal of family prospects. In all cases the families that form the basis of this book were constructed in the new world, three in Melbourne, Australia, and two in Christchurch, New Zealand. In occupational terms the families spread across two broad categories—the small colonial academic world that was taking root as an offshoot of its British parent and a legal profession that grew as colonial cities matured. Both occupations conferred status, but, as professionals operating within the private rather the public sphere, lawyers stood to become more obvious beneficiaries of expanding colonial economies. Both occupations were held to signify membership of the intellectual community and were fertile breeding grounds for the development of networks of men and women with enthusiasms and ideas.

Thematic collective biographies of the family have commonly ranged over larger numbers of families, sometimes as many as 60.[100] The preference for the more closely textured, qualitative case study of five families is founded in the contention that the dynamics of family life are best revealed in the more intimate exchanges of daily life. The historian is here constrained by the nature of the family records that remain. The professional classes of the late nineteenth century were steeped in the literary tradition of their age and, if some were more assiduous maintainers of family papers than others, have had much to say in diaries, letters and memoirs about their domestic or private lives and their network of friends and acquaintances. While there is unevenness between family records and within the records of an individual family, the lives observed here are richly present in the

---

100 John Tosh's *A Man's Place* draws on the papers of 60 families, though explores seven in-depth. Pat Jalland explores the lives of women in more than 50 families in *Women, Marriage and Politics 1860–1914*, Oxford University Press, Oxford, 1986. Helen Pfeil's thesis 'Raising Colonial Families' deals with 13 families. On the theory of collective biography, see, for example, Tosh, *A Man's Place*, p. 199; Jalland, *Women, Marriage and Politics*, pp. 1–5; Nolan, *Kin*, pp. 16–17, 23–33; Alison Booth, *How to Make It as a Woman: Collective Biographical History from Victoria to the Present*, University of Chicago Press, Chicago and London, 2004, pp. 4, 9–21; Diana K. Jones, 'Researching Groups of Lives: A Collective Biographical Perspective on the Protestant Ethic Debate', *Qualitative Research*, vol. 1, no. 1, 2001, pp. 325–46; Lawrence Stone, 'Prosopography', *Daedalus*, vol. 100, no. 1, 1971, pp. 46–79.

written word. It is a written word that is selective, subjective and in varying ways a literary occasion.[101] It nonetheless provides a text from which we may recover something of the fabric of family life amongst Australasia's professional class of the late nineteenth and early twentieth centuries. The process of interrogating these primary documents of family life has benefited in some cases from published biographies of individual family members. While not primarily concerned with relationships either within or between families, they have often provided useful insights and frameworks for the understanding of more private experience.[102] Moreover, although five families are a relatively small sample, there are enough differences as well as similarities between the migrants' backgrounds to suggest that these few may be indicative of the many.[103]

This book is developed within three sections. The first—Departures— locates each individual (or couple) within their family, professional and social contexts and attempts to explore their attitudes and assumptions about family and their broader philosophies, evident as they envisaged their lives in the new world. It is organised in two chapters that group together two married couples, Frederick and Julia Wilding and Orme and Mary Masson, and three young men, Henry Higgins, Alexander Leeper and John Macmillan Brown. This grouping embodies a fundamental difference: couples for whom marriage and migration are intimately related envisage family in idealistic and optimistic terms; individuals, (whether their migration experience is encased within a family group, such as Henry Higgins) or as part of a quest for professional advancement, dwell more upon social or personal realities and think in ways that reflect a mixture of hopeful idealism and cautious expectation.

---

101 Katie Holmes, *Spaces in her Day: Australian Women's Diaries of the 1920s and 1930s*, Allen and Unwin, Sydney, 1995, p. xiii; Harriet Blodgett, *Centuries of Female Days: Englishwomen's Private Diaries*, Allan Sutton, Gloucester, 1989, pp. 39–57, 181–93; Margo Culley, '"I Look at Me": Self as a Subject in the Diaries of American Women', *Women's Studies Quarterly*, vol. 17, parts 3 and 4, 1989; Nolan, *Kin*, pp. 16–17, 23–33.

102 Margaret Lovell-Smith, *Easily the Best: The Life of Helen Connon (1857–1903)*, Canterbury University Press, Christchurch, 2004; John Poynter, *Doubts and Certainties: A Life of Alexander Leeper*, Melbourne University Press, Carlton, Victoria, 1997; John Rickard, *H.B. Higgins: The Rebel as Judge*, George Allen & Unwin, Sydney, 1984; Len Weickhardt, *Masson of Melbourne: The Life and Times of David Orme Masson, 1886–1923*, Royal Australian Chemical Institute, Parkville, Melbourne, 1989. R. J. W. Selleck's, *Finding Home: The Masson Family*, Australian Scholarly Press, Melbourne, 2013, was published after the bulk of *Family Experiments* was written.

103 Nolan, *Kin*, pp. 23–33.

The second section—Arrival and Establishment—groups the newcomers according to occupation: lawyers and academics. It attempts to uncover the processes by which they made their way within an emergent professional society and realised the family lives they envisaged. The third section—Marriage and Aspirations— focuses upon the dynamics of family life. Organised thematically, it begins with a chapter that traces the nature of the individual marriages within which varying concepts of family evolved and devotes three chapters to an examination of the nurture of children that gave expression to these ideals. Here we observe, in the intense preoccupation with the education of their daughters and sons, the full flowering of family idealism. The fact that two of the three chapters are devoted to daughters reflects the importance these families attached to gender equality in education and provides an opportunity to examine their perceptions of the roles their educated daughters might play in the achievement of the better society.

The Five Couples

Dates and Places of Birth	Date of Departure from Britain	Date and Place of Marriage	Occupation (paid) at Marriage

Higgins, Henry Bournes
• b. 1851
  Newtownards,
  County Down,
  Ireland
 	
—, Mary Alice
(née Morrison)
• b. 1860
  Geelong, Victoria
	1869	1885
		Geelong,
		Victoria
			Lawyer

Leeper, Alexander
• b. 1848
  Dublin, Ireland
 	
—, Adeline Marian
(née Allen)
• b. 1853
  Sydney, NSW
• d. 1893
 	
—, Mary Elizabeth
(née Moule)
• b. 1859 Melbourne,
  Victoria
	1869, 1875	1879
		Sydney, NSW
		
		1897
		Melbourne,
		Victoria
			Scholar and Warden
			Trinity College,
			University of
			Melbourne

Macmillan Brown, John
• b. 1846
  Irvine, Scotland
 	
—, Helen (née Connon)
• b. 1857?
  Melbourne, Victoria
• d. 1903
	1874	1886
		Christchurch,
		New Zealand
			Academic
			
			Teacher (1877–94)
			Principal
			Christchurch,
			Girls' High School
			(1883–94)

Masson, David Orme
• b. 1858
  London, England
 	
—, Mary
(née Struthers)
• b. 1854
  Aberdeen, Scotland
	1886	1886
		Aberdeen,
		Scotland
			Academic (Scientist)

Wilding, Frederick
• b. 1852
  Montgomery, Wales
 	
— Julia
(née Anthony)
• b. 1853
  Hereford, England
	1879	1879
		Hereford,
		England
			Lawyer

Section One:
Departures

In their recent study of migration from England, Ireland and Scotland to New Zealand, Jock Phillips and Terry Hearn observe that the colony was 'comparatively attractive for those with a white collar background'.[1] Throughout the nineteenth century, their 'absolute' numbers were never great, perhaps representing 'one in eight' of all migrants in New Zealand and a similar proportion in Australia.[2] Attempts to characterise the motivations of these 'children of clerks and professionals', as Phillips and Hearn describe them, have been necessarily broad-brush.[3] The most prevalent characterisation is that as members of Britain's 'troubled middle classes' they were uncertain of their place in a rapidly changing society, and hopeful that they might find in the new settler societies of the Empire a less troubled future with widened opportunities for themselves and their families. Moreover, generalisations about a group as diverse as that embraced by such phrases as 'the children of clerks and professionals', imply greater coherence than is warranted. A recent study by K. Theodore Hoppen of the mid-Victorian generation (defined as the years between 1846 and 1886) provides a useful analysis of the group.[4] Hoppen classifies them as belonging collectively to an 'inclusive' middle class and calculates that roughly one-fifth of the non-agricultural

1   Phillips and Hearn, *Settlers: New Zealand Immigrants*, p. 83.
2   Phillips and Hearn, *Settlers*, pp. 83–84; Borrie, *The European Peopling of Australasia*, passim.
3   Phillips and Hearn, *Settlers*, p. 84.
4   Hoppen, *The Mid-Victorian Generation*, pp. 31–55.

male workforce fell within its boundaries. He then suggests that his 'middling sort of people' might be divided into a 'more affluent half made up of higher professionals, employers and managers, and a lesser one of lower professionals, foremen and clerks'.[5] Hoppen's analysis of these 'middling sort of people' sees members of the ancient or learned professions (law, medicine and the Church) as constituting something of an 'exclusive' middle class that was inclined to abrogate to itself the leadership of the 'great English middle class'.[6]

The mystique of moral leadership was protected by lengthy, costly and arcane processes of admission.[7] Aspirant professionals without the family connection or wealth that would smooth the pathway might often struggle to break into a seemingly closed shop. Indeed, by the late 1850s, books offering advice to middle-class parents on the prospective employment of their sons described the law as a 'sinking profession' and almost all professions as 'grossly overcrowded'.[8] While these perceptions have been judged to be exaggerated and overly pessimistic, at particular times and in some places aspirant professionals, in Hoppen's words, 'had a hard time of it'.[9] Prone to depict themselves as thwarted by traditions and customs of British society, the aspirant professionals were also inclined to idealise the liberating possibilities of British colonies and their emergent settler societies. It is an area of individual experience where 'illusions' often did 'sterling duty for reality', and which has been fruitfully explored in Miles Fairburn's *The Ideal Society and Its Enemies*.[10] Most accounts, however, while acknowledging the role of ideas and ideals, prefer the more concrete certainties provided by real or imagined economic circumstances.[11] And, insofar as the 'family' features in assessments of the motivations that lay behind migration, it is answered within broader economic considerations.

---

5   Hoppen, *The Mid-Victorian Generation*, p. 33–34.
6   Hoppen, *The Mid-Victorian Generation*, p. 42–43.
7   Reader, *Professional Men*, passim.
8   Hoppen, *The Mid-Victorian Generation*, p. 43.
9   Hoppen, *The Mid-Victorian Generation*, p. 43; Richards, *Britannia's Children*, pp. 174–206.
10   The phrase, used in a slightly different context, is from Hoppen, *The Mid-Victorian Generation*, p. 40; Fairburn, *The Ideal Society and Its Enemies*; Miles Fairburn, 'The Rural Myth and the Urban Frontier, 1870–1940', *NZJH*, vol. 9, no. 1, 1975, pp. 3–21.
11   Borrie, *The European Peopling of Australasia*; Janet Doust, 'English Migrants to Eastern Australia 1815–1860'; Jupp, *The English in Australia*; Nicole T. McLennan, 'From Home and Kindred: English Emigration to Australia 1860–1900', PhD thesis, The Australian National University, 2009; Phillips and Hearn, *Settlers: New Zealand Immigrants*.

In his seminal *The Rise of Professional Society: England since 1880*, Harold Perkin sets out an argument that links the growing number of middle-class professionals with an increasingly coherent and distinctive world view.[12] Put simply, he argues that as English society became more industrialised in the nineteenth century, the opportunities for professionals expanded. As the number of their possible employers grew, they became freer to profess their own opinions, and less inclined to adjust such social ideals as they individually possessed to suit the values of the landed aristocracy, whose interests they served and from whom they derived their income. Faced with rapid industrial growth, and what many of them saw as incipient disorder and squalor, middle-class professionals, Perkin argues, appropriated the gentlemanly aristocratic ideal in a way that often combined a paternalistic sense of social responsibility with claims to provide the expertise that would enable progress and lay the basis for a better and more efficient society. He demonstrates how, in the twentieth century, these ideas, developed and extended by the middle-class professional experts, fed into and influenced the shaping of the British welfare state.

Perkin's argument has significance for the exploration of the middle-class professional family. He depicts a group ideology that emerges at the precise point at which individuals and young married couples from within this group increasingly migrate to British settler societies now moving beyond the pioneering stage of development. By exploring more closely the thinking that prompted migration, it is possible to explore particular ways in which the professional ideal identified by Perkin is beginning to take shape amongst the emergent young professionals of mid-Victorian Britain. The case studies presented here deal with a generation of middle-class professionals struggling to put together a world view at a time when science was coming to be seen as the key to the future and religious beliefs were increasingly being challenged. Their individual responses to this ferment took a variety of forms, but common to them all is a sense of experimentation, of testing how individuals and their collective expression in the family could

---

12   Harold Perkin, *The Rise of Professional Society: England since 1880*, Routledge, London and New York, 1989, passim, especially pp. 116–70, 359–404.

contribute usefully to 'the better society'. Each displays, explicitly or implicitly, acceptance of a notion of individual social responsibility as the basis for a more collective response to perceived social ills.

Put simply, the Australasian environment offered more scope for the incipient professional ideal to take root. Perkin perhaps unwittingly demonstrates this point by observing that, in the early twentieth century, New Zealand Agent-General William Pember Reeves was an active participant in the intellectual discussions that influenced the shape of the early British welfare state.[13] Reeves, a colonial-born, professionally trained lawyer, had been an architect of New Zealand's state experiments of the 1890s and the historian of Australasia's precocious burst of collectivism. His role in the network of middle-class professional families that developed between the migrant professional newcomers and the home-grown species demonstrates the process of adoption and adaptation by which the professional ideal developed an Australasian form.

The case studies are presented in two chapters. They are drawn from three professions: the law, academia and the Church. The first brings together the Wildings and the Massons, two young couples for whom marriage and migration are linked and wedded to a set of clearly articulated idealistic expectations. The second groups together Henry Higgins, Alexander Leeper and John Macmillan Brown, individuals for whom marriage came after migration, whose articulation of the professional ideal is less explicit, and for whom the struggle to reconcile the apparently competing claims of religion and science was a painful one. In all cases migration to Australia or New Zealand was the prelude to fuller endorsement of the professional ideal.

---

13   Perkin, *The Rise of Professional Society*, p. 159; Keith Sinclair, *William Pember Reeves: New Zealand Fabian*, Clarendon Press, Oxford, 1965.

1

The Family and Mid-Victorian Idealism

Julia Anthony and Frederick Wilding: In the spirit of John Stuart Mill

On 24 June 1879, 26-year-olds Julia Anthony and Frederick Wilding were married in their hometown of Hereford in England. Neither the bustling West Midlands town on the banks of the picturesque River Wye nor the county of Herefordshire, of which Hereford was capital, possessed a tradition of migration. Yet, little more than a month later, they set sail from Gravesend, London, bound for New Zealand, where they intended to make a new life. Their decision to migrate had clearly been made long before their wedding: marriage and migration were for them inextricably linked. At first glance, the pair seemed unlikely candidates for migration, with perhaps more to lose than to gain in the process. Frederick Wilding had commenced his training as a barrister in London chambers and was already a well-respected solicitor in Hereford, where he served as an advocate in the local courts. Julia Anthony enjoyed considerable social status as a talented pianist trained in Germany at the Cologne Conservatoire, and as a member of a well-known, wealthy and politically influential Hereford family. The comfortable lifestyle the pair already enjoyed seemed destined to continue after their marriage. Indeed, the attractions life held for them in a settler society over 12,000 miles away are not immediately apparent. To understand why they chose New Zealand over Britain we need to examine the forces, both personal and societal, that made their marriage a migratory moment.

Julia Anthony's family had risen to prominence on the strength of mercantile wealth. Originally members of the skilled artisan class in Abergavenny, Wales, the Anthonys had established a successful textile manufacturing business, Thos. Darker, Samuel and John Anthony. Julia's father, Charles (born in Hereford in 1803), managed the Hereford branch of the family firm until about 1831, when he sold his shares in the business and launched, with the assistance of local commercial interests, the *Hereford Times* as the mouthpiece of local liberal opinion in opposition to the long-established organ of conservative county opinion, the *Hereford Journal* (1663).[1] Anthony outlined the newspaper's political creed in unequivocal terms: it would advocate the 'protection of individual freedoms, the preservation of property, the practical acknowledgement of the rights of every member of the community, promote education and the abolition of the slave trade and monopolies in the Bank of England and the East India Company, and expose injustices and corruption in the Church'. It would act as a forum for the exchange of ideas, and aimed to 'accelerate the advancement of civilisation'. At the very least, Anthony promised that the *Hereford Times* would publish the 'clear and copious analyses of parliamentary discussions' that would lead to 'the elucidation of truth' and a 'better informed public'.[2]

Here, in such terms, Anthony placed himself squarely at the forefront of Hereford's version of the attack on the 'citadel of privilege' that was the hallmark of emergent middle-class liberalism. The position provided him with a springboard into local government politics. Over the next half century as councillor, alderman, Justice of the Peace, municipal trustee of charities and mayor for five terms, he was at the centre of local affairs.[3] It was a period that saw Hereford increase its

---

1   John Armstrong, 'The Hereford Times Desk: Its History and Associations', ms, Colwall, 1982, Hereford and Worcester County Record Office Reference (HWRO), BC 97, pp. 1–7; *Littlebury's Directory and Gazetteer of Herefordshire 1876–1877 with Private and Commercial Resident*, (transcription by Rosemary Lockie, 2005), p. 27.

2   Charles Anthony (senior), *Hereford Times Prospectus*, 1 May 1832, Hereford Times Office, Hereford, HWRO, BH 32/47/1; *A Story Most Interesting as Touching All but Five: A Birthday Souvenir of the Hereford Times*, 1927, HWRO, BH 32/34.

3   Charles Anthony senior was mayor of Hereford 1852–55, 1868–69.

population from 12,000 to 18,000, throw off the appearance of an isolated and struggling market town and develop railway links with Swansea to the south, Gloucester to the east and westwards into rural Wales.[4] Anthony was to benefit by association with this growth and the concomitant expansion of town services, and came to be seen as the 'founder of modern Hereford'.[5]

By the time of Julia's birth in 1853, Charles Anthony had consolidated his proprietorship of the *Hereford Times* and the Anthony family had become firmly embedded at the centre of the town's social and cultural life. Her childhood coincided with the full flowering of family fortunes. Over the next 20 years, the *Hereford Times* became a family enterprise that provided avenues of advancement for the older male Anthony children, Charles and Edwyn, who assumed its editorship and management respectively and followed their father into local Liberal politics.[6] Family success brought increasing wealth as well as status and was reflected in their newly built home set in five-and-a-half acres on a hill overlooking the city: a classically styled mansion, complete with a ball-room and music studio, and servants.[7]

To understand fully the making of Julia Anthony, we need to look behind these trappings of middle-class success and explore more closely the family structure that developed within it. The youngest of four children born between 1841 and 1853, Julia Anthony was raised in an environment where the male influence loomed large. Her mother had died when she was an infant, and, while her father remarried in 1856, her stepmother, aged 48 at the time of her marriage, seems to have exerted little influence over Julia's life and died when Julia was 22. Instead, it was her father and considerably elder brothers, Charles (born 1841) and Edwyn (born 1843), who largely shaped the adults Julia and her elder sister Blanche (born 1852) were to become.

---

4   *Littlebury's Directory and Gazetteer of Herefordshire, 1876–1877*, pp. 1–2.

5   Armstrong, '*Hereford Times* Desk'; *Hereford Times* (*HT*): 17 February 1885, 26 August 1911; Preface to William Collin's, *The Mayors of Hereford*, Wilding Family Papers (WFP), Canterbury Museum Documentary Research Centre, ARC.1989.124, box 42/1.

6   Charles Anthony junior was vice-president of the *Hereford Times* in the 1870s. Despite sustained pressure to stand as the Liberal candidate for Hereford, he did not do so. He also declined the mayoralty of Hereford offered to him in 1884 after his father died. Edwyn Anthony was a Hereford County councillor, alderman, Justice of the Peace, and Chairman of the South Herefordshire Liberal Association and the Hereford Liberal Club. Armstrong, 'The *Hereford Times* Desk', p. 22; 'Obituary: Charles Anthony junior', *HT*, January 1931, WFP, box 42/3.

7   Armstrong, 'The *Hereford Times* Desk', p. 12.

As a result, the sisters received a somewhat unconventional upbringing for girls of their class at the hands of three males deeply committed to their education and with a progressive attitude to women's rights in general.

Charles Anthony's career enabled him to provide the opportunities necessary to fully encourage the talents of his children. A warm and actively involved father, his public offices and newspaper business also made him an extremely busy one, and increasingly sons Charles and Edwyn assumed the dominant roles in their sisters' upbringing. Indeed, they may be seen as providing something of a generational bridge between the ideas of a father in his late 40s and early 50s when his daughters were born, and those of educated young men more in touch with the changing intellectual currents of mid-Victorian England. Their influence was to moderate and expand the education of their sisters in ways that freed it from the narrow confines of the middle-class household.[8]

The education of Charles and Edwyn Anthony was typical of that of young men of their class, background and social status. After a period at Hereford Cathedral School, both had been sent to Cheltenham College, 20 miles away in nearby Gloucester, established in 1841 as an Anglican school for boys and as one of the newer public schools, judged by one historian as more 'willing to experiment' with modern studies than many of the older public schools.[9] Thereafter, the combination of an indulgent father, considerable family wealth, and the boys' own wide-ranging interests and talents produced a period of travel and experimentation in a variety of fields. The prospect of a career in the family newspaper provided a secure basis for this exploration. A prizewinning scholar, Edwyn pursued further study at home with a private tutor and at the Sorbonne in Paris before establishing himself as a sort of intellectual in residence at Christ Church College, Oxford, between 1868 and 1876, where he studied law in the Inner Temple. After completing an MA honours degree, he was admitted to the Bar as a barrister in 1877 but never practised.

---

8   Cora Wilding, 'Notes and Information about Julia Wilding', ms, WFP, box 36/168/8; Armstrong, 'The *Hereford Times* Desk', pp. 7–24.

9   Reader, *Professional Men*, p. 111.

After a short period as an equity draughtsman and conveyancer, he became something of a resourceful gentleman scholar and established a reputation as a mathematician, active within the London Mathematics Society. His talents extended to engineering, invention and architecture. In the 1870s he designed and supervised the construction of a new Anthony family home and devoted himself to improving printing presses and inventing a newspaper-folding apparatus for the *Hereford Times*. In 1878 he sold several patents for newspaper-folding machines to an American company in New York for £9,000. The raw energy of American society fascinated him, and a short business trip to New York was followed by approximately six years living in the United States. He returned to Hereford with an American wife in 1884 to run the business side of the *Hereford Times*. Edwyn's influence over Julia's life was necessarily less direct but at times as significant as that of elder brother Charles.[10]

After leaving Cheltenham College, Charles's life took a number of turns. At the age of 18, he embarked upon a military career, his father having purchased a commission for him as a subaltern (Cornet) in the Queen's Lancers. After two years service, he retired and embarked upon a two-year tour of Europe and America and despatched articles to the *Hereford Times* and the *Pall Mall Gazette*. He had already revealed himself as a precocious literary talent of liberal political sympathies. His first essays for the *Hereford Times* were 'a plea for the enfranchisement of women' and 'a tirade against the evils of drunkenness'.[11] Upon his return to the Anthony household in 1865, with his Canadian wife Elizabeth and a young son, Charles began a writing career with the *Hereford Times*. In 1867 he published *The Social and Political Dependence of Women*, a work that established him as a 'disciple of John Stuart Mill'.[12] After assuming the editorship of the *Hereford Times* in 1876, he wrote a number of political tracts, including *Popular Sovereignty* and *Duty and Privilege*.[13]

---

10 Armstrong, 'The *Hereford Times* Desk', pp. 20–22; 'Obituary: Charles Anthony, jnr.', WFP, box 41/1.

11 *HT*, 20 November 1909; *HT*, 15 February 1919.

12 *HT*, 15 February 1919; Charles Anthony, jnr., *The Social and Political Dependence of Women* [1867], Longmans, Green and Co., London, 1880; Nicholas Capaldi, *John Stuart Mill: A Biography*, Cambridge University Press, New York, 2004.

13 Charles Anthony, jnr., *Popular Sovereignty*, Longmans, Green and Co., London, 1880; Charles Anthony, jnr., *Duty and Privilege*, National Press Agency, London, 1886.

The shared scholarly inclinations and progressive instincts of the Anthony brothers represented two strands of early Victorian public school education: the classical, literary and bookish, and the stirrings of the scientific and social inquisitiveness that were to strip away its religiosity. It is at the confluence of the traditional and the new that we can locate the shaping of Julia Anthony's education. Here Charles (junior), Edwyn and, to a lesser extent, their father confronted the 'woman question'. Their reading of the feminist political tracts, most notably those of Mary Wollstonecraft, John Stuart Mill and Harriet Taylor Mill, sharpened their awareness of the deficiencies inherent in the traditional education of young girls. Both were publicly highly critical of a system which produced 'narrow and little minded' middle-class women lacking in knowledge and incapable of applying their minds to political and intellectual ideas in anything but a cursory manner. As he was to write in *The Social and Political Dependence of Women* (1867), heavily dependent upon Harriet Taylor Mill's *Enfranchisement of Women* (1851), Charles Anthony argued that it was the *type* of education provided for girls that lay at the heart of a social system that oppressed women.[14] By 'confining the education and knowledge of women', society ensured that they had 'weak minds in weak bodies'.[15] Many women became wives and mothers, he wrote, 'only because there is no other career open to them, no other occupation for their feelings or their activities' and girls were 'brought up with the one idea, "marriage" continually dangled before their minds'.[16]

Together, Charles and Edwyn fashioned an education for their sisters that they believed would allow them to break the shackles of their confinement. It combined elements of the traditional instruction thought appropriate for women of their social standing and much that was unconventional. Its intention was to provide an academic rigour and intensity that would provide knowledge and train the mind in the processes of reasoned analysis. In practice, this meant that the Anthony girls were taught at home by a governess, with additional instruction provided by specialist tutors and the Anthony brothers. Alongside ladylike accomplishments such as painting, needlework, singing and music, the girls studied subjects deemed appropriate for the upper middle-class female mind: art, poetry, literature, history,

---

14   Charles Anthony, jnr., *Social and Political Dependence*, pp. 26–86.
15   Charles Anthony, jnr., *Social and Political Dependence*, p. 61.
16   Charles Anthony, jnr., *Social and Political Dependence*, pp. 56, 72.

English grammar and composition, French and German languages. Julia's particular talent for music was exploited to its full potential, and a music room created within the family home. To this conventional fare was added Latin, mathematics and an introduction to scientific knowledge and methodology that went far beyond the realms of botany and nature studies which were the staple diet of the average middle-class girl, and indeed, beyond that which the brothers Anthony had received as public schoolboys at Cheltenham.

At the core of the heavily prescriptive curriculum was a reading program. Drawn up by Charles, it had the teenage Blanche and Julia grappling with the latest scientific, political, economic and social theories and was designed to provide a familiarity, or at least an awareness, of the latest currents of intellectual thought. There was a significant emphasis on evolutionary theories, both of the animal world and the development of human society, along with contemporary critiques of the Victorian world. The list of writers is daunting: John Ruskin (1819–1900), Thomas Carlyle (1795–1881), Johann Wolfgang Goethe (1749–1832), Auguste Comte (1798–1857), Herbert Spencer (1820–1903), John Stuart Mill (1806–1873), Charles Darwin (1809–1882), Thomas Huxley (1825–1895) and Francis Galton (1822–1911).[17] Whatever else this immersion in the intellectual discourse of the day achieved, its emphasis upon intellectual theories was the common currency of a household sheltered from the economic realities of the marketplace. For conscientious and talented young women, it was at once a stimulus to high thinking and idealism—and perhaps also a recipe for personal frustration.

By its very nature, the education of Julia Anthony raised expectations. Accustomed to equal treatment within the family, Julia and her sister Blanche faced an outside world of legal, social and economic inequality that barred them from the professions and occupations open to their brothers. As a family enterprise, however, the *Hereford Times* provided an avenue of advancement that did not unduly challenge conventional restraints. In its pages, Julia developed a recognised talent for writing, albeit anonymously, and with family editors and encouragers at her

---

17   Cora Wilding, 'Notes and Information about Julia Wilding'.

shoulder. Between 1870 and 1876 she contributed a series of articles from which it is possible to glean an emerging philosophy or set of attitudes.[18]

There are, of course, dangers inherent in accepting her written words at face value. The articles represent, like all publications, a self-conscious literary occasion. They were often derivative, with the influence of John Stuart Mill's works clearly discernible and they are likely to have been suggested and shaped by brothers Charles or Edwyn.[19] At times, they also take on the character of exercises in deductive reasoning, rather than expressions of deeply held convictions. Historians also warn of the pitfalls of assigning to individual writers the assumptions and ideologies of the entire school of thought from which they draw. These caveats notwithstanding, it is perhaps worth noting the observation of historian G. M. Young that 'to understand' a person we should 'consider what was happening, what ideas were in the air' when they were 'around twenty, "because what sixteen to twenty-four is talking about, twenty-four to sixty-four will usually write, or think, or do. Those are the charging years".'[20] In this light, Julia Anthony's *Hereford Times* articles offer a useful snapshot of her developing preoccupations, beliefs and attitudes between the ages of 17 and 23 and might be seen as providing clues for an understanding of her subsequent departure from Britain at the age of 26.

The articles fall into two broad categories: some 20 columns written on trips to the Continent, mostly from Cologne between 1870 and 1873 when Julia was furthering her musical education, light in tone and striving to develop her writing talents; and a further 20, written mainly between 1873 and 1875 as the hopes which middle-class progressives had harboured for Gladstone's Liberal Government

18   The most important of these articles, published in the *HT* between 1873 and 1876 are as follows: Women's Suffrage', 15 February 1873; 'Women: Two Conflicting Tendencies', 14 October 1876; 'Marriage', 7 November 1874; 'Utilitarianism', 'John Stuart Mill', 17 May 1873; 'Peace and War', 8 November 1873; 'The Tyranny of Custom', 6 December 1873; 'Scientific Investigation', 9 August 1873; 'Scepticism v Orthodoxy', c. 1874; 'Education', c. 1875; 'The Power of Realization', 6 March 1875; 'Theory and Practice', 5 August 1876; and 'Early Influences', 9 December 1876.
19   John Stuart Mill, *The Subjection of Women* (1869), *Utilitarianism* (1861, 1863), *On Liberty* (1859), *On Representative Government* (1861).
20   George M. Young, *The Victorian Noon-Time*, cited by Philip Collins, 'Dickens and his Readers', in Gordon Marsden (ed.), *Victorian Values: Personalities and Perspectives in Nineteenth Century Society*, Longman, Essex, 1990, p. 44.

began to fade.[21] The latter reveal a young woman grappling with the intellectual theories of the day. A mixture of abstract expressions of her philosophy and a reaction to the events around her, they reveal an optimistic view of the future evolution of society alongside a deepening dissatisfaction with the present. The optimism sprang from a belief in the capacity of science to advance civilisation and provide a new way of thinking based on fact and observation and freed from the obfuscations of religion, custom and tradition. Science, she believed, provided the foundation for an ethical commonweal implicit in Comte's 'religion of humanity': 'this religion, this faith and hope in the future progress and perfection of mankind is as ennobling and exalting a guide to the conduct as any we can conceive'.[22] Scientific discoveries and material improvements, if wedded to a spirit of internationalism, would enable the world family to march forward in unison.[23]

Scholarly, almost Olympian in tone, the articles are infused with an increasing disappointment, as Gladstone's reforming Liberal Party was ground down by the inertia of the electorate.[24] As Julia saw it, Liberalism had lost its nerve in the face of a widespread and irrational fear of change. Entrenched customs and a stern orthodoxy inhibited the open expression of opinions and novel ideas were thwarted by a 'tyranny of custom' that stymied progress.[25] Nowhere was this collective failure more clear to her than in the progress of feminism. She berates Liberal members of parliament who privately supported the enfranchisement of women as a matter of moral justice only to vote against it in parliament when confronted with widespread derision. A. N. Wilson has recently addressed the same issue and pointed to the

---

21 Hoppen, *The Mid-Victorian Generation*, pp. 237–71, 591–637; A. N. Wilson, *The Victorians*, Hutchinson, London, 2002, pp. 342–424.
22 Julia Anthony, 'Scepticism v Orthodoxy'.
23 Julia Anthony, 'Education', 'Peace and War', 'Scientific Investigation'; Andrew Wernick, *Auguste Comte and the Religion of Humanity: The Post-Theistic Program of French Social Theory*, Cambridge University Press, New York, 2001.
24 Hoppen, *The Mid-Victorian Generation*, pp. 590–637; Wilson, *The Victorians*, pp. 343–64, 379, 383–84, 417. Gladstone's Liberals came to power in 1868 with a 'landslide' majority of over 100 seats. They were defeated in the 1874 general election by Disraeli's Conservative Party with a majority of 112.
25 Julia Anthony, 'The Tyranny of Custom'.

mania for Gilbert and Sullivan musicals as 'induc[ing] affection for the most moribund and unjustifiable abuses'.[26] Julia plainly did not see the joke.

Her discussion of the rampant individualism that blocked the path to reform draws heavily upon Morris, Ruskin, Matthew Arnold and Anthony Trollope.[27] She adopts their representation of nineteenth-century English society as consisting of a parasitical aristocracy, a selfish middle class intent on money making and a working class brutalised by the effects of industrialisation.[28] On the issue of how the path to reform might be smoothed, she is attracted to Ruskin's ideas about the need to balance the interests of the individual and those of society as a whole. By temperament she is drawn inexorably into his belief in the transformative power of education. It was this, she believed, that would ultimately pave the way for the removal of legal inequalities, injustices and abuses that would allow individualism to be civilised and a liberal society to be liberated.

This analysis led naturally to an emphasis upon the role of the family and the part it might play in the reformation of society. If English society was dominated by narrow-minded, conservative, selfish and largely unthinking men and women, then the family, as the microcosm of the wider society, held the key to social regeneration. Intellectually, she was drawn to the idealism of Mill whose argument she paraphrased in the pages of the *Hereford Times*. Social improvement could be initiated by 'noble' reasoned beings with a higher 'conception of the rights and duties' that 'every member of society individually owes to each other'. Such individuals, guided by 'a love of humanity' and possessing elevated aspirations, would usher in the 'amelioration of mankind'.[29] Educated and enlightened mothers were essential to the eradication of deficient parenting and unenlightened family

---

26 Wilson, *The Victorians*, pp. 420, 417–22.

27 See Matthew Arnold, *Culture and Anarchy: An Essay in Politics and Social Criticism* (1869), John Murray, London, 1923; Anthony Trollope's critique of society, *The Way We Live Now*, Chatto and Windus, London, 1875; John Ruskin, *Unto This Last*, Collins Clear-Type Press, London, 1862.

28 See, for example, Arnold, *Culture and Anarchy*, ch. 2 and 3 (cited by J. D. Jump, 'Matthew Arnold', in Boris Ford (ed.), *The Penguin Guide to English Literature From Dickens to Hardy*, 5th edn, Penguin, Middlesex, 1966, pp. 319–23); Julia Anthony, 'Tyranny of Custom', 'Theory and Practice', 'Education', 'Early Influences'.

29 Julia Anthony, 'Education', 'Early Influences'.

environments. Ideally, the family would become a sphere where childrearing would be the joint responsibility of both parents, equally committed to the moral regeneration of mankind.[30]

The prospect of marriage to Frederick Wilding, a prominent Herefordshire lawyer, gave these idealistic and intellectual ponderings greater immediacy. Prominent in her personal life by around 1877, Frederick Wilding was regarded by his fellow Herefordians as a perfect match or ideal husband for 'the daughter of Hereford'. He was born in Montgomery, Montgomeryshire, Wales, in 1852, to Harriet Farmer and John Powell Wilding, a surgeon, and as such may be placed at the lower end of the professional classes.[31] One of four children, he attended Hereford Cathedral School, before proceeding in the 1860s to the ancient and prestigious Shrewsbury School for boys, one of the nine 'great public schools', as defined by the Public Schools Act.[32] At the time, its reforming headmaster, Benjamin Hall Kennedy, was in the throes of endeavouring to shrug off criticisms of the school's curriculum. Charles Darwin, one of the school's most influential old boys, put the issue bluntly: 'nothing could have been worse for the development of my mind as it was strictly classical, nothing else being taught except a little ancient geography and history'.[33]

The young Wilding thrived in the Shrewsbury environment, absorbing fully its code of gentlemanly and manly behaviour. He distinguished himself more as an athlete than as a scholar and drew from one historian comparison with C. B. Fry, regarded by Edwardian English commentators as the beau ideal of the gentleman sportsman.[34] After leaving Shrewsbury he studied law and qualified as a solicitor in the early 1870s after a five-year apprenticeship.[35] He entered a London counsel's chambers to qualify as a barrister, a profession

---

30   Julia Anthony acknowledged that, given the present structure of society, mothers shouldered much of the childrearing duties within the family.

31   Reader, *Professional Men*, pp. 16–20, 31–64, 151–52.

32   The other schools were Charterhouse, Eton, Harrow, Merchant Taylors', Rugby, St Paul's, Westminster and Winchester. The Public School Commission, 1864, expressed unease at the continued concentration upon classical studies in such schools at the expense of more 'modern' or relevant subjects such as science. See Reader, *Professional Men*, pp. 104–15.

33   Francis Darwin (ed.), *The Life and Letters of Charles Darwin, including an autobiographical chapter*, John Murray, London, 1887.

34   'A Quarter-Century of Cricket. Doyen of Canterbury Sportsmen. Frederick Wilding', newspaper clipping, 3 October 1925, WFP, box 43/3, pp. 167–68.

35   Reader, *Professional Men*, p. 118.

which required in England a further three years training.[36] The cost of remaining in London to complete these studies led him to abandon them. By 1877 he had established a legal practice in Hereford, and was working as an advocate in the Hereford law courts, often appearing in front of Julia's father in his role as Justice of the Peace. The move to Hereford was thus in part a frustrated response to the entrenched customs and traditions of a British legal profession, where family influence and wealth counted for much and newcomers struggled to find a place. Thwarted professional ambition was to become a significant ingredient in his contemplation of English society and in the process by which he came to contemplate emigration.[37]

Away from the courtroom and legal chambers the young Frederick Wilding's life presents a contrasting image. Here we see not a frustrated individual but a young man at ease with the society in which he finds himself, an enthusiast energetically participating in almost every aspect of sporting, cultural, intellectual and political life. He was acknowledged in the West Midlands as a rugby player unlucky to miss selection for England as international rugby took its first steps in the early 1870s. He captained Hereford in rugby and rowing, represented the town on the cricket field and made his mark locally in athletics and in boxing. It was a sporting résumé that prompted one writer to describe him as 'the best all-round athlete Herefordshire had produced'.[38] Nor was his enthusiasm for sport confined to the playing fields. By his own admission, he had at one time or another been the secretary of 'nearly every athletic club in Hereford'.[39] Away from the playing fields his talents allowed him to sustain an active, if relatively undistinguished, role in Hereford's Harmonic and Amateur Dramatic Society, and in the local Debating Society.

The young Wilding's enthusiasms and interests flowed into politics and led him into the intellectual and political circle of the Anthonys. As secretary of the Hereford Liberal Association, he worked alongside all three Anthony males. With Charles junior and Edwyn he shared a common educational background and an attraction to the emergent progressive philosophies of Mill and Ruskin. Something of his political

---

36   *Lyttelton Times*, 28 June 1913.
37   *Lyttelton Times*, 28 June 1913; Hoppen, *The Mid-Victorian Generation*, pp. 40–43.
38   'A Quarter Century of Cricket', WFP; Len and Shelley Richardson, *Anthony Wilding: A Sporting Life*, Canterbury University Press, Christchurch, 2005, pp. 16–17.
39   *HT*, 22 October 1878.

thinking can be seen in an address he gave, as retiring secretary of the Hereford Liberal Association, in which he surveys the destruction of Liberalism at the hands of Benjamin Disraeli's Conservatives:

> The period during which I have had the honour of being your hon. Secretary has been a most painful and humiliating period, not only to the Liberal party, but to the country generally. We have seen the good ship of Liberalism almost hopelessly wrecked on the treacherous and shifting sands of foreign politics. We have seen how individuals, once prominent in the good cause, have deserted the leadership of the best and wisest statesman of all times—led away by a mistaken feeling of patriotic devotion, to even a bad government in a time of national trouble and peril, under the supposed necessity for the moment of electing between their country and their party ... With even deeper pain we have marked how the country generally has fallen away from her adherence to the old principles of humanity, justice and fair dealing to all mankind, and how under the spell of the Jewish magician she has indulged for a brief period in a wild dream of aggression, annexation and military pre-eminence in every quarter of the globe ... Such, ladies and gentlemen, has been the policy and spirit of the Conservative Party.[40]

The comments display a disenchantment with the fickleness of the electorate and dismay that the reforming initiatives of Gladstone's Liberal Party have been sunk by Disraeli's unnecessary foreign entanglements. They stop short of pessimism and go on to express the view that the perversion of enduring British values would be short-lived. The address might also be read against the background of impending marriage to Julia Anthony, with its accompanying sense of change and new beginnings. Placed in this context, the comments can be seen as feeding into a shared pool of frustration, from which the couple were to draw in shaping their future. They were part of the soul searching that was gradually making their marriage a migratory moment. The calculations involved in the decision to leave Hereford for New Zealand were a finely balanced weighing of present frustration against the hopes of a better future. The decision in favour of the new world rested upon the perception that in the antipodes enduring British values and culture would be free from the restraining hand

---

40 'Hereford Liberal Association Presentation of a Testimonial to Mr. Frederick Wilding', *HT*, 28 June 1879.

of rampant individualism that was temporarily diverting the progress of humanity, and free of the obfuscations of religion imbedded in an established Church.

We may leave the newly-weds on their wedding day, little more than a month before they sailed for New Zealand from Gravesend. Their secular and rationalist inclination notwithstanding, the ceremony was conducted in the 'suburban' Anglican church of Tupsley by two clergymen. The occasion, captured at considerable length in the social pages of the local tabloid, the *Hereford Mercury*, reveals something of the social position the pair were leaving behind and offers tantalising glimpses of the motives that prompted departure. The roads leading to the church were, according to the *Mercury*'s social columnist, 'thronged by members of the higher and middle classes of society, chiefly ladies, of whom there must have been 500', all anxious to catch a glimpse of the bride who wore a style of dress 'precisely of the type worn at the marriage of the Lord Mayor of London … a few weeks ago'. After the nine carriages bearing the bridal party had arrived, guests unable to find space inside gathered around the entrance. The stirring strains of *Onward Christian Soldiers* played 'in a slightly accelerated movement', as Julia marched towards the altar on her father's arm, and filled the surrounding churchyard.[41] With its militarist phraseology—'marching as to war'—it seems an odd choice for a secular couple, for whom the notion of war was a negation of humanity. Yet it encompassed also a sense of mission—'one in hope and purpose'—and perhaps it was this that appealed to a young couple imbued with idealistic notions of marriage and family. Perhaps also they found in its words the element of defiance and 'protest against the establishment' that, as historians have pointed out, appealed later to the civil rights movement in America.[42]

---

41 *Hereford Mercury and Independent*, 25 June 1879.
42 See J. M. Jasper, 'The Emotions of Protest: Affective and Reactive Emotions in and around Social Movements', *Sociological Forum*, vol. 13, no. 3, September 1998, pp. 397–424; and *The Social Movements Reader*, Blackwell, Oxford, 1968; David Hamer, *The New Zealand Liberals: The Years of Power, 1891–1912*, Auckland University Press, Auckland, 1988, pp. 48–52. Hamer raises the question of whether the act of migration can be seen as a 'political gesture' (p. 49). He suggests that as such it might take 'conservative' or 'utopian' forms. In short, an emigrant might want to 'escape' the unwanted or embrace the prospect of change.

Mary Struthers and Orme Masson:
Science and the imperial university

On 5 August 1886 Orme Masson, a 28-year-old chemist of Edinburgh, married Mary Struthers, the 24-year-old daughter of Sir John Struthers, an anatomy professor from Aberdeen, and Lady Christina Struthers, an advocate of higher education for women. Their summer marriage, like that of Julia Anthony and Frederick Wilding seven years previously, was a prelude to migration. Within three weeks the aspiring academic and his new wife sailed for Australia and a chair at the University of Melbourne. At first glance it would seem an unexceptional decision. The embryonic universities of Australasia had sought to draw their academic staff from amongst the graduates of the British institutions they regarded as parent bodies. Yet explaining the Massons' decision solely or even primarily in terms of an employment opportunity would leave unexplored the attitudes and assumptions that propelled the young couple to make the move to Melbourne. By placing the young couple in their family, social and intellectual context it is possible to examine the wider motivations that underlay their departure. In doing so we find that, like the Wildings of Hereford, the Massons of Edinburgh and Aberdeen share much of the secular idealism of the mid-Victorian generation of intellectuals. Their idealism was less explicitly articulated but, as we shall see, just as optimistically wedded to notions of progress and the capacity of science and education to produce a liberal and civilised society.

Born in 1858 at the fashionable London home of his maternal grandparents, Eliza Andrews and Charles Orme, (David) Orme Masson was the second child and only son of Englishwoman (Emily) Rosaline Orme, a highly educated member of a large and relatively affluent family of intellectuals, and first-generation Scottish academic, David Mather Masson. In 1852 David Masson became a pioneering professor of English Literature at University College, London, the first degree-granting institution in Britain to establish a chair in the subject.[43] The intellectualism that was to be the defining element

---

43   Jenny Young, 'Family Tree Compiled By Jenny Young', David Orme Masson Family Papers (DOMFP), University of Melbourne Archives, Acc. no. 1980.0080 (80/80 and 106/54); Jo McMurtry, *English Language, English Literature: The Creation of an Academic Discipline*, Archon Books, Hamden, Connecticut, 1985, pp. 1–5, 111–35.

of the young Orme's development was stronger on the maternal side, where it spanned several generations and blended artistic, literary, scientific and professional interests. His mother Rosaline, a scholar by disposition, had been one of the first students to attend Bedford College for Women, established in 1849 with the intention of providing a higher education of a liberal and secular nature. She became a published author in 1876 when Macmillan produced her anthology, *Three Centuries of English Poetry*.[44] Her younger sister Lilie was the first female law graduate of London University. Another sister, Olivia Blanche Orme Fox, helped establish Falmouth High School for Girls. A brother, Temple, taught chemistry at University College, London, while sister Julia married Henry Charlton Bastian FRS, physiologist, neurologist and Professor of Clinical Medicine at University College Medical School, and a participant in the scientific debate over spontaneous generation.[45] The Ormes' household in Regent's Park, London, was consequently a lively one and was made the more so by the comings and goings of artists, literary figures, social theorists and critics including Alfred Tennyson, Coventry Patmore, Ralph Waldo Emerson and Thomas Carlyle, as well as the leading figures of the Pre-Raphaelite circle, William Holman Hunt, Dante and William Rossetti. In such an environment the discussion of contemporary concerns such as the condition of Britain, the nature of 'progress' and the evolution of British society flowed naturally.[46]

It was also a setting into which Orme's father, David Mather Masson, with his literary credentials and later academic position, fitted neatly. Born in Aberdeen, in 1822, into a highly religious and literate family, he had in 1839 at the age of 17 commenced theological studies under Thomas Chalmers at the University of Edinburgh. He was to remain a deeply devout man, but abandoned his religious studies to carve out a career as a man of letters. Chalmers continued to be something of a mentor and his reconciliation of recent scientific findings with traditional religion formed the bedrock of Masson's spiritual life.[47] As editor of the *Banner* magazine (1842–43), he actively supported

---

44   Rosaline Masson (ed.), *Three Centuries of English Poetry*, Macmillan, London, 1876.
45   James Strick, 'Darwinism and the Origin of Life: The Role of H. C. Bastian in the British Spontaneous Generation Debates, 1868–1873', *Journal of the History of Biology*, vol. 32, no. 1, 1999, pp. 51–92.
46   Weickhardt, *Masson of Melbourne*, pp. 3–4.
47   Thomas M. Devine, *The Scottish Nation: A History 1700–2000*, Allen Lane and Penguin Press, London, 1999, pp. 364, 370–80.

the formation of the Free Church of Scotland, and Chalmers, who led the dissidents out of the Church of Scotland in 1843. After a decade in Edinburgh and London editing, and writing a number of articles and essays for the Chambers publishing firm, Masson accepted a professorship at University College, London, in 1852. During this time, he aligned himself with John Stuart Mill on all matters, except religion, and established a reputation for being liberal, progressive and something of an internationalist. As secretary of the London-based Friends of Italy Society he hosted the visiting Italian patriot Mazzini.[48]

In his writing and teaching Masson assumed the role of moral guide. He employed the works of writers grappling with the great social questions and theories of the day—the condition of England, the nature of progress, the development of society—to point the way forward to a better future. His most notable work, a *Life of John Milton, narrated in connection with the Political, Ecclesiastical and Literary History of His Times*, was published in seven volumes between 1859 and 1884.[49] His ideas were brought together in a survey of *Recent British Philosophy*, published in 1865, and an expansion of his lectures delivered to the Philosophical Institution of Edinburgh and the Royal Institute of London.[50] Described as a historian at heart, his studies of English literary figures were interspersed with several histories of the classical and medieval period. Between 1880 and 1884, after his appointment as Historiographer Royal for Scotland, he produced the 'four massive volumes' of the *Register of the Privy Council in Scotland 1578–1604*.[51]

David Masson had his greatest influence as Professor of English and Chair of English Literature and Rhetoric at Edinburgh University (1865–95).[52] An inspiring teacher, he was depicted by an anonymous writer as having shaped a future generation by moulding his students' characters as well as their minds:

48 Newspaper clippings: 'David Masson: December 2, 1822', *Glasgow Herald*, 2 December 1922; 'Death of Professor Masson', *Times*, 8 October 1907; 'The Late Emeritus Professor Masson: A Distinguished Literary Career', *Scotsman*, 8 October 1907, DOMFP, box 7/10/3.
49 David Mather Masson, *Life of John Milton*, 7 vols, Macmillan & Co., London, 1854–94.
50 David Mather Masson, *Recent British Philosophy*, Macmillan, Cambridge and London, 1887.
51 'Death of Professor Masson', 'The Late Emeritus Professor Masson', 'David Masson', newspaper clippings, DOMFP, box 7/10/3.
52 McMurtry, *English Language, English Literature*, pp. 111–35.

> all that he has said and written accepts the high responsibility and
> maintains the dignity of the true man of letters. He has done much
> to show to heedless undergraduates and thoughtless 'general readers'
> that he who worthily studies the language and literature of our race
> is not chiefly concerned how most gracefully ... to turn a paragraph
> ... The student must also face for himself the problems with which the
> strong souls of Knox and Hume, Hooker and Milton, George Eliot and
> Carlyle struggled not in vain ...[53]

Carlyle, more than any other contemporary writer, influenced Masson.
The pair were lifelong friends, and contemporaries noted that Masson
shared a certain moral earnestness with his friend, though without the
pervasive gloom. Rosaline Masson described her husband as 'a happy
Carlyle'.[54] Carlyle himself pronounced Masson a 'true thinking man,
sincere and sure of purpose'.[55] Contemporary observers were struck by
the irony that amongst Masson's greatest admirers and most successful
former students were three Scottish authors known for imaginative
works mixing fantasy, Scottish folklore and nostalgic tales of
Scotland's rural past: Rev. Samuel Crockett (1859–1941); Ian Maclaren,
the pen-name of Rev. John Watson (1850–1907); and Sir James Barrie
(1860–1937). Part of the 'Kailyard School' of Scottish literature, which
was later criticised for being divorced from the reality of a highly
industrialised, urban Scotland of the late nineteenth century, the
trio acknowledged Masson's lectures as their inspiration.[56] Writing
in *Edinburgh Eleven*, Barrie described the vigorous, impassioned and
often dramatic delivery-style of Masson's image-laden lectures 'that
made his lectures literature'.[57] The huge numbers of students drawn to
his classes led to the introduction of the degree with Honours in English
(the first candidate graduated in 1895). A dedicated teacher, Masson
missed only three lectures in 30 years, and also played a prominent
role in the movement for women's tertiary education, student welfare
schemes, university administration and public lecturing programs.[58]
The earnestness and energy that Masson injected into his professional

---

53   'The Late Emeritus Professor Masson', newspaper clipping, DOMFP, box 7/10/3.

54   Rosaline Masson to Orme Masson, 16 July 1933, cited by Weickhardt, *Masson of Melbourne*,
p. 110.

55   'David Masson', newspaper clipping, DOMFP, box 7/10/3.

56   'Death of Professor Masson', newspaper clipping, DOMFP, box 7/10/3.

57   James Barrie, *An Edinburgh Eleven: Pencil Portraits from College Life*, Office of the British
Weekly, London, 1889; 'The Late Emeritus Professor Masson', 8 October 1907, newspaper
clipping, DOMFP, box 7/10/3.

58   Extract from volume of university portraits, DOMFP, box 7/10/3.

duties flowed through into family life so that Orme and his three sisters—Flora, Rosaline and Helen—grew up in an environment where ideas and their importance were part of the rhythm of daily existence. They picnicked with Herbert Spencer, played games with John Stuart Mill, entertained the Carlyles and the Patmores (Coventry and George) and generally became accustomed to hearing the great questions of the day debated in front of them.[59]

The young Orme Masson's formal education was consistent with such an environment; broad, liberal and loaded with expectations of subsequent tertiary studies. He attended 'Mr Oliphant's School', a small private establishment for boys, until 1869 when, at the age of 11, he embarked on four years of study at Edinburgh Academy, described as 'a private establishment patronized by the professional elite'. A relatively new private boys' school, the academy was established in 1823 with the intention of providing a first-class classical education that included instruction in Greek, to rival that of British public schools, and thus provide an entry route to Cambridge and Oxford universities. Its founders also desired to provide a pleasant educational environment with minimal corporal punishment, in contrast to their own experiences at Edinburgh High School.[60] Orme Masson excelled academically at the academy, frequently featuring in its prize lists. He matriculated at age 15 (enrolment at university at a young age was a distinct feature of the Scottish educational tradition) and embarked, in 1873, upon the 'uniform' four-year MA course at Edinburgh University. A broad and liberal undergraduate degree, it encompassed humanities, Greek, botany, mathematics, natural philosophy, natural history, rhetoric and English literature. A busy social life (sister Rosaline remembered him 'danc[ing] till three in the morning the night before an exam') and an active involvement in student life (the Diagnostic Society, a debating club; and the university theatrical company, of which Robert Louis Stevenson was also a member) probably resulted in academic performance described by Weickhardt as 'solid rather than brilliant'.[61] In his final year (1876), he came 20th in humanities, 13th in Greek, 5th equal in mathematics and natural

59   Flora Masson, *Victorians All*, Chambers, Edinburgh, 1931, pp. 53–69.
60   Weickhardt, *Masson of Melbourne*, p. 6; Magnus Magnusson, *The Clacken and the Slate*, Collins, London, 1974.
61   Weickhardt, *Masson of Melbourne*, p. 7; Rosaline Masson to Orme Masson, 25 July 1933, DOMFP, box 2/1/8.

philosophy, 9th equal in natural history, 7th equal in rhetoric and English literature, and 42nd in chemistry—though this meant first-class honours in chemistry with 77 per cent. Orme's performance was good enough to provide him with several options for specialisation, especially in natural philosophy, mathematics and English. Yet after gaining his MA in 1877 he chose to pursue postgraduate studies in chemistry at Edinburgh University.[62]

What was behind Orme Masson's decision to depart from the family literary tradition to specialise in scientific studies? In contrast, his sisters Flora and Rosaline were to become successful writers. Yet there was enough interest in science and connections with the scientific world within the Orme and Masson households to make a career in science appear an attractive possibility. Indeed, according to family accounts, it was Orme's mother, Rosaline, a published author, who more than anyone else influenced Orme's choices. She had attended chemistry classes at Edinburgh University, where she was inspired both by the subject and its teacher, Crum Brown, and encouraged her son in his direction.[63] The environment of the University of Edinburgh, with its world-renowned medical school, of which the chemistry course was a component, was also a stimulating influence. Orme and his parents were part of a generation that revered science as the key to progress; thus the relative sense of 'newness' and promise that surrounded the field of chemistry held some appeal. Moreover, the leap from his father's study of English, philosophy and history was not as great as it might first appear. David Masson's approach to the study of English literature, history and philosophy was essentially scientific, involving rigorousness, exhaustive analysis and the amassing of factual evidence. Contemporaries remarked upon the resulting absence of artistic merit in his critical literary studies. An obituary in the *London Times* remarked:

> His perception of English literature was perhaps at the opposite extreme from that of the 'belletristic trifler'. For him it was simply the highest expression of the national mind and character, and as such was to be mastered by study as laborious and systematic as is demanded

---

62 Weickhardt, *Masson of Melbourne*, pp. 6–15.
63 Flora Masson to Orme Masson, 16 December 1936, DOMFP, box 3/1/12; Weickhardt, *Masson of Melbourne*, pp. 7–9.

in the case of the severest sciences. Hence the great burden of his teaching was the necessity of strenuous effort alike for enjoyment and the production of what is best in any form of literature.[64]

While his father searched for answers to the great questions of their time in literature, history and philosophy, Orme went in search of the 'chemical truth'.[65] Unlike his sisters, Orme came to reject the religion of his father. He later claimed that clergymen had 'been brought up to declare the truth of what they know to be untrue'.[66]

Orme Masson became one of the new breed of research scientists, trained in methodologies developed in Germany. In April 1880, after two years further study in botany, natural history, chemistry and practical, he was awarded a Bachelor of Science degree. He followed this with a brief, but much sought after stint in Frederick Wohler's laboratory at Göttingen, Germany, before returning to England in 1880 to take up an appointment as lecturer and research assistant to chemistry professor William Ramsay at University College, Bristol. Masson was to remain in close contact with Ramsay, who received the Nobel Prize in Chemistry for his discovery of inert gases. Masson resigned, however, from this post a year later in 1881, presumably to advance his career prospects, and returned to Edinburgh University, where his research work on the composition of nitroglycerine (facilitated by a prestigious scholarship and several fellowships) led to his attainment of a PhD in 1884.[67] There followed the problem of finding a suitable academic position.[68]

To understand the motivations that prompted migration, we need to explore the trends at work within the parent institutions that made up the 'British university' and the place that this university established

---

64 'Professor Masson', *Times*, 8 October 1907, DOMFP, box 7/12/1. His life of John Milton spanned six volumes and was written over 10 years.

65 Orme Masson, 'The Scope and Aims of Chemical Science and its Place in the University', Inaugural lecture, *Argus*, 24 March 1887.

66 Orme Masson to Flora Masson, 12 January 1936, University of Melbourne Archives (UMA), quoted by Weickhardt, *Masson of Melbourne*, p. 180.

67 Orme Masson served as one of three joint presidents of the first Students' Representative Council at the University of Edinburgh, formed in 1884, possibly as a more democratic answer to the elitist 'Speculative' society within the university. He was heavily involved, along with his father, in the celebrations for the university's tercentenary held in April 1884. Weickhardt, *Masson of Melbourne*, pp. 15–17.

68 R. J. W. Selleck, *The Shop: The University of Melbourne 1850–1939*, Melbourne University Press, Carlton, Victoria, pp. 285–86; Weickhardt, *Masson of Melbourne*, pp. 9–14, 20–23.

in the new settler societies. The first Australasian universities were products of the mid-Victorian age: Sydney (1850), Melbourne (1853), Otago (1869), Canterbury (1873) and Adelaide (1874).[69] Historians have described their gestation in terms that underline the old world attachments that underlay their foundation. W. J. Gardner's path-breaking *Colonial Cap and Gown: Studies in the Mid-Victorian Universities of Australasia*[70] discusses them within the framework of Louis Hartz's 'fragment' thesis.[71] As institutions or 'fragments' of the old world, they looked backwards not forwards and took on forms that were conservative and derivative.

Yet, as Gardner and others have demonstrated, such a generalisation obscures as much as it reveals. It needs to be seen in the context of the diversity of models available to colonial universities from within the mid-nineteenth-century British university system. Oxford and Cambridge stood as the exemplars of rural retreats of contemplation, whose exclusivity was maintained by religious tests and a curriculum built around Greek and Latin. The urban, more secular and cheaper universities of Scotland and Ireland had developed in ways that were less exclusive.[72] When the founding fathers of colonial universities discussed what sort of academy they wished to create, they did so in terms that reflected their individual understandings of this diversity.[73] They were also aware of the growing body of criticism that held the universities, especially Oxford and Cambridge, to be retarding the advancement of science by their traditional concentration upon Latin and Greek.[74] It was from within this mixed framework of inherited tradition that the Australasian colonies established their universities.

---

69   Selleck, *The Shop*; W. J. Gardner, E. T. Beardsley and T. E. Carter, *A History of the University of Canterbury 1873–1973*, University of Canterbury, Christchurch, 1973; W. G. K. Duncan and Roger Ashley Leonard, *The University of Adelaide, 1874–1974*, Rigby, Adelaide, 1974; H. E. Barff, *A Short Historical Account of the University of Sydney*, Angus and Robertson, Sydney, 1902; W. P. Morrell, *The University of Otago: A Centennial History*, University of Otago Press, Dunedin, 1969.

70   W. J. Gardner, *Colonial Cap and Gown: Studies in the Mid-Victorian Universities of Australasia*, University of Canterbury, Christchurch, 1979, p. 11.

71   Hartz, *The Founding of New Societies*, p. 3.

72   Selleck, *The Shop*, pp. 9, 18, 21–22, 26–27; Reader, *Professional Men*, pp. 134–35.

73   Selleck, *The Shop*, pp. 25–27; Gardner, *Colonial Cap and Gown*, pp. 10–11.

74   Reader, *Professional Men*, pp. 127–45; Selleck, *The Shop*, pp. 17–20, 46–52, 284–85.

Where then can we place Orme Masson as aspiring academic? A young, talented English-born but Scottish-educated chemist, son of a professor of English literature, he gained his PhD in Edinburgh. Although one of the 'ancient' universities, the University of Edinburgh, founded in 1582, had a decidedly more democratic tradition, providing a less expensive and more professionally orientated education to greater numbers of students.[75] There was also more emphasis on research. Masson, in the words of Richard Selleck, was 'one of the new British academic scientists for whom training in research was part of the preparation for professional life'.[76] Yet the newly qualified and ambitious Masson faced difficulties securing an academic appointment in a relatively new field where suitable positions were scarce and competition fierce.

Opportunities for academic advancement for scientists were limited in Britain for a number of reasons. Chemistry as a scientific discipline distinct from that of medicine was a relatively recent development. Indeed, the two subjects had only begun to be separated at Edinburgh University in 1844, and a Chemical Society founded at the university (refounded) in 1874. One of Masson's inspirational teachers, Alexander Crum Brown, Professor of Chemistry and Chemical Pharmacy, University of Edinburgh, had become the first holder of the London Doctor of Science degree in 1862 and was at the forefront of the pioneering movement to professionalise the chemistry field by establishing proper qualifications and standards. Crum Brown aided the formation of the Chemical Institute of Great Britain between 1876 and 1877 specifically for this purpose.[77] Yet Weickhardt points to the relatively stagnant state of chemistry research in Britain in the 1880s when Masson was searching for a suitable appointment:

> There was … evidence of a sad decline in the research productivity of British chemistry, as measured by the number of original papers read before the Chemical Society, which had fallen from 113 in 1880 to 63 in 1883. In fact the 1881 *Transactions* contain no papers at all from any of the professors of chemistry at Oxford, Cambridge, Edinburgh, St Andrews, Aberdeen, University College, London, or the Royal College of Chemistry.[78]

---

75 Reader, *Professional Men*, p. 134.
76 Selleck, *The Shop*, p. 286.
77 Weickhardt, *Masson of Melbourne*, pp. 7–9.
78 Weickhardt, *Masson of Melbourne*, p. 22.

Furthermore, despite growing criticism, the continuing emphasis placed by English public schools and universities upon the classical and liberal educational programs at the expense of science and the newer technical professional trainings, further limited employment opportunities for men such as Masson.[79]

Engaged since 1884 to Mary Struthers, daughter of Sir John Struthers, Professor of Anatomy at Aberdeen University, the matter of securing an academic position was becoming for Orme Masson a pressing matter both professionally and personally.[80] In keeping with the family tradition and upper middle-class social convention of the day, the timing of Masson's marriage was dependent upon his ability to support a wife (and future family) in suitable style. Throughout 1884–5, while on a research fellowship at the University of Edinburgh, Masson applied unsuccessfully for the limited number of chemistry chairs on offer in Britain; early in 1886 he turned his attention to an advertisement in the *Lancet* and *Nature* for the chair at the University of Melbourne. On 10 June the university selection committee notified him of his successful appointment, Masson formally accepted on 3 August and he and Mary Struthers were married on 5 August 1886.[81]

Masson's application for the Melbourne position had been timely. There was growing receptivity in the colonial universities towards scientific research and its perceived potential to aid industrial and agricultural development. The sudden death of the sole chemistry professor, John Kirkland, on 22 October 1885, imperilled the future of the discipline. Moreover, the need to find a replacement for Kirkland came after a number of 'unsatisfactory' appointments and a series of public scandals involving accusations of drunkenness, nepotism and irregular practice.[82] The University Council was more than ever anxious to adopt a selection process that would stand up to public scrutiny and deliver a first-class academic. Kirkland's appointment had itself been much criticised. A Melbourne University graduate, and already

79   Reader, *Professional Men*, pp. 104–15.
80   John Struthers, *Memoir of Dr Alexander Wooler* [printed pamphlet, n.d., publisher unknown], DOMFP, box 7/10/3; *In Memoriam: James Struthers, M.D. of Leith*, Oliver and Boyd, Edinburgh, 1891 [reprinted from the *Edinburgh Medical Journal*, July 1891], DOMFP, box 7/10/3; 'Obituary: Lady Struthers', *The Journal of Education*, September 1907, DOMFP, box 7/10/3; 'Mamma's Forbears', ms, DOMFP, box 7/10/3.
81   Weickhardt, *Masson of Melbourne*, pp. 13–14, 17, 23.
82   Selleck, *The Shop*, pp. 206, 297.

a chemistry lecturer at the university, he had been appointed to the newly created Chair of Chemistry in 1882, after a farcical application process in which the position was only advertised locally, and for less than three weeks. Four other Melbourne University graduates, three of whom were also members of the teaching staff, were appointed to newly created chairs at the same time, and it is possible to see elements of economy and Victorian assertiveness in the appointments.[83] Historians, commenting specifically on Kirkland's appointment, have judged the process deficient and observe that Kirkland lacked 'thorough' training in chemistry. Both Richard Selleck and Geoffrey Blainey agree that Kirkland would not have been appointed if the university had followed its earlier practice of using a British selection panel.[84]

Whatever the motives behind these appointments, the public criticism that ensued led the University Council to revert to looking further afield for Kirkland's replacement. A panel of British experts chaired by the Victorian Attorney-General was assembled in London to receive applications, interview British and European-based candidates, and rank them. The position was advertised locally and in Britain, Europe and the United States, although the selection committee ultimately decided not to wait for American applications to arrive. There were generous inducements to draw scholars to the other side of the world: an annual salary of £750 for the first five years, an increase of £150 pounds every five years within a salary cap of £1,200. Moreover, the criteria provided to guide the selection panel's deliberations were designed to point them towards a younger scholar—neither under 25 'nor much over 32'. Teaching experience was paramount in the quest for a man of 'moral character' and 'gentlemanly manners' and the secular nature of the new university was underlined by the injunction that 'men in holy orders' were not to be considered.[85] Masson was judged to meet the criteria admirably and was ranked first of the 34 candidates. Significantly, as Weickhardt points out, he was placed ahead of a scientist regarded by some members of the London

---

83 Selleck, *The Shop*, pp. 176–78, 196–210; Weickhardt, *Masson of Melbourne*, p. 21.
84 Selleck, *The Shop*, pp. 196–99, 285; Geoffrey Blainey, *A Centenary History of the University of Melbourne*, Melbourne University Press, Carlton, Victoria, 1957, p. 102; Weickhardt, *Masson of Melbourne*, p. 21.
85 University of Melbourne Council Minutes, 16 December 1885, cited by Weickhardt, *Masson of Melbourne*, pp. 20–22.

selection committee as possessing superior scientific qualifications, but seemingly judged as lacking the innovative, pioneering spirit or drive thought appropriate in a colonial university.[86]

For their part, Orme and Mary Masson would have found the prospect of employment by the University of Melbourne attractive for a number of reasons. The potential for financial security and the determinedly secular nature of the university held obvious appeal. Perhaps equally important was the presence of Edinburgh University acquaintances in Australia, albeit in Sydney, who confirmed for them that there were enough similarities between the University of Edinburgh and the University of Melbourne's teaching style to provide a sense of familiarity.[87] Those who had gone before them provided insights into the possibilities a new university offered scholars with agendas for the future. Significantly, there were signs during the 1880s of an increasingly sympathetic attitude within the university towards the study of science and scientific research.[88] The place of classical studies in a rapidly expanding colonial society with specific labour requirements had been questioned since the university's foundation and 'attack[s] on "useless" knowledge' had become 'a colonial preoccupation'.[89]

Selleck suggests that the 1880s witnessed a change in the general conception of the idea of a university, whereby it came to be seen not simply as a disseminator of information, but as a creator of knowledge via research. His definitive history of Melbourne University demonstrates that this change revealed itself most clearly in the endorsement of science. Furthermore, it was linked to claims such as those made by a member of the university Senate, Charles Topp, that in the natural sciences, particularly, colonial universities possessed 'greater facilities for original research than did the universities at "home"'.[90] Against this background, a Senate Committee chaired by Henry Higgins, already making his mark in Victorian society, formally

---

86   Weickhardt, *Masson of Melbourne*, pp. 21–23.
87   Weickhardt, *Masson of Melbourne*, pp. 24–25.
88   Selleck, *The Shop*, pp. 284–300.
89   Selleck, *The Shop*, p. 19.
90   Selleck, *The Shop*, p. 284.

drew attention in 1885 to the paucity of scientific instruction within the university and successfully proposed the introduction of a BSc degree and the creation of a chair in biology.[91]

These stirrings within the university suggested to Masson that the environment at Melbourne University offered fertile ground for the development of his ideas. He was aware that behind the grand proclamations of intent there lurked the realities of a new and relatively raw institution, most notably a lack of equipment, and unsuitable buildings and laboratories.[92] He was also well aware that, notwithstanding the expressed desire for the university to become a significant contributor to the advancement of knowledge rather than primarily a disseminator of established knowledge, teaching would loom large in his duties. As his inaugural lecture at Melbourne was to make clear, Masson harboured the hope that from within the university he would be able to influence the development of science in Australia. He would train a 'small band' of students in scientific research methods, so that they could contribute to 'original work' and strive to raise the status of chemistry to that of a discipline in its own right.[93] In prosecuting this personal mission, he was to be recognised by contemporaries and subsequently by historians as part of a 'brilliant triumvirate of young scientists'.[94]

91   Selleck, *The Shop*, pp. 284–85.
92   Selleck, *The Shop*, pp. 289–90.
93   Orme Masson, 'The Scope and Aims of Chemical Science and its Place in the University'.
94   Selleck, *The Shop*, p. 298 and also pp. 287–89, 297. The other members of the triumvirate were Walter Baldwin Spencer, a Lancashire man and Oxford graduate, appointed Professor of Biology at the University of Melbourne in January 1887, and Thomas Ranken Lyle, Irishman and graduate of Trinity College Dublin, appointed Professor of Natural Philosophy (Physics) at the University of Melbourne in March 1889.

2

The Family and Mid-Victorian Realities

John Macmillan Brown: Scottish scholar and colonial mission?

In 1874, some 12 years earlier than Orme Masson, fellow Scottish academic John Macmillan Brown (1845–1935) departed from Britain to take up the foundation chair in classics and English literature at Canterbury College. Established at Christchurch in 1873, the college was an affiliate of the University of New Zealand. Like Masson, Macmillan Brown's main migratory motivations were career advancement and financial gain. The 28-year-old was a graduate of both the University of Glasgow and, more recently, the highly regarded Balliol College, Oxford. His previously brilliant academic record had been marred by an illness during his final exams at Oxford, resulting in a disappointing second-class degree instead of the predicted first-class honours. The outcome severely limited his prospects of an academic post in Britain and he turned his mind to the schools and universities being established throughout the Empire. There was no shortage of opportunities and Macmillan Brown was offered posts in India and Canada, as well as at Canterbury College.[1]

---

1   John Macmillan Brown, *The Memoirs of John Macmillan Brown*, Whitcombe and Tombs, University of Canterbury, Christchurch, 1974, pp. 69, 73–75.

Macmillan Brown later ascribed his choice to a curiosity about Māori culture, the perceived freer life of a pioneering country and an ingrained sense of adventure.[2] As the son of a North Ayrshire shipmaster and ship owner working from Irvine, which was then second only to Glasgow as a Scottish seaport, Macmillan Brown grew up with a heightened interest in the world beyond the narrow confines of his home town. In his *Memoirs*, he recalls the excitement of watching the arrival of incoming ships, the 'romances we wove round the distant lands the schooners had voyaged to' and the exotic foods and curios that his father brought home from his voyages.[3] 'By nature' a 'migrative' community, mid-nineteenth-century Irvine represented for Macmillan Brown all that 'made the British Empire so wide-ranging in its interests and prosperity. It would be like a tour over the world to tell of all the fates that overtook my schoolmates.'[4] Moreover, as Macmillan Brown contemplated his future in 1874, his family and extended family provided both examples of mobility and sources of advice: his married sister had settled in Sydney and a retired sea-captain cousin was living in Hokitika, the New Zealand goldfields town across the Southern Alps from Christchurch.[5]

If Macmillan Brown grew up at a time and place where migration was a commonplace, the family environment provided a philosophical outlook in which the prospect could flourish. The long absences of his shipmaster father meant that his 'deeply religious' mother exerted the greatest influence during his childhood. It was his mother who organised the establishment of the family household in Irvine to take advantage of the opportunities the town offered for the education of her children: well-respected ladies' colleges for the girls and the coeducational Irvine Academy for the boys. For John and older brother Francis, the academy of some 200 students offered the sort of traditional education that prepared capable boys for university study and entry to the professions. For an extra fee, it was possible to have additional lessons in Greek, Latin and mathematics. The coeducational experience would help shape Macmillan Brown's later views about higher education for women. Like his elder brother, he displayed talent in mathematics, but blossomed as the sort of all-rounder his

---

2   Macmillan Brown, *Memoirs*, p. 73.
3   Macmillan Brown, *Memoirs*, pp. 4, 13.
4   Macmillan Brown, *Memoirs*, p. 5.
5   Macmillan Brown, *Memoirs*, pp. 81, 98.

generation so admired. His intellectual talents were regarded as leading naturally to a career in the Church.[6] Indeed, as Macmillan Brown later acknowledged, he accepted life as a clergyman as his 'destiny': 'I cannot imagine any career but that of the church likely to entangle my ambitions and aims.'[7]

It was a future that fitted family expectations. He grew up within a family that was religious 'by tradition and upbringing', where 'sober enthusiasm … based on the old covenanting view of life and the world' went largely unchallenged.[8] Indeed, as he was later to write, Puritan Scottish families like his own exhibited minds 'steeped in the tenets of their special sect even before they know what they are'.[9] In such an environment, the Bible became both the young Macmillan Brown's frame of reference for interpreting the world and also his literary guide. Family and religion provided the setting in which Macmillan Brown first confronted the philosophical issues of his age. He was later to identify the experience of listening with other family members to churchyard discussions, sparked by the weekly sermon, as shaping his youthful attitudes and laying the foundation for a mode of thought that was to influence his life choices.[10]

Macmillan Brown's experience as a student at the universities of Edinburgh, Glasgow and Oxford between 1864 and 1874 was transformative. His university years coincided with the beginnings of a concerted response by a school of British philosophers, known as the British Idealists, to Darwin's theories of biological evolution and what they saw as the individualism of Herbert Spencer, the empiricism of John Stuart Mill and the developing dominance of scientific materialism. At the University of Glasgow and at Balliol College, Oxford, Macmillan Brown was to be greatly influenced by three of the more prominent leaders of this group, Edward Caird, Thomas Green and Benjamin Jowett. Caird's attempts to reconcile religion and science and his efforts to rebut the disciples of Comte's 'religion of humanity' helped sustain Macmillan Brown's conventional religious beliefs, and he became something of an acolyte of the Glaswegian professor

6   Macmillan Brown, *Memoirs*, pp. 5–12.
7   Macmillan Brown, *Memoirs*, p. 9.
8   Macmillan Brown, *Memoirs*, p. 9.
9   Macmillan Brown, *Memoirs*, p. 7; Devine, *The Scottish Nation*, pp. 365–66.
10   Macmillan Brown, *Memoirs*, pp. 8–9.

of moral philosophy.[11] In Caird's classes Macmillan Brown discovered that prose was his natural medium. Moreover the 'gentleness and sympathy' that he found so attractive in Caird's teaching struck a responsive chord.[12] The sinking of his father's uninsured ship, along with its cargo, as Macmillan Brown set out for university, had made it necessary for him to find tutoring work. He enjoyed assisting students from a variety of social backgrounds to cope with their studies and especially the first-hand experience of the less exclusive nature of the Scottish university system.[13] The experience also stimulated a change of his own direction of study, which came gradually to point in the direction of journalism or academia rather than the Church.[14]

Upon completing his MA in 1865, Macmillan Brown was awarded the coveted Snell Exhibition Prize in Classics and Philosophy, which provided a five-year scholarship to Balliol College, Oxford. Founded by Scottish academics, Balliol was Caird's old college and the spiritual home of British Idealism. Noel Annan later described it as a place to which 'hard working hard-headed Scots came to irritate the gentleman idlers'.[15] In its Scottishness and ethos of earnest endeavour, it proved a congenial college for the diligent, if spiritually troubled, Macmillan Brown. One of Oxford's most academically prestigious colleges, Balliol exhibited, in Macmillan Brown's view, much of the cloistered elitism of the older English university, and he was never to lose his preference for the general degree and more democratic ethos of the Scottish university.[16] Nevertheless, he arrived at Balliol just as the college was being revitalised under the mastership of the theologian and classicist Benjamin Jowett (1870–93). Jowett's attempts to sustain Christianity by advocating a more liberal theology built around the more critical analysis of the Bible initiated by German

---

11   John Passmore, *A Hundred Years of Philosophy*, Gerald Duckworth & Co. Ltd, London, 1957, pp. 50–59; Geoffrey Thomas, *The Moral Philosophy of T. H. Green*, Clarendon Press, Oxford and New York, 1988, passim; A. Vincent and R. Plant, *Philosophy, Politics and Citizenship: The Life and Thought of British Idealists*, Blackwell, Oxford, 1984; George Davie, *The Democratic Intellect: Scotland and her Universities in the Nineteenth Century*, Edinburgh University Press, Edinburgh, 1981.

12   Macmillan Brown, *Memoirs*, pp. 56, 23–64.

13   Gardner, *Colonial Cap and Gown*, pp. 59–64.

14   Macmillan Brown, *Memoirs*, pp. 20–26.

15   Noel Annan, *The Dons: Mentors, Eccentrics and Genuises*, HarperCollins, London, p. 62; John Jones, *Balliol College: A History* [1988], 2nd edn, Oxford University Press, Oxford, 2005.

16   W. J. Gardner, 'Part I: The Formative Years, 1873–1918', in Gardner et al., *A History of the University of Canterbury*, pp. 91, 96, 103; Gardner, *Colonial Cap and Gown*, pp. 59–63.

theologians, was controversial. Between 1873 and 1893, however, he had a profound influence upon a generation of young men who were later to make their marks as politicians, statesmen, lawyers, educators, writers and clergymen.[17] As the following exhortation delivered by Jowett to students makes clear, it was an influence that carried with it a strong moral imperative and sense of responsibility:

> The object of reading for the Schools is not primarily to obtain a first class, but to elevate and strengthen the character for life … What does matter is the sense of power which comes from steady working … the power in a man to control and direct his own life instead of drifting on the currents of fortune and self-indulgence.[18]

To the young Macmillan Brown, these injunctions offered direction at a time when the 'freethinking' atmosphere and the 'variety of opinions and beliefs' of his fellow students had created doubt.[19] He was, he later recalled, clinging to a 'creed which was slowly becoming a hopeless wreck'.[20] In an attempt to understand what he described as the 'aggressive dogmatism' of the professed sceptics, agnostics and atheists amongst the student body, he joined a 'speculative group' that met for Sunday morning breakfast and took long walks in the countryside, during which the ramifications of Darwin's *Descent of Man* (1871) were earnestly discussed.[21] The liberal Christianity, hard work and inculcation of individual responsibility offered by Jowett provided the industrious Macmillan Brown with a congenial philosophical framework. As an able and enthusiastic student he caught the eye of the Master and was soon regarded as one of his protégés. He became a frequent guest at 'Jowett's Jumbles'—Sunday evening dinners at his mentor's home, where the bright young students of Balliol were given the opportunity to mix with members of the intellectual elite, who made their way to Oxford. Such exposures to great minds were intended as a stimulus to excellence and carried with them the lofty implication that by emulation and hard work, each student could become part of the nation's intellectual leadership.[22]

---

17 Macmillan Brown, *Memoirs*, pp. 28–34; Annan, *The Dons*, pp. 61–72; Passmore, *A Hundred Years of Philosophy*, p. 55.

18 Annan, *The Dons*, pp. 62–63.

19 Macmillan Brown, *Memoirs*, p. 35.

20 Macmillan Brown, *Memoirs*, p. 42.

21 Macmillan Brown, *Memoirs*, pp. 35–37, 40–64.

22 Macmillan Brown, *Memoirs*, pp. 29–32; Annan, *The Dons*, pp. 71–72.

Jowett's exercise in grooming placed a high value on social usefulness and implied a commitment to the needs of the wider community. Learning was not to be an end in itself but a means to both individual and social improvement. The link between the academy and society was to be made more obvious to Macmillan Brown in the teaching of two Oxford scholars, Thomas Green of Balliol and William Wallace of Merton. In the lectures of the 'two great Hegelians', as Macmillan Brown describes them, he was 'saturated with the idealism of that modern resurrection of Plato, Hegel'.[23] To Macmillan Brown and the more earnest of Jowett's students, a deep commitment to social betterment through education could and did take on the air of academic evangelism. This sense of moral purpose and engagement with the world outside the university was to issue in the 'university settlement programmes', whereby recent graduates lived among the working class in an attempt to narrow the gap between the social classes.[24] More immediately, it was an influence that informed the sense of mission with which Macmillan Brown approached life after university.

In 1874 as Macmillan Brown confronted his academic future this sense of mission took its place among the host of thoughts, emotions and impulses that surrounded an important transition point of his life. An illness during the final examination period had led to a second-class degree. The disappointment was in part assuaged by a consoling letter from Jowett urging him, as Macmillan Brown writes in his *Memoirs*, 'not to accept that as my rank in life; I was, as a student and a man, in the first class'.[25] Against this, some of his university friends reacted with trepidation to the idea of leaving Britain for 'a land isolated from the great centres of civilisation and still untouched by the cultural movements of the world, till at last [he] came to believe them'.[26] He began to defend the prospect by presenting the move as but a temporary 'exile' and an opportunity to rebuild a blemished academic career. The defence was buttressed by a professed determination to avoid forming any attachment to people or places while away from 'Home'. This professional predicament left no space for marriage. In an academic sense, the tyranny of distance from

---

23   Macmillan Brown, *Memoirs*, p. 56.
24   Passmore, *A Hundred Years of Philosophy*, p. 55; Wilson, *The Victorians*, pp. 519–20.
25   Macmillan Brown, *Memoirs*, p. 69.
26   Macmillan Brown, *Memoirs*, pp. 82–83.

civilisation would impose great costs upon a scholar endeavouring to remain in touch with current thinking.[27] However accurately these thoughts reflect Macmillan Brown's attitude to migration in 1874, they do less than justice to the beliefs and assumptions that were to shape his future. Appointment as a foundation professor in a new colonial university, proposing a general degree based upon Scottish rather than English precedents and desiring to produce teachers rather than cloistered scholars, offered an environment in which a latent sense of academic evangelism could flourish.[28]

Alexander Leeper: Irish gods and Australian passions

In July 1869, Alexander Leeper, the 21-year-old Dublin born and bred son of an Anglican curate, after whom he was named, and Catherine Porter, the highly educated daughter of William Porter, surgeon and President of the Royal College of Surgeons, temporarily put aside his undergraduate studies at Trinity College Dublin and sailed for Australia. He had been diagnosed with phthisis, an inflammation of the lungs more commonly known as consumption, and advised to spend some time in Victoria, which was, in Ireland, widely believed to possess a congenial climate. An elder brother, William (1846–1873), also a Trinity College student, had 'voluntar[il]y transport[ed]' himself to Victoria after a failed love affair and a succession of scandals, and had lost contact with his family.[29] Alexander's departure came to be seen as a quest for improved health and a search for a lost brother. Sailing for Australia was thus not an act of migration but rather something of an antipodean sojourn. That it was, in a succession of stuttering steps, to lead to migration provides an opportunity to explore an example of Ireland's part in the construction of Victoria's nineteenth-century urban, professional middle class.

---

27 Macmillan Brown, *Memoirs*, pp. 82–83.
28 Gardner, 'The Formative Years, 1873–1918', pp. 92–106; Gardner, *Colonial Cap and Gown*, pp. 59–67.
29 Poynter, *Doubts and Certainties*, pp. 23–25; Freda Leeper to Alexander Leeper, 15 June 1893, Alexander Leeper Papers (ALP), Trinity College Archives, University of Melbourne Archives, T1, box 30/69. William Leeper's siblings attributed his behaviour to being prevented by his parents from marrying Sophie Bell, niece of Alexander Bell, because the Bell family lacked 'prospects'.

What began as a visit came to be a life-changing experience. After locating his brother on a sheep station, 'Terricks' in Victoria, the brothers moved together to Sydney, where Alexander secured a teaching position at the Collegiate School, Eglinton House, Glebe Point. The time in Sydney was not an altogether happy experience. His brother William's continued dissolute behaviour was, as Alexander observed bluntly, 'a powerful inducement for me to go home'.[30] Homesickness and worry about his health produced bouts of anxiety. His biographer, John Poynter, emphasises the young Alexander's propensity for depression and volatile moods.[31] The following passage from Alexander's diary, written while he was teaching in Sydney in 1869, captures something of this tendency and neatly summarises how the young Irishman perceived his prospects:

> I am destined to be short-lived. Born with a good constitution and with prospects of a prosperous and distinguished career. What a failure I have made! … Here I am an underpaid usher in a second-rate Australian school snubbed and slighted in Society in consequence of what is regarded as a menial position. And what might I have been … I might now be holding an honourable position in the Legal or Medical profession at home, or might be winning my way to affluence and distinction in the Indian Civil Service. But what have I gained to compensate for what I have lost? A more than average knowledge, (but little aesthetic appreciation) of the Greek and Latin language; but at best an inaccurate knowledge of <u>everything</u>. I am nearly as much as ever afflicted with *mauvaise honte*, and have not gained what I anticipated would be produced by travel, namely free, manly, outspoken ways. I sneak and cringe, and lie as much as ever.[32]

The melodramatic diary entry reflects a life hedged in by a propensity for complicated personal entanglements, and it is to those that we must turn to understand the forces that shaped his ultimate decision to become a settler rather than a sojourner. An embarrassing situation at home in Dublin, where he had misled a young woman into thinking they were engaged, made him reluctant to return and face the wrath of her family.[33] The admonition of a friend, as he was leaving Ireland, to avoid such entanglements because Australian girls were 'a low common

---

30   Poynter, *Doubts and Certainties*, p. 26. William Leeper died in Melbourne on 17 July 1873 after being transported to Victoria from Sydney to face a charge of bigamy.
31   Poynter, *Doubts and Certainties*, pp. 5, 19.
32   Diary of Alexander Leeper, 1870, ALP, T5, box 35.
33   Diary of Alexander Leeper, 1870.

sort' did not seem to dampen his ardour.[34] His teaching position at Collegiate School brought him into contact with Adeline Allen, the 16-year-old sister of two of his pupils. The daughter of George Allen (1824–1895), a prominent and wealthy Sydney Methodist lawyer, who was Mayor of Glebe, shortly to become Speaker of the New South Wales Legislative Assembly and knighted in 1877, seems to have been somewhat indifferent to Leeper's obvious infatuation. George Allen was blunt: his daughter was too young for romantic involvement and Leeper's career and health prospects were unfavourable. In despair, and convinced that his life would be short, Leeper returned to Dublin in May 1870.[35] There he began a complex, long-distance 'courtship' that spanned almost a decade, largely conducted via correspondence with Adeline's mother and brother. It would bring family interference on both sides, misunderstandings and confusion.

There can be little doubt that this affair of the heart must be placed at the centre of any discussion of Leeper's attitude to the prospect of a life in Australia. In 1875, after some five years largely crippled by hypochondria and making little progress with his attempts to win over a reluctant Adeline and gain the consent of her father, he secured a position as Second Master and Senior Classics Master at Melbourne Grammar School, the leading Anglican school for boys. Melbourne was not Sydney, but acceptance of the post placed him closer to Adeline and her family and allowed him to look for other positions more to his taste. Within a few months he negotiated a three-year contract as principal of the Anglican Church's Trinity College, later to become affiliated to the University of Melbourne. Important as this position was to become in Leeper's life, it does not mark any change in his attitude to Australia or the question of where he saw his future. Nor does it seem to have been based on any particular fondness for Melbourne. Any sense of permanent commitment to Melbourne or Australia was to await his eventual marriage to Adeline Allen, a second-generation Australian, in December 1879.[36]

Leeper's acceptance of a future life in Australia needs also to be set within the context in which his world view was shaped. Indeed, it is at least arguable that the significance of Ireland in his Australian life

---

34   George Wildig to Alexander Leeper, 16 January 1870, ALP, T1, box 21b/11.
35   Poynter, *Doubts and Certainties*, pp. 27–31.
36   Poynter, *Doubts and Certainties*, pp. 45–99.

was to increase rather than diminish with the passage of time. Leeper's family background places him and his nine siblings firmly within the ranks of Dublin's privileged professional Anglo-Irish Ascendancy and on the fringes of the more wealthy, yet socially aware, intellectual and cultural Irish elite. His mother Catherine Porter (born 1817) was the daughter of Trinity College–educated, leading Dublin surgeon William Porter and grew up with her three younger siblings in some affluence in Kildare, a south Dublin suburb. Physically hardy, strong-minded and academically orientated, Catherine received a somewhat unorthodox education at the hands of her father, who taught her at home and shared his interest in science with her. She developed into an earnest, well-read, articulate and opinionated young woman with a talent for horse riding, music, art and writing and had several works published in later life. Her Anglicanism was low church rather than high and, as a teenager, she taught Sunday school in St Anne's Church, Dublin.[37]

Catherine's politics, as far as we can assess them, can be placed at the liberal end of the spectrum. Her grandfather had been involved in the late eighteenth-century movement known as the United Irishmen, who sought parliamentary reform and Catholic emancipation, and opposed the Act of Union of 1800. We know little of her adult life before her marriage in 1842, at the age of 25, to Alexander Leeper (1815–1892), a young Anglican assistant curate at St Mary's Church, where she was now teaching Sunday school. Ten children and 14 years of childbearing followed. From them we gain few clues of her beliefs and preoccupations. She named her eldest son William Melanchthon, after Philip Melanchthon (1497–1560), a German professor of Greek, humanist theologian and supporter of the Lutheran reformation, who favoured moderation and the peaceful reconciliation of Catholicism and Protestantism.[38] After the pressures of domestic life diminished, she published an article on the Irish theologian Alexander Knox (1757–1831), who supported Catholic emancipation and defended religious liberty and differences.[39]

---

37 Canon Alexander Leeper, 'In Memoriam. Catherine Leeper', ms, ALP, T6, box 35; 'Obituary: Mrs Leeper', *Church of Ireland Training College Magazine*, July 1889, ALP, T6, box 35; Poynter, *Doubts and Certainties*, pp. 7–10.

38 Poynter, *Doubts and Certainties*, pp. 10–14; Canon Alexander Leeper, 'In Memoriam. Catherine Leeper', ms, ALP, T6, box 35; 'Obituary: Mrs Leeper', *Church of Ireland Training College Magazine*, ALP, T6, box 35.

39 Catherine Leeper, 'Alexander Knox', *The Churchman*, July 1889, ALP, T6, box 35.

Catherine Porter's husband came from considerably more modest origins. Rev. Alexander Leeper was the son of a Dublin-based artisan and merchant (saddler and harness maker). A brilliant scholar, he won a scholarship to Trinity College Dublin, where he excelled in modern and ancient languages, winning several prizes before graduating in 1841. In 1842 he was ordained into the Church of Ireland and served as curatorial assistant at St Mary's Church between 1843 and 1859. He and Catherine initially lived with their young and growing family in one of the less well-off Dublin suburbs until a new and better paid posting enabled them to move to a still relatively modest home in the more fashionable Kildare Place, across the road from wife Catherine's childhood home. It was from this comfortable and genteel setting that the Leepers experienced the volatile economic, social and political realities that confronted Ireland as famine ravaged and divided the country. It was from here, too, that in 1846 Alexander Leeper was appointed catechist at the teacher training school of The Society for Promoting the Education of the Poor in Ireland, also known more popularly as the Kildare Place Society. Formed in 1811 by a group of philanthropic Dubliners who wanted to establish a non-denominational institution for educating the poor, it was affiliated with the Church of Ireland in the 1830s and eventually became subsumed by the Church Education Society in 1855. In 1853 Leeper became chaplain and superintendent of the Kildare Place Society, and secretary of the Church Education Society in 1855.[40]

From this perspective, Catherine and Alexander Leeper and their family experienced the realities of Irish poverty, both urban and rural. The experience nurtured an increasing belief in the transformative power of education as a means of alleviating the lives of the poor, and a deepening sense of duty. In combination, these beliefs produced an emotionally close family environment that was deeply religious and committed to high academic goals. Theirs was an Anglo-Irish middle-class professional lifestyle lived within the intellectual context of that social position, and they were comfortable within an imperial framework. The education of the children took place in the family home, as well as private schools, and in the Church of Ireland, where Alexander preached. Son Alexander and his siblings attended their

---

40   Poynter, *Doubts and Certainties*, pp. 10–12; Susan M. Parkes, *Kildare Place: The History of the Church of Ireland Training College 1811–1969*, CICE, Dublin, 1984.

father's weekly High Church sermons, from which they took not only a sense of religious duty and moral mission, but also a preoccupation with personal moral worth, guilt and sin and the need for redemption. These were themes that troubled the earnest amongst their generation and were to play a significant role in young Alexander's life in Australia.[41]

Academic ability appears to have been a Leeper family trait, though the intellectually precocious Alexander seems to have been singled out by his parents as destined for academic success. After being taught by his father until the age of 13, Alexander received the typical private school education of a middle-class boy destined for university and a professional career. He attended Kingston Grammar School in south Dublin, where he showed a leaning towards the classics and tutored the younger boys to earn some money. In 1866, at the age of 16, he embarked upon the customary, Scottish-modelled, general undergraduate degree at Trinity College Dublin, having won a scholarship for boys of 'limited means' and four entrance prizes in Latin and Greek composition.[42] His elder brother William had preceded him to the ancient university, which was thought to be a bastion of privilege and learning equivalent to the English universities of Oxford and Cambridge, though more liberal in its course of study by this stage. The college remained, however, as Poynter describes it, a 'finishing school for the rich and a university for the clever'. Though there was no religious entry requirement, in reality the university was dominated by Anglicanism. Like Oxford and Cambridge, Trinity College Dublin students were taught in small groups with private tutors, a practice that influenced Alexander Leeper in his later role as principal of Trinity College, Melbourne. The environment suited the young Leeper, and he became something of a protégé of Reverend John Mahaffy (1839–1919), the distinguished classicist and Professor of Ancient History.[43]

---

41 Poynter, *Doubts and Certainties*, pp. 7, 14–17.
42 Poynter, *Doubts and Certainties*, p. 17.
43 Poynter, *Doubts and Certainties*, pp. 16–23; William Stanford and Robert McDowell, *Mahaffy: A Biography of an Anglo-Irishman*, Routledge & Kegan Paul, London, 1971; C. H. Holland (ed.), *Trinity College Dublin and the Idea of a University*, Trinity College Dublin Press, Dublin, 1991. Oscar Wilde (1854–1900), a student at Trinity College Dublin (1871–74) was also taught by Mahaffy and became an acquaintance of Alexander Leeper.

Content within the scholarly and cloistered Trinity College environment, Leeper's view of life after university took shape slowly. He considered the 'family professions' of medicine and the Church. There was little pressure from his family to choose religious orders; his mother thought he lacked the requisite seriousness. Teaching did not appeal.[44] To increase his options, he undertook the newly established courses in law in addition to his BA degree. As we have seen, illness and a subsequent trip to Australia interrupted his studies, as did a five-month tutoring job when he accompanied a young aristocrat on a tour of the Middle East (December 1870 – April 1871). It was not until December 1871, five years after he began at Trinity College Dublin, that Leeper graduated with a BA (placed at the top of the First Class), an LLB degree and a number of academic prizes.[45]

By now Leeper's mind was dominated by his desire to return to Adeline Allen, and for the next five years his life took a series of bizarre twists and turns that resemble a Victorian melodrama. At the end of 1871, he applied unsuccessfully for positions at the University of Melbourne and Sydney Grammar School. Then, when correspondence with Adeline Allen's mother convinced him to further his education, and preferably at some distance from Australia, he obliged. Taking up a suggestion from Adeline that he should go to Oxford, he successfully applied for a five-year scholarship to St John's College. There, in October 1872, he embarked on another degree in classics and literae humaniores. A letter from Mrs Allen with news of Adeline's engagement produced a bout of despair. When that engagement was broken off, Leeper sent a supplicatory appeal to Adeline, in which he undertook to follow 'any wish you might express—to try to gain a Fellowship at Oxford, or be a Parish Clergyman in Australia—I care very little what—with you to share my lot I believe my life would be happy and noble anywhere'.[46]

When his entreaty was rebuffed, Leeper was dispirited. Never as happy at Oxford as he had been at Trinity College Dublin, he nonetheless immersed himself in life at Oxford and became librarian of the Oxford Union and Secretary of St John's College Missionary

---

44   His younger brother Charles (b. 1850) qualified as a lawyer while brothers George (b. 1856) and Richard (b. 1858) qualified in medicine.

45   Poynter, *Doubts and Certainties*, pp. 31–35; *The Melburnian*, 14 November 1877.

46   Alexander Leeper to Adeline Allen, 17 April 1873, ALP, T1, box 21c/13.

Association. In 1874, he gained a First in classical moderations, but a misunderstanding led Leeper to go on a walking tour of Norway in June 1874 without sitting all of his final exams or fulfilling the residential requirements, with the result that he could not be awarded an Oxford degree. Returning to Dublin, he seems to have done some tutoring and acted as an assistant for Mahaffy, while he continued searching for work in Australia. An application for the headmastership of Melbourne Grammar School was unsuccessful, but the appointee, an older Oxford graduate named Edward Morris, offered him the position of Second Master.[47] With his health largely restored, and determined to see Adeline Allen, he accepted the position. Thus, in February 1875, he sailed once more for Australia, better qualified than previously and hopeful that his future might be spent with Adeline, wherever that might take him. At 27 years of age, Alexander Leeper, a product of both the English and Irish university systems, had travelled very little distance from the beliefs and value systems of the family environment in which he had been raised. He had remained within the Anglicanism of his parents; religion, education and scholarship had formed the cornerstones of his career and were to be intertwined with his subsequent career as principal of Trinity College, Melbourne.[48]

Henry Bournes Higgins: Irish woes and Australian opportunities

In November 1869 Irishman Henry Bournes Higgins (1851–1929), an 18-year-old clerk and son of Wesleyan minister John Higgins and Anne Bournes, left his home country bound for Melbourne, Victoria. He did so not as an individual, but as part of a large and close-knit family group in search of a healthier environment.[49] He sailed for Australia with his mother and his five younger siblings: George (14), Samuel (12), Ina (9), Anna (7) and Charlie (5). Until the family was joined a year later by brother John (17) and their father, who had remained

---

47   Olive Wykes, 'Morris, Edward Ellis (1843–1902)', *The Australian Dictionary of Biography* (*ADB*), vol. 5, Melbourne University Press, Carlton, Victoria, 1974, pp. 293–94.

48   Poynter, *Doubts and Certainties*, pp. 36–57.

49   See F. B. Smith, *Illness in Colonial Australia*, Australian Scholarly Publishing, Melbourne, 2011, pp. 117–31; and Richards, *Britannia's Children*, p. 185, for a discussion of the 'therapeutic migrant'.

in Ireland until he had completed a three-year circuit as Wesleyan preacher in Wexford, Henry stood alongside his mother as joint head of household. The separation was an act of desperation precipitated by family tragedy. The youngest child, William, had died in infancy in 1867; the eldest child, James, died on 30 June 1869, aged 20, after a two-year battle with consumption, contracted when he joined the stream of young Irish men attempting to find work and a better life in New York.[50] A seemingly inherited family weakness in the lungs meant that chest complaints such as asthma and bronchitis had continually dogged the family. Years of shifting around Ireland on the Methodist circuit had plainly failed to help mitigate the deleterious effect of the cold, damp Irish climate. Migration was thus a matter of family survival.

Ireland had a powerful and lifelong influence upon Higgins and shaped his understanding of the family. As his niece, Nettie Palmer, was later to write:

> [he] carried his youth about with him always, renewing himself with its memories … Scenes and sayings, that had been without meaning for him at the time, remained in his mind and illustrated the opinions that he came to hold later on. Looking back, he felt that, with all its suppressions, Ireland in the [eighteen-]sixties had been a place of germinating ideas.[51]

His parents, Anne Bournes and John Higgins, both from small rural towns in the west of Ireland, had married in 1848, when the potato blight was at its worst. Both were from well-educated, small landowning families that, in Irish terms, had achieved modest prosperity, although on the eve of their marriage the Higgins family was in some financial difficulty.[52] Anne Bournes had attended a Dublin boarding school, where she excelled at music and French, and John Higgins had received the classical education typical for boys of the professional classes, before taking a job in the Bank of Ireland in accordance with his Anglican father's wishes.[53]

---

50 Rickard, *H.B. Higgins*, pp. 6, 25–33.
51 Nettie Palmer, *Henry Bournes Higgins: A Memoir*, George G. Harrap & Co., London, 1931, pp. 4, 48.
52 Rickard, *H.B. Higgins*, pp. 2–4.
53 Palmer, *Higgins: A Memoir*, pp. 5–8.

John Higgins's decision to enter the Wesleyan ministry in 1842, aged 21, in answer, as one writer puts it, to the business of 'saving souls', dramatically altered his social status and economic position.[54] It was a choice that placed him and later his wife and children unequivocally in the ranks of the lower middle classes and ensured a life of 'genteel frugality'.[55] The meagre stipend and itinerant nature of the Wesleyan preacher's circuit—ministers were posted to a different area of the country every three years—contributed to the lowly status of the Methodist minister. The society in which the Higgins family moved was that of shopkeepers and clerical workers. It was also a constantly changing one. Henry, for example, was born in Northern Ireland in 1851 and experienced, throughout his childhood, small, struggling rural townships and the larger, industrial cities of Northern Ireland, where religious, class, social and political differences were more obvious. 'Home' to Henry Higgins was simply where his family was. As well as providing a range of experiences, the constant moves contributed to a deepening of family ties, mutual obligations and responsibilities, as individual members came to depend on each other for companionship and support.[56]

The Higgins family environment combined warmth and affection with a religious earnestness, 'high moral expectations' and intellectual ambitions for their children.[57] In combination with the ever-present cloud of illness and financial strain, the family setting was to produce a tendency towards anxiety and over-seriousness in the young Henry. His introspection was reinforced by attendance with his siblings at his father's chapel prayer meetings, held three times a week, where the emphasis was upon constant examination of the 'soul' and exaltation of truth and goodness as the talismans of moral behaviour. Moreover, Henry's serious and thoughtful demeanour was accompanied by a love of reading, which he satisfied by immersing himself in the Bible. This enthusiasm was welcomed by his father as an indication of a highly religious nature rather than a quest for imaginative and literary stimulus. The judgement was to underlie parental expectations of the young Henry and shape his education.[58]

---

54 Rickard, *H.B. Higgins*, p. 4.
55 John Rickard, 'Higgins, Henry Bournes (1851–1929)', *ADB*, vol. 9, Melbourne University Press, Carlton, Victoria, 1983, pp. 285–89.
56 Rickard, *H.B. Higgins*, p. 7.
57 Palmer, *Higgins: A Memoir*, p. 12.
58 Rickard, *H.B. Higgins*, pp. 7–15; Palmer, *Higgins: A Memoir*, pp. 11–21.

The Wesleyan Connexional School in St Stephen's Green, Dublin, to which the scholarly 10-year-old Henry was sent in 1861 as a boarder, was in essence an extension of the moral atmosphere of his home. The headmaster, the Reverend Dr Crook, a young Wesleyan minister and distinguished classics graduate of Trinity College Dublin, oversaw a somewhat austere regime, establishing what John Rickard has labelled a 'moral dictatorship'—'opening the eyes of the boys to their moral infirmities'.[59] A small and financially struggling school intended to prepare boys for Trinity College Dublin and the professions, it provided Higgins with a sound classical education. In the summer of 1865, after four years at the school, 'inflammation of the lungs' forced the 14-year-old Henry to return to his family, now based in Newry, a seaport and industrial town in Northern Ireland. Apart from a brief interlude engineered by his mother at Dr Potterton's school in Newry, where he excelled in classical studies, he spent the next three years (1866–69) in paid employment. The prospect of his proceeding to Trinity College Dublin was now judged too great a strain for his delicate disposition and too great a drain upon family finances.[60]

In retrospect, this move away from the narrow world of home and school proved to be a turning point in the making of Henry Higgins. Immersion in the world of work began falteringly. An apprenticeship with a wholesale drapery warehouse in Belfast ended abruptly as deteriorating health, attributed by his father to poor living arrangements above the warehouse, saw Henry return home. After a period of recuperation, during which he attended Dr Potterton's school in Newry, Henry began work as a shop assistant with a merchant tailor in Clonmel. Finally, in January 1868, he moved to a furniture warehouse, Arthur John in St Stephen's Green, Dublin, where better wages and conditions enabled him to send money home to his family, now based in Wexford. These life experiences, his first outside the boundaries of a Methodist framework, broadened his horizons and brought him into contact, albeit in a limited fashion, with people of different religious backgrounds and political beliefs. They stimulated a sense of injustice and the beginnings of an awareness of Ireland's troubles. Politically uninformed, if not naive, he had been bewildered by the comments of tailors in the Clonmel shop, who supported

---

59   Rickard, *H.B. Higgins*, p. 21.
60   Rickard, *H.B. Higgins*, pp. 16–25; Palmer, *Higgins: A Memoir*, pp. 22–31, 33.

a Fenian rebellion. In Dublin, as his health improved and his financial worries eased, the maturing Henry Higgins's interests and concerns widened. He was drawn to the slums of Dublin, where he attended the Cork Street Chapel and distributed religious reading material to the poor, and read widely; he also joined a branch of the YMCA, where he attended the debates of Trinity College graduates and students. Here he was exposed to the ideas of Auguste Comte and the English positivists. Lacking an intellectual mentor or guide, he was out of his depth, yet hungrily soaked up the new knowledge.[61]

It is not possible to know what Henry contributed to the family decision to leave Ireland, but his understanding of the motivations that impelled his parents was grounded in the family and Irish experience. Since the potato blight first sparked a mass exodus to America in 1845, migration had become an unwelcome reality of the Irish experience. It was frequently discussed within the Higgins family. When illness forced Henry to leave school at 14, his parents could not quite find the money to send him to recuperate in Australia in the care of a Wesleyan minister. When eldest son James sailed for New York in October 1866 to 'try his luck', the family was prepared to follow if they received a favourable report from him. The merits of South Africa, Australia and India were canvassed at various times. There can, however, be no doubt of the sequence of events within the family that precipitated the decision to sail for Australia. In May 1867 James returned from New York. Winter had proved debilitating, and, after being diagnosed with consumption, he returned home, where he died on 30 June 1869, Henry's eighteenth birthday. A distraught Anne Higgins consulted a well-respected Dublin physician, Dr Stokes, who advised that the entire family migrate to Victoria's warmer, drier climate.[62] By securing the monetary value of her share in a Bournes family property, it was just possible, by taking the cheapest passage available on a cargo ship, for six of her seven surviving children to sail for Australia with her.[63]

Thus in November 1869, Anne Higgins and the bulk of her family sailed for a land where they knew no one, had no accommodation arranged and no employment prospects. John Higgins senior and son John remained in Ireland to fulfil work commitments, and it was intended

---

61   Palmer, *Higgins: A Memoir*, pp. 33–36, 40–46; Rickard, *H.B. Higgins*, pp. 25, 27–30.
62   Smith, *Illness in Australia*, pp. 117–31.
63   Rickard, *H.B. Higgins*, pp. 25–27, 30–42; Palmer, *Higgins: A Memoir*, pp. 32, 36–40, 46–48.

that the former would send remittance payments. As Higgins's niece Nettie Palmer later wrote, 'even the youngest of them was conscious to some degree' of the 'finality' of their migratory act. As Palmer explains, 'it was no mere casual experiment for them: they had definitely pulled up their roots in the old country and entrusted their future to the new'.[64] The decision to leave Ireland was surrounded by a sense of urgency and seriousness; the departure for Australia was enveloped in tragedy even before the voyage to the antipodes was completed. Charlie, aged five, the youngest Higgins child, fell ill at sea and died two days before the family reached Australia's shores.[65]

When we come to place Henry Higgins's arrival in Australia within the framework of middle-class migration to Australasia, we are clearly confronted by a different set of dynamics than those evident in our previous case studies. His departure for Australia was not, like that of the Wildings, infused with a sense of wider social betterment and the hope of a better world to come for all. Personal circumstance and the plight of those dearest to him dominated his thoughts. His educational and work experiences thus far had, unlike those of Frederick Wilding, Orme Masson, John Macmillan Brown and Alexander Leeper, provided little certainty of what direction his life in Australia might take. Insofar as his migration can be linked with a conception of the family, it is one nurtured within a close family drawn closer by the exigencies of life within the tiny Methodist community of mid-nineteenth-century Ireland. From within this environment, with its strong sense of mutual dependence and obligation, Henry Higgins was, in the Australia of the 1870s and 1880s, to formulate a commitment to family that became an amalgam of old world Ireland and new world Melbourne.

---

64 Palmer, *Higgins: A Memoir*, pp. 1–2.
65 Rickard, *H.B. Higgins*, pp. 34–42; Palmer, *Higgins: A Memoir*, pp. 55–56.

Section Two: Arrival and Establishment

This section outlines the process by which five middle-class professional families established themselves within the colonial environments of Melbourne and Christchurch. Individual case studies are grouped together by occupation of the male breadwinners: Wilding and Higgins as representatives of the legal families; Macmillan Brown, Leeper and Masson as academic families. To a degree, this is a categorisation of convenience, yet it rests upon day-to-day realities that helped shape the pattern of family life. The differences between the two categories were ones of emphasis rather than kind, and all five families shared a broad conception that they had a capacity to contribute significantly to the community-building processes in which their settler societies were engaged. They also shared a sense of duty which was grounded in notions of citizenship that owed much to their understanding of the civic democracies of the ancient world. Theirs, however, was an expanded notion of citizenship that included women to a greater or lesser extent.

It was an expanded understanding, as Frank Turner argues, that rested upon an 'abstract and idealised "ancient world"', leavened by 'a set of more or less traditional English humanist values long employed to oppose commercialism ... and social individualism'.[1] These ideas lay at the heart of British philosophical liberalism, which, influenced by John Stuart Mill, had developed a significant communitarian

---

1   Dale, *The English Men*, p. 24 (citing Turner, *The Greek Heritage in Victorian Britain*).

dimension. Its central concept—that of 'active citizenship'—derived from Mill's study of Athenian democracy, and undoubtedly shaped the five colonial families at the centre of this study.[2] Each may be shown to have been influenced by what Eugenio Biagini has described as Mill's 'zeal for the cultivation of civic virtue'.[3] As relatively new communities, colonial Melbourne and Christchurch provided contexts in which the values of nineteenth-century liberalism might flourish. Moreover, Mill also provided a way of linking the public and private spheres of family: to each individual there was attached, in his view, a duty to pursue 'eudaimonia'—'human flourishing' or personal development—as the surest way of achieving the fullest expression of humanity.[4] Viewed in this light, the family could be thought of as a microcosm of the wider community, in which ideal citizens and civic virtue could be cultivated and social relations harmonised.

That is not to say that this group of mid-nineteenth-century professionals laid out these philosophies in coherent form (although the Wildings were broadly aware of where they stood within English liberal thought). Rather, their liberalism acted as a prism through which they interpreted the world and offered a guide as to how they might live their lives.[5] Within the embryonic professional communities of the colonial societies they entered, their world view and the language in which it was advanced were instantly recognised.[6] Among the networks of like-minded families taking shape in the colonies, they were welcomed as potential recruits in the task of achieving the idealised society they envisaged. Within these colonial family networks we can glimpse ways in which a generation of professional migrants move beyond the classical liberal position that involved a negative conceptualisation of individual freedom to confront the apparently conflicting concepts of liberty and community. In this they might be seen as acting as a bridging generation, linking older conceptions of liberalism and newer ones that accepted that a more ethical and fairer society might require a degree of social experimentation.

---

2   Biagini, 'Citizenship, Liberty and Community', p. 6, and more generally, pp. 1–9.
3   Biagini, 'Liberalism and Direct Democracy: John Stuart Mill and the model of ancient Athens', in Biagini (ed.), *Citizenship and Community*, pp. 23–24, and more generally, pp. 21–44.
4   Biagini, 'Liberalism and Direct Democracy', p. 23.
5   This interpretation owes much to Stuart Macintyre's definition of colonial liberalism in *A Colonial Liberalism*, pp. 10–13.
6   Dale, *The English Men: Professing Literature*, pp. 15–19.

The pursuit of a social ideal was sustained by material and professional success. None of the families in this study was to retreat from the community they entered. The lawyers Henry Higgins and Frederick Wilding left estates of £69,000 and £30,000 respectively—sufficient to place them amongst the very comfortably off colonial upper middle class.[7] John Macmillan Brown, whose wealth derived in large part from shrewd investments that produced an estate of some £80,000, stands closer to the rich of his day than was normal for academic families.[8] The Leepers and Massons are more representative of their profession: comfortably housed within the cloisters of Melbourne University, they neither benefited from the rising property values that home ownership provided, nor shared Brown's capacity for shrewd investment.

Thumbnail sketches of the professional careers of the male breadwinner in each family underline the successful trajectory of the group within their respective legal and academic professional communities. After completing a classical and legal education at Melbourne University, Higgins established himself in equity law, was appointed to the judicial bench, and presided over the Federal Court of Arbitration. Wilding, likewise, established himself as a prominent barrister and in 1913 was appointed King's Counsel. Masson's services to the advancement of science within the university and in the forging of links with industry were recognised in 1918 by the award of CBE and by a knighthood in 1923. Macmillan Brown gained a reputation as teacher and scholar of English literature that transcended the cloistered environment of a colonial university and established himself as arguably the most influential New Zealand academic of his age. After leaving academia in 1895, he was to become something of a public intellectual on the international academic circuits as a frequently controversial and idiosyncratic student of anthropology and as a utopian novelist. Alexander Leeper's career developed within the academic world of Melbourne University, where he is credited with pioneering the Australasian university college system, consolidating the place of the

---

7   Rickard, *H.B. Higgins*, p. 310; Probate records of Frederick Wilding, Probate Register, Christchurch 24606/1945, Christchurch branch of National Archives, New Zealand.

8   Angus Ross, 'The Macmillan Brown Lectures 1977: The Slow Progress of the Favourite Child', (typescript), Macmillan Brown Library (MBL), University of Canterbury, Christchurch, pp. 2–3.

classics, and playing a crucial role in the establishment of Anglican education for girls, which he saw as a first step towards increasing their number within the university.

Such a summary speaks of successful male careers within an expanding professional community. Establishing the family households that both sustained and were sustained by these careers needs to be set within the context of migration. For young married couples the most obvious consequence was the loss of the support structure of immediate and extended families. The average British family had since the 1850s been producing fewer children. As Leonore Davidoff has demonstrated, 'the number of children born to a couple had declined from, on average, over six for those married mid-century to around three' by the end of the century.[9] One consequence of this was the demise of the big family and the subsequent decline in the extensive cousinage that produced 'clan-like groupings' and made it possible for individuals to live out their lives almost entirely within the confines of the family.[10] The frontrunners in embracing the new, smaller British family were the professional classes. It was from them that the families of this study are drawn. As members of a mid-century generation of professionals, they effectively traded whatever comfort was to be had from their extended families at Home for the prospects of the family they were about to create in the new world.

In practical terms, the absence of the extended family placed a premium upon engagement with the new communities they entered. In the cities of New Zealand and Australia, as in Britain, the big family that had characterised the early pioneering communities was becoming less common.[11] The new migrant professionals of the 1870s and 1880s were to be as instrumental in its demise as their British counterparts. Their idealised conception of the family demanded much of them as individuals and, as the following case studies attempt to show, migration intensified these demands. Their responses to the immediate

---

9   Leonore Davidoff, *Thicker than Water: Siblings and their Relations, 1780–1920*, Oxford University Press, Oxford, 2012, p. 103.

10   Davidoff, *Thicker than Water*, p. 84.

11   Ian Pool, Arunachalam Dharmalingam and Janet Sceats, *The New Zealand Family From 1840: A Demographic History*, Auckland University Press, Auckland, 2007, passim, and especially pp. 18–19, 55–56, 59–66, 72–79, 81–84, 93–99, 106–8, 123–43, 156–57, 160; Ann Larson, *Growing Up in Melbourne: Family Life in the Late Nineteenth Century*, Demography Program, The Australian National University, Canberra, 1994, pp. 27–30, 37–63.

challenges of translating ideal into reality provide a way of exploring the roles played by men and women in both the public and private spheres of colonial life. They do so in a way that suggests that, in the establishment phase of their colonial lives, they both realised and, at times, transcended the Victorian ideal of the family built around 'domesticated husbands' and 'supportive wives'.[12]

---

12   Tosh, *A Man's Place*, p. 54; Davidoff and Hall, *Family Fortunes* [2002 edn], pp. 149–92.

3

The Academic Evangelists

Between 1874 and 1886 Macmillan Brown, Leeper and Masson headed to Christchurch and Melbourne, where they settled immediately into professional positions that they had secured before leaving home. In this way, their act of migration involved less risk and uncertainty than that of the Wilding and Higgins families. Their incomes had been negotiated, and their professional positions brought, if not automatic authority, then at least a degree of recognition within the wider community. Only Macmillan Brown regarded his appointment as a colonial sojourn. Each was to bring an almost missionary zeal to the self-imposed task of ensuring that the colonial universities they entered established themselves firmly within the international community of scholarship. It was on these terms of activist academic engagement that they set out on their colonial careers. They were terms that were to have a significant, if not determining, influence upon the family environments they were simultaneously helping to establish. The case studies that follow attempt to gauge more precisely the extent to which their academic evangelism became the axis around which family was constructed. In doing so, they also explore such negotiated terrain as remained within households, where the separation of work and domestic life was blurred.

John Macmillan Brown: 'I am Canterbury College'[1]

Twenty-eight-year-old John Macmillan Brown set sail from England, resigned to a temporary exile at Canterbury College, which he hoped might be relieved by the beauty of New Zealand's scenery and a constant supply of books sent from Britain. It was an exile viewed as an opportunity to build up capital and he did not see marriage as a prospect. He was to remain in New Zealand for the rest of his life, and throughout his 23-year tenure as professor, established himself as the dominant academic influence of the college's foundational years. W. J. Gardner depicts him as an 'Encyclopaedic God-Professor', a generalist rather than a specialist, who exerted a far-reaching personal influence over the college and its students.[2] The extent of this influence, and the speed with which it was achieved, appealed to Macmillan Brown's self-assured and egocentric personality, and produced a fondness for declaring: 'I am Canterbury College'.[3] Indeed, the story of John Macmillan Brown's establishment is also the story of Canterbury College's establishment. It is bound up with the issue of defining the purpose and role of a colonial university, and rests upon a considerable body of personal academic achievement and a reputation as a champion of women's higher education. It is also a story whose denouement is a marriage constructed around two separate professional careers. The 'other' of this tale is Helen Connon, Macmillan Brown's first student at Canterbury College, the first woman within the British Empire to gain an MA honours degree, the pioneering principal of a leading academic girls' school in Christchurch, and later, in 1886, his wife.

In 1874 Macmillan Brown encountered the bustling South Island town of Christchurch and the wider province of Canterbury enjoying a short-lived period of economic growth built on the back of high wool

---

1   A former student of John Macmillan Brown, Lillian Harriet Williams (Mrs J. W. Blyth) claimed that this was a much repeated phrase of his. D. J. O. Caffin, 'Interviews with former staff and students', 18 April 1986, (typescript), p. 2, W. J. Gardner Papers, MB 107, 5b, MBL; Gardner, *Colonial Cap and Gown*, p. 59.

2   Gardner, *Colonial Cap and Gown*, pp. 43–67; W. J. Gardner, 'The Formative Years, 1873–1918', in W. J. Gardner, E. T. Beardsley and T. E. Carter, *A History of the University of Canterbury 1873–1973*, University of Canterbury, Christchurch, p. 104.

3   Lovell-Smith, *Easily the Best*, p. 108; Gardner, 'The Formative Years', pp. 89–90; Charles Brasch, *Indirections: A Memoir 1909–1947*, Oxford University Press, Wellington, 1980, p. 119.

prices, Vogel's public works programs, borrowing, and immigration. In education and in politics, the trend was towards centralisation. The University of New Zealand, established in 1870 as an examining body only, had invited affiliations from institutions providing higher education and offered operational grants. A national system of elementary education was established in 1877 by which primary schooling became free, compulsory and secular. The provinces that formed the basis of a federal system of government were abolished in 1876. Christchurch civic leaders envisaged their city as playing a pre-eminent role in the nation's educational development and saw Canterbury College and the city's museum, established in 1870, as forming the hub of an educational and cultural precinct that would embrace a city library, and be framed by botanical gardens.[4]

The establishment of a university college in Christchurch had been a utopian part of the Wakefieldian Canterbury settlement of 1848. The idea was kept alive by a small, educated elite. In 1872, in alliance with a cluster of progressive politicians and run-holders, they hastily established an institution of higher learning (the Canterbury Collegiate Union) as the first step in the creation of a university. Their haste reflected a desire to thwart the ambition of the newly created University of Otago (1869) to become the colony's sole teaching university.[5] Whatever interprovincial rivalry was involved, their actions also indicated a preference for regional universities, and their professed objectives were progressive: the 'encouragement of talent without barriers of distance, wealth or class'.[6] This dictum embraced the admission of women, although no formal policy was enunciated. Women attended from the start on equal terms with the men. Teachers, mostly Oxford and Cambridge graduates, were recruited from within Christchurch, and a liberal course of studies offered that included classics, mathematics, physical science, modern languages and, from 1873, jurisprudence, English languages and literature, physiology, and geology. Classes were held in late afternoon or evening, to allow

---

4   'The Origin of University Education in Canterbury by Dr J. Hight, Prof. of History, Canterbury College', *Lyttelton Times*, 12 May 1923, p. 14; Gardner, 'The Formative Years', pp. 29–46; Gardner, *Colonial Cap and Gown*, p. 33; Burnard, 'Artisanal Town', pp. 115–37; Macintyre, 'Outwards and Upwards', pp. 85–89, 95–98; Lovell-Smith, *Easily the Best*, p. 25.
5   Gardner, 'The Formative Years', pp. 22–32.
6   Gardner, 'The Formative Years', p. 32. Here Gardner is summarising the inaugural address of John Tancred, Chancellor of the University of New Zealand, at the opening of the Canterbury Collegiate Union on 22 July 1872.

part-time study. The Union began with 83 students, of whom only a small proportion had matriculated. When the Union was dissolved in 1874, the university that replaced it, Canterbury College, formalised the essence of the original curriculum.[7] Its original board of governors prescribed a Bachelor of Arts degree that followed the more generalist Scottish model; both arts and science subjects were included, and Latin and mathematics were compulsory. They planned to establish chairs in chemistry, classics, history and English literature, mathematics and natural philosophy, and five lectureships in biology, modern languages, mental science, jurisprudence and political economy.[8]

Its founders were well aware of the various strands in the heated British public debate, which reached a crescendo in the 1870s, about the purpose of a university and its relation to the wider society. James Hight, historian and former early Canterbury College student, argued that many of the university's founders had been Cambridge University students in the 1850s and 1860s, when the ancient university was 'more receptive to change' than Oxford, and that this experience helped to shape the foundational ethos of Canterbury College.[9] In a similar vein, Gardner argues that the Canterbury College founders wished to achieve British standards of scholarship within a colonial-style university, by which they meant democratic—'open to rich and poor alike'.[10] They looked to Scotland and the newer, dissenting British universities of London and Durham, the secular nature and combination of vocational and general education of which seemed to match colonial needs. The prospects of reconciling scholarship and democracy were better at Canterbury College than in the Sydney or Melbourne universities, in Gardner's view, because it was founded later. Unlike the University of Sydney, for example, Canterbury College did not aspire to become 'the same under … different skies'.[11] Colborne Veel, editor of the Christchurch *Press* and later to become a close friend of Macmillan Brown, captured the pragmatic attitude that prevailed in the creation of the city's university:

---

7   The Canterbury College Ordinance was passed by the Canterbury Provincial Council on 16 June 1873. The Canterbury College Union was officially dissolved on 19 May 1874, with the university's first term technically beginning in June 1874.
8   Gardner, *Colonial Cap and Gown*, pp. 30–34; Gardner, 'The Formative Years', pp. 17–88.
9   Hight, *Lyttelton Times*, 12 May 1923.
10   Gardner, *Colonial Cap and Gown*, p. 39.
11   Gardner, *Colonial Cap and Gown*, pp. 17, 22.

a system must be moulded to suit the state of society in the colony. We must strike out a line of our own. We must adapt the scheme of University education to the peculiar requirements of our own case. We cannot reproduce Oxford, Cambridge or Edinburgh in New Zealand. The state of society in the colony will not admit of such an idea.[12]

Within this context the establishment of Canterbury College was a haphazard, piecemeal and unsystematic affair that left room for individual professors to play a defining role. This allowed innovation and experimentation within a framework shaped by customary understandings of what a university should be. It was a formula that suited the peculiar mix of pragmatism and idealism that historians have detected in the academic career of John Macmillan Brown.[13] He held degrees in classics and philosophy and had also studied in the newer field of English literary studies. From Oxford University he imbibed the spirit of Arnoldian idealism.[14] His Scottish background and university experience encouraged a democratic approach and allowed Macmillan Brown to argue that education might be both utilitarian and moral in its purposes. These two 'seemingly paradoxical ideologies', as Erica Schouten calls them, were to inform Macmillan Brown's university career.[15]

At the centre of the paradox stood modern literature or, more precisely, *English* literature. There was much resistance from the older universities to the introduction of modern languages and literature as a formal academic discipline. English literary studies, often referred to as 'mere chatter about Shelley', were seen to have an inferior intellectual status to classics. Latin and Greek were the traditional languages of scholarship in Britain and Europe. They required, or so it was believed, greater intellectual effort than the study of literature in one's own language and possessed a repository of 'spiritual and aesthetic inspiration' not apparent in modern literature.[16] Knowledge of English, French and German literature, though regarded as a necessity for the

---

12   *Press*, 13 August 1873; Gardner, 'The Formative Years', pp. 34–35.
13   Erica Schouten, 'The "Encyclopaedic God-Professor": John Macmillan Brown and the Discipline of English in Colonial New Zealand', *Journal of English Literature*, vol. 23, part 1, 2005, pp. 109–23; Gardner, *Colonial Cap and Gown*, pp. 59–60, 63, 65–67; Gardner, 'The Formative Years', pp. 87–89.
14   Matthew Arnold emphasised the moral value of literary studies.
15   Schouten, 'The "Encyclopaedic God-Professor"', p. 109.
16   Dale, *The English Men*, p. 12.

cultured gentleman, was seen as a matter for private study rather than systematic academic analysis. Courses in English literature were seen, as Leigh Dale writes, 'as the obvious refuge for women, working-class boys and "third class" men'.[17] To this, perhaps, could be added 'colonials'. Jo McMurtry has established how the newly established colonial universities of America, unencumbered by tradition and open to experimentation, were relatively quick to embrace the new discipline, and that nostalgia for the British homeland was a factor in the acceptance of English literature as a university subject.[18] These factors may have played a part in the emergence of Macmillan Brown as the founding father of such studies in Australasia.[19]

Macmillan Brown's commitment to literature as an instrument of moral development and a vehicle of public discourse blossomed relatively quickly in the colonial environment. He was later to present in his *Memoirs*, as an indicator of his views about the place of classical studies in a colonial society, an exchange in 1874 with Lord Lyttelton, the chairman of the London selection committee that recommended his appointment to Canterbury College. To Lyttelton's observation— 'You cannot write Greek verse'—John Macmillan Brown responded: 'God help me, what would be the good of Greek verse for pioneers in a new colony?'[20] The exchange has been largely accepted at face value. Schouten suggests, for example, that Lyttelton was highlighting Macmillan Brown's 'failure to possess the cultural capital that was still most important in the English university system ... a solid mastery of classics', and Macmillan Brown's retort could be seen as rebutting a piece of old-world snobbery.[21] The pattern of Macmillan Brown's future teaching role, and in particular the speed with which literature assumes a larger role in it, suggests that such an interpretation may

---

17   Dale, *The English Men*, p. 12.
18   McMurtry, *English Language, English Literature*, pp. 1–5, 16–17, 21–23, 65, 78–82.
19   Dale, *The English Men*, pp. 25–37. Though English literature was taught at the ancient universities of Cambridge and Oxford, it was as part of the School of Medieval Languages; Cambridge did not have a full chair in literature until 1911. Oxford established a chair of English literature in 1893, though a philologist, rather than an English literary specialist, was appointed to it. John Macmillan Brown led the way for English literary studies in Australasia. English was taught in the Australian universities under the umbrella of modern languages and literature, until the appointment of Mungo MacCallum in 1887 to the foundational chair of Modern Languages and Literature at Sydney University. Unlike Macmillan Brown he maintained that classical studies should take precedence over English literary ones.
20   Macmillan Brown, *Memoirs*, p. 75.
21   Schouten, 'The "Encyclopaedic God-Professor"', pp. 113–14.

not do justice to a developing commitment to literature as a form of presenting moral values in a way that was consistent with the lessons of the ancients.[22]

Whatever interpretation is attached to it, Macmillan Brown's initial appointment to Canterbury College required him to teach classics and English.[23] By 1879, as student numbers had increased, he had relinquished the teaching of classics to concentrate upon English literature, history and political economy. He argued in support of such a step that it would be far easier to find another classics professor 'from home' than it would be to find an English literature professor.[24] In public his justification of modern literature was couched in pragmatic and utilitarian terms. 'Even to the most enthusiastic student of ancient classics there is a dead and foreign matter clinging round them that makes his enthusiasm an effort', he told the student audience at the inaugural meeting of the Canterbury College Dialectical Society in 1881. The 'ordinary student' would be better off 'reading good translations' of the original classical texts; 'the mere effort of getting to know their meaning is so great that it rises to the rank of exquisite torture'.[25] Schouten presents this pragmatism as a denial of the relevance of classical literature and 'decidedly un-Arnoldian'—in the sense of rejecting the notion that the ancient works contained truths of 'universal worth'.[26] It is perhaps equally arguable that Macmillan Brown was not so much questioning the relevance of classical literature and the intrinsic value of its moral compass for modern times, as suggesting a need for representation of such ideas in a more recognisable form:

> [E]very age must have its own version of the common thoughts and emotions of humanity ... we need a re-utterance of the old thoughts and old expressions—a renaissance such as we had before the Elizabethan era ... the scholar in a new country, whilst studying the past, must look more to the future; he must not use the past as his

22   John Macmillan Brown, *Student Life and the Fallacies that Oftenest Beset It: An Inaugural Address Delivered to the Canterbury College Dialectic Society at the Commencement of Its Session 1881*, The Canterbury College Dialectic Society with Tombs and Co., Cathedral Square, Christchurch, pp. 23–24.
23   The University of Otago also lumped the two subjects together.
24   Macmillan Brown, *Memoirs*, pp. 89–92.
25   Macmillan Brown, *Student Life*, pp. 23–24.
26   Schouten, 'The "Encyclopaedic God-Professor"', pp. 115–16.

tyrant to trample upon his own impulses, but as his guide, whom he must reverence, but never bow to without the use of reason. No age is incapable of being great; no great past should shut out the possibility of a great present.[27]

Regardless of the rationale that lay behind it, John Macmillan Brown pioneered the study of English literature in New Zealand and, indeed, Australasia. Such was 'his mastery', argues Gardner, that he 'became a legend in his lifetime' and in doing so ensured that Canterbury College 'moved more quickly and more successfully into the field of English literature' than any 'other Australasian university'.[28] Apart from his experiences in the English literature classes of John Nichol, Regius Chair of English Literature at Glasgow University, and Benjamin Jowett's essay-writing tutorials at Oxford, Macmillan Brown had little upon which to model his courses. The system he ultimately developed was an extension of the method he was using in his teaching of classics and was designed to suit colonial conditions. It consisted of essay classes, composition classes and what he termed 'art lectures', in which he aimed in four years to give his students a familiarity with all the great writers and works in English literature.[29] Sermon-like and rhetorical in their delivery, the lectures were primarily vehicles for the exposition of deep philosophical and moral themes.[30] Typical of them was his 5,000-word lecture on Carlyle's 'Sartor Resartus' which ended in dramatic and stirring terms:

> the noblest of the old beliefs ... the brotherhood of man ... the kinship of all human souls with their divine source puts human love upon a new and loftier footing. We feel that all we do for our fellows, for our race, is a part of the highest worship; we labour that those who come after us may be more noble. And there is a new meaning in the divine mandate, 'Whatsoever thy hand findeth to do, do it with all thy might. Work while it is called to-day, for the night cometh when no man can work.'[31]

---

27   Macmillan Brown, *Student Life*, pp. 24, 30.
28   Gardner, *Colonial Cap and Gown*, p. 60.
29   Macmillan Brown, *Memoirs*, pp. 86–88, 92–93, 109–11, 128–29.
30   Gardner, 'The Formative Years', pp. 90, 104.
31   John Macmillan Brown Papers (JMBP), Macmillan Brown Library, University of Canterbury, Christchurch, MB 118, B3/1/18.

As performances made available to the public, such lectures attracted a large following—especially among middle-class women—and did much to build his popular reputation.[32] Upon his retirement in 1895 the Christchurch *Press* gave formal recognition of this achievement:

> It is due to him alone that the teaching of English literature has taken its proper place in the curriculum of the University. He had no precedents to go upon. When he began his work English was not seriously thought of as a subject of study in any University ... He had to invent his own methods, to formulate his own system. And the thoroughness and completeness of that system is demonstrated not merely by the results it has achieved within the University, but by its adoption in nearly every institution of learning in the colony ... the system pursued by Professor Brown makes mediocrity at least serviceable; and where talent exists it stimulates and directs it.[33]

In Macmillan Brown's view, the utilitarian aspect of his English studies system had important ramifications for social development. The ability to write clearly, to present a logical, balanced reasoned argument, was predicated upon the ability 'to think out any subject in a systematic and logical way' and was, he argued, the fundamental characteristic of a rational human being and the basis of a humane society.[34] Similarly, he exhorted his students to read the great works of literature in ways that helped improve the way they lived their lives. In this way he believed, language and literature would inform and improve the tenor of civic life and cement its place within the British cultural tradition.[35]

If the establishment of English literature as a discipline was the critical aspect of the John Macmillan Brown legend, it is rivalled by his role as 'the first practical promoter of higher education for women in Australasia'.[36] The precursor of Canterbury College, the non-degree granting Canterbury Collegiate Union, had freely admitted female students. At its establishment Canterbury College had no formal policy regarding the admittance of female students to degrees. When its officials received a request in 1874 from the mother of 17-year-old Helen Connon for her daughter to study at the college for a BA degree, they directed the request to the newly appointed John Macmillan

---

32 Agnes Gribling to John Macmilllan Brown, JMBP, A7/81.
33 'Professor Brown', *Press*, 2 April 1895, p. 4.
34 Macmillan Brown, *Memoirs*, pp. 92–93.
35 Macmillan Brown, *Student Life*, pp. 9–19, 22, 25–31.
36 Gardner, *Colonial Cap and Gown*, p. 69.

Brown, then on his way to Christchurch. The much 'celebrated' and now legendary meeting between Helen Connon, her mother and Macmillan Brown took place shortly after his arrival, in December 1874. Without hesitation he enrolled the young woman as his first BA degree student, offering, as he did so, to smooth her way with the other professors and students.[37] Thereafter he publicly championed the rights of women to a university education and entry into the professions, and acted as a guide and mentor to women within the university, often providing special group tuition for them.[38] Helen Connon became one of the first two women to graduate with a BA in 1880 from Canterbury College, and in 1881 the first woman in the British Empire to graduate with an MA honours degree.[39]

Though women themselves sought entry, they did not have to fight to gain admission to Canterbury College. Rather than a story of the politics of exclusion and admission, the Helen Connon episode was at the time celebrated as a sign of Christchurch's liberalism and an example of a wider colonial progressivism.[40] As its facilitator, John Macmillan Brown thus became almost immediately thrust to the forefront of progressive thinkers within the colony and assumed something of a patron-like status for the embryonic suffrage movement. As such, he was consulted by its leading advocates Kate Sheppard, Edith Searle

37 J. Macmillan Brown, 'Early Days and Early Students', *Canterbury College Jubilee, Lyttelton Times* supplement, 12 May 1923, p. 1; Gardner, 'The Formative Years', pp. 156–57; Gardner, *Colonial Cap and Gown*, pp. 82–83; Lovell-Smith, *Easily the Best*, pp. 26–27.

38 Macmillan Brown became more conservative with age in his attitudes towards women's education and role: see J. Macmillan Brown, 'Woman and University Education', Wilding Memorial Lecture, No. 2, Christchurch, 1926, p. 31.

39 The other was the Australian Anne Bolton, who came from Sydney to get her degree. Australian universities were later in admitting women to degrees than New Zealand's. These developments were part of a wider international movement for women's higher education, with parallel, albeit slower, developments at Otago University, the Australian universities and the newer British institutions. See, for example, Gardner, *Colonial Cap and Gown*, pp. 68–89, 92, 101; Lovell-Smith, *Easily the Best*, pp. 28–29, 31–39; and Theobald, *Knowing Women*, p. 61.

40 See, for example, Lovell-Smith, *Easily the Best*, pp. 71–72; McAloon, 'Radical Christchurch', pp. 162–92; Theobald, *Knowing Women*, pp. 56, 64–66; Macintyre, *Colonial Liberalism*, passim; Grimshaw, *Women's Suffrage in New Zealand*, pp. 2–4. Gardner, in *Colonial Cap and Gown*, pp. 86–87, argues that 'colonial apathy' also had a part to play in the admission of women to degree courses on the same terms as men.

Grossmann and Ada Wells.[41] Writing in 1923, Macmillan Brown added a gloss to his reputation as an advocate for women students by claiming that his admission of Helen Connon to Canterbury College in 1874 had 'committed the new college to a new attitude to women's education in the history of the world; that which gave them equality with men in university life; it determined Canterbury College as a coeducational university institution, the first of its kind in the world'.[42] A more considered appraisal might, as Gardner argues, suggest that Canterbury College's pre-eminence in this respect was confined to the British Empire.[43]

Macmillan Brown's support for the admission of women to the university is perhaps best seen as part of his wider view of education. Central to his thinking was a belief in the potential for colonial societies to be swamped by a tide of vulgar materialism.[44] In Gardner's view, Macmillan Brown saw teachers as the foot soldiers in a 'cultural revolution', which would reshape society and allow it to shrug off the dangers of the rawness of colonial society.[45] This was a view that sat well with the conception of Canterbury College's founding fathers, that the BA should be a teacher's rather than a scholar's degree, reflecting both the needs of the developing colony and inevitably low standards of academic attainment at first.[46] Most Canterbury students who sat before Macmillan Brown pursuing degrees were teachers or teacher trainees of middle or lower middle-class origin, with little formal

---

41   For examples, see letters to John Macmillan Brown from Kate Sheppard, 1893, JMBP, A8/15, A8/20, Ada Wells, c. 1893, JMBP, A8/29, Edith Grossmann, 2 May 1907, JMBP, A9/103, Edith Grossmann c. 1910, JMBP, A9/109, Edith Grossmann, 31 May 1910, JMBP, A13/107, Edith Grossmann, 21 June 1911, JMBP, A13/107. All three were prominent in the New Zealand women's movement. Both Ada Wells and Edith Grossmann studied with Helen Connon and John Macmillan Brown. Wells (1863–1933) attended Canterbury College (1881–82), followed by a brief period working at Christchurch Girls' High School, under Helen Connon's principalship, as an assistant teacher; Grossmann (1863–1931) attended Christchurch Girls' High School in 1879, where she was head girl, then studied at Canterbury College, graduating with an MA (Hons) in Latin, English and Political Science in 1885.

42   Macmillan Brown, 'Early Days and Early Students', *Lyttelton Times*, 12 May 1923.

43   Gardner, 'The Formative Years', pp. 155–56; Barbara Solomon, *In the Company of Educated Women*, Yale University Press, New Haven, 1985, pp. 45, 63; Lovell-Smith, *Easily the Best*, p. 26. American colleges led the way in coeducation.

44   'Prof. Brown's Opening Speech', *Press*, 12 May 1878; Macmillan Brown, *Student Life*, pp. 28–29.

45   Gardner, *Colonial Cap and Gown*, p. 64. See Raymond William's *Culture and Society 1870–1950*, Pelican, Harmondsworth, 1982, on the association during the Industrial Revolution of the arts with human improvement, civilisation and culture.

46   Gardner, 'The Formative Years', p. 96.

education themselves. Classes were held in the early morning, late afternoon, evening, and all day Saturday to allow country teachers to attend.[47] Such was the range of educational attainment within the college that one of the governors was, in 1878, prompted to proclaim that 'they had not a College here in the home acceptation of the word—it was halfway between a College and a big public school'.[48]

The comment may have been meant as a criticism, but it would not have gained support from Macmillan Brown. In his view, teaching was the 'noblest' of professions, and he promoted it in terms that were as much spiritual and moral as educational.[49] The roles of the school teacher and the university lecturer were to be complementary. The former aimed to train the recollection and promote good citizenship, while the university's aim was 'to stir into active life the higher faculties' and promote the 'independence of thought and originality of research' essential for 'a leader of progress'.[50] Teachers, he believed, would spread the civilising influence of the university throughout the wider society. Thus, if his Oxford mentor Benjamin Jowett envisaged his 'boys' as future statesmen of Empire, Macmillan Brown saw his most notable students—'boys' and 'girls'—as its headmasters and headmistresses.[51]

If the teacher within a secular educational system was to replace the priest as moral guardian, Macmillan Brown came increasingly to argue that the 'spiritual destiny' of the nation might rest also upon its journalists. Newspapers offered a daily pulpit from which an educated priesthood of letters might inform and guide society. It was this lofty conception of the potential of the press that had initially shaped his

---

47 Gardner, 'The Formative Years', pp. 94–100, 139, 141–43; Gardner, *Colonial Cap and Gown*, pp. 91–99, 106–7; Kay Morris Matthews, *In Their Own Right: Women and Higher Education in New Zealand before 1945*, NZCER Press, Wellington, New Zealand, 2008, pp. 12–14.
48 W. J. Hamilton, quoted by Gardner, 'The Formative Years', p. 100.
49 'Advice To Teachers: Professor Brown's Address', *Lyttelton Times*, 25 March 1889, p. 5.
50 'Prof. Brown's Opening Address', *Lyttelton Times*, 12 May 1878.
51 Perhaps the most notable of Macmillan Brown's students during this period who went on to become secondary school principals were Helen Connon (MA Hons 1881), Principal of Christchurch Girls' High School; Kate Edger (MA Hons 1882), Principal of Nelson College for Girls from 1883; Jeanette Grossmann, Principal of Maitland Girls' High School, Sydney, 1890–1913, and North Sydney Girls' High School from 1914; and Frank Milner (MA Hons 1896), Principal of Waitaki Boys' High School (1906–44). Gardner, in *Colonial Cap and Gown* (p. 107), points out that the majority of male university graduates at this time also expected to enter the teaching profession.

university studies in Scotland and later found its fullest expression in *Modern Education: Its Defects and their Remedies*, published in 1908. In a chapter on 'Religion, Morality and Education', he argues that:

> The daily paper is the preacher and priest for six-sevenths of the life of the community, and colours … a dye that not all the Sundays of the year could wash out. The editors of our local papers are the true bishops of the diocese … journalism is on the fair way to becoming the conscience and the religion of mankind.[52]

Whether teacher or journalist, members of this educated elite were, in Macmillan Brown's view, more likely saviours of civilisation than politicians and the political parties they were in the process of creating.[53]

In asserting his role as a protector of civilisation, Macmillan Brown willingly embraced much of what A. P. Rowe had in mind when he wrote of the 'Encyclopaedic God-Professor' especially prevalent within colonial universities, where economic constraints required professors to teach a broad range of subjects.[54] It was a role that made them instant public figures and provided a pedestal for men with a sense of personal mission. It is in this sense also, perhaps consciously modelling himself on the character of Benjamin Jowett, his Oxford mentor, that Macmillan Brown simply assumed the role of de facto rector at Canterbury College and exercised an overall pastoral supervision of all students. He took each of his male students for a meal at least once a term and insisted that they join him for long walks (again reminiscent of his own Oxford experience), where

---

52   J. Macmillan Brown, *Modern Education: Its Defects and their Remedies*, Lyttelton Times Company Limited Printers, Christchurch, 1908, p. 13. See also Schouten, 'The "Encyclopaedic God-Professor"', pp. 119–20.

53   Gardner has argued in *Colonial Cap and Gown*, pp. 64–65, that Macmillan Brown's apolitical stance cast a long shadow in the history of the University of Canterbury. See also Macmillan Brown's *Memoirs*, p. 127, and *Modern Education*, pp. 5–7.

54   Gardner, *Colonial Cap and Gown*, p. 66; Schouten, 'The "Encyclopaedic God-Professor"', pp. 113, 118.

the discussion often took the form of an intense grilling rather than a relaxed conversation.[55] His female students were given extra group tuition in groups of three or four at his university study.[56]

Embracing the role of 'God-Professor' did not encourage universal admiration, but it did provide a status that guaranteed a public voice. Macmillan Brown was more than willing to accept invitations to write leading articles for either of the city's newspapers, whether they came from William Pember Reeves's *Lyttelton Times*, the organ of liberal and radical opinion within the city, or the conservative Christchurch *Press*.[57] Equally, he rarely declined a public appointment. In 1877 he became a member of the University of New Zealand Senate, and the following year he was appointed to a royal commission into higher education in New Zealand. The annual meetings of the Senate, the controlling administrative body of the federal University of New Zealand, in different parts of the colony helped to provide the profile of a national figure and brought him into contact with members of political, professional and commercial elites. His appointment as an examiner for matriculation and junior university scholarship exams added further to his colonial status. Locally, he became an inspector of secondary schools and, in 1885, chairman of the North Canterbury Education Board. In short, within a decade he had immersed himself in just about every facet of the education system and exerted considerable influence on it.

A critical factor in Macmillan Brown's establishment was the relative ease with which he found 'kindred spirits' within the professional community that was taking shape within the colony. None more so than Robert Stout. A Scot from the Shetland Islands, he had reached New Zealand in 1864 as a qualified teacher and surveyor. When Macmillan Brown arrived a decade later, Stout had completed articles in law, was finishing a degree at the University of Otago while lecturing in law, and about to embark upon a political career, in which he attempted to place himself at the forefront of colonial liberalism. Opposed to the

---

55   Gardner, *Colonial Cap and Gown*, p. 62; Macmillan Brown, *Memoirs*, pp. 180–83; 'Prof. Brown', *Press*, 2 April 1895; O. T. Alpers, 'Recollections of an Under-graduate', special supplement to the *Press*, 12 May 1923, p. ii; James R. Wilkinson, 'Educational Reminiscences from 1866', Canterbury Museum, ARC 1992.54, p. 38, cited by Lovell-Smith, *Easily the Best*, p. 38.
56   K. W. Evans, 'The First Girl Graduates', *Lyttelton Times*, 12 May 1923, p. 16; Lovell-Smith, *Easily the Best*, pp. 38–39.
57   Macmillan Brown, *Memoirs*, pp. 89–90.

notion of party politics, he nonetheless played a significant role in attempts to bring together a Liberal 'party' in parliament in the 1880s and 1890s. Like Macmillan Brown, he was steeped in the writings of John Stuart Mill and Herbert Spencer. He is said to have stood in the House of Representatives with the works of Mill 'piled "three feet high" in front of him'.[58] Above all else, their friendship grew around a shared belief in the fundamental importance of education. Each thought of the teacher and not the priest as the custodian of public morality and argued that social improvement would ultimately rest upon education rather than legislation. It was this philosophy that led each to champion women's rights and to support the suffrage movement. By 1885 Stout had served two brief terms as premier, and while his political career withered, his role within higher education made him a powerful ally.[59]

Of the multitude of friendships that Macmillan Brown developed amongst the professional elite, two others stand out as providing representative strands. Among the earliest was that with Julius von Haast. The son of a well-to-do merchant and burgomaster of Bonn, he had come to New Zealand in 1858 and, after establishing an international reputation as explorer and geologist, played an important role in the foundation of Canterbury's museum, as well as being one of the founders of the Canterbury Collegiate Union (1871), the precursor of Canterbury College. As the college's first professor of Geology from 1877, he became an academic colleague and close friend of Macmillan Brown. In 1879 he joined Macmillan Brown on the Senate of the University of New Zealand, to be followed in 1885 by Robert Stout. All three were on reciprocal visiting-terms with Frederick and Julia Wilding, who, as we observe elsewhere, were prominent shapers of the new professional elite that was developing within Christchurch.

---

58   David Hamer, 'Stout, Robert 1844–1930', *The Dictionary of New Zealand Biography (DNZB)*, *Volume Two, 1870–1900*, Bridget Williams Books and Department of Internal Affairs, Wellington, 1993, pp. 484–87; Macmillan Brown, *Memoirs*, pp. 83–84.
59   Robert Stout was New Zealand's Premier (1884–87), Attorney-General (1878–79), and Chief Justice of the Supreme Court (1899–1926).

As a group, they frequently attended musical concerts in the city, where on occasion Julia Wilding and Lady von Haast as pianists and Julius von Haast as violinist were amongst the performers.[60]

Macmillan Brown's friendship with James Collier, now remembered for his pioneering work on Australian pastoralism, illustrates both how quickly a newcomer might become a patron, and the way in which individual professional migrants sought each other out and recognised the familiar elements in each other's circumstances. Born in 1846 in Dunfermline, son of a Scottish handloom weaver, Collier had in 1882, like Macmillan Brown, left the old world, as a disenchanted academic. He had read classics and mathematics at St Andrews (1863–67) without graduating and spent some 10 years as assistant to Herbert Spencer, initially as an amanuensis, but later played a much larger role in the preparation of *Descriptive Sociology*. Macmillan Brown helped Collier obtain a number of tutorships and sought the assistance of Robert Stout in gaining his appointment as the colony's Parliamentary Librarian in 1885. Their common interest in literature and history and a shared propensity to see links between the biological and sociological worlds were the basis of a friendship that spanned some 40 years. Collier resigned as Parliamentary Librarian in 1891 and lived precariously off earnings from tutoring posts, secured for him by Macmillan Brown, until 1895 when he left New Zealand for Sydney. Macmillan Brown retired from his post at Canterbury College

---

60   Peter B. Maling, 'Haast, Johann Franz Julius von (1822–1887), *DNZB, Volume One, 1769–1869*, Allen & Unwin and Department of Internal Affairs, Wellington, 1990, pp. 167–69; Macmillan Brown, *Memoirs*, pp. 102–3, 128; 'Lady von Haast', press cutting WFP, box 42/3-4, p. 116; Jonathan Mane-Wheoki, 'The High Arts in a Regional Culture: From Englishness to Self-Reliance', in Cookson and Dunstall (eds), *Southern Capital Christchurch*, p. 302.

in 1895 also. Thereafter, as both pursued careers as prolific writers and commentators, the nature of their relationship changed; Macmillan Brown became less of a patron and more of a scholarly colleague.[61]

Within this emerging cultured community that he himself was helping to create, Macmillan Brown developed a reputation as 'a people's professor'. It is a reputation that rested, as we have noted, on the popularity of his Saturday 'art lectures' that examined the 'great works' of literature and drew large audiences comprised predominantly of middle-class women. There was similarly significant support from within this community for his public proclamations that Canterbury College should shun the 'pedantic narrowness' of the ancient universities, and that its graduates should avoid the 'limp superciliousness' of their Oxford and Cambridge equivalents.[62] Yet while it is clear that Macmillan Brown took great pains to assist students from humble backgrounds, it is also clear that the 'people' he had at the forefront of his mind were the educated elite capable of exerting moral leadership within the community. When he spoke of life as an 'unending battle' with labour as its essence, he was championing a 'purification of the soul'.[63] In this sense he was advocating an educated, scholarly elite absorbed in a life of solitary study and asceticism that would assume the moral guardianship of a secular society.[64] These were views that were seen by the aspirant lower middle class as consistent with their desire to gain the academic credentials that would allow them to find a place within the city's expanding professional ranks. They had particular appeal to the

---

61   Macmillan Brown, *Memoirs*, pp. 146, 184–85; Jill Waterhouse, 'Collier, James (1846–1925)', *ADB*, vol. 8, Melbourne University Press, Carlton, Victoria, 1981, pp. 69–70; J. Collier to Macmillan Brown, 2 April 1910, JMBP, A4/33; J. Collier to Macmillan Brown, 25 March 1908, JMBP, A7/22; J. Collier to Macmillan Brown, 24 November 1907, JMBP, A7/66; J. Collier to Macmillan Brown, n.d., JMBP, A7/79; J. Collier to Macmillan Brown, 22 December 1912, JMBP, A13/81, J. Collier to Macmillan Brown, 31 May 1914, JMBP, A14/35; Herbert Spencer, *Descriptive Sociology, or Groups of Sociological Facts, parts 1–8*, classified and abstracted by David Duncan, Richard Schepping, and James Collier, Williams and Norgate, London, 1873–81; James Collier, Introduction to D. Collins, *An Account of the English Colony in New South Wales*, Whitcombe & Tombs, Christchurch, 1911; James Collier, *The Pastoral Age in Australasia*, Whitcombe & Tombs, London, 1911; James Collier, Introduction to E. G. Wakefield, *A View of the Art of Colonization*, Clarendon Press, Oxford, 1914. Collier also wrote articles on contemporary Australasian topics such as the old age pension and land legislation for the New York *Nation*, religious reconstruction in France and Germany (*Hibbert Journal*, 1906), as well as articles on sociology (*Knowledge*, 1902–4) and colonisation (*American Journal of Sociology*, 1905–6).

62   'Prof. Brown's Opening Address', *Press*, 12 May 1878.

63   Macmillan Brown, *Student Life*, pp. 4, 5, 29.

64   Macmillan Brown, *Student Life*, pp. 20–21, 28–31.

parents of academically inclined young women for whom a career in teaching was thought to satisfy prevailing expectations of what was socially acceptable for women.

Macmillan Brown's prescription was a high-minded one. It was also an accurate enough description of his first decade as a 'God-Professor'. His life now conformed in all essentials, save that of campus residence, to that of the traditional Oxbridge don. By his own account, a typical day of scholarship and teaching stretched some 16 hours.[65] Board at a private suburban household catered for his domestic arrangements for the first five years after which Macmillan Brown took up residence at the Christchurch Club on the fringe of the developing educational precinct, in which the university was taking shape. As the meeting place of the city's rural and professional classes, the Christchurch Club was the hub of the social networking that facilitated community activity. It was here that Macmillan Brown's high-mindedness rubbed up against the acquisitive instincts of the commercial classes. He himself acquired a capacity for investment that laid the foundation for the accumulation of considerable personal wealth. It was here also that he met migrant professionals like himself, seeking to find a place in the society they had just joined, and keen not to recreate Britain, but find ways to a better one.[66]

The club-land of Macmillan Brown's daily life was by its very nature a male preserve. Membership denoted a degree of acceptance, but continued permanent residence might be read as indicating ambiguous commitment to and involvement in the community. For an educationalist proclaiming a life of asceticism and scholarship, and the nurturing of talent amongst the young regardless of gender, club-land was an unsuitable address. It brought into question an individual's understanding of the family and the dynamics of domestic life. Macmillan Brown's apparent reluctance to abandon the life of the academic don wedded to his books and embrace family life has produced speculation amongst historians.[67] The discussion has taken shape around his eventual marriage to his protégé Helen Connon in

---

65   Macmillan Brown, *Memoirs*, p. 112.

66   Macmillan Brown, *Memoirs*, pp. 89, 90–92, 134–39; Megan Woods, 'Behind Closed Doors: A Study in Elite Canterbury Masculinity 1856–1900', BA (Hons) essay, University of Canterbury, 1995; McAloon, 'The Christchurch Elite', pp. 196–97.

67   Lovell-Smith, *Easily the Best*, pp. 56–63, 87, 107–9; Gardner, *Colonial Cap and Gown*, p. 111.

1886 and will be discussed in this context in the next chapter. It is sufficient here to observe that his marriage was a critical component in his establishment and acceptance within the city.

Viewed purely as an example of the migration process, Macmillan Brown's establishment years were ones in which family played few of its familiar roles. His departure from Britain was not influenced by the prior migration of family members. The fact that a younger sister was soon to migrate to Sydney with her shipping-merchant husband was a fortuitous development that was to provide Macmillan Brown with a family base, from which he could engage directly with the Australian academic and intellectual community.[68] Rather, the manner in which Macmillan Brown took his place amongst the colonial elite is best seen as illustrating the workings of the academic imperial network that developed as part of the expansion of the British world in the last quarter of the nineteenth century.[69] The transplant of the British university to the settler societies provided a ready status for migrant academics and a cocoon within which the personal adjustment to colonial life might take place. This was an environment in which men like Macmillan Brown, imbued with a sense of mission, were able to build for themselves a role that fulfilled any needs they had to identify with their new home. For Macmillan Brown this sense of identification grew naturally from his academic career and required little external stimulus.

There is little evidence that Macmillan Brown cultivated leisure or sought escape from work. Saturday evenings were spent with his 'club friends' at musical concerts and the theatre. There are some signs, however, that he recognised and enjoyed the sanctuary of the domestic haven. On Sundays and during trips to Dunedin, he spent time in the family homes of his academic colleagues, which encompassed a range of domestic settings, from the New Brighton open homes of the controversial chemistry and physics professor Alexander Bickerton to the more conventional environments of the households maintained by

---

68   Macmillan Brown's *Memoirs*, p. 81; Malcolm S. Earlam, 'Craig, Robert Gordon (1870–1931)', *ADB*, vol. 8, 1981, pp. 133–34. The husband of Macmillan Brown's sister Elizabeth (Bessie), Ayrshire-born shipping master Capt. Robert Craig (1837–1917), was appointed marine superintendent of the Eastern and Australasian Steamship Company, Sydney, in late 1874. Craig and his wife settled in Neutral Bay, Sydney.
69   See Tamson Pietsch, *Empire of Scholars: Universities, Networks and the British Academic World 1850–1930*, Manchester University Press, Manchester and New York, 2013.

von Haast, Sale and Stout.[70] He readily accepted and possibly sought invitations to join in the family activities of academic colleagues. Yet there seems little doubt that the missionary-like zeal and total absorption that characterised Macmillan Brown's engagement with the world of scholarship and education called for a high degree of self-reliance and left little room for other forms of community involvement.

Walking may have provided a partial exception. Among the professional classes of the mid-nineteenth century walking had come to be seen as a healthy pursuit in its own right, a means of escaping the city and communing with nature.[71] Macmillan Brown absorbed these attitudes at Oxford, and, as we have seen, introduced walks with students as a part of his teaching, very much in the manner of his patron Jowett. As well as an educational tool and a form of exercise, walking also provided a point of contact with young, migrant and unmarried members of the Australasian academic community, keen to explore the flora and fauna of their new antipodean environment. Amongst them were two very different Irish friends making their mark in Australia: the deeply religious, vigorous, athletic John MacFarland who, in 1881, had become Master of Ormond College at the University of Melbourne; and Henry Higgins, later a keen foundation member of the Wallaby Club (1894), a 'walking and talking' society of professional men.[72]

---

70 For a description of Sunday 'open homes' at the Bickertons attended by Macmillan Brown, see E. S. White, 'A Lady Student's Recollections'; S. Page, 'An Enthusiastic Genius'; Thomas Rowe, 'Forty Years Ago', and K. W. Evans (Kate Edger), 'The First Girl Graduates', in *Canterbury College Jubilee, Lyttelton Times*, 12 May 1923 (*Press* supplement). In 1895–96 Bickerton formed a 'federative home' in Wainoni: see Jim McAloon, 'Radical Christchurch', pp. 172–73; Gardner, 'The Formative Years', p. 110; Jane Tolerton, *A Life of Ettie Rout*, Penguin, Auckland, 1992, pp. 28–31.

71 Millicent Baxter, John Macmillan Brown's daughter, later wrote in her introduction to Macmillan Brown's *Memoirs* (p. xvii) that they were a family of 'inveterate walkers, always in Indian file, my father in the lead'. See also John Lowerson, *Sport and the English Middle Classes 1870–1914*, Manchester University Press, Manchester, 1995, pp. 30–31; Melissa Harper, *The Ways of the Bushwalker*, University of New South Wales Press, Sydney, 2007; Frederic Gros, *A Philosophy of Walking*, Verso Books, UK, 2014; Rebecca Solnit, *Wanderlust: A History of Walking*, Granta Books, UK, 2014.

72 Rickard, *H.B. Higgins*, pp. 58–59, 165–66; Geoffrey Serle, 'MacFarland, Sir John Henry (1851–1935)', *ADB*, vol. 10, Melbourne University Press, Carlton, Victoria, 1986, pp. 266–67; Macmillan Brown, *Memoirs*, pp. 35, 130–31. Macmillan Brown notes that most of the Melbourne University professors holidayed in the South Island while those from Sydney generally went to the North Island, presumably a result of the available shipping routes. Macmillan Brown accompanied Melbourne professors Herbert Strong (Classics) and Edward Nanson (Mathematics) on a trip through the Otira Gorge on the West Coast of the South Island. His old Oxford friend, Pitt Cobbett, appointed to the Challis Chair of Law at the University of Sydney, holidayed in the North Island. See F. C. Hutley, 'Cobbett, William Pitt (1853–1919)', *ADB*, vol. 8, 1981, pp. 40–41.

Whatever the context in which these explorations of the Australasian environment were formulated, they represent a level of engagement with the new world. In some degree they reflect a shift in Macmillan Brown's attitude to colonial life. At the time of his emigration from Scotland, he spoke of a period of exile that lay before him and envisaged an eventual return to claim a place within the British university system. A decade later, when he took six months leave to return 'Home', he came as a representative of the Australasian academic community and as a pioneer of English literary studies. The world of writers, poets, academics and publishers opened up to him in ways that reveal the interconnectedness of the British intellectual world and its smallness. He discussed literary developments with David Masson, pioneer of English literary studies and father of Orme Masson, soon to make his way to Melbourne. As a close friend of Herbert Spencer, David Masson's recommendation, together with a letter of introduction from James Collier, Spencer's former assistant now in Christchurch, smoothed the way for several meetings.[73] Stopping off in America on the return journey, Brown discussed developments in the teaching of English literature with Professor F. J. Child, its pioneering exponent at Harvard, and was greatly impressed by Walt Whitman, whose poetry and particular brand of humanism he admired.[74]

The return to Christchurch at the beginning of 1885 was beset by none of the doubts that surrounded his arrival in 1874. At Merton College, Oxford, he had been offered the newly established chair in English literature. There was also an offer from Ormond College at the University of Melbourne. By his own later account, Oxford weather held no appeal, and neither appointment matched his current earnings at Canterbury. Such recollections may contain an element of truth but they sit awkwardly alongside other developments in his life.[75] Within months of returning to Christchurch, Macmillan Brown became engaged to his protégé Helen Connon, now Principal of Christchurch

73 Macmillan Brown, *Memoirs*, pp. 139–50.
74 Macmillan Brown, *Memoirs*, pp. 162–67, 174–75; McMurtry, *English Language, English Literature*, pp. 65–110. Harvard professor Frances James Child (1825–1896), author of *The English and Scottish Ballads*, had studied at Harvard, Göttingen and Berlin, and took up a Harvard professorship in Rhetoric and Oratory in 1851, going on to occupy Harvard's first chair of English literature in 1876. Macmillan Brown also met Professor Lounsbury, English professor at Yale.
75 Macmillan Brown, *Memoirs*, pp. 94, 143–44; Gardner, *Colonial Cap and Gown*, p. 61; J. Macmillan Brown, 'University Pioneering', special supplement, *Press*, 12 May 1923.

Girls' High School. The courtship, conducted away from the public gaze, had been a protracted affair, as the city's two most influential educationalists sought to envisage a marriage that would accommodate not one but two careers.

Alexander and Adeline Leeper

For Alexander Leeper, academic life in the new world was to be an 'experiment of an anxious kind'.[76] His pathway to Melbourne University had been strewn with false starts. He had returned to Australia in 1875 to marry Sydneysider Adeline Allen, whom he had met on his first sojourn to Australia in 1869–70. To facilitate his return and make marriage possible, he applied for the advertised principalship of Melbourne Grammar School, but was offered and accepted the position of Second Master and Senior Master of Classics.[77] He had sailed to Melbourne with his closest friend, John Winthrop Hackett, a young barrister fully conscious of the difficulties Leeper had experienced teaching in Sydney.[78] Always morbidly concerned for his health, he was on the brink of abandoning his teaching post and taking up a tutoring position in the country, when he was offered the principalship of Trinity College, established in 1872.[79]

The college was to become the 27-year-old's 'life's work'.[80] His initial establishment period was not without its problems. His preoccupation with his health continued. There was opposition to his appointment from members of the Melbourne Anglican community concerned about his youth and lack of experience, and opposition to the new college itself as a drain on Church finances. Money for the college was short. Leeper's salary was a modest £300, and he was required to run Trinity College as a private business funded out of student

---

76   Alexander Leeper's speech at the opening of the Bishops' Building, Trinity's Theological School, on 17 June 1878, ALP, T9a, box 29/1.
77   Poynter, *Doubts and Certainties*, pp. 45–46.
78   Lyall Hunt, 'Hackett, Sir John Winthrop Hackett (1848–1916)', *ADB*, vol. 9, 1983, pp. 150–53.
79   Poynter, *Doubts and Certainties*, pp. 48–49, 58–59. For a general history of the boys' school see Weston Bate and Helen Penrose, *Challenging Traditions: A History of Melbourne Grammar*, Australian Scholarly Publishers, Melbourne, 2002.
80   Poynter, *Doubts and Certainties*, p. 60.

fee-payments and private contributions. Indeed, so precarious was his financial position, that his marriage to Adeline had been delayed until 1879, four years after their 'engagement' in 1875.[81]

When Leeper took over Trinity College, it was little more than a hostel with five residents. The fact that he was able to establish it as the hub around which Melbourne University built its version of the collegial system speaks of persistence and dedication. His observation that initially he 'did not get much encouragement from anyone' accurately reflects his crucial role.[82] His brief was to establish a theological school and ensure that the college was successful financially. From the outset, however, Leeper was considerably more ambitious and was determined that Trinity College should not suffer the fate of earlier university colleges. In Sydney, St Paul's Anglican College (1856) had by 1878 a grand building and only three students; St John's, the Roman Catholic College (1860), had been reduced to the residence of the coadjutor Bishop.[83] Leeper welcomed the challenge to succeed where others had failed: 'It would be so much a greater glory to raise this miserable place and make a decent college of it than to begin with everything so smooth and perfect as at St Paul's. There is a strange satisfaction in overcoming difficulties.'[84] His determination to achieve academic affiliation of the college to the University of Melbourne aroused opposition from those who saw the very existence of an affiliated church college as a threat to the secular foundational principles of the university and from others who thought it an unwanted agent of class and snobbish elitism best left in the old world.[85]

Such a characterisation of Leeper's vision for Trinity College was a harsh assessment of what Leeper had in mind. His personal experience of residential colleges, at Trinity College, Dublin, as well as St John's, Oxford, did not leave him uncritical of them. There was no place in Australia, he told a Social Science Congress held in October 1880, for what he regarded as the 'aristocratic exclusiveness', 'petty cliquism' and 'luxury and apathy' of the Oxbridge colleges. It would be 'indeed

---

81   Poynter, *Doubts and Certainties*, pp. 66–71, 78–99, 121.
82   Alexander Leeper's 'Reminiscences', *Argus*, 13 July 1918.
83   Poynter, *Doubts and Certainties*, pp. 61–73.
84   Alexander Leeper to George Boyce Allen, 6 December 1876, ALP, T1, box 30/68.
85   Poynter, *Doubts and Certainties*, pp. 68–71. Those that opposed the move included the foundation chancellor of the University of Melbourne, Redmond Barry, the Melbourne *Age's* David Syme and Charles Henry Pearson.

deplorable', he thought, if Australian colleges 'became aristocratic clubs for the idle, from which the poor or humbly born student could be practically shut out'.[86] The Trinity College he envisaged for Melbourne was by contrast to be a place of strenuous effort. Scholarships would enable gifted but economically constrained students to enjoy the benefits of residential student life. The college would operate on two levels—academic and moral. A tutorial system like that of Oxford and Cambridge was in Leeper's view essential, because lecture classes at the University of Melbourne were too large and the number of university professors too few for teaching to be adequate. The students' need for more individualised tuition was borne out, he believed, by the popularity of the 'university coach'. At the same time, in a break with Oxbridge tradition at least, Leeper envisaged that colleges might become the centres of research within the university. The overworked lecturers, confronted by large classes, often inadequately prepared for university, were, he argued, in no position to carry out much research of their own. The encouragement of competition within a residential college and between the other colleges, which Leeper thought would follow in the future, would raise the university's academic standards, contribute to an increase in new knowledge, and provide an esprit de corps which was the lifeblood of a university.[87]

Moreover, Leeper believed it to be imperative that the sense of moral purpose that infused the ancient universities should be replicated in their colonial offspring. Indeed, he sought to establish himself within Trinity College as a patriarchal head of a household of young men, standing, as it were, in loco parentis. He insisted upon twice-daily attendance at what he called 'family prayer' and saw supervised study as a means of inculcating steady work habits and self-discipline among students.[88] For Leeper '[n]o better preparation for the world exists than free association with one's contemporaries' that such guided communities of scholars provided.[89] As Geoffrey Blainey has put it, Leeper's ideal college would be 'a disciplined democracy and a training school in citizenship, a forum of unrestrained intellectual

---

86 Jubilee Calendar of Trinity College, 1897.
87 Poynter, *Doubts and Certainties*, pp. 100–102. The research ideal was derived from German universities.
88 *Australasian*, 12 February 1876; Poynter, *Doubts and Certainties*, pp. 67–68.
89 *Australasian*, 12 February 1876; Poynter, *Doubts and Certainties*, p. 67. Poynter speculates that Leeper 'must have briefed the author personally, if not written the piece personally'.

fellowship for students …'.[90] The Trinity College tutors would, like their Oxbridge and Trinity College Dublin counterparts, have a considerable role in shaping the characters and outlook of those who in Leeper's conception would be leaders of the next generation. Leeper aimed at establishing nothing less than, as John Poynter puts it, a 'training [school] for the nation's intellectual élite'.[91]

Leeper pursued this goal with a steadfastness derived from a moral certainty. At its centre lay a deeply ingrained belief in the importance of classical studies as the basis of a 'liberal education' that would 'furnish the community with its best leaders and thinkers'.[92] It was a set of beliefs kept alive and refreshed by his personal scholarship, as he continued to publish even as his administrative teaching and pastoral duties grew. He collaborated with Professor H. Strong to publish *A Guide to Classical Reading Intended for the Use of Australian Students* (1880), published a translation of *Thirteen Satires of Juvenal* (1882), and for several decades worked on an annotated edition of Liddell and Scott's Greek–English lexicon.[93] More immediately important in establishing his place amongst Melbourne's cultural elite was his production of classical plays performed by Trinity College students and, for the first time in the city, delivered in Latin. Further Latin plays followed in 1884 and 1887, and the staging of a more ambitious Greek tragedy in 1898, the first Greek play performed (in the Greek language) in Victoria, attracted a large audience.[94]

The energy that Leeper poured into classical studies undoubtedly cemented his reputation within academe and amongst the educated community. Such constant engagement with the ancient world reinforced a frame of reference that inspired a teaching regime stressing the importance of civic values. Leeper took from his studies

90   Blainey, *A Centenary History of the University of Melbourne*, p. 80.
91   Poynter, *Doubts and Certainties*, p. 102.
92   Alexander Leeper, *A Plea for the Study of the Classics. Inaugural Lecture delivered before the Classical Association of Victoria, 22nd April, 1913*, Melville and Mullen, Melbourne, 1913; *Age*, 23 April 1913.
93   Alexander Leeper (with H. A. Strong), *A Guide to Classical Reading, Intended for the Use of Australian Students*, George Robertson, Melbourne, 1880; Alexander Leeper (with H. A. Strong), *Juvenal: Thirteen Satires*, translated into English, after the Latin text of J.E.B. Mayor, Macmillan, London, 1882. Leeper also had published his *Fourteen Satires of Juvenal*, translated into English, Macmillan, London, 1912.
94   The Greek tragedy performed in 1898 was *The Alcestis of Euripides*, for which Leeper provided the audience with an English translation. Another Greek play, Aristophanes's *Wasps*, took place in 1906. See Poynter, *Doubts and Certainties*, pp. 107–8, 124–25, 135, 269–72, 326.

an understanding of how human beings might seek to behave in ethical ways, and of how a sense of community might be encouraged amongst the educated few. Historians have recently drawn attention to the ways in which late-Victorian and Edwardian philosophers were drawing upon the ancient world and developing a 'theory of "community" and of collective social action' previously 'lacking in the established mainstream of English political thought'.[95] Leeper's advocacy of the ancient world as an exemplar was consistent with this analysis. His understanding of the ancients led him to place them at the centre of thinking, informed his vision for Trinity College, and lent his stewardship a missionary zeal and moral certainty that has led historians to describe him as both liberal progressive and bigot.[96]

Evidence of both can be found in his long tenure at Trinity. It is argued here that in the establishment of Trinity College Leeper's role was constructive, energetic and directed towards an understanding of community building. Once the college had achieved affiliation with the University of Melbourne in 1876, opened its Theological College and been suitably rehoused in grounds within campus, Leeper proceeded to develop his ideal tutorial system. Classical studies occupied central place, but the program he constructed was broad and at times innovative. Among its early features were an essay and debating club and a Dialectical Society based on the Trinity College Dublin model designed to develop collegial spirit. An annual public lecture sought to provide engagement with the wider educated community. In response to the widening of the University of Melbourne's matriculation exams to include four science subjects, and the looming introduction of a Bachelor of Science degree in 1887, Leeper established a biology and chemistry laboratory and appointed tutors in practical and medical chemistry, biology, histology and physiological chemistry. Despite his personal preference for classical languages and literature, by 1889 he had added modern languages—French and English—to his tutorial program.[97] Nothing better testifies to the success of Leeper's endeavours to establish Trinity College than the appearance of two further colleges, the Presbyterian Ormond College (1881) followed by

---

95   Jose Harris, 'Platonism, Positivism and Progressivism: Aspects of British Sociological Thought in the Early Twentieth Century', in Biagini (ed.), *Citizenship and Community*, p. 354.
96   Poynter, *Doubts and Certainties*, pp. 2–4; O'Farrell, *The Irish in Australia*, p. 190.
97   Poynter, *Doubts and Certainties*, pp. 75, 103, 105.

the Wesleyan Queen's College (1888).[98] Leeper would become locked into a rivalry with MacFarland's better-endowed Ormond during the 1880s.

Leeper's enthusiastic advocacy of learning within a collegial system was at its most progressive and controversial when he championed the inclusion of women students. He had taken up the cause after the admittance of women to courses and degrees at the University of Melbourne in 1881. Two years later, he admitted the first non-residential female student to Trinity College lectures. A visit to Girton College, England, in 1884 spiked his enthusiasm further and he persuaded Melbourne University authorities to approve, on a 12-month trial basis, a residential hostel for women students. From the outset, Leeper intended women students to be integrated fully into Trinity College life and strove to provide them with access to the same educational opportunities as the male students, namely tutorials, lectures and use of his personal library. Leeper made the experiment something of a personal crusade. Initially there were few women students and little demand for a woman's hostel. As originally conceived, the hostel was farmed out to a principal appointed by Leeper and run as a private business concern. In practice Leeper personally provided scholarships and bursaries for female students, and his wife, Adeline, propped the hostel up financially.[99]

As well as financial hurdles, there was scepticism, misunderstanding and controversy. Bishop Moorhouse probably spoke for many within the Anglican community when he expressed a fear that 'penniless' female students would trap wealthy Trinity College men into marriage.[100] The generally sympathetic *Daily Telegraph* thought the experiment contained the 'germ of an Australian Girton', but this was an emphasis that did not quite do justice to Leeper's conception of full integration.[101] It was certainly true that Leeper had looked initially to Girton and Newnham Women's colleges at Cambridge and Somerville

---

98   Stuart Macintyre (ed.), *Ormond College Centenary Essays*, Melbourne University Press, Carlton, Victoria, 1984; Owen Parnaby, *Queen's College, University of Melbourne: A Centenary History*, Melbourne University Press, Carlton, Victoria, 1990.
99   On the establishment of Trinity College Hostel see Poynter, *Doubts and Certainties*, pp. 131–50, 202–23; Lyndsay Gardiner, *Janet Clarke Hall 1886–1986*, Hyland House, Melbourne, 1986, pp. 1–69; Theobald, *Knowing Women*, pp. 40, 75–80.
100 Poynter, *Doubts and Certainties*, p. 133; Morna Sturrock, *Bishop of Magnetic Power: James Moorhouse in Melbourne 1876–1886*, Australian Scholarly Publishing, Melbourne, 2005.
101 *Daily Telegraph*, 5 December 1885.

at Oxford University for legitimising models, but he came increasingly to favour the more integrated American practice of coeducation. As Leeper saw it, integration offered the surest way to the full participation of women students. Establishing independent women's colleges in the manner of the English universities would, he believed, be a backward step for women that would lower their academic standing.[102] It was a position that did not always sit comfortably with the Ladies Council appointed to assist in the management of the hostel. The lady councillors, perhaps partly influenced by the establishment in Sydney of a government-funded independent (non-denominational) women's college in 1892, sought publicly and unsuccessfully to push Leeper aside.[103] In the slanging match that ensued in the pages of the Melbourne *Age*, Leeper's patriarchal and authoritarian tendencies are well revealed. Whatever the merits of the integrated versus independent models propounded, and whatever the motivations behind the skirmish, Leeper rode out the controversy. His role in the admission of women to the university stands as positive, encouraging and persistent. The first intakes of the women's hostel distinguished themselves academically and produced a steady stream of teachers and doctors, as well as an outstanding classical student, Melian Stawell.[104] By any assessment, Leeper had made good his claim to have established at Trinity College 'a fair Home of Religion and Learning' for women students.[105]

The phrase 'religion and learning' describes Leeper's academic evangelism and defines the parameters of his engagement with the wider community of his time. As warden of Trinity College, essentially a private business affiliated to the university, he was always conscious of the need to attract funding and publicise university and college wherever and whenever possible. To this end he willingly assumed and assiduously cultivated a public role as a champion of Melbourne's

---

102 Poynter, *Doubts and Certainties*, pp. 133–42.
103 On the Women's College at Sydney University, see Theobald, *Knowing Women*, pp. 80–90; Ursula Bygott and K. J. Cable, *Pioneer Women Graduates of the University of Sydney, 1881–1921*, University of Sydney, Sydney, 1985, pp. 15–23.
104 Gardiner, *Janet Clarke Hall*, pp. 5, 6, 49, 52, 65, 67. Melian Stawell (1888), daughter of the Chief Justice, 'completed her degree at Cambridge, became Classics tutor at Newnham and later published several books on classical literature and translations of classics texts'. See also K. J. McKay, 'Stawell, Florence Melian (1869–1936)', *ADB*, vol. 12, Melbourne University Press, Carlton, Victoria, 1990, pp. 55–56; Charles Francis, 'Stawell, Sir William Foster (1815–1889)', *ADB*, vol. 6, Melbourne University Press, Carlton, Victoria, 1976, pp. 174–77.
105 Alexander Leeper to Lillian Alexander, 30 August 1888, cited by Gardiner, *Janet Clarke Hall*, p. 8, and by Poynter, *Doubts and Certainties*, p. 140.

cultural community. He founded and maintained an active lifelong involvement in a Shakespeare Society (1884); from 1887 until 1928 he was a trustee of the omnibus organisation that oversaw the city's Public Library, museums and National Gallery; and founded the Classical Society of Victoria in 1913. In a similar and complementary way, the essentially religious component of his role as secretary of the Theological Faculty at Trinity College and warden of the Anglican Trinity College allowed Leeper to quickly become increasingly influential within the Anglican Church in Victoria.[106] As a lay canon of St Paul's Cathedral and a member of the Synod, he was a visible participant in Church affairs and attracted public attention promoting the rights of the laity, as opposed to that of the bishops, and supporting the ordination of women. It is a measure of his growing status within Melbourne that in 1888, 13 years after settling in the city, Leeper was nominated for membership of the prestigious Melbourne Club. Leeper's description of his acceptance—involving an expense he thought extravagant—as presenting a further opportunity to promote Trinity College suggests an academic evangelism tinged with more than a touch of entrepreneurial vigilance.[107]

The religiosity of Leeper's academic evangelism places him closer to the clerical Oxbridge dons who characterised the ancient English universities than either Macmillan Brown or Masson, whose minimal religious convictions continued to wither in the colonies. It is tempting to see Leeper's Anglicanism as intensifying the evangelical element of his personality and shaping the nature of his marriage and family life. He was to be married twice. It is his first marriage, in 1879, to colonial-born Adeline Allen, of Sydney, that sealed his commitment to life in Australia and helps define the nature of the Leeper family. The eldest

---

106 For Anglicanism in Victoria and Australia see: James Grant, *Episcopally Led and Synodically Governed: Anglicans in Victoria, 1803–1997*, Australian Scholarly Publishing, Melbourne, 2010; Reginald Stephen (ed.), *The First Hundred Years: Notes on the History of the Church of England in Victoria*, Executive Committee of the Anglican Assembly, Melbourne, 1934; Brian H. Fletcher, *The Place of Anglicanism in Australia: Church, Society and Nation*, Broughton Publishing, Mulgrave, Victoria, 2008; Bruce Kaye (ed.), *Anglicanism in Australia: A History*, Melbourne University Press, Carlton, Victoria, 2002; James Grant, *Old St Paul's: The Story of St Paul's Church, Melbourne, and its Congregation, 1850–1891*, Melbourne, 2000.

107 Alexander Leeper was nominated as a member of the Melbourne Club by two prominent businessmen, R. Murray Smith, a member of the University Council (1887–90) and F. A. Keating. See Poynter, *Doubts and Certainties*, pp. 114–19, 444, n. 37; Ronald McNicholl, *Number 36 Collins Street, Melbourne Club 1838–1988*, Allen & Unwin/Haynes, Sydney, 1988; Ernest Scott, *Historical Memoir of the Melbourne Club*, Specialty Press, Melbourne, 1936; Paul de Serville, *Pounds and Pedigree*.

daughter of a wealthy and prominent Sydney legal and politically active family, Adeline undoubtedly improved Leeper's social and professional standing and she brought to the marriage sufficient capital to prop up Leeper's often-shaky personal finances. Throughout the marriage, it was frequently Adeline who provided the money that was remitted to Leeper's Irish relatives and underwrote the struggling Trinity Women's Hostel in its earliest years.[108] She also chaired the Ladies' Committee appointed to assist in running the hostel and often bore the brunt of day-to-day management when Leeper was absent. It could be said that life for the Leepers revolved around operating a family enterprise within the cloistered and institutional environs of Melbourne University.

More than any other of the women in this study Adeline brought extended family to her marriage. The role of her Sydney-based family during the establishment years at Trinity College took several forms. Adeline spent the greater part of her four 'confinements' at her parents' home in Glebe and stayed for lengthy periods until each of her newborns had settled into a routine. During busy or stressful times her sister Ida often joined the Leepers' Trinity College household to provide an extra pair of hands. For Adeline, her Sydney family and friends remained a central component of her life and offered a respite from the intensity with which her husband lived his life. That her family recognised this and readily facilitated it is made clear in letters that passed between Alexander Leeper and Adeline's brother, Boyce.[109] There can be little doubt that the extended family and its preoccupations necessarily lessened Adeline's engagement with the Melbourne community in which her own family took shape. She spent little time, for example, forging social networks in the traditional female manner of paying calls, and devoted herself to the domestic arrangements of college and family.[110] Within this small community of academic families clustered within the confines of Melbourne University, Adeline participated in the networks that developed amongst university wives and was closest to Mary Masson, with whom she shared a preference for the private and domestic aspects of family life.[111] It was a preference

---

108 Poynter, *Doubts and Certainties*, pp. 120–21, 144. Adeline Leeper received a £200 annuity from her father upon her marriage.
109 For example, Boyce Allen to Alexander Leeper, 20 August 1892, ALP, T1, box 30/68.
110 On social calls and networking, see Russell, '*A Wish of Distinction*'.
111 Adeline Leeper to Alexander Leeper, 30 June 1889, 5 July 1889, 10 July 1889, 26 July 1889, 4 August 1889, ALP, T1, box 23/52.

facilitated by the institutional environment of Melbourne University, which minimised many of the more mundane elements of maintaining a household and gave greater scope to women who sought to play active roles in the education of children.

In this collegial and family context Adeline's life conforms to the prevailing norm of her class and generation: the supportive wife whose talents complemented those of her husband. If there was one area of her life more than any other that illustrates the point, it was her love of music. She possessed sufficient talent as a pianist to take her beyond 'accomplishment' to the margins of performance quality. Whether she judged the gap too large or lacked the confidence to pursue the opportunity is unclear. But she chose, instead, a less conspicuous and conventional means of giving expression to her musical talent. As organist for the Trinity College chapel, she assumed responsibility for church music, and, somewhat shamefacedly at the age of 36, took singing lessons, so that she might offer a more effective lead.[112] Religious settings such as these had long been an acceptable semi-public performance platform for women.[113] That Adeline confined public expressions of her musicality to chapel and concert-going reaffirmed to contemporaries her status as a supportive wife who shared her husband's religious beliefs.

In summary, the Leeper family established by Alexander and Adeline Leeper occurs within a cloistered household dominated by an intense and anxious academic evangelist, whose energy and persistence had carved out a niche within Melbourne's educated establishment. The extent to which his mercurial personality and intellectual certainty shaped the nature of the family that lived out its life within the sheltered environs of a colonial university is pursued in later chapters. At this point, it is safe to say that Alexander's controversialist tendencies and certainties loom largest and point to pronounced patriarchal and paternalistic tendencies, embedded in a high-minded liberalism derived from an understanding of the classical world. Family life was to take its place within this framework and, as the following chapters reveal, became infused with a similar anxiety to make the idealised colonial family a reality.

---

112 Adeline Leeper to Alexander Leeper, 28 July 1889, ALP, box 23.
113 Paula Gillett, *Musical Women in England, 1870–1914*: *'Encroaching on all Man's Privileges'*, St Martin's Press, New York, 2000, pp. 33–62.

Orme and Mary Masson

The process of establishment was smoothed for the Massons by a university system dependent for its continued expansion upon a steady stream of new academic staff from Britain. The smallness of the academic enclaves that were taking shape in the metropolitan centres, and the eagerness with which they embraced replenishment from 'Home' British universities, had been evident to Orme and Mary even before they reached Melbourne. They were nonetheless surprised when, en route to Melbourne, they were greeted in Adelaide by Archibald Watson, Chair of Anatomy at that city's university, who declared himself a 'fervent' admirer of Mary's father, John Struthers's work in comparative anatomy.[114] In fact, both Massons came from academic families: David Masson, Orme's father, was Chair of English Literature and Rhetoric at Edinburgh University. Less surprising was the presence in the welcoming party of Edward Henry Rennie, Australia's first native-born professor of Chemistry. Newly appointed to the University of Adelaide's foundation chair, Rennie had completed a DSc in London in 1882. He was to develop a close friendship with Masson and they became collaborators in the quest for a greater research focus within the universities.[115] When the Massons reached Melbourne on 16 October 1886, their welcome on board the Orient-liner *Garonne* at Port Williamstown was similarly conducted, at least in part, in old world accents and accompanied by academic familiarities, although a number of medical students had ducked off to watch the Caulfield Cup.[116] Mary and Orme Masson did not join the Australian university as unknowns, but as accepted, if not yet proven, members of a select and socially narrow community.

---

114 Weickhardt, *Masson of Melbourne*, p. 1.

115 Ann Moyal, *A Bright and Savage Land: Scientists in Colonial Australia*, Collins, Sydney, 1986, pp. 165–66, 173; I. Inkster and J. Todd, 'Support for the Scientific Enterprise, 1850–1900', in R. W. Home (ed.), *Australian Science in the Making*, Cambridge University Press in association with the Australian Academy of Science, Cambridge and Melbourne, 1988, p. 115; Ian Rae, 'Chemists at ANZAAS: Cabbages or Kings?', in Roy MacLeod (ed.), *Commonwealth of Science: ANZAAS and the Scientific enterprise in Australasia, 1888–1988*, Oxford University Press, Melbourne, 1988, p. 167. E. H. Rennie (1852–1927) was a graduate of Sydney University (1871) and London University with a doctorate in organic chemistry. He held the Chemistry chair at the University of Adelaide from 1885–1927.

116 Marnie Bassett, *Once upon a Time*, Royal Historical Society of Victoria, South Melbourne, 1985, pp. 57–58; Orme Masson to Irvine Masson, 13 January 1927, DOMFP, box 6/8/1.

The practicalities of establishing a household were similarly eased by university authorities. Even so, more than two years went by before they were installed in a recently completed professorial house within Melbourne University grounds, one of five identical houses in domestic-Gothic style. The first months of life in Melbourne were spent in rented accommodation of various kinds: a boarding house in Fitzroy, furnished rooms in East Melbourne, and a 'small brown brick villa' in Bruce Street, Toorak, close to the 'large mansions set in spacious grounds' of Melbourne's professional and business classes.[117] It was in this 'little brown house', as Marnie Masson was later to describe it, that the process of adjustment to the new world began and the first of the Masson children was born.[118] From here also the Massons made their first social contacts with members of the city's establishment. Inside this suburban villa, they were able to surround themselves for the first time with their wedding presents, comforting reminders of 'Home'. Prominent among them was a grand piano, made possible, Marnie Masson speculates, by 'combined family cheques'.[119]

The surrounds of Melbourne University, rather than suburban Toorak, were to shape the Massons' establishment in Melbourne. As we have observed, Masson was one of the new generation of career academics recruited by the universities of Sydney, Melbourne, Adelaide, and the foundational universities of New Zealand during the 1870s and 1880s.[120] Their appointments reflected a commitment to expanding the teaching of scientific subjects in the wake of the growing specialisation, whereby natural history, previously approached as one overriding subject, was divided into separate fields. Research was

---

117 Bassett, *Once upon a Time*, p. 58.
118 Bassett, *Once upon a Time*, p. 59.
119 Bassett, *Once upon a Time*, p. 59.
120 The chemistry professors were: John Black (University of Otago, Dunedin, appointed 1869); Archibald Liversidge (University of Sydney, appointed 1872), Alexander Bickerton (University of Canterbury, Christchurch, appointed 1874), F. D. Brown (University of Auckland, appointed 1883), E. H. Rennie (University of Adelaide, appointed 1885), Orme Masson (University of Melbourne, appointed 1886). In 1898, T. H. Easterfield was appointed at Victoria University, Wellington. Apart from Rennie, who was Australian-born, all came from Britain. Rennie completed degrees at Sydney University and was the first Australian to complete a DSc (London, 1882). Neither Black, who was pre-eminently a natural scientist, nor Bickerton, who was more interested in cosmology and university politics, played much part in chemical research. See Ian D. Rae, 'Chemists at ANZAAS: Cabbages or Kings?', in *Commonwealth of Science*, pp. 166–70. At the University of Melbourne, Masson was part of a trio of research-orientated scientists and teachers appointed during the late 1880s: biologist Walter Spencer Baldwin joined him at the university in January 1887; mathematician and physicist Thomas Lyle was appointed in 1889.

seen as a desirable concomitant, rather than an essential component, of this expansion. With varying degrees of success, Masson and his cohort of research-minded scholars attempted to shift the balance between the teaching and research functions of the universities they entered.[121] As Masson discovered and historians of science confirm, research in chemistry was stronger outside the universities. Based in industry, mining and medicine, its concerns primarily lay in applying established methods and knowledge rather than in pure research. By comparison the universities were laggards on both fronts. Within the University of Melbourne, chemistry remained encased within the School of Medicine, and it was to be some years before Masson was able to establish its right to be considered a separate discipline.[122]

Against this background, Masson introduced himself in his inaugural lecture at Melbourne University on 23 March 1887. Titled 'The Scope and Aims of Chemical Science', it can be read as the manifesto of the foundational generation of university research scientists.[123] Expressed in idealistic and high-minded terms, it rested upon the classical concept of knowledge as the ultimate truth and sought to enshrine scientific research as offering the surest road to social progress: 'The Science of chemistry is organised knowledge of natural truths, and it is an instrument of natural truths, and it is an instrument for the discovery of new truths.' The pursuit of these truths was best achieved by academic scientists, whose fundamental duty was 'the development of science itself'.[124] Universities should thus become centres of research unfettered by the constraints of the marketplace. As creators of new knowledge rather than pre-eminently purveyors and examiners of established knowledge, they would thus contribute more to the development of humankind.

The language in which Masson's inaugural lecture was delivered was the language of a rising generation of research scientists, who saw science as the handmaiden of progress. It was a view that looked backwards to classical antiquity for its validation, and from it derived a moral certainty that had the potential to turn its advocates into

---

121 Moyal, *A Bright and Savage Land*, pp. 164–68, 173; Home (ed.), *Australian Science in the Making*, pp. xii–xiii, 111–18, 125.
122 Rae, 'Chemists at ANZAAS: Cabbages or Kings?', MacLeod (ed.), *Commonwealth of Science*, pp. 167–70.
123 Melbourne *Argus*, 24 March 1887.
124 Melbourne *Argus*, 24 March 1887.

crusading apostles. The ideal of the research university had begun in Germany, initially with a cultural and indeed religious orientation, which it quickly discarded to emphasise the nature of science as open inquiry. In Masson's subsequent career, there is much that might be read in terms of secular evangelism, nowhere more clearly than when he confronted and sought to define the relationship between science and the state. To pursue 'truth', as Masson and his generation appreciated, required them to profess public neutrality. Such proclamations of '"disinterestedness" implied that their judgements deserved special respect'.[125] When their opinions were discounted, the moral certainties in which they were grounded ensured that those who ignored them were seen as enemies of progress. For Masson and his generation of scientific idealists, the ranks of the enemy were thick with bureaucrats and politicians.[126] This did not mean that Masson and his generation avoided engagement with the marketplace or politicians. Indeed, Masson's idealism, as sketched in his inaugural lecture, had skilfully pointed to the utilitarian value of research and the importance of strengthening the links between research and industry, manufacturing and government agencies. To this end he had proposed the establishment of a Victorian section of the British Society of Chemical Industry, formed in 1881.[127]

The desire to create a research environment that encouraged the 'scientific idealist', as he categorised the university scientist of the future, dominated Masson's establishment years and indeed his academic career.[128] As he confronted the realities of Melbourne University, he became increasingly conscious of the gap between aspiration and realisation. A small university staff had limited time to devote to research and was confronted with students inadequately prepared for scientific study. The laboratories upon which research depended did not exist. His initial goals were tailored to meet the circumstances. He envisaged 'a small band of students devoting the

---

125 Stefan Collini, *Public Moralists: Political Thought and Intellectual Life in Britain, 1850–1930*, Clarendon Press, Oxford, and Oxford University Press, New York, 1991, p. 224, and more generally: pp. 2–3, 68–69, 204–9, 224–25.
126 See here A. G. Austin (ed.), *The Webbs' Australian Diary 1898*, Sir Isaac Pitman & Son, Melbourne, 1965, p. 65; Weickhardt, *Masson of Melbourne*, pp. 77–97, 106–9, 115–18, 124–29, 135–46, 149–57; Orme Masson to Marnie Masson, 27 November 1917, DOMFP, box 6/9/1; Marnie Masson to Orme Masson, 24 March 1918, DOMFP, box 3/2/1.
127 Melbourne *Argus*, 24 March 1887.
128 Melbourne *Argus*, 24 March 1887.

bulk of their time for a few years to the study of chemistry', guided by teachers whose task was to instil a 'practical familiarity with the methods of inquiry'.[129] The university's standing as a school engaged in original work would ultimately depend, Masson argued, upon such elite groups of scholars.

Masson's mission statement encapsulates the idealism of the foundational-generation research scientists, of which he stands as exemplar. The extent to which this collective idealism was realised has been variously assessed, as historians have sought increasingly to understand the process by which science developed in Australia. Until the 1970s, the prevailing view depicted the science practised in Australian universities from the 1850s until after World War Two as dependent, suffering from isolation from the main scientific centres of research, parochial, teaching-focused rather than research-orientated, derivative and incapable of making original contributions to knowledge. Within this stunted scientific community, university science is seen as inferior, but capable of attracting a small band of brilliant young British scientists, who had missed out on the limited number of new positions available at 'Home'. Once in Australia, they remained unsettled and anxious to end the 'colonial interludes' in their careers as soon as they could. A critical historiographical shift in this understanding followed a path-breaking study by Donald Fleming and George Basalla that applied core–periphery analysis to the transfer of western science and provided a diffusionist framework that allowed for increasingly independent scientific activities at the periphery.[130] Within this paradigm, Australian historians, most notably Michael Hoare and Ann Moyal, developed a periodisation of Australian scientific development that sees Masson and his generation as representing the final phase of Australia's struggle to achieve an independent scientific community with its own institutions and research agenda.[131]

---

129 Melbourne *Argus*, 24 March 1887.
130 Home, 'Introduction', in Home (ed.), *Australian Science in the Making*, p. ix–xi; Jan Todd, *Colonial Technology: Science and the Transfer of Innovation to Australia*, Cambridge University Press, Melbourne, 1995, pp. 7–8.
131 Moyal, *A Bright and Savage Land*, pp. 162–73; Todd, *Colonial Technology*, p. 7.

Neither framework nor conclusion has gone unchallenged.[132] The thrust of the critique, however, is directed at the persistence of the imperial connection. For Roy MacLeod, Australian science remained, even in the 1930s, a pawn in the imperial plan. Such changes of focus as occurred within Australian science were directed from the core, reflected changes in imperial policy and the changing needs of Britain for markets and products. Inkster concedes that, while Australia developed its own scientific societies in the late nineteenth century, the 'mental map' of its scientists remained fixed on Britain, 'even into the early twentieth century'.[133] Nevertheless, these characterisations contain little that diminishes Ann Moyal's assessment of Masson and his generation of Australian scientists. They were, she argues, a band of energetic young British scientists, trained in research methodology, who took up positions in the Australian universities during the 1870s and 1880s in their respective specialist fields, established schools of scientific research, carried out their own research, made significant contributions to both the local and international scientific community, and enjoyed long, rewarding careers in the colonies.[134]

However historians have judged the efforts of his generation, Masson endeavoured to make the most of the opportunities his appointment as Melbourne University's first formally qualified professor of Chemistry offered.[135] His blueprint for the establishment of chemistry laboratories, presented to the University Council six weeks after his arrival in Melbourne, was ambitious without being excessive.[136] Its implementation was soon complicated by the straitened economic realities that followed a severe downturn in the Victorian economy in 1889. It is a measure of the persistent financial constraints under which Masson operated that in 1901 he offered to contribute £100 to help maintain science laboratories.[137] If money was in short supply,

---

132 Todd, *Colonial Technology*, pp. 7–8.

133 Todd, *Colonial Technology*, pp. 7–8.

134 Moyal, *A Bright and Savage Land*, pp. 162–73.

135 Weickhardt, *Masson of Melbourne*, p. 21; Selleck, *The Shop*, p. 196. Orme Masson succeeded the first chair of Chemistry, John Drummond Kirkland, senior, who died in 1885, three years after the chair was established. Kirkland was largely self-taught in chemistry and acquired medical qualifications while lecturing in Chemistry at the university's medical school.

136 The University Council considered Orme Masson's 'Memorandum on the Requirements of the Chemistry Department of the University of Melbourne' on 29 November 1886.

137 His colleague, biologist Walter Spencer Baldwin offered £100 and to withhold part of his salary to prevent the reduction of the Engineering Department. Weickhardt, *Masson of Melbourne*, p. 59; Selleck, *The Shop*, pp. 354–55, 359.

so also were the science students who might become Masson's band of elite researchers. In 1888, just two undergraduate chemistry majors enrolled, and by 1893 Masson had four research students.[138] Indeed, most of Masson's energies were directed to teaching a first-year chemistry course with as many as 160 students, most of whom were medical students, and supervising their chemistry laboratory work.[139] The slowness with which these circumstances changed and the frustration involved is manifest in a report Masson presented to the University Council some 22 years after he took up his post.[140] Large first-year classes continued, he claimed, to be made up of students with little scientific training, which meant that much time needed to be devoted to elementary teaching, and opportunities for research were limited. There were few serious students of science wishing to pursue postgraduate research. Most students, Masson lamented, regarded time in the laboratory as 'merely an agreeable amusement'.[141] Enrolments in science as a whole had indeed grown slowly from eight in 1888 to 17 by the turn of the century, and 58 by 1914.[142]

Masson's frustrations were widely shared within the scientific community. Beatrice Webb, visiting Sydney and Melbourne universities in 1898, recorded a general dismay among university scientists, and in her characteristically acerbic manner, she attributed it to the 'utter indifference of well-to-do Australians for learning of any kind'.[143] This judgement nonetheless echoed the views of Sydney University scientist Edgeworth David, who in 1902 condemned the general lack of interest in science. Similarly, Sir Samuel Griffith,

---

138 Masson and his colleague Spencer, professor of Biology, designed the science course, with Masson offering Chemistry Parts I, II, and III to undergraduates. Weickhardt, *Masson of Melbourne*, p. 180; Orme Masson to Irvine Masson, 12 January 1936, DOMFP, box 6/8/1. The first science students enrolled in 1888. On the introduction of the BSc and DSc, see Selleck, *The Shop*, pp. 284–85.

139 Amongst these students were the first female medical students, who gained admittance to the University of Melbourne's medical school in 1887. Orme Masson was to give them particular encouragement.

140 Masson presented his report in 1908 on the state of science courses at the University of Melbourne in his capacity as Dean of the Faculty of Science, established in 1903. Masson became Dean in 1905.

141 Weickhardt, *Masson of Melbourne*, p. 62.

142 Selleck, *The Shop*, pp. 182, 496. The University of Melbourne's total number of students was 539 in 1888, 647 in 1900, and 1,375 in 1914. Roy MacLeod notes that, in 1904, 1,104 arts degrees were awarded at the University of Sydney and only 47 science degrees, none of which were doctorates: Roy MacLeod, 'From Imperial to National Science', in MacLeod (ed.), *Commonwealth of Science*, p. 55.

143 Austin (ed.), *The Webbs' Australian Diary 1898*, p. 33.

Queensland's Chief Justice and former premier, suggested that the apparent lack of interest pointed to '[t]he great defect of Australian life ... the want of apprehension of the value of knowledge in itself'.[144] A brief meeting with Masson led Webb to describe him as a 'charming person and an enthusiast', developing a 'thoroughgoing contempt for democratic institutions'.[145] Whatever prompted Webb's assessment, Masson's thwarted scientific idealism was evident enough. The difficulties of establishing science within the universities weighed heavily upon him, and his absorption as practitioner and proselytiser in finding ways to overcome them and foster scientific development generally dominated his working life. They were also to dominate a domestic and family life that was lived out within the confines of Melbourne University.

Science also defines the nature of the family's integration within Melbourne's professional community. Within two years of his arrival in Melbourne, Masson was one of two University of Melbourne academics appointed to a royal commission set up after an outbreak of typhoid to investigate the need for improved sanitation in Melbourne. Chaired by Professor Harry Allen, Dean of Melbourne University's medical school, the commission which Masson joined was a cross-section of Melbourne's commercial, professional and medical establishment, and thrust Masson into direct engagement with the industrialist community. He visited industrial sites in Sydney, Adelaide and Melbourne to observe the discharge of industrial pollutants into the water supplies. So began an engagement with industry and government which was to produce a knowledge of Australian industrial practices that was, in the judgement of one historian, 'unrivalled by any of his successors' at the University of Melbourne.[146] More immediately, the consequences were twofold: it led to appointment, in 1890, to the

---

144 T. W. Edgeworth David, 'University Science Teaching', *Record of the Jubilee Celebrations of the University of Sydney*, Brooks and Co., Sydney, 1903, p. 24 (cited by MacLeod, 'From Imperial to National Science', p. 55).

145 Austin (ed.), *The Webbs'*, pp. 65, 88.

146 Weickhardt, *Masson*, pp. 48–49, 180; Orme Masson to Irvine Masson, 12 January 1936, DOMFP, box 6/8/1; Selleck, *The Shop*, p. 312, 740 n. 59; Progress Report of the Royal Commission to inquire into and report upon the Sanitary Conditions of Melbourne, *Victorian Parliamentary Papers 1889*, vol. 2, part 2.

newly formed Board of Public Health; and it encouraged Masson to double his efforts to establish a society of chemical industry—realised in 1900—as a means of widening the research base for chemistry.[147]

Participation in the royal commission confirmed for Masson the belief that, in Australia, the expansion of science would ultimately rest upon the scientific evangelism of its university component. Missionary activity was at times as pragmatic as it was idealistic. Industry was a source of employment and a recruiting ground for the universities (Herbert Gepp, one of Masson's four honour students in 1896–97, worked at an explosives factory).[148] Whatever the mix of motives, Masson put his support enthusiastically behind the creation of institutions designed to advance scientific knowledge. He played a prominent role in the development of the Australasian Association for the Advancement of Science, based in Sydney and founded by Professor Archibald Liversidge in 1888, and, in 1891, as president of the association's chemistry section. In this role he assiduously developed working relationships with the scientific communities of Australasia and internationally.[149] Moreover, as a frequent presenter of papers, he joined a cluster of academics bent upon injecting a theoretical perspective into the proceedings of the association.[150]

Less visible, though perhaps more crucial to an understanding of Masson's academic evangelism, was his commitment to a mode of teaching that has much in common with the intense and morally laden tutorship commonly ascribed to Balliol.[151] In Masson's case,

---

147 Weickhardt, *Masson*, pp. 48–49; Len Weickhardt, 'Masson, David Orme (1858–1937)', *ADB*, vol. 10, 1986, pp. 432–35; Selleck, *The Shop*, p. 312, Orme Masson to Irvine Masson, 12 January 1936, DOMFP, box 6/8/1.

148 Herbert Gepp (1877–1954) was a junior chemist at the Australian Explosives Factory at Deer Park. Masson recruited him to his chemistry course and Gepp continued to work at the factory while attending university. The factory was taken over by Nobel Industries Scotland in 1897. Gepp was taken on as a cadet by the company in Scotland in 1897, returning to Victoria to head the Melbourne plant. He was to become a leading industrialist in Australia. Weickhardt, *Masson*, pp. 48–49.

149 Selleck, *The Shop*, p. 299; Home, 'Introduction', in *Australian Science in the Making*, pp. xiii, 117–18.

150 See here MacLeod, 'From Imperial to National Science', Ian D. Rae, 'Chemists at ANZAAS', in MacLeod (ed.), *Commonwealth of Science*, pp. 43, 166–67, 173. Other such chemists included professors Archibald Liversidge (Sydney), John Booth Kirkland (Masson's demonstrator at the University of Melbourne), Norman Wilsmore (former student of Masson) Edward Rennie (Adelaide) and T. H. Easterfield, (Wellington, New Zealand). By 1911 Masson was president of the entire association.

151 Jones, *Balliol College*, pp. 202–24.

as we have seen in an earlier chapter, the more direct link is to the literary tradition that prevailed within Scottish education. Moral in its purposes and heavily reliant upon the mentoring resources of the individual tutor, it provided a model for how the young Masson might go about encouraging others to share his enthusiasm for and faith in science as an agent of progress. The model placed great demands upon the teacher and, as John Macmillan Brown's early retirement at the age of 50 attests, could be crippling in its effects.[152] In Masson's case it proved effective. His reputation as an energetic, adventurous if not exciting lecturer, who couched his message skilfully and with literary flair, brought converts from the ranks of arts students and produced acolytes.[153] He took pains to ensure that his best students were able to pursue their studies with either his former colleague William Ramsay, at University College, London, or at one of a number of German universities.[154] 'Masson's men', as they came to be called, were noted overseas for the quality of their research training. Many returned to Australia to take up leading scientific roles, and, as they did so, Masson's network of influence grew.[155] Throughout all this Masson managed to continue his own research, publishing a number of papers in British and European journals that were acknowledged in 1903, when he was made a Fellow of the Royal Society.[156]

By any assessment, Orme Masson's adjustment to his new environment was a successful and productive one. For his young wife Mary the process of adaptation and establishment took longer and was fraught with the anxieties of the unsettled. Indeed, her migration story is, by her own later admission, one of failure to adapt and withdrawal from the public gaze. In a sense, Mary Masson was to remain an expatriate

---

152 Macmillan Brown, *Memoirs*, pp. 128–30, 139, 183–84, 186–87; 'Canterbury College: Farewell to Professor Brown', *Lyttelton Times*, 6 March 1896. During his farewell speech Macmillan Brown went so far as to encourage his students to 'cultivate idleness to some extent'.

153 Weickhardt, *Masson*, pp. 185–86; I. W. Wark, Notes on Masson, 31 August 1972, p. 22.

154 The 1851 Exhibition science research awards were established in 1891 to allow outstanding colonial science students to continue their studies overseas. Several of Masson's postgraduate students won these and other scholarships. Weickhardt, *Masson*, pp. 49, 50, 54, 58, 69.

155 Weickhardt, *Masson*, p.190. Weickhardt writes that Masson's 'style and influence' was maintained by Rivett and Hartung in particular. Furthermore, by 1989 'seven out of the twelve recipients of the Royal Australian Chemical Institute's Leighton Memorial Medal, awarded since 1965', were product of the Masson-Rivett-Hartung epoch. Two were professors and later vice-chancellors, one was president of the Australian Academy of Science, three held senior posts in the CSIRO, and two were industrialists who served as university chancellors.

156 Masson has been credited with providing the inspiration, during his trip 'home' in 1895, for friend William Ramsay's later discovery of gases neon, argon, krypton and xenon.

all her life, and it was around this very migrant identity that she assumed a more public role. Attempting to explain why Mary should experience more difficulty adjusting to married life in the colonies than the other young migrant wives of this study would require deeper exploration of the individual personalities involved than is possible here. It is possible, however, to place Mary's experience within the context of changes that were taking place within the nineteenth-century family, and to explore the ways in which migration affected these changes.

In her recent study, *Thicker than Water: Siblings and their Relations, 1780–1920*, Leonore Davidoff describes these changes in a manner that characterises professional couples, such as Mary and Orme Masson, as part of a transitional generation that looked backwards to the 'long family' with its intricate network of cousinage, and anticipates the smaller, more socially isolated family that was gradually replacing it. As children of professionals, they possessed the social advantages that might enable them to enter the professions at a time when entry was becoming increasingly competitive. But, as we have seen, they had done so at a time when professional opportunities were shrinking and women stood on the fringes. It was from within this more constrained environment that the professional classes were in the vanguard of the trend towards smaller families that saw family size fall from between 'over six for those married mid-century to around three' at the end of the nineteenth century.[157] Migration improved professional prospects for men and solidified the trend to smaller families, but it also effectively severed the vestiges of cousinage that had, in a variety of ways, provided a support structure which, as Davidoff points out, made it possible for lives to be lived out very largely within family contexts.[158]

Perhaps the 24-year-old Aberdeen-born and raised Mary Masson (1862–1945), daughter of a famous Aberdeen professor, engaged at 22, three weeks after meeting Orme Masson (26), and married 26 days before sailing for Melbourne, underestimated the impact migration would have upon her life. Like so many other middle-class migrant wives, she arrived in Melbourne with *Mrs Beeton's Book of Household Management* (1880 edition) and little practical knowledge

---

157 Davidoff, *Thicker than Water*, p. 103
158 Davidoff, *Thicker than Water*, pp. 84–85.

that would help in the establishment of a household.[159] She took a methodical approach to the task, recording lists of wedding presents and household equipment she had gathered before leaving Scotland, and colour-coding dusters according to their purpose, as a guide to servants.[160] Once she had engaged a general domestic servant to take care of household duties in the Fitzroy boarding house at which they first lived, Mary was left with little to occupy herself, apart from shopping and returning the calls of 'Melbourne matrons'.[161] Looking back upon these times, Mary conceded that there had been too much time to indulge in 'comparisons' between Melbourne and Scotland, and that the habit bred a homesickness and nostalgia that continued to impair her engagement with the new community she had entered.[162]

Pregnancies came swiftly and easily for Mary Masson. Unlike Julia Wilding, Helen Connon and Mary Higgins, she was untroubled by fertility problems and untouched by infant mortality. While the pregnancies were welcomed and lent purpose to her life, they also increased her loneliness, isolation and longing for distant family members. Embarrassed by her changing shape, a feeling common amongst her generation, Mary cloistered herself within the bounds of her home during the day and emerged in the evenings to go for walks with Orme. Without the familiar family networks of Aberdeen, this retreat from the public gaze was all the more isolating.[163] Her withdrawal largely cut off whatever potential there may have been for developing, as Julia Wilding was able to do, friendships with females, who might act as surrogate mothers, sisters or cousins and ease both the transition from the old world to the new and the approach of motherhood. The experience of Sydney-born Adeline Leeper suggests that the dominantly masculine university environment in which she and Mary lived most of their married lives was not a congenial one for young, expectant mothers. During each of her four pregnancies Adeline departed from Trinity College's Warden's Lodge and sought refuge in her parents' home in Sydney, where she remained for a lengthy period after each child was born.[164]

---

159 Bassett, *Once upon a Time*, pp. 56–57.
160 Bassett, *Once upon a Time*, p. 59; Mary Masson, 'Household Lists', ms, 1886, DOMFP, box 7/10/5; Weickhardt, *Masson of Melbourne*, p. 24.
161 Bassett, *Once upon a Time*, pp. 58, 60.
162 Bassett, *Once upon a Time*, pp. 58–59.
163 Bassett, *Once upon a Time*, pp. 61–63.
164 Poynter, *Doubts and Certainties*, pp. 119–20.

Whatever role the university environment played in Mary Masson's troubled early years in Melbourne, she later described the early phase of motherhood as the loneliest time in a woman's life.[165] By September 1890, she was the mother of three children under four years of age. Irvine, born in 1887, in the villa the Massons rented in Toorak, had been followed by Flora Marjorie (Marnie) in 1889 and Elsie in 1890. Both girls were born in the professorial house the family was to call home until Orme Masson retired. So similar were these spacious two-storey red-brick homes to the family residences built during the 1870s at Oxford University to house the first Oxford dons permitted to marry without forfeiting their fellowships, they may, as Marnie Masson suggests, have been modelled on them.[166] The Massons named it Chanonry after Mary's childhood home in Aberdeen.[167] As the institutional residence of a domesticated don and family, Chanonry made few demands upon either of the Massons. The almost half-acre in which it was set offered the potential to create a garden, and, with Mary's enthusiasm and the labour of university groundsmen, it became a reality. Three servants—cook, general housemaid and nursemaid—provided the domestic labour.[168]

As mistress of the household and mother of three young children, Mary's days were busy ones. They were also ones passed in an environment that relieved the domestic dons of the worries of home ownership and maintenance, but offered limited opportunities for wives apart from those they created for themselves as individuals. Such involvement as Mary developed outside the confines of the university took place in contexts that were expatriate in nature, related to her husband's interests or both. At no time was this more clearly the case than when, in 1892, she became a foundation associate lady member and one of two inaugural vice-presidents of the ladies'

---

165 Bassett, *Once upon a Time*, p. 71.
166 Bassett, *Once upon a Time*, pp. 61–63; Selleck, *The Shop*, pp. 223–24.
167 Bassett, *Once upon a Time*, p. 61. Mary Masson's home in Aberdeen was situated in a street called The Chanonry, according to Selleck, *Finding Home*, p. 10. Apart from the Leepers, whose home was imbedded within Trinity College, all the families in this study followed a practice common amongst the professional migrant class of naming their homes after some known old world rural arcadia or nostalgic reminder of 'Home'. See Davison, *The Rise and Fall of Marvellous Melbourne*, pp. 137–38, on the Melbourne custom of naming homes.
168 Bassett, *Once upon a Time*, pp. 62–64.

section of the Royal Melbourne Golf Club.[169] As John Lowerson points out, there is much that is 'mythical' about the spread of golf from a base amongst eighteenth-century Lowland Scots as following 'the spider's web of Caledonian *emigrés*'.[170] But in Melbourne the role of migrant Scots is manifest. Of the 100 foundation subscribers to the Royal Melbourne Golf Club (RMGC), the good majority were Scots by birth or parentage.[171] Orme Masson was one of 100 willing to pay 15 guineas to become a foundation subscriber. In doing so, he was joining a body of 'predominantly successful businessmen and pastoralists' leavened with a 'sprinkling of lawyers, doctors and high-ranking civil servants', of whom 32 were or became members of the Melbourne Club, 52 were members of the Australian Club, and 15 belonged to both.[172] In short, the RMGC mirrored in social composition the cross-section of society to which Mary and Orme were accustomed.

The manner in which the RMGC made space for women reflects both the social nature of the new pastime and attitudes prevalent amongst the educated professional sections of society, of whom it was composed. Most of the 69 women who joined during the first year were the wives and daughters of members. There was a core of enthusiastic players among them, but a large percentage of associates (and, for that matter, members) did not play. Many who did play were, as the club historian delicately puts it, not 'conversant with the rules'.[173] A great many of the members' wives fell readily into the role of tea-makers, just as most members readily assumed they would. Mary Masson was not one of them, or at least not before she had played the customary 11 shorter holes then allotted to the women's game. She took part in the first ladies' competition in August 1893, for which she had donated a prize of three custom-made balls, and was chosen for the first interclub match against Geelong and the return home-game in October.[174]

---

169 Joseph Johnson, *The Royal Melbourne Golf Club: A Centennial History*, Royal Melbourne Golf Club, Black Rock, Victoria, 1991, pp. 27–35, 50–51; Weickhardt, *Masson of Melbourne*, pp. 51, 181; Orme Masson to Irvine Masson, 12 January 1936, DOMFP, box 6/8/1. Orme Masson was a foundation member of the Royal Melbourne Golf Club, established in 1892, a member of the club council and vice-captain of the club.
170 Lowerson, *Sport and the English Middle Classes*, p. 126.
171 Johnson, *The Royal Melbourne Golf Club*, p. 27.
172 Johnson, *The Royal Melbourne Golf Club*, p. 27.
173 Johnson, *The Royal Melbourne Golf Club*, p. 51.
174 Johnson, *The Royal Melbourne Golf Club*, pp. 50–51.

Nonetheless, golf was never to become a sporting passion for Mary Masson. It did not in any way become an expression of public individuality or a rejection of domesticity in the way Eric Hobsbawm has suggested sport did for some late nineteenth-century European women.[175] Indeed, it may be more accurate to see her involvement in golf as standing closer to issues of psychological adjustment to colonial life. The golfing community was a congenial one, redolent of the Scotland she had left behind. That it was also a setting that reinforced and extended developing colonial networks is evident when we note the names of Mary's acquaintances, who joined her as associate members of the RMGC. As well as the wives of the academic colleagues, we find Mary Alice Higgins and Kate Morrison.[176] The daughter of George Morrison, Headmaster of Geelong College, Mary Alice was the wife of Henry Higgins and linked to the academic community through her husband's membership of the Melbourne University Senate. Her cousin Kate, daughter of Alexander Morrison, Headmaster of Scotch College, was similarly a familiar face within the extended academic community.[177] Both were Australian-born of Scots parentage and drawn into the golfing fraternity by its Scottishness rather than by any sporting enthusiasm. Whatever their sporting prowess, the 'twenty ladies' who had established the women's section of the RMGC shrewdly convinced Lady Janet Clarke, the city's pre-eminent social 'lioness' and philanthropist, to become its inaugural president.[178]

Golf was a diversion that could briefly dispel homesickness, but did little to aid Mary's acceptance of her life in Melbourne. The prospect of a return 'Home' was a realistic one that became more so as Orme Masson's career flourished. Indeed, of all the subjects of this study, his career possessed an international dimension, built around the

---

175 E. Hobsbawm, 'Mass-Producing Traditions: Europe 1670–1914', in E. Hobsbawm and T. Ranger, *The Invention of Tradition*, Cambridge University Press, Cambridge, 1983, p. 29.

176 William Harrison Moore (Law), Thomas R. Lyle (Natural Philosophy) and Thomas Tucker (Classics) had been encouraged by Orme Masson to take up golf, and, together with their wives, they were the core of an active university set within the early Royal Melbourne Golf Club. See Johnson, *The Royal Melbourne Golf Club*, p. 35; Weickhardt, *Masson*, pp. 51, 181.

177 E. L. French, 'Morrison, Alexander (1829–1903)', *ADB*, vol. 5, 1974, pp. 295–97; B. R. Keith, 'George Morrison (1830–1898)', *ADB*, vol. 5, 1974, p. 298. Amongst the academics' wives were law professor Moore Harrison's wife, Edith Eliza à Beckett, suffragist (daughter of a judge, Sir Thomas à Beckett); physics professor Thomas Lyle's wife, Frances Clare (a grazier's daughter) and classics professor Thomas Tucker's wife, Lancashire-woman Annie Muckalt.

178 Johnson, *The Royal Melbourne Golf Club*, pp. 50–51.

nurturing of links with scientific and academic institutions. Such networks gave rise to offers of posts that allowed a return, if not to Scotland, then at least to the old world.[179] Such prospects encouraged a sense of temporariness and made engagement with new and unsettling surroundings seem to Mary less necessary or pressing. In 1895, they returned to Scotland for six months leave without salary to introduce their three children to their grandparents and the extended Masson and Struthers families. We do not know whether Orme took the opportunity to explore the job market. If he did, he was unsuccessful. Marnie Masson has suggested that the visit added to her mother's sense of loss and separation.[180]

The disabling impact of nostalgia and the withdrawal that accompanied it gradually lessened. It was not until the 1920s that the Massons abandoned thoughts of seeking a post in Britain, or contemplating a return 'Home' upon retirement.[181] But their joint decision in 1912 to decline the chair in chemistry at University College, London, marks a growing acceptance by Mary that she was now, for better or worse, committed to life in Melbourne and Australia.[182] Two decades had passed since the pair had arrived in Melbourne. The demands of children and household had diminished, and, as the wife of a now well-established professor of chemistry, Mary made the transition from the domestic to the public sphere in ways that were consistent with the prevailing expectations of middle-class professional women of her day: to pursue charitable and philanthropic endeavours and act as an advocate of social causes. This neat bifurcation of Mary's life in Melbourne mirrors a common enough pattern: an early phase dominated by the demands of motherhood and domesticity, followed by a more public presence as these demands lessen. Yet Mary's depiction of her establishment years as blighted by nostalgia and

---

179 Orme Masson declined the position of foundational principal of the proposed Indian Research Institute, offered to him in 1901. A posting as head of the Chemistry department at the Imperial Institute of Technology at South Kensington, England, was mooted in 1911. Six months later he declined the chair of Chemistry at University College, London, about to be vacated by his colleague, William Ramsay. See Weickhardt, *Masson*, pp. 51–53, 72, 84–87.

180 Marnie Bassett, *Once upon a Time*, pp. 67–72.

181 Weickhardt, *Masson of Melbourne*, pp. 85–86, 129; Marnie Bassett to Elsie Malinowski, 6 December 1921, DOMFP, box 5/5/2.

182 Bassett, *Once upon a Time*, p. 72.

withdrawal and a reluctance to commit to her new environment seems also to rest upon a sense of lost opportunity or perhaps even unfulfilled obligation.

This ambiguity is best discussed by examining briefly the nature of the public activity in which Mary became increasingly involved. The public phase of Mary Masson's Melbourne years may be described as having four characteristics: it took its initial shape within the university environment familiar to her; its focus drew heavily upon her own migrant experience; it was given full expression during World War One; and it was a persistent aspect of her life thereafter. As her husband's status within the university hierarchy grew, she came to play the traditional role of hostess of social gatherings, some of which took place in the Chanonry. It was a function that allowed her to play 'an increasing and influential part in University affairs'.[183] Mary devoted considerable time to assisting newly arrived academic families combat the loneliness and isolation with which she was only too familiar. She aided the small group of female students to find their way amongst the male-dominated student body by putting their case to university authorities for representation on the university students' union committee.[184] When most male university staff ignored Lucy Archer, the Principal of Trinity College Hostel for Women (1906–18), because she lacked academic qualifications, she joined Mary Moule Leeper and insisted upon 'proper recognition'.[185]

The university environment also allowed Mary Masson to develop intellectual interests. She regularly attended meetings of the University of Melbourne's Chemical Society, founded in 1900 by Orme's students. Her support of female students flowed through into their efforts after graduating to establish cultural societies for women. In 1910, for example, she became a foundation member of the Melbourne Lyceum Club, established by a small group of women graduates. In discussion of membership qualifications, Mary led opposition to following the

---

183 Orme Masson was chairman of the Professorial Board between 1912 and 1916 and had much to do, in this capacity, with the vice-chancellor, John MacFarland, a confirmed bachelor. Mary Masson assumed some of the university roles of a vice-chancellor's wife, drawing the wives of the 'sub-professorial staff' into the university social life and suggesting ways to improve the institution. See Marnie Bassett, *Once upon a Time*, pp. 71–73; Weickhardt, *Masson of Melbourne*, p. 75.
184 Selleck, *The Shop*, pp. 523–24.
185 Weickhardt, *Masson of Melbourne*, p. 75; Joan M. Gillison, *A History of the Lyceum Club*, Lyceum Club, Melbourne, 1975, pp. 32–33; Bassett, *Once upon a Time*, pp. 72–73.

example of its British counterpart and accepting women purely on the basis of the achievements of their fathers or husbands. Rather, women would qualify for admission on the basis of a university degree and/or distinction in art, music, literature, philanthropy, education and public service. In this way, intellectual purpose would be preserved and the club could take its rightful place alongside its male equivalents.[186]

It was the outbreak of war in August 1914 that provided the opportunities which allowed Mary to transcend the sheltered confines of the University of Melbourne and assume a public space of her own. Her experience mirrors that of countless middle-class women, who assumed leadership roles in the myriad ladies' service organisations that sprang quickly into life throughout the British Empire after the outbreak of war. Mary's first tentative steps into community service are visible in her involvement with the Victoria League for Empire, the initial purpose of which was to achieve closer bonds with Britain by entertaining overseas visitors. Women's role within the league was, however, primarily that of hostess.[187] Her first direct engagement with the service community began with her election as President of the University Branch of the Australian Red Cross Society in 1914. From this position, her talent for organisation, already evident within the university setting, led to participation in the administration of a host of organisations, most notably as an executive member of the Australian Comforts Fund, which provided provisions for soldiers. In the judgement of her daughter Marnie, these positions gave Mary 'her own activities', 'brought that now-diminished nostalgia to an end', and provided 'opportunities for wide human contacts [that] gave her greater satisfaction than her music, or even her experiences of Scotland'.[188] With liberation came community recognition: in 1918, she was awarded a CBE.

What made her experience different, however, was the extent to which, after the war had ended, she continued her civic involvement. She did so in ways that hark back beyond the exigencies of wartime to her own difficulties as a young, married migrant. In 1921, she became

---

186 Gillison, *Lyceum Club*, pp. 26–28, Selleck, *The Shop*, pp. 523–24.
187 Ann Else (ed.), *Women Together: A History of Women's Organisations in New Zealand*, Daphne Brasell Associates Press and Historical Branch, Department of Internal Affairs, Wellington, 1993, p. 292.
188 Bassett, *Once upon a Time*, p. 72; Weickhardt, 'Masson, Sir David Orme Masson (1858–1937)', pp. 432–35.

a foundation member of the New Settlers League, which sought to help young British women who came to Australia as the wives of Australian servicemen. She was similarly a foundation member of the Country Women's Institute of Victoria, attracted by its concern to seek to minimise the isolation of rural life by providing communal opportunities for country women. Her concern for the unsettled or isolated extended also to helping Australians going abroad, especially students, writing countless letters of introduction, and providing contacts that might prevent them from having their experience blighted by an inability to cope with an unfamiliar environment. That such activity gave Mary particular satisfaction has been well attested by her daughter Marnie. The satisfaction may have stemmed from the belated fulfilment of a sense of duty and a quest for social usefulness.

4

The Lawyers

This chapter charts the establishment of two legal families, those of Julia and Frederick Wilding in Christchurch and Henry and Mary Alice Higgins in Melbourne. The process differs in its emphases from that observed within the academic families of the previous chapter and unfolds within markedly different individual circumstances. The Wildings arrived in Christchurch in 1879 as a professional couple, with clearly developed notions of the family, needing only to satisfy the none too onerous qualifying conditions of the New Zealand legal system before commencing practice. The tale of their establishment thus emphasises the manner in which they attached themselves to the city's professional elite, integrated themselves into a range of social and cultural activities and developed networks of friends and acquaintances. By contrast, the establishment of Henry Higgins is intimately bound into the migration story of his Irish parents. Eighteen years of age in 1869 when he arrived in Melbourne with his mother and siblings, his passage to the legal profession and marriage spreads over 16 years. The passage was negotiated through ethnic and religious networks, engendered a sharp awareness of the realities of social class and consolidated the central place of family in his thinking. Ultimately, Henry's intellectual abilities and talents allowed them to flourish within the colonial society.

Julia and Frederick Wilding: 'We certainly transplant very well'[1]

Unlike their academic contemporaries heading for the University of Melbourne and Canterbury College safe in the knowledge that a salaried position awaited them, 26-year-old solicitor Frederick Wilding and his wife Julia faced greater uncertainty and risk as they set sail for New Zealand shortly after their marriage late in June 1879. Julia was in the early stages of pregnancy when they first set foot in New Zealand in September 1879. They entered a debt-ridden country moving into a lengthy period of economic stagnation. The 'long depression' as it was once called by historians lasted arguably until 1895.[2] Though the Wildings came armed with some capital to tide them over the early establishment period and the promise of further family financial support, their success in New Zealand was largely dependent upon Frederick's ability to negotiate the hard economic times to establish himself as a barrister and build a successful legal practice.

Within three years of settling in Christchurch they had become a recognisable couple within the community. Their 'arrival' can be measured in a succession of milestones: Frederick's admittance to the New Zealand Bar as a barrister and solicitor in 1880; the establishment of a legal practice in 1881; Frederick's inclusion in the Canterbury cricket team in 1881; the purchase, in 1883, of Fownhope in Opawa, on the fringe of suburban Christchurch, which remained the family home for 65 years; membership of the prestigious Canterbury Club; and, in 1884, the hosting of a garden party at Fownhope for 200 guests that marked their acceptance within the city.[3] We shall see that the speed and relative ease with which the Wildings established themselves owes much to their personal talents and interests. It was also made possible by the timing of their arrival and by the nature of the Christchurch

---

1 Frederick Wilding, 'Life in New Zealand', *HT*, 17 July 1880.

2 W. J. Gardner, 'A Colonial Economy', in Geoffrey W. Rice (ed.), *The Oxford History of New Zealand*, 2nd edn, Oxford University Press, Auckland, 1992, pp. 75, 614 n. 48; Jim McAloon, 'The New Zealand Economy, 1792–1914', in Giselle Byrnes (ed.), *The New Oxford History of New Zealand*, Oxford University Press, Melbourne, 2009, p. 213; Mein Smith, *A Concise History of New Zealand*, p. 93.

3 Julia Wilding's Events Diary (JWED) 1879–1908, WFP, box 11/54/54: 8 June 1880, 1 September 1881, 21 April 1883; Julia Wilding's Household Diary (JWHD) 1883, WFP, box 1/5/5: Household Diary Expenditure Summary for 1883; 6 February 1884, JWHD 1884, WFP, box 2/6/6.

society they entered. As a predominantly English city, a couple from Hereford could more easily make their way in Christchurch, and there remained, as the 1880s began, enough fluidity and flexibility to accommodate newcomers within its developing professional urban culture.

Indirectly, these markers of the Wildings' 'arrival' tell also something of the commitment that infused the act of migration and the family experiment that was at its centre. Julia and Frederick were 'joiners', enthusiasts with a wide range of interests and talents, who, almost as soon as they arrived, became involved in a range of societies and clubs that signalled an enthusiastic engagement with their new community. These included the Debating Club, the Glee Society, the Library Society, the Lancaster Park Cricket Club, the Canterbury Cricket Club, the County Athletic Club, the Cranmer Square Tennis Club, the Christchurch Musical Society and the Philosophical Society.[4] If Julia's presence seems at first less prominent than that of her husband, this reflected the fact that the material and public manifestations of building a new home are more easily measured. The human dimension of the family experiment upon which the Wildings embarked proceeded at its own pace. Their first child, a son who they named Frederick Archibald, died in December 1880 of dysentery when nine months old. By October 1883 Julia had given birth to a daughter and another son and the family experiment was ready to begin.[5]

There can be no doubt that the attraction of New Zealand for Frederick and Julia Wilding lay in what they believed to be its 'Englishness'. It was this perception that had led them to favour migration to New Zealand rather than one of the Australian colonies. Stopovers in Adelaide and Melbourne during the voyage to New Zealand provided an opportunity to test this judgement.[6] Frederick found his confirmation in what he perceived to be an emergent Australian national type, as distasteful as it was distinctive:

---

4   These societies and clubs are first mentioned in JWHD 1880, JWHD 1881, JWHD 1883, WFP, box 1/2/2, 1/3/3, 1/5/5 expenditure entries for the following dates respectively: 11 March 1880, 7 May 1880, 3 July 1880, 11 August 1880, 17 September 1880, 14 October 1880, 8 June 1881, 5 July 1881, 23 October 1883.

5   Frederick Archibald Wilding, 10 March 1880 – 30 December 1880; Gladys Julia Wilding, b. 1 November 1881; Frederick Anthony Wilding, b. 31 October 1883.

6   Frederick Wilding, 'Jottings of a Voyage to the Antipodes', HT, 22 November 1879.

though 'corn stalks', as the young Australians are called, are athletically and mentally up to the average of English youth [they possessed] bad, sallow complexions. An Englishman is struck by their lounging, loafing air, their proneness to strange uncouth slang and a nasal accent, not so pronounced as the American drawl, but most unmusical to susceptible ears.[7]

New Zealand, supposedly, did not possess such a type, and, in Christchurch, he observed, newcomers from England continued to be as 'anxious as the old settlers to perpetuate in the colony all that is best in English life'.[8] Indeed, Englishness had undergone 'no perceptible alteration' among the first settlers.[9] In a column contributed to the *Hereford Times*, he conceded that the 'the wrench of leaving one's friends and associations is sharper' than he had anticipated, but suggested that the transplant from England to New Zealand was 'little more, in many respects, than a change from Northumberland to Devonshire'.[10] At first glance, Christchurch, and indeed New Zealand as a whole, appeared to be a better Britain, where there was more social freedom, fewer and more relaxed social conventions and less pressure towards conspicuous consumption; a place where perceived British characteristics were maintained but in a more relaxed form.[11] Moreover, the very different conditions that existed in the colony had allowed English political institutions to be adapted in ways that provided 'almost perfect political freedom'.[12] Such was the initial judgement of a young lawyer sufficiently confident in his Englishness to proclaim enthusiastically to readers of the *Hereford Times* that 'we certainly transplant very well'.[13]

There was much that Wilding thought comforting and English about Christchurch. He was struck by 'the home-like look of everything and everybody' and suggested to readers of the *Hereford Times* that the city's 'beautiful public gardens, museums, theatres, steam trams and host of cabs [were] faintly, very faintly suggestive of London'.[14] The quest for such reassuring signs came naturally

---

7   Frederick Wilding, 'Life in New Zealand', *HT*, 17 July 1880.
8   Frederick Wilding, *HT*, 17 July 1880.
9   Frederick Wilding, *HT*, 17 July 1880.
10   Frederick Wilding, *HT*, 22 May 1880.
11   Frederick Wilding, *HT*, 29 November 1879, 27 December 1879, 22 May 1880, 17 July 1880.
12   Frederick Wilding, *HT*, 17 July 1880.
13   Frederick Wilding, *HT*, 17 July 1880.
14   Frederick Wilding, *HT*, 17 July 1880.

enough to migrants, but some historians seem as keen to diminish the Englishness of the city's past as Julia and Frederick Wilding were to welcome it. By describing the city's 22 February 2011 earthquake as a 'postcolonial moment' that would, by its destruction of monuments and buildings, provide a natural break from the city's English past, historian Katie Pickles has given this tendency its most controversial airing.[15] Historians have generally been more circumspect in their discussion of the city's Englishness. Most stress that its urban form was 'more recognisable as a colonial and New World town', and that its culture was no more English than Wellington's, but allow that its flatness enabled settlers to construct a more English-*looking* town than proved possible anywhere else in New Zealand.[16] The topography allowed for more brick and stone constructions, enclosed spaces and public gardens, and lacked Wellington's 'vistas of bush and wild hills'. Whatever Englishness it possessed in 1879, Christchurch appealed to the Wildings and seemed a good place not to replicate England, but rather to help in the construction of a better one.

Would the 'better England' allow the realisation of idealised aspirations that the young couple attached to migration? Middle-class professionals did not escape the general belt-tightening that accompanied the prolonged recession marking the 1870s and 1880s. Male newcomers at the lower end of the professional ladder now competed in a contracting job market against a growing number of colonial-born sons for a diminishing number of clerkships and secretaryships. 'Local influence' and 'private friendship', Wilding believed, determined such appointments in much the same way as it did at 'Home'.[17] Legal clerks and solicitors were finding their paths blocked by the sons of wealthy and influential families, who now dominated the field. Several longstanding firms of solicitors dating back to the 1850s and 1860s had garnered the shrinking volume of legal work. The situation was more promising for migrant barristers

---

15   Katie Pickles, 'A Natural Break from our Colonial Past', Perspective, *Christchurch Press*, 8 April 2011 (A15). For reactions to Pickles's article, see 'Past Present', *Press* editorial, 11 April 2011 (A12); Letters to the Editor, *Press*, 11 April 2011; Lorraine North, 'Victorian Legacy', Perspective, *Press*, 13 April 2011 (A19). See also Pickles's recently published book: *Christchurch Ruptures*, Bridget Williams Books, Wellington, 2016.
16   John Cookson, 'Pilgrims' Progress—Image, Identity and Myth in Christchurch', in Cookson and Dunstall (eds), *Southern Capital*, pp. 13, 28–32. See also Lyndon Fraser and Angela McCarthy, *Far from Home: The English in New Zealand*, Otago University Press, Dunedin, 2012.
17   Frederick Wilding, *HT*, 22 May 1880.

and especially, in Wilding's view, for qualified English medical men.[18] Those with capital could, he believed, buy into a practice on 'easier terms' than in England.[19] He was optimistic that, despite the temporary downturn, Christchurch would continue to be a 'rapidly increasing community' and offer fewer obstacles to establishing a new practice than Hereford, the 'stationary town' he had left behind.[20] In his view, professional men may have been 'badly paid', but most seemed 'to make pretty good livings'.[21]

Wilding's analysis of the city's legal scene was an accurate one and is largely endorsed by Daniel Duman's study, *The English and Colonial Bars in the Nineteenth Century*.[22] Duman's survey of the movement of English legal professionals to the colonies dismisses the commonplace assumption that the colonies served as a refuge for the failures of the English legal world and shows that Englishness did not guarantee a successful colonial career. Most colonial lawyers in his random sample of the colonial bars in 1885 were colonial-born and trained. Very few of the migrant English practitioners to establish themselves in colonial settings had practised before migrating, and thus possessed no form.[23] The attraction of the colonies for aspiring lawyers, in Duman's view, was that they offered alternative careers for 'less ambitious and competitive English, Scots and Irish lawyers'.[24] Frederick Wilding was neither a failed nor an unambitious lawyer, but an impatient one with different goals. A qualified and practising solicitor with his own legal practice in Hereford, he had some experience of advocacy work. He had, as we have seen earlier, undergone the required five-year solicitor's apprenticeship and was admitted to the English Bar as a solicitor in 1874. He had subsequently decided to qualify as a barrister, and had entered counsel's chambers for this purpose. The cost of the three years further study involved thwarted his desire

---

18   Frederick Wilding, *HT*, 22 May 1880. Wilding noted that this was particularly the case for British-trained medical newcomers, who were able to establish practices in Christchurch in a few short years. Similarly, he understood that 'parsons of all denominations' were in 'fair request' and 'freethought lecturers drew good crowds on Saturday afternoons'.
19   Frederick Wilding, *HT*, 22 May 1880.
20   Frederick Wilding, *HT*, 22 May 1880.
21   Frederick Wilding, *HT*, 22 May 1880.
22   Duman, *The English and Colonial Bars*.
23   Duman, *The English and Colonial Bars*, pp. 121–23, 137–38.
24   Duman, *The English and Colonial Bars*, p. 138.

to earn a living that would enable him to marry.[25] In New Zealand, the training of barristers and solicitors was less distinct. Within six months of arriving in Christchurch, Wilding had passed the New Zealand Law and Practice Exam, and was admitted to the Bar as a barrister and solicitor in June 1880.[26]

Progress within the legal profession was speedy, despite the fluctuating economic environment. Within a year of arrival in the city, at a cost of £150, Wilding formed a partnership with fellow Englishman Dr Charles Foster, a part-time law lecturer at Canterbury College, who had helped him prepare for his bar examinations.[27] Within a year the partnership was dissolved and Wilding established his own firm in Hereford Street at the heart of the city's commercial district.[28] Over the next 30 years, during which it underwent a variety of permutations, the practice provided an income that placed the family amongst what Jim McAloon has characterised as the third tier of urban wealth—the 'lesser rich' as opposed to those in the tier above with 'very large urban fortunes' of between £40,000 and £99,000.[29] The income it generated provided the bulk of family income and sustained a comfortable, yet unpretentious lifestyle that offered a pathway into the profession for the two eldest sons. One measure of the success of Frederick Wilding's transplant to the colonies, and the recognition afforded the family practice, was his appointment in 1913 as King's Counsel.

However important the practice of law was to be in the accumulation of wealth, its role in securing the family's place in late nineteenth-century Christchurch should not be seen in isolation from the experiment of which it was an important, but not the defining, part.

---

25 Press cutting, WFP, box 42/3. For an explanation of the English system of legal education and qualifications, see Selleck, *The Shop*, pp. 59–60; and Reader, *Professional Men*, pp. 21–31, 43–56, 118–21, 134.

26 JWED, 15 March 1880, 8 June 1880, WFP, box 11/54/54. Like most law students in New Zealand, he had studied privately, most likely with Englishman Dr Charles Foster, a practising lawyer and part-time law lecturer at Canterbury College (1873–80). Lectures in Jurisprudence had been offered at Canterbury College from the university's inception and the LLB degree offered from 1877. See Gardner, 'The Formative Years', p. 97; Jeremy Finn, *Educating for the Profession: Law at Canterbury 1873–1973*, Canterbury University Press, Christchurch, 2010, pp. 17–21.

27 JWED, 6 September 1880, 10 August 1880, WFP, box 11/54/54.

28 JWED, 1 September 1881, WFP, box 11/54/54.

29 Jim McAloon, *No Idle Rich: The Wealthy in Canterbury and Otago 1840–1914*, Otago University Press, Dunedin, 2002, pp. 55–62; Probate records of Frederick Wilding, Probate Register: Christchurch 2406/1945, National Archives, Christchurch. By his death in 1945 Frederick Wilding left behind him an estate worth £29,490, accumulated over 65 years, despite considerable expenditure on their children during that time (Julia had predeceased him in 1936).

The idealism with which migration had been infused was a shared one that, in theory at least, rejected the separate spheres of the new urban order. It did so by asserting the centrality of the family as an instrument of social betterment. Viewed from this perspective, the legal profession was a potentially noble occupation and a worthy family enterprise in its own right.[30] This sense of joint commitment sustained Julia and Frederick in efforts to find a place within the legal community. They rented a house with land and created a small farmlet, on which they produced vegetables for their own consumption, fattened livestock, milked dairy cows, churned butter, kept hens and sold produce at the gate to generate an income that would help them negotiate the years before the legal practice paid its own way. Despite an annual remittance of £200 from Julia's father and the investment of some of their capital in property, which they rented out before selling at profit, it was two years before their income exceeded expenses.[31] As a side interest, Frederick also quickly became involved in the apple-growing business, forming a partnership with another Herefordshire man in the Styx Mill Apple Company, though he was to find it unprofitable in a country where fruit was abundant and cheaply available.[32]

The speed with which the Wildings established a place for themselves within Christchurch society owes much to the fact that they were 'joiners' and keen to participate in community activities. Nowhere was this more evident than in the sporting sphere. Frederick Wilding's reputation for sporting prowess had not quite preceded him, but this was quickly discovered by his neighbour, the radical lawyer-journalist and aspiring politician, William Pember Reeves.[33] Reeves recruited him to play for the United Cricket team largely made up of young city professionals. The speed with which Wilding emerged from within this coterie of youthful cricketers to become arguably the most versatile of the city's sporting fraternity owes much to talent, but his arrival could not have been more timely. Greg Ryan argues that

---

30   Collini, *Public Moralists*, pp. 251, 284–85. Collini argues that the English legal system's initial emphasis on humanism gave it a moral tone and distinguished it from its European counterpart.

31   JWHD 1880: 31 March 1880, JWHD 1881: 13 September 1881, WFP, box 1/2/2, 1/3/3.

32   See JWHDs for quantities of fruit sold; 'Fruit Growers' Association', *Star*, 11 February 1886; 'Apple Culture in Canterbury', newspaper cutting, c. June 1910, 'Apples for Sale. Trade to Argentine. Canterbury Supplies Available'. newspaper cutting, c. April 1912, WFP, box 42/3.

33   Sinclair, *William Pember Reeves*; Fry, *Maud and Amber*.

'Between 1850 and 1930 Christchurch developed' New Zealand's 'most distinctive sporting culture'.[34] He has offered a convincing explanation for the city's sporting pre-eminence: the existence of ample flat land on which to play, as well as the presence of a disproportionately large number of English public school and university graduates in the city, fresh from the revolution in games and leisure, who were imbued with a genuine interest in sport and a desire to foster sport and the values it was thought to inculcate.[35] When Wilding arrived in Christchurch in 1879, the rhythm of sporting life and the formation of the institutions that supported it were still in their formative stage, and he found himself in the midst of something of a sporting boom that produced club, provincial and international dimensions.

Cricket and tennis were obsessions, but Wilding's enthusiasm for sport knew few bounds. By the beginning of the twentieth century he was commonly placed among the leading pioneers of the city's sporting fraternity and lauded as the 'father of lawn tennis in the province'.[36] His New Zealand sporting career began in 1880 playing cricket for the United Club, one of four beginning to take shape in the city. To increase competition in Christchurch, he helped establish the Lancaster Park Cricket Club in 1881, became its inaugural captain, and continued to play for its senior side until he retired from the game in 1909, aged 56. He first represented the Canterbury province during the 1881/82 season, and was to captain the side for over 20 years, scoring 1,000 runs and taking 100 wickets before being displaced by his son, Anthony, in 1902.[37] During his first summer in the city, he was among the founders of one of the city's earliest tennis clubs at Cranmer

---

34   Greg Ryan, 'Sport in Christchurch', in Cookson and Dunstall (eds), *Southern Capital Christchurch*, p. 325.
35   Greg Ryan, 'Sport in Christchurch', pp. 325–47.
36   'Birthday Greetings to Stalwart of Cricket. Prominent in Tennis too', 20 November 1942, newspaper cutting, WFP, box 42/3, p. 10; L. and S. Richardson, *Anthony Wilding*, pp. 21–22, 25, 27, 29–30; Shelley A. Richardson, '"Striving After Better Things": Julia Wilding and the Making of a "New Woman" and a "Noble Gentleman"', MA thesis, University of Canterbury, 1997, pp. 85–92.
37   'Prominent Men in Canterbury Cricket', newspaper cutting, WFP, box 42/3, p. 102; 'Early Cricket in Canterbury', *Press*, 25 March 1912, newspaper cutting, WFP, box 42/3, p. 114; 'A Quarter-Century of Cricket. Doyen of Canterbury Sportsmen. Frederick Wilding', newspaper cutting, 3 October 1925, WFP, box 43/3, pp. 167–68; T. W. Reese, *New Zealand Cricket, 1841–1914*, Whitcombe & Tombs, Christchurch, 1927, p. 326; D. O. and P. W. Neely, *The Summer Game: The Illustrated History of New Zealand Cricket*, Moa Beckett, Auckland, 1994, p. 31; Matthew Appleby, *Canterbury Cricket: 100 Greats*, Reed, Auckland, 2002, pp. 275–77; Lynn McConnell and Ian Smith, *The Shell New Zealand Cricket Encyclopedia*, Moa Beckett, Auckland, 1993, p. 167; Greg Ryan, *The Making of New Zealand Cricket 1832–1914*, Frank Cass, London, 2004.

Square, having first played the relatively new game on his wedding day in Hereford.[38] In 1882 he won the singles of the club's first-ever championship, known as the Canterbury Championship, and, with R. D. Harman, was to win the New Zealand doubles title five times before successfully partnering his son in the 1909 Championships.[39]

These sporting achievements arguably established a place for Wilding within the community more speedily than his endeavours within the legal and commercial world. The combination of talent and enthusiasm saw him emerge as one of a small fraternity of sports advocates, who became the sustaining force in the province. In 1880 the city possessed a single sports ground, Hagley Park. Local by-laws prohibited sporting clubs using the 500-acre public reserve from charging entrance fees. Wilding and the small cluster of young professionals and neighbours would walk to Hagley Park from the city after work for daily cricket practice, and then trudge home to Opawa, 'too hard up', as Wilding recalls, 'to catch a cab'.[40] On one of these excursions, they conceived the idea of a fee-charging ground near to their homes where a variety of sports could be played and the gate money used to encourage a wide range of sports. They formed the Canterbury Cricket and Athletics Company Ltd (later known as the Lancaster Park Company), purchased land, surrounded it with a seven-foot-high fence, and in 1881 Lancaster Park was opened as a cricket and athletics ground. Over the next 20 years cinder and grass tennis courts, a croquet lawn, bowling green, cycle track and swimming pool were added. These developments were sometimes controversial and the finances often precarious, but Lancaster Park

38 'Civic Reception to Visitors', newspaper clipping c. 1932, WFP, box 42/2.
39 'I Remember Early Canterbury Tennis. Interview With Frederick Wilding', c. 1911, newspaper cutting, WFP, box 42/3, p. 112; *100 Years Canterbury Lawn Tennis Association 1890–1990*, Canterbury Lawn Tennis Association, Christchurch, c. 1990; Canterbury Lawn Tennis Association Minute Books, vol. 1–4, April 1881 – 3 October 1888, Cantebury Museum Documentary Research Centre (CMDRC), Christchurch; Paul Elenio, *Centrecourt: A Century of New Zealand Tennis 1886–1996*, New Zealand Lawn Tennis Association, Wellington, 1986, pp. 14–16.
40 Script of a radio broadcast given by Frederick Wilding about William Pember Reeves, 29 November 1937, WFP, box 43/194/61 A.

became the focal point of the city's sporting life.[41] As one of Lancaster Park's most persistent advocates and as a talented sportsman in his own right, Wilding assumed an increasingly prominent place within the sporting fraternity nationally.[42]

Frederick Wilding's sporting talent found expression in the public arena, but this does not mean that he saw sport as a separate and male activity. It was, as subsequent chapters show, an integral part of family life, central to Wilding's conception of the balanced lifestyle. Julia's talents lay elsewhere, but her role in the sporting sphere was not a passive one. She came from a cricket-mad family, and her enthusiasm for it saw her attend every game Frederick and, later, son Anthony played, maintaining a scorebook with such efficiency that officials frequently verified their scores against hers. She was also active in fundraising for individual sports, took part in concerts to raise money for improvements to Lancaster Park and won public accolades as a popular patron of tennis. In 1900 the Lancaster Park Cricket Club recognised her consistent and energetic support by electing her a vice-president of the club, alluding, as they did so, to her known support of feminist causes with the comment that the club 'ought to be up-to-date'.[43]

It was in music and not sport that Julia was to make her most telling contribution to the family's integration into visible civic community. Her European musical training and skills were quickly recognised by Christchurch's small, but musically accomplished group of English immigrants. Gardner has described late nineteenth- and early twentieth-century Canterbury as 'perhaps the strongest musical centre of the colony', and one dominated by amateurs under professional leadership.[44] As John Thomson points out, it was also a musical scene

---

41 Such was Wilding's belief in the efficacy of sport that when he was unable to convince his fellow directors that they should purchase what became the South ground (known as the 'frog pond'), he purchased the land himself and rented it to them until they finally purchased it in 1900. See Gordon Slatter, *Great Days at Lancaster Park*, Whitcombe and Tombs, Christchurch, 1974, pp. 17–24; Ryan, 'Sport in Christchurch', pp. 336–39; Fiona Hall, 'Wilding, Frederick (1852–1945)', *DNZB*, vol. 2, pp. 576–97; A. T. Donnelly, 'The Late Mr. Frederick Wilding, K.C., Broadcast Tribute, Given from 3YA, Christchurch, on the 13 July, 1945', pp. 1–7, WFP, box 43/193/56.

42 He became president of the New Zealand Amateur Athletic Association in the 1890s, served as president of the Canterbury Cricket Association, 1903–23, and was three times president of the New Zealand Cricket Council.

43 Newspaper cuttings, WFP, box 41/1, p. 26.

44 The quote is from Gardner, 'The Formative Years', p. 99.

that, when Julia arrived in the city in 1879, was already exhibiting 'a capacity to form rival societies in similar fields, which waged internecine war against each other'.[45] This capacity was, he believed, to become a uniquely Christchurch phenomenon.[46]

Despite its fractiousness, the Christchurch musical community offered space to newcomers, and it did so for women in ways that were familiar to Julia. She was well acquainted with the inconsistencies in Victorian thought that had long limited women's participation in the paid world of musical performance by combining an 'ardent admiration of [women's] artistic talent' with a 'simultaneous denigration of those who made their living from it'.[47] In Hereford, as in Christchurch, those with a serious commitment to music developed ways of blurring the interface of private and public performance: they formed clubs that met and performed in domestic settings, and performed in the more socially acceptable context provided by philanthropic activity.[48] For Julia, this meant becoming a founding member of a musical club that met monthly in members' homes. The club displayed a high level of organisation; performances were prearranged and programs printed.[49] Moreover, within months of arriving in the city, she performed piano solos at an array of charitable events and fundraising occasions that included hospital concerts, rose shows and the sporting club fetes.[50]

Like many of her Victorian contemporaries, Julia looked upon music, to employ Gillett's phrase, 'as a unique and potent moral influence' and her own performance as a 'striving after better things'.[51] Her sense of personal and social earnestness, matched by a talent as a pianist, won appreciation and attracted opportunities for more public performances. Throughout the 1880s and 1890s Julia played regularly in the Christchurch Musical Society's subscription concerts.

---

45   John M. Thomson, *The Oxford History of New Zealand Music*, Oxford University Press, Auckland, 1991, p. 45.

46   Thomson, *The Oxford History of New Zealand Music*, pp. 45–46.

47   Gillett, *Musical Women in England, 1870–1914*, p. 6. Concerns about the respectability of performing music in public under the male gaze added another layer of consideration for women musicians.

48   Gillett, *Musical Women in England*, pp. 33–62.

49   See WFP, box 12/58-61. The club consisted of both men and women; the fact that they met privately is also perhaps an indicator of their enthusiasm and genuine musical interest.

50   JWED, 11/54-55.

51   Gillett, *Musical Women*, p. 36, 'Note by Julia Wilding about her music', ms, January 1924, WFP, box 12/61/142.

In the winter of 1893 she was asked by the society's conductor, Frank MacKenzie Wallace, to be part of a series of Chamber Concerts that would 'produce a class of music seldom heard in Christchurch'.[52] Acceptance of an invitation to perform for composer Alfred Hill (1870–1969) in a concert of his own work, held in the city in 1893, is testimony to a willingness to involve herself in colonial musical innovation. Endorsement from Hill, regarded as 'the most significant of the first-wave of composers in New Zealand and Australia', marked her growing status within the city's musical community.[53] In 1901 she accepted an invitation to play a solo piece at a reception held for the Duke and Duchess of York. Such was her lifelong commitment to music that, on 4 December 1931, some 50 years after she and Frederick had settled in the city, and despite the onset of arthritis, she performed live on radio.[54]

In their persistence and achievements on the different performance platforms of sport and music, the Wildings had placed themselves firmly within what we might term a community of talent. As joiners and enthusiasts, they had successfully attached themselves to and helped define what one historian has described as an essentially English transplanted culture.[55] That they saw themselves as contributing to the making of an improved version of their parent society was to invest their colonial experiment with a sense of moral purpose. This sense of purpose, which saw the family unit and individual self-betterment as fundamental to a humanist quest for social progress, makes the Wildings the most ideologically explicit of our migrant couples. Their departure from Hereford was based on a rejection of the political and economic environment of mid-Victorian England. That rejection came after active involvement in Hereford's political life. For Frederick, this had meant membership of the town's Liberal Association and, in Julia's

---

52   Frank Wallace to Julia Wilding, 1 June 1893, WFP, box 12/61/143. Frank MacKenzie Wallace (1852–1908), cousin of the English composer Sir Alexander Wallace, studied the violin in Leipzig and spent 10 years as first violinist in the Philharmonic and Crystal Palace orchestras in London, before settling in Christchurch as a violin teacher. He was appointed conductor of the Christchurch Musical Society in 1881. See Gardner (ed.), *A History of Canterbury*, vol. II, pp. 440–56; Thomson, *Oxford History of New Zealand Music*, p. 45.
53   John Mansfield Thomson, 'Hill, Alfred Francis (1870–1960)', *DNZB*, vol. 2, pp. 213–15; John M. Thomson, *Distant Music: The Life and Times of Alfred Hill, 1870–1960*, Oxford University Press, Auckland, 1980, pp. 95–104; Alfred Hill to Julia Wilding, 21 June 1896, WFP, box 12/61/138.
54   Radio 3YA, 4 December 1931, 8.00 pm, WFP, box 12/61/144.
55   Jonathan Mane-Wheoki, 'The High Arts in a Regional Culture—From Englishness to Self-Reliance', in Cookson and Dunstall (eds), *Southern Capital*, p. 299.

case, participation in the newspaper debates that surrounded the issue of women's suffrage. It remains to assess whether their engagement in public political debate was transplanted to the colonies.

Migration to the new world was conceived by the Wildings as a means of throwing off the dead hand of custom and tradition, which they believed impeded social progress and defied democratic reform. The New Zealand they encountered was an English colony where:

> there is no overgrown state church rank with time-honoured abuses, where the law of primogeniture and a host of other feudal absurdities which still disgrace the English jurisprudence have been swept away; and where land is abundant and cheaply and expeditiously transferred.[56]

In such an environment, Frederick Wilding explained to readers of the *Hereford Times*, 'political warfare must be carried on different lines ... Men and not measures furnish the watchwords at elections'.[57] His first impressions of colonial politics confirmed the expectations: 'Outwardly, nearly everyone professes Liberal opinions, and the only well-defined division of political parties, is that all important one between the "ins" and the "outs".'[58]

Thereafter, the Wildings gravitated naturally and without deliberation towards the company of a cluster of young professionals led by William Pember Reeves, a near neighbour and cricketing companion, around whom a progressive urban political party was beginning to emerge in the city.[59] Throughout the 1880s, as the economic climate worsened and class-based political groups, which were later to carry the labels Conservative and Liberal, took clearer shape, the Wildings moved politically closer to Reeves. Now the defining voice of the city's Liberals and courting the support of the city's nascent labour movement, dominated by the skilled artisans, Reeves was later to test the Wildings' capacity for radical change.[60] What drew the Wildings to

56   Frederick Wilding, *HT*, 17 July 1880.
57   Frederick Wilding, *HT*, 17 July 1880.
58   Frederick Wilding, *HT*, 17 July 1880.
59   Script of a radio broadcast given by Frederick Wilding on William Pember Reeves, 29 November 1937, WFP, box 43/194/61 A, p. 4; 'Early Cricket in Canterbury', *Press*, 25 March 1912, WFP, box 42/3, p. 114; Sinclair, *William Pember Reeves*, pp. 46–58.
60   Too 'advanced' in his 'political opinions' for most of his own social class, 'only a few of his cricketing friends who knew him best, supported him', Frederick Wilding, radio broadcast on William Pember Reeves, 29 November 1937.

Reeves was his advocacy of an increased role for the state as a promoter of a series of strategic experiments to unlock land, reform labour relations and create a more civilised society that facilitated the 'family ideal of land and home ownership'.[61] Inasmuch as these goals were the cornerstone of the Liberal Party philosophy, then the Wildings sat comfortably within its ranks.

By 1890, the Wildings had aligned themselves with the political ideology that dominated New Zealand politics arguably for the next 50 years. Among its earliest legislative achievements was the enfranchisement of women in 1893. The campaign that preceded its enactment had gathered pace shortly after the Wildings arrived, though there is no evidence that Julia became involved in its public activities. There is, however, evidence that within the overlapping and essentially English communities that she moved—sporting, musical and neighbourhood—she encouraged discussion of the 'woman question'. She pressed her brother's book, *The Social and Political Dependence of Women*, upon Maud Reeves, who later acknowledged Julia's role in stimulating her to become involved in working for women's rights in New Zealand and in Britain.[62] Above all else, as the following chapters on the education of her children reveal, her feminism was most in evidence as she sought to create well-educated, civically minded sons and daughters, whose talents would make a useful and equal contribution to the betterment of society. In her hands the family thus became the crucible in which the personal became the political.

In late 1893, as the Wildings looked out from the large and comfortable, rather than stylish wooden house that they had named Fownhope, they could justifiably have felt they had successfully established themselves within Christchurch's professional community and put in place a home that would enable them to achieve the idealised family

---

61   The quote comes from Mein Smith, *A Concise History of New Zealand*, p. 100. On Reeves, and the political and economic situation of the 1880s and 1890s more generally, see, for example: Mein Smith, *A Concise History of New Zealand*, pp. 93–105, 108; Sinclair, *Reeves*, ch. 5–15; McAloon, 'Radical Christchurch', pp. 162, 166–70; McAloon, 'The Christchurch Elite', pp. 198–99, 206; Cookson, 'Pilgrim's Progress', pp. 22, 25–26; Raewyn Dalziel, 'The Politics of Settlement', in Rice (ed.), *Oxford History of New Zealand*, pp. 107–11; Len Richardson, 'Parties and Political Change', in Rice (ed.), *Oxford History of New Zealand*, pp. 202–11; Tony Ballantyne, 'The State Politics and Power 1769–1893', in Byrnes (ed.), *The New Oxford History of New Zealand*, pp. 99–124; Fry, *Maud and Amber*, pp. 1–27.

62   Maud Reeves to Cora Wilding, 30 January 1938, WFP, box 43/194/60.

life they had envisaged. Set in the midst of a four-and-a-half-acre farmlet that sloped down to a small stream, possessing a picturesque, park-like garden with an extensive orchard, it was also a sporting paradise. With two tennis courts—grass and cinder, a cricket pitch, croquet lawn and possibly the first swimming pool in Christchurch, they had created an environment that expressed their aspirations.[63] An extant visitor's book reveals that already a wide cross-section of the city's sporting, cultural, intellectual and professional communities made their way to Fownhope. Collectively they formed what Wilding liked to call a 'community of tastes, habits and manners', and he prized the 'bond of union' that he believed united the large and often lively gatherings, rather than 'equality of wealth'.[64] Bohemian in a slightly mannered sort of way and determinedly devoid of conspicuous display, Sunday afternoon gatherings, where the injunction against play on the Sabbath was openly flouted, provided a setting in which the Wildings were accepted on their own terms as members of a new urban society that they were at the same time helping to shape.[65]

'We talked over the matter fully, and have come to the conclusion that we must, as a family, make a combined effort'[66]

The story of Henry Bournes Higgins and his family charts the fortunes of a somewhat different slice of professional family migration, namely that of Ireland's Protestant, genteel, educated and struggling middle class. The decision to migrate, unlike that of the Wildings, was born of desperation

---

63   F. M. B. Fisher describes Fownhope and the social gatherings that took place there in A. Wallis Myers, *Captain Anthony Wilding*, Hodder and Stoughton, London, 1916, pp. 11–13. The Wilding home was named after a village on the Wye near Hereford.
64   Frederick Wilding, *HT*, 17 July 1880.
65   The term 'Bohemian' changed and broadened out over time. Emerging in early nineteenth-century France, the term was initially confined to artists, writers, musicians and roving gypsies living alternative and unconventional lives of free love and frugality. In the American context, during the 1870s, the term underwent a redefinition, as respectable family men and pillars of the community sought to shape their own form of Bohemianism to include people like themselves: sportsmen and appreciators of fine art leading simple lifestyles. See Kate Sheppard, 'A Noble Bohemianism', *White Ribbon*, February 1897, pp. 7–8 (Reprinted in Margaret Lovell-Smith (ed.), *The Woman Question: Writings by the Women Who Won the Vote*, New Women's Press, Auckland, 1992, pp. 122–23); Lovell-Smith, *Plain Living High Thinking*, pp. 46–54, passim.
66   John Higgins [senior] to Mr [Robert] Acres, 11 April 1873, Henry Bournes Higgins Papers (HBHP), NLA, MS 1057, box 6, series 2/2444.

and sustained by the conviction that their combined resources as a family would ensure a successful outcome. The hard-headed realism and optimistic faith in the family as a collective entity came naturally from a context in which the 'cohesive force' of the family as an integral part of social and economic structures was highly developed.[67] In the view of Patrick O'Farrell, this united Irish family was to exercise 'particular power in atomised colonial Australia [and] to hold its members together in coherence against the world'.[68] Whatever importance we attach to 'Irishness' in defining the nature of the Higgins family, there can be no doubt that Henry Higgins—an 18-year-old of indifferent health, possessed of a schoolboy's classical liberal education, with limited work experience in the commercial world of Dublin—became both the chief beneficiary of the family enterprise and, as John Rickard has pointed out, 'the architect of his family's fortunes'.[69] If the phrase has been seen by some as limiting the individual initiatives of other Higginses, it is nonetheless one which directs attention to what distinguishes the Higgins family experience from the other case studies examined in this book, namely, that in Australia they constructed the middle-class professional family that in Ireland had remained a thwarted aspiration.[70]

Nothing marks the transition in the history of the Higgins family more starkly than the initial separation that migration to Australia involved. Anne Higgins, eldest son Henry (18), and four of his five siblings (George, 13; Samuel, 11; Georgina, 10, and Anna, 8) arrived in Melbourne on Saturday 11 February 1870 after 88 days on board the *Eurynome*. The youngest child, Charlie (born 1864) had died two days earlier of diphtheria and was buried at sea. Both John Higgins senior and junior remained behind in Ireland to complete work commitments and earn enough money to support the family in Australia until the eldest boys found work. Anne had a small sum of money for emergencies, to which she hoped to add such remittances as her husband could send her.[71] It was to be nine months before the

---

67   O'Farrell, *The Irish in Australia 1788 to the Present*, p. 16.
68   O'Farrell, *The Irish in Australia 1788 to the Present*, p. 16.
69   Rickard, *H.B. Higgins*, p. 126.
70   Deborah Jordan writes that 'H. B. Higgins has been painted as the founder of the Higgins' fortunes in Australia, but other members also made substantial contributions to the family finances'. See Deborah Jordan, *Nettie Palmer: Search for an Aesthetic*, History Department, University of Melbourne, Carlton, Victoria, 1999, p. 20.
71   Autobiography of Henry Bournes Higgins, ms, HBHP, box 7, series 3, p. 56.

family was reunited in Melbourne; this critical period in the evolution of the family confirmed the matriarchal influence and required Henry to assume greater levels of responsibility.

Irish and Methodist connections were pursued from the start, with varying degrees of success. John (senior) had alerted Reverend James Waugh, an Irishman and president of Wesley College, to his family's impending arrival.[72] They were met by Reverend Martin Dyson, local resident Wesleyan minister at Sandridge, and enveloped by a web of Wesleyan/Methodist kindness and practical assistance. There were offers of financial aid, advice about breaking into the Melbourne labour market and, critically, help finding accommodation. Within three days of their arrival, with the help of Waugh, Anne and Henry had located a suitable rental property: a humble detached cottage in Henry Street, Windsor, a train-ride away from town, for nine shillings per week.[73] Indeed, such was the extent of the Methodist community's involvement in the family's settling-in period, that the young Henry formed the impression that Methodism was 'the most numerous denomination in Australia'.[74]

Anne Higgins played a pivotal role in establishing the family in Melbourne from the earliest days of their arrival, employing a mixture of cunning and pragmatism. She diligently pursued all the Irish connections John had provided and took special care to dress the family in what she described as the more fashionable Melbourne style in order to fit in.[75] But as the 'most "Irish" of Australian colonies', Victoria perhaps presented the new migrants with fewer assimilation problems, and, within four months, Anne admitted that while 'at first we felt very friendless ... now that we are known ... we have many

---

72   John Higgins senior to Anne Higgins, n.d. (c. March 1870), HBHP, box 5, series 2/2412.
73   Diary of Henry Bournes Higgins 1869–1870, (typescript), HBHP, box 7, series 3, pp. 47–53.
74   Henry Higgins to John Higgins senior, 26 March 1870, HBHP, box 4, series 2/2409; H. R. Jackson, *Churches and People in Australia and New Zealand 1860–1930*, Allen and Unwin/ Port Nicholson Press, Wellington, 1987, pp. 104–5. Melbourne seems to have had more active practitioners of Methodism than any other denomination.
75   Anne Higgins to John Higgins senior, c. 14 April 1870 – 22 April 1870, 13 May 1870, HBHP, box 5, series 2/2418.

[friends] … but I worked until I found them'.[76] To her husband she confided that 'the chief thing you will want here is a bold exterior, maintaining your own dignity, and then others will admire you— in this respect Henry is vastly improved'.[77]

Finding work for the two boys proved more difficult. Melbourne's population had now reached 207,000—a result of an influx of goldminers in search of employment, sponsored and unassisted immigration and natural increase, and the city struggled to provide employment for the newcomers.[78] Henry and George had arrived with the intention of seeking work in the commercial world, of which Henry at least had some experience in Ireland. They were advised by their father to take, in the first instance, 'any lawful, healthful employment, while continuing to 'look for something better'; 'do not fret … Get health first'.[79]

It was several months before George secured employment, at seven shillings a week, in a wholesale stationery store, after the recommendation of an old Irish friend of the family.[80] Henry's quest for employment was at first more chequered. After a week's work in the hosiery department of a warehouse, he was deemed unsuitable and promptly dismissed.[81] Despite having 'applied for everything' and the efforts of 'influential people' on his behalf, he was unable to break into either the commercial world, or a public service currently in retrenching mode.[82] Henry's analysis of Melbourne's labour market in letters to his father accurately described the problem that

---

76   The first quote is from O'Farrell, *The Irish in Australia*, p. 148; the second is from Anne Higgins's letter to John Higgins senior, c. 22 April 1870, HBHP, box 5, series 2/2417. Don Garden, *Victoria: A History*, Thomas Nelson, Australia, Melbourne, 1985, p. 80, places the Irish-born in Victoria as the third largest ethnic group in 1861 (16.3 per cent), after English and Welsh-born (31.39 per cent), and Victorian-born (25.55 per cent). Scots made up 11.23 per cent of Victoria's population, Chinese-born 4.58 per cent and Germans 1.93 per cent by 1861. Though, unlike Alexander Leeper, the Higgins family were not part of the Anglo-Irish professional elite on arrival, the fact that they were well-educated, genteel middle-class Protestants made them well able to fit into the dominant English culture. See, for example, O'Farrell, *The Irish in Australia*, p. 100.
77   Anne Higgins to John Higgins senior, 14 April 1870, HBHP, box 5, series 2/2417.
78   Garden, *Victoria*, pp. 74–75, 79–80, 124–35, 172.
79   Letter from John Higgins senior to George Higgins, 20 January 1870, HBHP, box 5, series 2/2395; Letter from John Higgins senior to Henry Higgins, Melbourne, 18 May 1870, HBHP, box 5, series 2/2419.
80   Henry Higgins to John Higgins senior, 22 April 1870, HBHP, box 5, series 2/2413.
81   Henry Higgins to John Higgins senior, 26 March 1870, HBHP, box 4, series 2/2409; Autobiography of Henry Bournes Higgins (ms), p. 56, HBHP.
82   Henry Higgins to John Higgins senior, 26 March 1870, HBHP, box 4, series 2/2409.

confronted him: unemployment, though lower than in other colonies, was high in Melbourne; business was 'slack'; competition for jobs was acute; wages were depressed; and 'there is not sufficient employment for the thousands of immigrants continually arriving'.[83] In particular, he noted, there were a limited number of positions for those seeking clerical work, but 'that class will avail themselves of the emigrant ships'.[84] The problem embraced 'colonial people' who were 'find[ing] it very difficult to get their sons into suitable openings'.[85] Conversely, those with specialist knowledge and experience were in demand and well remunerated.[86]

After three months of fruitlessly searching for a job in Melbourne's business sector, the Irish and Wesleyan connections helped him draw the obvious conclusion that his old world, liberal education would allow him to negotiate a path into teaching and university study.[87] Through James Waugh and James Corrigan, respectively president and headmaster of Wesley College—arguably Melbourne's most successful boys' boarding school, Henry was made familiar with the opportunities that were on offer for well-educated young men.[88] By 1870, Corrigan was the dominant voice on the Victorian Board of Education, and about to become its chairman, and was well placed to sketch out the peculiarities of the city's educational needs. The numerous and prosperous gold-rush generation of immigrants, now parents in their 50s and 60s, were anxious to provide the solid secondary education for their sons that would allow them to find

---

83   Henry Higgins to John Higgins senior, 26 March 1870, 22 April 1870, HBHP, box 5, series 2/2409, 2413.

84   Henry Higgins to John Higgins senior, 14 May 1870, HBHP, box 5, series 2/2417.

85   Henry Higgins to John Higgins senior, 14 May 1870, HBHP, box 5, series 2/2417.

86   Henry Higgins to John Higgins senior, 14 May 1870, HBHP, box 5, series 2/2417.

87   Henry Higgins to John Higgins senior, 22 April 1870, 14 May 1870, HBHP, box 5, series 2/2413, 2417.

88   James Swanton Waugh (1822–1898), a Wesleyan minister, was born in Newtownbarry, County Wexford, Ireland. After working on Dublin circuits in the 1840s, he migrated to Victoria, where he worked as a Wesleyan minister. In 1865 Waugh was elected president of the Australasian Conference and in the following year appointed president of the newly established Wesley College, Melbourne, a position he retained until 1883. His close friend, James Corrigan (1823–1871), also Irish, was a graduate of Trinity College Dublin (MA, LLB, 1861; LLD, 1864), mathematician and teacher. He was appointed headmaster of Wesley College, Melbourne, in 1866. See Peter Gill, 'Corrigan, James (1823–1871)', *ADB*, vol. 3, Melbourne University Press, Carlton, Victoria, 1969, pp. 464–65; G. Blainey, James Morrissey and S. E. K. Hulme, *Wesley College: The First Hundred Years*, The President and Council Wesley College, in association with Robertson and Mullins, Melbourne, 1867, pp. 14–41; Andrew Lemon, *A Great Australian School: Wesley College Examined*, Helicon Press, 2004.

a place in a tightening labour market.[89] Melbourne was, as journalist Marcus Clarke put it, 'boiling with boys'.[90] Demand for teachers in private schools for boys modelled on English public schools was such that the expanding profession had become an increasingly lucrative one and headmasters were reportedly earning between £500 and £600 per year.[91] Most headmasters were recent recruits from England, Scotland and Ireland, and they were inclined to favour young men whose educational backgrounds they understood and trusted. After explaining these elements of the city's educational system, Corrigan suggested Henry could seek an assistant teacher's position in the city and prove his merit by studying for the Board of Education teaching certificate and the University of Melbourne matriculation exams to be held in July and November respectively.[92]

One month later, in May 1870, Higgins successfully applied for a position as teaching assistant at Turret House Academy, Victoria Street, Fitzroy, run by James Scott. He was surprised to find teaching at the school to his liking and spent the evenings working on his own studies.[93] In this way he hoped to find a way into academic study, which had been denied him in Ireland. That this aspiration had been a parental as well as an individual one is clear in the delighted tones in which Anne Higgins relays the development to husband John in Ireland:

> I wished for him something in the literary way for I believe there he will excel … Well Providence points [to teaching and a university education] … & he can get nothing desirable in business … [I am] glad he is turning to what he loves … his face lights up when he speaks of it [the University of Melbourne] and the fees are small here,

---

89   Davison has pointed to Melbourne's 'kinked age structure'—the 'bunching' of gold-rush immigrants and their children, coming of age in the 1880s. Davison, *Marvellous Melbourne*, pp. 2–3, 131.

90   Marcus Clarke, 'What To Do with Our Boys' (*Australasian*, 5 March 1870), in L. T. Hergenhan (ed.), *A Colonial City: High and Low Life. Selected Journalism of Marcus Clarke*, University of Queensland Press, St Lucia, 1972, p. 73.

91   Henry Higgins to John Higgins senior, 22 April 1870, HBHP, box 5, series 2/2413; Anne Higgins to John Higgins senior, 22 April 1870, HBHP, box 5, series 2/2417. Such schools would later struggle through the economic depression of the 1890s.

92   Henry Higgins to John Higgins senior, 22 April 1870, HBHP, box 5, series 2/2413, 2417.

93   Henry Higgins to John Higgins senior, 14 May 1870, HBHP, box 5, series 2/2413. Henry had previously expressed his 'very great aversion to teaching of any kind' to his father.

£2 entrance only … all say he has got a splendid education, he can make well of it here, and afterwards he may rise to eminence—I know you regretted his giving up his studies.[94]

Henry's assessment of the family's prospects after three months in Melbourne, written in the afterglow of his own achievements, is similarly optimistic:

I do not think we shall ever regret our coming out here. Things were very dark at first but, taking the family as a whole, I am confident that, with God's help we will gain health and many other things … I feel happy to be able to say we are all well and hopeful.[95]

The teaching position at Turret House Academy was a turning point for Henry Higgins. Principal James Scott, a former student at the University of Glasgow and graduate of Melbourne University (BA), reignited Henry's intellectual interests by granting access to his library, discussing Carlyle's ideas with him and listening as Henry read Carlyle's *Sartor Resartus* aloud to help him overcome his stutter. In July, he sat the common schools' teaching examination, passing in all subjects except writing, as he had misunderstood the instructions for the latter. In November, he distinguished himself in the university matriculation examination, passing with credit, and, a few months later, won the University of Melbourne Classical Exhibition for 1871.[96]

Between 1871 and 1875 Henry Higgins attended the University of Melbourne, at a time when annual fees were approximately £30 per year.[97] It was a critical experience that shaped his future and consolidated in a number of ways the importance he was to attach to family. Higgins lived at home while studying at university and paid his way, contributing to the family funds, by winning further academic prizes, as well as working, firstly, as a tutor at Alexander Morrison's Scotch College, where he supervised boarders' evening studies and taught scripture lessons. This was followed by a period teaching at Melbourne South Grammar School (1872–73), and later giving private instruction to the Carlton-based sons of squatter Andrew Chirnside, for which he earned a lucrative £20 per month.

94   Anne Higgins to John Higgins senior, 22 April 1870, HBHP, box 5, series 2/2417.
95   Henry Higgins to John Higgins senior, 14 May 1870, HBHP, box 5, series 2/2417.
96   Autobiography of Henry Bournes Higgins (ms), pp. 56–58, HBHP. Henry remarked that 'The standard at our schools in Ireland was much higher than matriculation standard' (p. 57).
97   Davison, *Marvellous Melbourne*, p. 95.

University study in 1870s Melbourne remained a minority experience, limited to a comparatively small number of young, middle-class males. In 1871, when the population of Melbourne, Australia's largest city, had reached 207,000, the university had a total of 116 matriculated students (51 in arts, 42 in law, 13 in engineering, and 29 in medicine).[98] But while he was surrounded by the first generation of Australian-born sons of the Victoria's landed, mercantile and professional elite, there were others like himself from more middling economic positions (most notable amongst them Alfred Deakin, also paying his way through) and hoping for professional careers.[99]

The university experience would seem at first glance to mark out an essential difference between Higgins and Frederick Wilding, who came, as it were, as a finished item resplendent with old world credentials. The LLB, introduced at the University of Melbourne in 1860 in the hope of increasing student numbers and improving the status of the colony's lawyers, was a four-year course combining the traditional classical liberal education of an arts degree with that of a law degree. It was intended as a professional degree for those who would have to earn their living, rather than being merely a part of a gentleman's education. In this sense it was, as Selleck has pointed out, less like the ancient universities of Oxford, Cambridge and Trinity College Dublin, and more in line with the universities of Germany and Scotland.[100] Higgins's university education introduced him to the same strands of liberal thought that had shaped the Wildings' world view. The outlines of contemporary intellectual thought presented at Melbourne University were delivered in the old world voices of professors from Cambridge, Oxford and Trinity College Dublin and took the more systematic form of the lecture room, rather than

---

98 Garden, *Victoria: A History*, p. 172; Selleck, *The Shop*, p. 112.
99 Henry Higgins's closest friends at the University of Melbourne were: Alfred Deakin (1856–1919), Alexander Sutherland (1852–1902) and Richard Hodgson (1855–1905). Sutherland (BA, 1874; MA, 1875), son of a draftsman, commercial artist and art teacher, migrated from Scotland at the age of 12 with his family and later became a journalist, schoolmaster, English professor and then registrar at the University of Melbourne from 1902. Richard Hodgson, Melbourne-born son of a Wesleyan Methodist importer and mining speculator (BA, 1874; MA, 1876; LLD, 1878), later became a 'psychical researcher'. Rickard, *H.B. Higgins*, p. 58.
100 Selleck, *The Shop*, pp. 58–65. See Davison, *Marvellous Melbourne*, ch. 4, for a discussion of the state of Melbourne's legal profession in the 1880s and 1890s.

independent study. But it was part of the same discourse with which the Wildings had engaged, within the more leisured world of private reading and public discussion.[101]

The Anglo-Irish voice of Professor William E. Hearn at the University of Melbourne introduced the young Higgins to the central tenets of liberal thought, through the works of John Stuart Mill, Auguste Comte, Herbert Spencer and George Grote. He also presented the great intellectual issues of the day that centred upon religion, science and evolution.[102] A clergyman's son, member of the Irish Bar (1849), graduate of Trinity College Dublin (1853), and 'advocate of laissez-faire economics', Hearn was no mere transmitter of the public discourse, but a participant in it, and his published works have been judged 'remarkable books to have emerged from a colonial society'.[103] His perspective has been characterised as conservative in its Australian context, but Rickard has argued that Hearn, as a supporter of free trade, might be better characterised as a liberal in the 'English sense'.[104] Higgins thought him a 'most interesting and stimulating teacher', and Hearn's ideas and teachings precipitated in Henry something of a religious crisis, common to his generation, as he began to question the validity of long-held religious beliefs and the concepts of hell and eternal punishment.[105]

These questionings later provided a point of tension within the Higgins family and complicated Henry's relationship with his parents. Of more immediate concern to the family was Henry's induction into the legal profession. His decision to specialise in law was born of necessity, rather than any long-held ambition to pursue a career in law. A law degree would enable him to earn a comfortable living

---

101 Autobiography of Henry Bournes Higgins (ms), pp. 59–60, 59–65; see Selleck, *The Shop*, pp. 31–42, 118–19, 187, for information about the foundational professors of Melbourne's university.
102 William Hearn (1826–1888), professor of Modern History and Literature, Political Economy and Logic, as well as Latin and Greek in 1871, until appointed Dean of Law in 1873. See Selleck, *The Shop*, pp. 37, 84–85; Rickard, *H.B. Higgins*, pp. 47–48; Autobiography of Henry Bournes Higgins (ms), pp. 59–60.
103 The first quotation comes from Selleck, *The Shop*, p. 39, the second from J. A. La Nauze's *ADB* entry on Hearn, *ADB*, vol. 4, Melbourne University Press, Carlton, Victoria, 1972, pp. 371–72. Hearn wrote four books in Australia: *Plutology or the Theory of the Efforts to Satisfy Human Wants* (Melbourne 1863, London 1864); *The Government of England* (1867); *The Aryan Household* (1878) and *The Theory of Legal Duties and Rights* (1883).
104 Rickard, *H.B. Higgins*, p. 48.
105 Autobiography of Henry Bournes Higgins (ms), pp. 59–60, 64–65.

and provide greater family security, as well as requiring him to overcome his stutter. He aimed nonetheless for the more lucrative role of barrister rather than that of solicitor. Higgins emerged from the University of Melbourne with an LLB (1874) and MA (1876) after winning several prizes. He had taken elocution lessons and worked hard with the assistance of his mother to improve his speech, with only a trace of a stammer remaining.[106] The job market for lawyers was contracting in similar fashion to that of the old world, and patronage, social connections and networks had become increasingly important. Colonial-born sons from established legal families in Melbourne, or with connections to them, had a distinct advantage over newcomers. Those with enough money were also able to weather the typically lean early years of the young barrister.[107]

A young man of proven merit, however, supported by old world connections, might also find a pathway into the profession. Higgins was right to recall in his autobiography that 'No one knew me' in Melbourne, outside the city's academic circles.[108] His admission to the Bar was readily facilitated by obtaining the endorsement of his law lecturer, Frank Dobson (1835–1895), and his mother's own social connections within the Irish community secured the support of George Higginbotham, the city's leading Anglo-Irish barrister and radical liberal and politician.[109] With the support of these two sponsors, Henry was called to the Bar on 14 September 1876 and chose to pursue a career in Equity 'rather than common law', as he later explained, 'because I might succeed in laborious work, but [I felt] that I could hardly succeed in addressing jurors'.[110]

---

106 Autobiography of Henry Bournes Higgins (ms), pp. 65–66.
107 Duman, *The English and Colonial Bars*, pp. 122–23; Davison, *Marvellous Melbourne*, pp. 95–96.
108 Autobiography of Henry Bournes Higgins (ms), p. 66.
109 Frank Dobson was an Australian-born, Cambridge-educated and English-trained barrister (common law), and politician. For the connection with Higginbotham, see Henry Higgins's autobiography, p. 66.
110 Autobiography of Henry Bournes Higgins (ms), pp. 66–68; the quote is from p. 68. After being called to the Bar Henry read in the chambers of Edward Holroyd (1828–1916), an English-born, Cambridge-educated equity lawyer, whom he assisted with briefs. He also acted as junior counsel for Thomas à Beckett. The early years of his legal career were, according to Henry, financially lean ones. In his first year at the Bar he earned 24 guineas, in his second 13 guineas, and in his third year 10 guineas. Between 1876 and 1879 he supplemented his legal income by tutoring the sons of David Symes, editor and proprietor of the *Age*. Nevertheless, in 1877, he was able to purchase a 20-acre block of land in Gippsland.

Henry's achievements, considerable as they undoubtedly were, never took primacy over the welfare of the Higgins family unit. A sense of reciprocity within the family had been evident in his father's response to intimations that his prospects in Australia as a Methodist minister were not assured:

> you know I did not build on that ... I hardly expected to be placed in favourable circumstances in that respect. We made up our minds to make a large sacrifice for the good of our beloved children ... and I trust that they will do well and prosper.[111]

During Henry's years of university study and the early phase of his legal career, Henry had lived with his family in a series of rented homes in Windsor, Fitzroy and Carlton.[112] It soon became clear that there was little if any chance of circumventing the Methodist Conference's decision to implement their own form of 'colonial protectionism' and give preference to locally trained men.[113] When John's application to join the Australasian Methodist Conference was declined, he was forced to take up casual work for the Presbyterians in rural areas. His frequent and lengthy absences from the family during the 1870s and 1880s meant that the fortunes of the family fell increasingly on Henry as the eldest son, and it was his rising earning capacity that allowed the gradual improvement in rented accommodation.

If the novelist Ada Cambridge was correct in her assertion that 'money is the gauge of social consequence in Melbourne', Henry Higgins had 'arrived' and brought his family with him.[114] The most tangible marker of his arrival was the purchase of one-and-a-half acres of land on

---

111 John Higgins senior to Anne Higgins, c. March 1870, HBHP, box 5, series 2/2412.

112 The Higgins family lived, firstly, in a detached cottage in Henry St, Windsor, then moved to 40 Rose St, Fitzroy, and moved again in 1877 to a two-storey home in Rathdowne St, Carlton, listed variously under Henry or his father's name in the Melbourne *Directory*, and then, in 1880, to a similar home in Sydney Road (173 Royal Parade) in the more fashionable Royal Park area in Carlton. Rickard, *H.B. Higgins*, p. 55.

113 Rickard, *H.B. Higgins*, pp. 41, 48–49. The Australasian Methodist Conference had passed a resolution in 1867 that discouraged ministers from other countries seeking positions within the Australian Methodist Church, for they had more than enough of their own locally produced ministers. A Provisional Theological (Training) Institution had been established at Wesley College in 1867, with James Waugh as its theological tutor. Furthermore, says Rickard, the numbers of Methodists in Victoria decreased as the gold rush petered out. See here also O'Farrell, *The Irish In Australia*, p. 105; Renate Howe, 'The Wesleyan Church in Victoria, 1855-1901', MA thesis, University of Melbourne, 1965, pp. 30, 167.

114 Ada Cambridge, *Thirty Years in Australia*, London, 1903, quoted by Davison, *Marvellous Melbourne*, p. 190.

Glenferrie Road, Malvern, for £1,200.[115] The opening of the Gippsland railway-line, beginning in 1879, stimulated an influx of middle-class professionals to the area, and, amongst their 'stucco "Italian palaces," with domes and colonnades', Higgins commissioned the construction of an architecturally designed, two-storeyed, red-brick house consisting of 14 rooms, including a billiard room, set in landscaped grounds and resplendent with croquet lawn.[116] Henry named the estate Doona after a castle his mother had seen on the coast of County Mayo, Ireland, and it was to function more as a family home rather than as the gentleman's residence of an unmarried barrister. For the first time in their lives, the Higgins family had a permanent base from which its individual members might come and go as circumstances dictated.

If Doona marked Henry's arrival, the income that made its realisation possible provided the foundation for subsequent family achievement. Precisely how much money Henry Higgins was earning by the mid-1880s is difficult to calculate. By Davison's assessment, most Melbourne professionals in the 1880s belonged on the second rung of the city's ladder of wealth below the business class, and a few joined them on the top rung. At a time when the lowest earners, semiskilled and unskilled manual workers, could hope to earn £90 to £105 pounds per annum, leading barristers were earning 'as much as' £1,500 a year, or about three times as much as a solicitor.[117] Whatever Higgins's income, Rickard has rightly pointed out that his career illustrates 'the speed with which a young member of the profession, in those days before income tax, could gather around him the perquisites of wealth and position'.[118]

---

115 Autobiography of Henry Bournes Higgins (ms), p. 84.
116 In 1888 the house was valued at £1,800 and the land at £1,500. Stonnington History Centre Catalogue, MP 12540; auction notice for Doona Estate, 1929, Stonnington History Centre Catalogue, MP 353. See Davison, *Marvellous Melbourne*, pp. 158–59, for a discussion of railway-led suburban growth. The quotation is from Nettie Palmer's biography of her uncle, *Henry Bournes Higgins: A Memoir*, p. 103. Doona was designed by architect William Salway, who had previously, according to Palmer, won prizes for the designs of two Melbourne railway-station buildings.
117 Davison, *Marvellous Melbourne*, pp. 191–93.
118 Rickard, *H.B. Higgins*, pp. 56–57. T. à Beckett, as leader of the equity bar, had earnt £5,000 in one year and, in 1886, led Higgins to expect similar amounts in the future.

Doona increasingly became the hub of family life and the base to which Henry's younger siblings could retreat, as they sought the training that would enable them to establish professional careers. By the turn of the century, the Higgins family had found a place in a wide range of professions, both ancient and more modern: the church, law and medicine, accountancy, engineering, journalism and landscape design. We will follow Henry's relationship with his siblings in a later chapter but it is sufficient for the moment to make two observations. Firstly, while each was to establish an independent career path, their futures were more disrupted by the ebb and flow of economic and personal circumstance, and both Henry and Doona provided stability at difficult times.[119] Secondly, in this patriarchal role, Henry's influence extended beyond his siblings to their children, whose education he supported and careers he fostered.

The process of Henry Higgins becoming an established member of the Australasian professional middle class encompassed marriage, as it did for John Macmillan Brown. In August 1885, a year after Doona had been completed, Higgins (then 34) became engaged to Mary Alice Morrison, some nine years his junior, and they were married on 19 December 1885. Mary Alice was the daughter of George Morrison, the staunchly Presbyterian Principal of Geelong College. They met while Henry was working briefly at Scotch College, where her uncles Alexander and Robert Morrison were principal and president respectively. Mary Alice had grown up at Geelong College with her younger sisters, Hilda and Violet, and five brothers. Her education, conducted by a governess and supervised closely by her father, had been a conventional one. Before the announcement of Henry's

---

119 John Higgins junior qualified as an accountant in the 1880s and was moderately successful. He pursued opportunities presented by the quartz mining boom in Bendigo in the 1880s, returning with its decline to Melbourne, where he set himself up as an independent accountant, and required financial assistance from his family at various times throughout his life. George Higgins qualified as a civil engineer and worked in railway construction outside New South Wales in the 1880s, before returning to work in Melbourne. In 1904 he was appointed lecturer in engineering at the University of Melbourne and became Dean of Engineering. Samuel Higgins (1858–1887) studied medicine at the University of Melbourne's medical school (1875–80), worked at Melbourne Hospital, as a surgeon at Tenterfield, New South Wales, and as a locum at Geelong, 1883–84, before returning to Melbourne with tuberculosis. He died in 1887. Ina Higgins, a foundational student of Presbyterian Ladies' College Melbourne (PLC) in 1875, was amongst the first females to study landscape gardening and design at Burnley Horticultural School, Melbourne, and worked intermittently as a landscape designer. Anna, the youngest surviving sibling, attended PLC with Ina, graduated from the University of Melbourne with an MA, and became a journalist.

engagement, the Higgins family knew only that the future mistress of Doona was 'tall, well-built, strong and a good tennis player'. They learned in time that her commitment to the Protestant ethic and highly developed sense of duty rivalled and perhaps exceeded that of her husband. It was to be a year or more before the family confronted the practical implications of Henry's marriage upon the household. Such was Henry's confidence in the future that almost immediately after his marriage he hung a notice on the door of his legal practice: 'Back on or about the 15 Jan. 1887' and embarked on a year-long European tour with his wife.

The absence of the newly-weds provided a useful transition period and prefigured a transformation of the extended Higgins family.[120] While in Ireland, Henry ensured that a useful inheritance—land valued at £1,200 and the rental from various buildings on the property—found its way to his father. It was sufficient to enable his parents to buy a piece of land a short walk from Doona, and to build a 'comfortable home' they were to call Killenna in 1888.[121] That made the transition at Doona a smooth one. When Mary Alice was installed as mistress of the household and provided with three servants, Henry Higgins's parents and siblings moved to temporary accommodation until Killenna was completed.[122] Thereafter, Killenna and Doona became the joint axis of a network of extended kinship ties that stands in sharp contrast to the nuclear model traditionally ascribed to the urban middle class of this period.[123] In this sense, Henry's marriage, like those of his siblings John and George, widened the Higgins family sphere, and placed them within the ambit of prominent Victorian family groupings. Moreover, as Mary Alice and Henry had only one child, Mervyn (born 1887),

120 Autobiography of Henry Bournes Higgins (ms), p. 84.
121 Autobiography of Henry Bournes Higgins (ms), p. 84; Jordan, *Nettie Palmer: Search for an Aesthetic*, p. 20.
122 Although Marnie Bassett (née Masson) remembered two domestic maids at Doona, there would also have been a nursemaid when Mervyn was an infant. A French governess, Mademoiselle Dumont, was later employed for Mervyn. The services of a gardener and odd jobs man would also have been employed. (Rickard, *H.B. Higgins*, pp. 55–60, 127, 323–24). Davison, in *Marvellous Melbourne*, p. 202, estimates that a Melbourne family with an income of £800–1,000 would have been able to afford two female domestic servants and a man servant, though the continual servant shortage and high wages rates commanded by servants in Australia could make this number difficult to achieve.
123 Jordan, *Nettie Palmer: Search for an Aesthetic*, p. 14, notes that 'the Higgins were not the simple model of the nuclear family'.

their wealth and social position encouraged them to embrace even more readily the obligations and pleasures of the wider family network of nieces and nephews.

The establishment of this Higgins family within Melbourne's professional class thus provides an opportunity to observe the ways in which old world practices are reproduced within the circumstances of the new. The migratory experience in the Higgins's case, encased within a Methodist and Irish framework, provided mechanisms and connections that allowed the negotiation of local circumstance in ways that permitted an improvement in the collective family condition. As the eldest of the children, Henry was both beneficiary and architect of this transformation. His role within the Higgins family was rooted firmly in a professional career that continued to flourish. In 1903, the year he was created a King's Counsel, he purchased for £1,100 a 'country residence', Heronswood, in Dromana, set amidst 35 acres. The seaside property was intended as a summer retreat from the heat for his wife, son, parents, siblings and friends.[124] If the purchase of Heronswood has prompted Deborah Jordan to describe the Higgins lifestyle as 'aristocratic', others have been more generous.[125] To an architectural historian, Heronswood was an early expression of the 'Australian bungalow' style and stood 'midway between the grandeur of the Victorian mansions and the mean working man's cottages of the time'.[126] This description sits comfortably alongside John Rickard's observation that Henry Higgins 'neither flaunted nor apologised for the trappings of success'.[127] He was comfortable as a successful professional man, who enjoyed fulfilling the obligations borne of a family enterprise, and framed by Irish circumstance and Melbourne's opportunities.

---

124 Autobiography of Henry Bournes Higgins (ms), pp. 120–21; Rickard, *H.B. Higgins*, pp. 127–28. As Rickard notes, Nettie Palmer described Heronswood as her uncle's 'country residence' in *Henry Bournes Higgins: A Memoir*, opposite p. 184.
125 Jordan, *Nettie Palmer: Search for an Aesthetic*, p. 18.
126 Neil Clerehan, *Historic Houses of Australia*, Australian Council of National Trusts, Cassell Australia, North Melbourne, 1974, p. 180; Rickard, *H.B. Higgins*, p. 128.
127 Rickard, *H.B. Higgins*, p. 129.

Wilding family, May 1886. Front row, from left: Julia, Anthony, baby Frank held by nurse (?). Back row: Gladys and Frederick.

The Macmillan Brown family at Holmbank, c. 1899. From left: Millicent, Helen, Viola and John, with their gardener in the background and a maid on the balcony above.

Helen Connon in BA graduation robes, July 1880. The white
camellias symbolise 'excellence in women'.

19.12.86

Mary Alice Morrison Higgins on her wedding day, 19 December 1885.
Source: Stonnington History Centre, Malvern, MP 12541

Henry Bournes Higgins and his wife, Mary Alice Higgins, c. 1920.
Source: Stonnington History Centre, Malvern, MP 12543

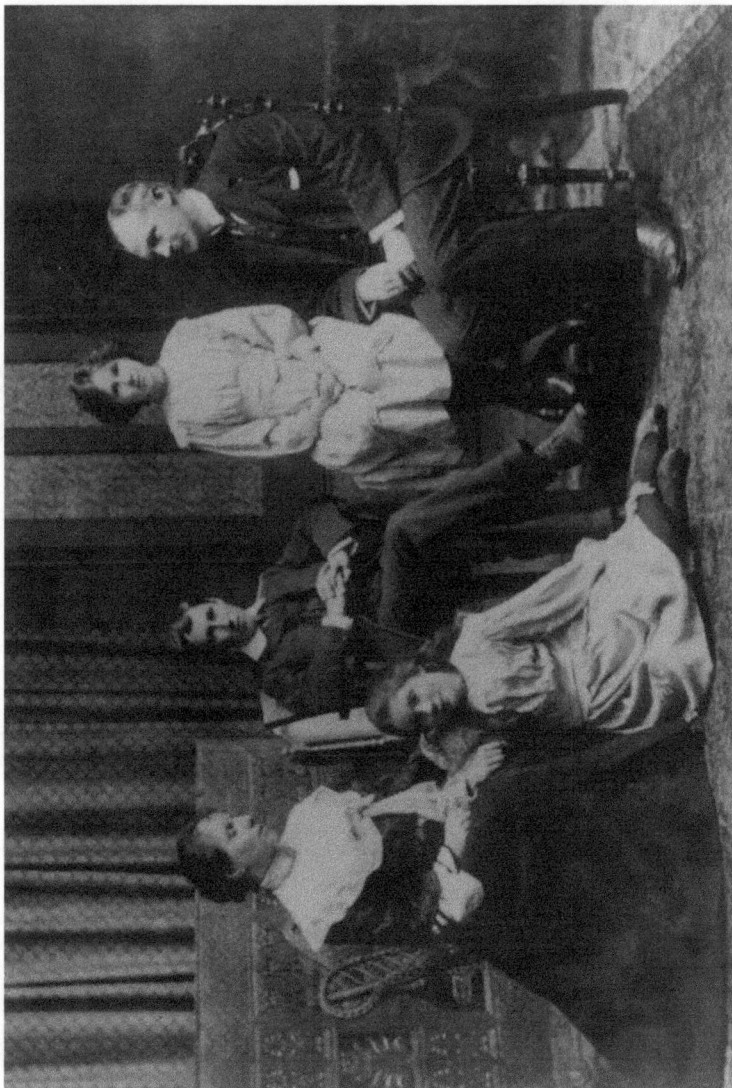

Masson family, Chanonry, University of Melbourne, Christmas 1902.
From left: Mary, Elsie, Irvine, Marnie and Orme.

Source: T. Humphrey & Co., UMA, BWP/7328

Alexander Leeper as a young married man in his thirties, in the 1880s

Alexander Leeper in the 1880s.

Source: Valentine Leeper Collection, Trinity College Archives, University of Melbourne (Cited by John Poynter, *Doubts and Certainties: A Life of Alexander Leeper*, Melbourne University Press, Carlton, 1997, p. 206.)

Adeline Leeper as a young married woman in the 1880s

Adeline Leeper in the 1880s.
Source: Valentine Leeper Collection, Trinity College Archives, University of Melbourne. (Cited by Poynter, *Doubts and Certainties*, p. 206.)

The children of Alexander and Adeline Leeper. From left to right: Kitty, Rex, Katha and Allen.
Source: UMA, BWP/7669

Mary Moule, September 1891. She became Alexander
Leeper's second wife in 1897.

Source: Foster & Martin, Valentine Leeper Collection,
Trinity College Archives, University of Melbourne

Mervyn Higgins, Irvine Masson and Robert Bage on holiday at Pentlands, Lorne, summer 1905–6.

Section Three:
Marriage and Aspirations:
Colonial Families

This section of the book examines the dynamics of family life that evolved as the five colonial families confronted the realities of marriage and raising children. It begins with an exploration of the implicit and explicit understandings present within each individual marriage. Four of the marriages evolve within the single male breadwinner mould; one develops within the framework of a professionally employed couple, whose prominent positions within a small educational community raised expectations. As the standard bearer of the city's feminist aspirations that focused on the suffrage and access to higher education for women, Helen Connon, as university graduate and headmistress, raised the prospect of a different future for middle-class women within marriage. Her marriage to John Macmillan Brown may be seen as an experiment which moved into new territory and raised questions about relationships within marriage that reached beyond the common experience of her class and generation. The understandings in which the other four marriages are anchored belong to those of the previous generation, when the university study that might unlock a professional career was not available to women. Within each marriage we observe men and women endeavouring to build family anew and give effect to a generalised goal of social betterment.

The distinctive understandings that inform each couple's attempt to create a colonial family is most clearly expressed in the education of their children. Historians have drawn attention to the role of the middle classes in the push for higher education for girls, and two chapters have been devoted to tracing the education of daughters within the families observed in this study. Put simply, and in advance of the argument, all play instrumental roles in the education of their daughters. There is, however, variation in the intensity with which education for daughters was pursued. It is difficult, for example, to imagine a more observant and meticulous mother than Julia Wilding, or a more compliant and dutiful daughter than Gladys. If there is an element of ambivalence to be found in attitudes to the education of daughters, it lies at the junction between school and university. The pursuit of a university education for daughters may be seen as a useful indicator of progressive liberal thought, but one strand of middle-class thinking saw it as an indulgence. The pursuit of a professional career through university qualification prevented the full realisation of middle-class social obligation by limiting a young woman's involvement in philanthropic and charitable activities. Such was the view of Mary Masson.

Until recently, the education of sons within the middle-class family had received somewhat less historical attention than that of their sisters. One of the outcomes of the recent literature on masculinities has been to put the father back in the family. It has done so primarily by emphasising the father's role in the upbringing of his son, but it also acknowledges greater fatherly involvement in the education of his daughters. The case studies that follow point to ways in which, in their colonial settings, there is an increase in both maternal and paternal influences in the lives of their sons. If the public dimension of the woman question in some instances lends something of an obsessive dimension to the mother/daughter relationship, so, too, does the day-boy status that prevailed throughout a son's schooling provide the opportunity for a greater maternal influence. Conversely, a father's role often seems to be ubiquitously present within the family, but harder to isolate. The case studies presented here point to direct paternal engagement in the upbringing of daughters, in ways that reflect individual preoccupations or enthusiasms. If fathers were judged, as Tosh suggests, they were judged according to their ability to induct sons into the ranks of the professional middle class.[1] Those observed here thought deeply about the education of their sons. That all chose to send sons 'Home' to a British university is testimony to their recognition that the problem of what to do with boys was as real in the new world as it was in the old.

---

1   Tosh, *A Man's Place*, pp. 79, 82, 84–85, 89–90, 98, 100–1, 114–19, 122.

5

Marriage

The institution of marriage was central to debates about the position of women in nineteenth-century Britain. The gendered and classed notions of equality limited extensions of the political franchise to middle-class men, restricted women's rights within marriage and denied them access to higher education. Any prospect of women's participation in the professions was similarly severely limited and subjected to scrutiny in ways that had implications for understandings of marriage and the role of men and women within it. The most influential of the critics of this orthodoxy were arguably John Ruskin and John Stuart Mill, whose views on women's role in society and marriage contributed to reshaping individual expectations and aspirations among professional and educated elites.[1] To Ruskin, women were innately different from men. Their particular nurturing capacities and sensitivities were better suited to the domestic and private world of the family. By contrast, Mill rejected innate difference and saw the confinement of women to the domestic sphere as a social construction that could be unmade. Fundamental as this difference of views was, there was common ground to be found. Each wanted higher education open to women. Each saw the family as the crucible in which the better society might be nurtured. Ruskin emphasised the role of the mother as moral guardian and was thus closer to the tradition of evangelical motherhood than Mill, whose rational secularism sought a pooling

---

1   John Ruskin, 'Lecture II.—Lilies Of Queens' Gardens', in John Ruskin, *Sesame and Lilies* (1865), Ward, Lock and Co., London, 1911; John Stuart Mill, *The Subjection of Women* (1869).

of talent in the quest for the useful citizen. It is here, somewhere in the gap between Ruskin and Mill, that the marriages of the five couples of this study took shape in new world societies.

Helen Connon and John Macmillan Brown: A marriage of two professionals

On 9 December 1886, Helen Connon, Principal of Christchurch Girls' High School, married her former Canterbury College professor, John Macmillan Brown, in the living room of her rented Lichfield Street home. The wedding and subsequent honeymoon in Sydney took place during the school and university vacation. Helen had instructed a pupil sitting a junior university scholarship examination that day to bring the exam papers to her shortly after the ceremony, so that they might review them together.[2] Thus, in her wedding as in much else, the historical image of Helen Connon bequeathed to us by her contemporaries is that of the dedicated, if not saintly, teacher. As student, graduate and teacher, she had come to symbolise an emerging womanly ideal that was taking shape amongst the educated colonial elite. Her particular combination of intelligence, colonial spirit and reassuring femininity provided comforting evidence that higher education for women was neither a masculinising nor de-sexing force. Indeed, her university and teaching successes were celebrated in self-congratulatory fashion within the city's professional community as an endorsement of colonial liberalism and as offering evidence that women's involvement in professional life did not threaten the social structure.

Any understanding of the Connon–Macmillan Brown courtship and marriage needs to be set against this public idealisation. Helen continued for eight years as a married principal of Christchurch Girls' High School, and the combination of professional career, marriage and motherhood was viewed with admiration by the city's educated community. In this sense, it was a marriage that was woven around their shared promotion of the higher education of young women. The difficulty in separating myth from reality has been exacerbated

---

2   'Marriage', *Lyttelton Times*, 10 December 1886, p. 4; Lovell-Smith, *Easily the Best*, p. 60.

by the unique nature of its creation.[3] The received version derives from the biography written in 1905, shortly after Helen's death at the age of 46, by her close friend Edith Searle Grossmann.[4] As a protégé of Helen Connon at Christchurch Girls' High School and Macmillan Brown at Canterbury College, Grossmann brought intimate sympathy and personal crusade to the task of biographer. Her account stresses the deliberative and idealistic elements of her mentor's life. She emphasises Connon's commitment to transforming the position of women, stresses the innovative and radical nature of her contribution to girls' education, and presents her effort to combine the traditional woman's role of wife, mother and household manager with a professional career as driven by contemporary feminist perspective.

Like much else in the Macmillan Brown–Connon relationship, the story of their 'meeting and mating' is complex. Daughter Millicent claimed in her memoirs that her parents had become secretly engaged when Helen was a 20-year-old student and seven years prior to their marriage.[5] Grossmann suggests that the courtship began when Helen was studying at Canterbury College in the evenings, across the hall from Macmillan Brown's study. Contemporaries seem not to have noticed. James Reeve Wilkinson, a spurned suitor who had frequently walked Connon home from the university on such occasions, had not 'perceived the trend' of her affection for Macmillan Brown.[6] Margaret Lovell-Smith's recent biography sees such a relationship as unlikely, given the determination with which proprieties were observed in the interests of deflecting criticism from women students.[7] The firmest evidence points to a relationship that began sometime after Helen Connon assumed the principalship at Christchurch Girls' High School. In his *Memoirs*, Macmillan Brown places his decision in the context of his desire to put club life behind him:

3   Lovell-Smith, *Easily the Best*, pp. 7–8, 25–26, 56–57, discusses the problems with sources about Helen Macmillan Brown.
4   Grossmann, *Life of Helen Macmillan Brown*; Heather Roberts, 'Edith Searle Grossmann, (1863–1931)', *DNZB*, vol. 2, pp. 180–81. Grossmann attended Christchurch Girls' High School in 1879 (and was head girl), graduated from Canterbury College in 1885 with an MA in Latin, English and Political Science, and went on to work as a teacher, novelist and journalist. She was active in the New Zealand women's movement and wrote novels with a feminist slant, including *In Revolt* (1893) and *The Heart of the Bush* (1910).
5   Millicent Baxter, *The Memoirs of Millicent Baxter*, Cape Catley, Whatamongo Bay, 1981, p. 16.
6   James R. Wilkinson, 'Educational Reminiscences from 1866', p. 38, CMDRC, ARC.1992.54; Lovell-Smith, *Easily the Best*, p. 59.
7   Lovell-Smith, *Easily the Best*, pp. 57–58.

> I had long contemplated a domestic life, as I could not ask any students to the Club or offer them other hospitality. My eye had long rested on one of my earliest lady students, Miss Helen Connon, who had been the first woman to take an honours degree in the British Empire. She was a very beautiful girl, much admired by some of the most successful men students and by others who were not students. She was now head of the Girls' High School and was making it a great success ...[8]

Whenever the romantic attachment began, it flourished in a protégé–mentor relationship of unusual intensity. To Macmillan Brown, Helen's university successes and teaching career added lustre to his growing status within the colonial academic environment. For Helen, Macmillan Brown's constant support and guidance had paved the way for a career that held out the beguiling prospect of playing a part in transforming the lives of young women of talent. In accepting his proposal on the condition that she continue as principal of Christchurch Girls' High School after their marriage, she was in effect ensuring that in marriage, as in her career, she would be entering new and largely uncharted territory.[9] While the concept of a married female principal was a socially acceptable one with precedents in the old world as well as the new, it remained a novel one in the 1880s and was widely embraced as such by the city's liberal, educated elite.[10]

This deeply inculcated and shared sense of mission gave rise to idealised views of marriage. Grossmann describes the defining characteristic as a rare union of minds, which, for Helen, 'came near the true ideal

---

8   Macmillan Brown, *Memoirs*, p. 180.

9   Elementary schools run by married couples were popular in mid-nineteenth-century Australia. Small private schools headed by a woman, offering an accomplishment-style curriculum in a home-like setting were a common enough feature of the period also. Many of them were run as family businesses, and some by married women. Yet Helen Connon (and her fellow pioneering headmistresses), a university degree-holding certificated teacher and principal of a state school with an academic bias, represented something different. See Theobald, *Knowing Women*, ch. 2, 4, 5.

10   Lovell-Smith, *Easily the Best*, p. 73, points to 'Another prominent Christchurch example', Emily Brittan, who had continued to teach at West Christchurch School after her marriage in 1882 and succeeded Helen Macmillan Brown as principal of Christchurch Girls' High School in 1894. Helen had something of a counterpart in the principal of state secondary school Sydney Girls' High, British-born Lucy Wheatley Walker Garvin, appointed in 1883, though she 'belonged to the pre-university generation' of female educational pioneers. She married in 1891 and proceeded to have three children while continuing as principal of the school (Theobald, *Knowing Women*, pp. 115–16). New South Wales introduced a marriage bar for female teachers in 1895, following the earlier example of the state of Victoria in 1893. New Zealand introduced a marriage bar for women working in the public service, including teachers, in 1913.

of Plato'.[11] To this fundamental, intellectual understanding, Macmillan Brown grafted a set of attitudes and expectations that derived from heroic literary models. Shakespeare's female characters loom large in the literary markers of his feminine ideal: Portia from the *Merchant of Venice*, Beatrice from *Much Ado About Nothing*, Rosalind from *As You Like It*, Viola from *Twelfth Night* (after whom the couple named their second daughter) and Coriolanus's wife, Virgilia, whom Ruskin had described as the 'loveliest' of Shakespeare's female characters.[12] From Greek mythology and literature Macmillan Brown found much to admire in Homer's wily, resourceful Penelope—faithful wife of Odysseus. Like Ruskin, Macmillan Brown found in these literary figures 'the highest type of humanity': a combination of physical and spiritual beauty, intelligence, and strength of character, infused with gentleness, self-sacrifice and submissiveness. The 'true woman', he said, discussing Portia in the *Merchant of Venice*, possessed a 'brave self-controlling gentleness and yieldingness'.[13] Helen, for John Macmillan Brown, came to represent his ideal heroine.[14]

The intellectual partnership to which the Macmillan Browns aspired in marriage has its origin in the development of Christchurch Girls' High School. Effectively an adjunct of Canterbury College, the school provided an academic education for girls that aimed to develop the 'whole being' and prepare them for university. Helen Connon had joined the staff while a student at Canterbury College, after being recommended by Macmillan Brown, and became 'Lady Principal' with his support. During her 11-year term as principal, as Gardner has demonstrated, her success at preparing students for university helped feminise the arts faculty and made Canterbury College New Zealand's leading women's university.[15] Her dedicated mentoring of talented girls for university was focused upon the close textual study of English literature and drew heavily upon methodologies she had

---

11   Grossmann, *Life of Helen Macmillan Brown*, p. 26.
12   Ruskin, 'Lecture II: Lilies', pp. 65, 62–93.
13   John Macmillan Brown, *Julius Caesar: A Study*, Whitcombe & Tombs, Christchurch, 1894, p. 148.
14   See, for example, Macmillan Brown's *Memoirs*, pp. x–xi, 180, 183, 188, 213–14.
15   Gardner, *Colonial Cap and Gown*, pp. 97–98, 106. See also Matthews, *In Their Own Right*, pp. 88–92, 105–6, 108–9, 111.

imbibed from Macmillan Brown.[16] Her influence, as he observed in a report on the girls' school written for Canterbury College in the years preceding their marriage, was such that the girls stopped 'little short of worship'.[17] This was precisely the mix of emulation and identification that he had sought to cultivate through his own teaching, and the combination is neatly captured in the diary jottings of a young pupil: 'I wonder shall I rise as Mrs Brown has risen? I am not in such a low position as she was and what is she now!'[18]

Historians of girls' education have discerned in women teachers who spearheaded the quest for higher education a set of progressive motivations they describe as 'discreet coterie feminism', which 'co-existed with the agendas of the traditional clientele'.[19] Such thinking lay behind Helen Connon's dedication to her most able academic students, but we may also observe similar democratic purpose in her development of the school curriculum, especially in the promotion of vocational education.[20] To Helen and the women who taught with her, the introduction of shorthand and typing in 1884 was not simply catering for a new labour market demand, but provided young girls of modest backgrounds a pathway to economic independence. Similarly, the introduction of optional Saturday morning cooking classes was viewed not as a preparation for the domestic sphere, but as a skill that would facilitate independent womanhood.[21] To the elements of feminist expectation and academic evangelicalism that lay at the

---

16   Canterbury College Girls High School Prize List and Prospectus, December 1883, pp. 8–9; Lovell-Smith, *Easily the Best*, pp. 46–47; Grossmann, *Life*, pp. 35–36; Barbara Peddie, *Christchurch Girls' High School, 1877–1977*, Christchurch High School Old Girls' Association, Christchurch, 1977, pp. 15–48.

17   Macmillan Brown, *Memoirs*, p. 180.

18   An entry from Elsie Lowe's 1891 diary, cited by Lovell-Smith, *Easily the Best*, p. 67.

19   Theobald, *Knowing Women*, p. 94.

20   Coral Chambers, *Lessons for Ladies: A Social History of Girls' Education in Australasia, 1870–1900*, Hale & Iremonger, Sydney, 1986, p. 99, writes that the public girls' schools were arguably 'better adapters' to colonial circumstances than the public boys' schools, which strove to emulate English models with their emphasis on classics and mathematics and reluctance to introduce specialist vocational subjects.

21   Peddie, *Christchurch Girls' High*, pp. 40–48; Grossmann, *Life*, pp. 34–36; Lovell-Smith, *Easily the Best*, pp. 41–51; Ruth Fry, *It's Different For Daughters: A History of the Curriculum for Girls in New Zealand Schools, 1900–1975*, New Zealand Council for Educational Research, Wellington, 1985, pp. 26–36; Theobald, *Knowing Women*, pp. 90–129; Melanie Nolan, *Breadwinning: New Zealand Women and the State*, Canterbury University Press, Christchurch, 2000, pp. 112–22; Chambers, *Lessons for Ladies*, pp. 94–103.

heart of Connon's teaching career, marriage added an intensity which derived much of its strength from the protégé–mentor basis upon which it was built.

The gender roles within the Macmillan Brown household at Holmbank remained essentially the traditional ones. Their joint incomes allowed them to employ two domestic servants, a gardener and odd-jobs man. Helen seems to have assumed the role of household-manager as her natural territory, and John just as naturally assumed it so. After years residing at a men's club, he took particular pleasure from the creation of Holmbank's five-acre garden, notable for its native trees and plants, and in many ways it represented the putting down of roots, and of laying the sense of exile that had infused his departure from Scotland to rest.[22] With Helen as a 'splendid helpmate', the domestic world of Holmbank enabled the full realisation of the academic ideal that he had absorbed at Oxford from Benjamin Jowett.[23] Sunday became an 'at home' day, when he held breakfasts for specially chosen students and friends—all members of the professional establishment, all of them male and all of them *his* rather than Helen's friends. At such times, it fell to Helen to be the busy hostess, overseeing the cooking and the serving of breakfasts by her sister, Maria, and trusted young girl pupils.

Parenthood came quickly. Their first child, Millicent, was born a little more than a year after their marriage, in January 1888, three weeks before the school year resumed.[24] The practicalities of Millicent's day-to-day physical care were left to others. As a baby she was bottle-fed, and the carers were drawn from a pool of trusted former pupils and students chosen for their capacity to follow Helen's instructions and preferred methods meticulously. In this initial nurturing, we glimpse the beginning of an educational experiment, designed and overseen, if not implemented, by Helen and John themselves. In essence, as we shall observe in greater detail in Chapter Six, it sought to implement, in the domestic context, their belief that the best form of education for young children was one based upon the careful nurturing on

---

22 Thelma Strongman, *The Gardens of Canterbury: A History*, A.H. & A.W. Reed, Wellington, 1984, pp. 158–60.
23 Macmillan Brown, *Memoirs*, p. 183.
24 Baxter, *Memoirs*, p. 16.

a one-to-one level of individual needs and talents.[25] Whatever its educational merits, it was an idealistic experiment that relied for its implementation upon Helen.

Both the Macmillan Browns believed that the experiment would be enriched by the presence of another child, but it was to be some eight years before their second daughter was born.[26] A frustrating succession of miscarriages undermined the couple's confidence and seemed a fateful confirmation of the widespread general belief that the strain of higher education and paid employment undertaken by women would jeopardise maternal health. By 1892 Helen was exhausted.[27] The pair took six-months leave and travelled to Europe, where they consulted a leading Edinburgh obstetrician. Macmillan Brown took Helen to visit Oxford, where his mentor Benjamin Jowett, according to Grossmann, took 'her aside and told her how greatly he admired her fulfilment of the double duty and how much he thought it would do for the cause and development and position of women if she could continue … in the principalship'.[28]

Upon their return to New Zealand, Helen continued to perform her 'double duty'. The strain under which the pair now laboured soon manifested itself in insomnia. In a bid to exhaust her body as well as her mind, Helen threw herself into a vigorous exercise program of rowing, cycling, hiking and horse riding. Throughout 1894 it became even more evident that the 'double life' had become an insuperable burden. At the urging of her husband, who thought that the miscarriages had taken an irreversible toll on her well-being and state of mind, Helen resigned the principalship in 1894.[29] She had held the position for 11 years, eight of them as a married woman and seven as a wife and mother.

---

25   'Diary of Millicent Amiel Macmillan Brown Born 8 January 1888', JMBP, A11/13; Grossmann, *Life of Helen Macmillan Brown*, pp. 48–52; Macmillan Brown, *Modern Education*, pp. 18–21, 23–30; Lovell-Smith, *Easily the Best*, pp. 63–66.

26   Macmillan Brown, *Memoirs*, pp. 186–88.

27   'Girls' High School Lady Principal asking for leave', 17 May 1892, Canterbury College Inwards Correspondence, MBL 5334/1892.

28   Grossmann, *Life of Helen Macmillan Brown*, pp. 52–53; Helen Connon to Maria [Connon Brown], 24 and 26 October 1892, JMBP, A18 Correspondence 1870–1934; Macmillan Brown, *Memoirs*, pp. 187–88.

29   Grossmann, *Life of Helen Macmillan Brown*, pp. 52–54; Lovell-Smith, *Easily the Best*, pp. 68–69, 73–75; Macmillan Brown, *Memoirs*, p. 187.

The consequences of her retirement for the marriage may be briefly stated. Helen became a veritable headmistress of the household. She involved herself more directly in her daughter's education, personally taking control of lessons for several hours each day. A governess, however, continued to implement the educational program as prescribed and supervised by Helen. She continued to mentor former pupils as they endeavoured to pursue careers, but in other respects seems to have made a conscious decision to make a clean break from her former career. Indeed, she slipped quietly into the traditional female activities of her class: she made and received calls, managed the household, and diligently maintained her exercise regime.[30] Those women closest to her—her mother and sisters and friend, and later biographer, Grossmann—thought her behaviour and demeanour indicated restlessness and dissatisfaction. They point to her wanderings in the Port Hills, continued insomnia and a growing preoccupation with physical and mental fitness that flowed over in to an obsession with Millicent's health and development.[31] Such a reading suggests an intellectually oriented woman struggling to find fulfilment within the traditional female role of wife and mother.

Helen's dilemmas were lost in the more public nature of her husband's resignation from Canterbury College in March 1896.[32] The decision derived from an academic disillusionment, in which he began to question the importance he had placed upon the study of English literature as a guide to building the better society. Whatever its intellectual origin, the decision to retire came as his perception of failing personal health reached new levels of hypochondria. The eyestrain that had troubled him during his student days returned. A six-month holiday in Europe followed almost immediately. Its benefits were quickly realised: within a year of the couple's return to Christchurch their second daughter, Viola, was born.[33] The arrival of the new child confirmed the increasing conventionality of the marriage. For Helen

---

30   Baxter, *Memoirs*, p. 28; Lovell-Smith, *Easily the Best*, pp. 79–82.
31   E. B. Craig to Helen Macmillan Brown, 5 February 1896, 28 February 1896, 8 May 1902, JMBP, A19/7-9; Pata [Maria Brown] to Helen Macmillan Brown, 25 April 1902, 13 June 1902, JMBP, A19/10, A19/13; Mrs Connon, 'Mother', to Helen Macmillan Brown, 4 July 1902, JMBP, A19/11; Grossmann, *Life of Helen Macmillan Brown*, pp. 82–88; Lovell-Smith, *Easily the Best*, pp. 109–12; Penny Griffith, *Out of the Shadows: The Life of Millicent Baxter* [October 2015], PenPublishing, Wellington, February 2016, p. 53.
32   'Canterbury College: Farewell to Professor Brown', *Lyttelton Times*, 16 March 1896, p. 2; 'Professor Brown', *Press*, 2 April 1895, p. 4; Lovell-Smith, *Easily the Best*, p. 76.
33   On 16 November 1897.

this meant absorption in the domestic routines of the household and the education of her daughters. Conversely, freed of his university obligations, Macmillan Brown could now follow his intellectual interests wherever they led him, becoming something of a public intellectual with a particular interest in education and anthropology, and a proclivity for publishing his lectures and writing utopian novels.[34] It was in these conventional roles and within a context of deteriorating health that the final years of the marriage were played out. Early in 1900, the entire family embarked on a European tour that lasted nearly two years. Helen suffered a further miscarriage early in 1901, from which she 'never fully recovered'. Upon their return to Christchurch in January 1902, she withdrew to the family cottage in the seaside suburb of Sumner, leaving the children with her husband at Holmbank. In February she was diagnosed with diphtheria and died on 22 February 1903, aged 46.[35]

What sets the Connon–Macmillan Brown marriage apart from the others in this study is the extent to which it was publicly associated with the expectations of the embryonic feminist movement. It is an association that has produced considerable scrutiny of her marriage. As the nation's first female principal and the most prominent of Christchurch's first generation of middle-class educated women, Helen's attempt to combine marriage, motherhood and career posed fundamental questions about the institution of marriage and gender roles within it. Grossmann's assessment, written in 1905 shortly after Connon's death and from a feminist perspective, confronts the limitations of Connon's achievement. Helen had 'proved perfectly that a profession does not make a woman forfeit her womanliness, but the question of married women carrying on a public career she left unanswered'.[36] For Grossmann, the ambiguities grew from the particularities of colonial circumstances. The absence of a developed servant class that underpinned the achievements of middle-class women in the old world made the domestic aspects of the professional

---

34 Macmillan Brown's utopian novels, *Riallaro*, Putnam, New York, 1901, and *Limanora, the Island of Progress*, Putnam, New York, 1903, were published under the pseudonym Godfrey Sweven.

35 Grossmann, *Life of Helen Macmillan Brown*, pp. 86–88; Baxter, *Memoirs*, p. 29; Macmillan Brown, *Memoirs*, pp. 213–14; Lovell-Smith, *Easily the Best*, pp. 93, 105–6, 110–14.

36 Grossmann, *Life of Helen Macmillan Brown*, p. 53; Grossmann, 'Employment of Married Women as Teachers', *Canterbury Times*, 26 October 1893, p. 8.

marriage comparatively more difficult in newer communities.[37] The 'double duty' that she and contemporaries perceived as the preserve of women became insuperably more difficult for those like Helen Connon, whose marriage was imbued with a sense of personal mission.

Viewed from a wider historical perspective, the Connon–Macmillan Brown marriage can be seen as being shaped by a highly personalised form of academic evangelicalism and colonial middle-class feminist aspiration. The fusion of these lofty goals produced a marriage that both partners saw as possessing a shared intellectual basis. As Noel Annan has observed of intellectuals in another context, 'those who have clear ideas on what life ought to be always have difficulty in reconciling themselves to reality'.[38] The realities that operated within the domestic world required of the professional couple a capacity to cast aside prevailing gender assumptions—not only the male-as-sole-breadwinner, but also the female domestic manager. There is no evidence that the Macmillan Browns ever discussed their marriage in these terms. Each accepted roles that conformed to prevailing conventions and they did so in ways that reflected their individual personalities. The gentle, quiet, reserved Helen simply shouldered the 'double duty' and added the absolute control of the domestic sphere to her teaching responsibilities. The energetic, charismatic, self-absorbed John Macmillan Brown welcomed the ordered domesticity at Holmbank as a congenial setting for his academic endeavours and as a symbol of the moral verities of life. In short, the Macmillan Brown marriage sits on the cusp of social changes, the consequences of which were in the 1880s and 1890s only dimly understood. The intellectual union and equality that they sought and believed they had achieved as a professional couple required adjustments within marriage that neither contemplated.[39]

---

37   Grossmann, *Life of Helen Macmillan Brown*, pp. 53–54.
38   Annan, *The Dons*, pp. 21–22.
39   A notable comparison is Macmillan Brown's former colleague, chemistry professor Alexander Bickerton and his wife Phoebe, who established a federated home in 1896 at Wainoni, Christchurch, in which domestic chores were meant to be shared between the female and male residents. See Tolerton, *A Life of Ettie Rout*, pp. 28–31.

Orme and Mary Masson: 'A kind of decent partnership'[40]

Orme Masson's aunt, Emily Andrews (1823–1862), was immortalised in 'The Angel in the House', a popular narrative poem written by her husband Coventry Patmore (1823–1896), which depicts the ideal wife of the Victorian era as selfless, submissive and docile.[41] While it was not an image that appealed to either Orme or Mary, their marriage nevertheless took a more conventional, middle-class form than that of the Macmillan Browns and was built around the notion of husband as breadwinner and wife as household manager, helpmate and mother. Mary proved to be the more conservative and traditional, nowhere more so than in the education of their adolescent daughters. On this issue and others, the Masson marriage and family experience encapsulates some of the ambivalence that characterises late nineteenth-century redefinitions of femininity.[42] For an understanding of these ambiguities, we are reliant upon correspondence between family members, observations made by friends, and the published reminiscences of the Masson daughters, Elsie and Marnie.

Orme Masson and Mary Struthers's whirlwind romance was anything but pragmatic or rational. They had become engaged three weeks after a first meeting in Edinburgh, arranged in traditional fashion from within the closed network of family and friends by Orme's sister Nell. Two years passed before marriage, as Orme conformed to the middle-class expectation that a gentleman should not embark upon marriage until he had secured a future that provided material comfort for his wife and family.[43] The nuptials and departure were in accord with the norms of Scottish middle-class professional family life: the marriage

---

40   Elsie Masson Malinowski to Bronio Malinowski, n.d., in Helena Wayne (ed.), *The Story of a Marriage: The Letters of Bronislaw Malinowski and Elsie Masson, vol. 1, 1916–1920*, London, Routledge, 1995, p. 183.

41   The poem was first published in 1854 and expanded until 1862, but did not become popular until later in the late nineteenth century; Ian Anstruther, *Coventry Patmore's Angel: A Study of Coventry Patmore, His Wife Emily and the Angel in the House*, Haggerston Press, London, 1992; Weickhardt, *Masson of Melbourne*, p. 3.

42   Tosh, *A Man's Place*, pp. 145–94; Desley Deacon, 'Reorganising the Masculinist Context: Conflicting Masculinism in the New South Wales Public Service Bills Debates of 1895', in Magarey et al. (eds), *Debutante Nation*, pp. 50–58.

43   Orme Masson, 'Notes', ms, DOMFP, box 7/10/3; Mary Masson, 'Household Lists', ms, 1886, DOMFP, box 7/10/5; Weickhardt, *Masson of Melbourne*, pp. 17, 23–24.

took place in the drawing room of the Struthers's home in Migvie, Aberdeenshire; extended families and friends showered the couple with more than 100 wedding presents; the eight-day honeymoon was spent rushing about farewelling family and friends. In these familiar rituals, we may glimpse the ingredients that were to shape the Masson experience of marriage and migration: a companionable union of an educated couple comfortable within the middle-class Scottish environment, drawn to the new world by professional prospects, leaving the old with regret and a sense of separation, and jostling with the excitement of a future in their own hands.

It is possible to discern two phases in the evolution of the Masson marriage: an early phase in which the overlapping processes of establishing career and family defined marriage roles narrowly and in ways that are consistent with separate spheres; and a later phase in which individual and parallel lives are created that transcend the public/private categories of separate spheres. Our knowledge of the private working out of this transition is heavily dependent on the later reflections of the two Masson daughters, Marnie and Elsie. Such views bring with them emotional and generational judgements that demand caution. Nevertheless, the personalities and life experiences of the two daughters give their observations individual and complementary perspectives, and offer insights that might otherwise elude historians.

The early years of Mary Masson's marriage highlight a dilemma familiar enough amongst middle-class, educated young wives. Her education fitted her to become a companion to her educated husband—'a better wife and mother'—but left her ill-prepared for the domestically orientated and maternal role this would entail. Accustomed to depending upon servants, she had arrived in Melbourne clutching an 1880 edition of *Mrs Beeton's Book of Household Management* and, as her daughter puts it, barely able to make her own bed. Servants were quickly found—one general domestic/cook to begin with, and later three, including a nursemaid for the children—and Mary quickly became an efficient mistress of the household. She was to remain keenly aware of her lack of practical know-how and was rarely confident enough to work alongside servants in household tasks.

With the assistance of the university gardeners, she did, however, help create a garden at the Chanonry and filled the half-acre of land with the familiar plants of her Scottish homeland.[44]

Motherhood came quickly, intensified the sense of loneliness and bred doubts about whether she and Orme would be able to realise in Australia the 'kind of decent partnership' they sought.[45] She later confided something of these anxieties to her daughter Marnie. By her account, Mary had carried from childhood the image of her mother lying on a couch in the family drawing room, struggling to direct servants, as she recovered from the birth of one of her seven children or prepared for the birth of the next. It was an experience she did not wish to repeat. Sheltered from the practical realities of child-raising throughout her life by the presence of nursemaids, she came to motherhood in Australia ill-equipped to cope with its constant demands and, until the approach of her third child, without the assistance of a nursemaid. It was at this point, Marnie records, that her mother wept uncontrollably as she tried to dress her and at the same time respond to the demands of her older brother.[46]

It is also from Marnie that we learn something of the essential separateness of parental lives within their daily routines. In *Once upon a Time*, she writes of watching from the nursery window with her brother and sister each morning as their father walked swiftly towards his laboratory, 'absorbed in thought, trencher on bent head', and excitedly watching for his return home.[47] He took his evening meal with Mary and then retired to the 'private world' of his study or returned to the laboratory. Mary, after tucking the children into bed and reading them stories, retired to the equally 'private world' of her drawing room where she played her piano.[48] The failure of this routine to meet Mary's expectations of personal fulfilment contributed, in Marnie's opinion, to her continued bouts of homesickness.[49] It is an experience that points to the more general dilemma of the growing

44   Bassett, *Once upon a Time*, pp. 53–58, 63; Marnie Bassett, 'Once upon a Time', Address to the Lyceum Club, 1972, ms, Flora Marjorie (Marnie) Bassett Papers, UMA, 1980.0079, 7/26/13.
45   Elsie Masson Malinowski to Bronio Malinowski, n.d., in Wayne (ed.), *The Story of a Marriage*, p. 183, (cited in Michael Young, *Malinowski: Odyssey of an Anthropologist 1884–1920*, Yale University Press, New Haven and London, 2004, p. 584).
46   Bassett, *Once upon a Time*, (1985), p. 55.
47   Bassett, *Once upon a Time*, p. 64.
48   Bassett, *Once upon a Time*, p. 66.
49   Bassett, *Once upon a Time*, pp. 59–60, 61, 66, 71–73.

number of highly educated, upper middle-class married women frustrated within the narrow confines of the traditional domestic role. Society was increasingly allowing for the expansion of the horizons of the female mind, but provided limited opportunities for this to be put to practical purpose outside the role of 'better wife and mother'. In Mary's case, as for many others of her generation, it was a dilemma that was not resolved until World War One provided opportunities for an expansion of the voluntary and charitable work traditionally regarded as appropriate for women of her class and social position.

The disruption occasioned by migration that added to Mary's sense of unfulfilled aspiration was not accompanied by any lessening of commitment to the joint quest for 'a kind of decent partnership'. It does, however, highlight an unevenness of personal fulfilment within marriage, especially within the early years of childrearing. If Mary's problems were those of isolation—both from her homeland and those generated by the traditional confinement to the home during pregnancy—Orme's frustrations were those engendered by academe. Researchers have suggested that marriages between members of the same class and occupational category have historically produced more enduring intimate unions.[50] The observation is built around the notion that such couples are 'familiar with the work that characterizes their class' and 'more likely to share a similar understanding of one another and the world'.[51] In this sense, endogamy could scarcely have better illustrations than in the marriage of Orme and Mary Masson. Their understandings of the world and each other underpinned an enduring union.

Despite the tensions generated by migration and early motherhood, as the children grew older, the partnership to which the couple aspired took on its conventional, mature form. Mary now emerged from an almost self-imposed domestic seclusion to play an auxiliary role in Orme's professional and university life and assumed a separate and more public role for herself. As helpmeet within the university community, she fostered academic relationships and social networks and provided hospitality to Orme's colleagues. When Orme's career

---

50   Marco H. D. van Leeuwen and Ineke Maas, 'Endogamy and Social Class in History: An Overview', *International Review of Social History* 50, Supplement, 2005, p. 17; see also Tosh, *A Man's Place*, e.g. pp. 64–66; Peterson, *Family, Love and Work*, pp. 163–66.
51   Leeuwen and Mass, 'Endogamy', p. 17.

within the national scientific movement blossomed, Mary 'kept pace', as Marnie puts it, 'with sympathy and constructive ideas and by making Chanonry a hospitable meeting ground'.[52] As the daughter of a professor of anatomy, this was familiar territory for Mary and evidence of the advantages of 'occupational endogamy': a source of enhanced status by association and preparation for the more public and independent role she was to play during and after the Great War.

That the role of 'helpmeet' and voluntary philanthropic endeavour met Mary's expectations of the 'decent partnership' is perhaps best indicated in her attitude to the education of her daughters. This will be examined more fully in chapters 6 and 7; here it is sufficient to observe that the education of Marnie and Elsie Masson was a subject upon which the parents held different views, and that Mary's more traditional and conservative attitude prevailed. Despite her family background—both her parents had championed the higher education of women, including the right for women to undertake medical degrees—Mary did not think it appropriate for her daughters to study for degrees or paid employment. Orme deferred to his wife on the matter and was later to say that he had left it 'too late' to question an approach which he thought both wrong for their daughters and out of touch with changing attitudes.[53] In the gap between their views, Mary's stance held firm. It later became a point of tension between mother and daughters that reflected a wider generational conflict within middle-class families, as they confronted the redefinitions of femininity which accompanied changes in the position of women.[54]

52   Bassett, *Once upon a Time*, pp. 71–72; Weickhardt, *Masson of Melbourne*, pp. 72–73; Obituary: Marnie Bassett, *The Times*, 29 February 1980.
53   Marnie Bassett, 'Notes', ms, 8 February 1874, Marnie Bassett Papers, UMA, 7/26/13.
54   On the topic of intergenerational conflict see, for example, Caine, *Bombay to Bloomsbury*, pp. 294–326, 327–54; Carol Dyhouse, *Feminism and the Family in England 1880–1939*, Basil Blackwell, Oxford, 1989, pp. 22–27. Steve Mintz, in *A Prison of Expectations: The Family in Victorian Culture*, New York University, New York, 1983, focuses on family conflicts that reflect wider social changes.

It was this generational divide that gave rise to the most acute assessment of the marriage of Orme and Mary. It came from the pen of the younger Masson daughter Elsie, who, as a young woman in the 1910s, belonged to 'The Clan', the Melbourne equivalent of the English Bloomsbury set.[55] Her premarital relationship with Bronio Malinowski (1884–1942), a Polish anthropologist detained in Melbourne as an alien during World War One, shocked conservative circles in Melbourne, not to mention her parents. In a letter to Malinowski, after they married, she observed:

> Mother's idea of marriage seems to be a kind of decent partnership which forms a practical excuse for love, which otherwise is something which should be repressed; the husband's business in the firm lies in doing work which will raise him in repute and give him weight in the eyes of the world, and the wife's duties consist in helping him to get on.[56]

The suggestion of emotional emptiness and calculation, in which status is valued above any sense of intrinsic worth, is at times put even more bluntly: 'I'm sure I cared more for your work than she has ever really cared for father's, and I care for yours because I believe in its worth and value, not for what it will bring you.' To Malinowski's claim that 'love is like art and is really an end in itself, and one of the things making life worthwhile', she responded that her mother believed that 'love is only permissible when it is rendered disciplinary by the bringing up of children'.[57] These were harsh judgements. They sit somewhat uncomfortably alongside the considered response of her parents to her proposed marriage to Malinowski at a time when he was widely thought, within the Melbourne University community at least, to be a philanderer:

> Elsie has the right to decide for herself and—which is more to the point—it is too late to be raising objections when she and you have made up your minds. Elsie's happiness is really the only consideration that counts with her mother and me, and that now rests with you.[58]

---

55   Young, *Malinowski*, pp. 457–58.
56   Elsie Masson Malinowski to Bronio Malinowski, c. 1920, Wayne (ed.), *Story of a Marriage*, vol. 1, p. 183; Young, *Malinowski*, p. 584.
57   Wayne (ed.), *Story of a Marriage*, p. 183; Young, *Malinowski*, p. 584.
58   Orme Masson to Malinowski, 18 October 1918, Wayne (ed.), *Story of a Marriage*, pp. 177–78; Young, *Malinowski*, pp. 577–78.

Leeper's Angels: 'What a strange complex love story we have had'[59]

Alexander Leeper was married twice. His first wife, Sydney-born and raised Adeline Allen, died in 1893 when barely 40 years old after 14 years of marriage. His second marriage in 1897, at the age of 49, to 37-year-old Mary Moule, a Melburnian, lasted until his own death in 1934. Both unions brought children: four with Adeline and a further three with Mary. The first marriage involved differences in class and wealth largely absent from the second: Adeline was from a close, long-established, rich, influential, legal, political and philanthropic family, whose intense emotional ties and dynastic concerns exerted a major influence in her marriage and in the lives of her children after her death; Mary Moule was a member of an established, if somewhat less wealthy, Melbourne legal family and more comfortable in the city's professional society. At the heart of each marriage, and in sharp contrast to the other marriages discussed in this study, were strongly held religious beliefs. The Allens were a prominent and devout Wesleyan-Methodist family; the Moules were committed Anglicans. The interaction of these particular religious beliefs with Leeper's intense brand of Anglicanism shaped gender roles within both marriages. The discussion that follows will focus upon the marriage of Adeline and Alexander.

Writing of the mid-Victorian age, John Tosh argues that 'almost all forms of Christian belief were shot through with assumptions of sexual inequality. St Paul's injunction, "Wives, submit yourselves unto your own husbands, as unto the Lord" underpinned unequal marriages in countless devout households.'[60] The late Victorian period, to which Leeper's marriages belong, witnessed a liberalisation of such religious beliefs, the emergence of a 'gentler pattern of family relations' and a trend toward declining deference of wives and children to their husbands and fathers.[61] Something of this transition can be observed in both of Leeper's marriages. Adeline and Mary were cast, and *cast themselves*, firmly in the traditional role of their husband's helpmeet and supporter. The mercurial Leeper is not so readily categorised.

---

59 Adeline Leeper to Alexander Leeper on her deathbed, 1893.
60 Tosh, *A Man's Place*, p. 72.
61 Tosh, *A Man's Place*, pp. 146–69.

Though often paternalistic in his attitude towards women, he rarely assumed a patriarchal stance. Ambivalent towards the changing role of women, he championed their right to higher education, admired professional women who retained their feminine charms, and promoted the ordination of women within the Anglican Church, but did not think women were ready for the vote. A romantic, he adored and idealised women.[62] Tormented by a fear of death, racked by religious doubts and a deep sense of personal sin and inadequacy, he saw a sweetness, gentleness and purity in Adeline that could bring about his own redemption.[63] To Adeline, Leeper seemed a troubled and worthy man in need of emotional and practical support.

Adeline Allen and Alexander Leeper first met in Sydney in 1869. After a tortuous 10-year courtship that rivalled the machinations of *Pride and Prejudice* and *Romeo and Juliet*, they were married on 30 December 1879 in a private chapel at Toxteth, the Allen family's estate. Much of the courtship had been conducted by correspondence, initially between Leeper and Adeline's mother and younger brother Boyce. Leeper was first invited to the Allen household in 1869 as a teacher for the two eldest boys. To the family, he seemed a somewhat romantic figure; a charming conversationalist, a clever, cultured, devout and earnest young man. The nature of Adeline's early response to Alexander is well captured in her diaries:

> I have thought of him a good deal lately—It seems to me that he is the only man I have ever met who in any way comes up to my ideal of what a man should be. I cannot help thinking about him—wishing to see him so that I may know him as he is. If he really is what I think I should like to have him as a friend. He would raise me—make me better, nobler, wiser—and I could almost worship him.[64]

Whatever his considerable virtues, Leeper's poor health and precarious financial position made him, in the considered assessment of Sir Wigram Allen, a dubious marriage prospect for Adeline. In 1870 Alexander returned to Ireland, his captivation with Adeline thwarted,

---

62 Poynter, *Doubts and Certainties*, p. 27.
63 Tosh, *A Man's Place*, pp. 54–56.
64 Adeline Allen's 1875 diary, (day and month not recorded), ALP, T5, box 38; Poynter, *Doubts and Certainties*, p. 54.

unrequited, but undiminished: 'What a bright shining little creature she is. Oh I would to God that I were fine and noble enough to win or deserve to win her love!'[65]

The correspondence with Adeline's mother and brother continued unabated, and, in the process, Leeper seems to have become obsessed with the *idea* and the *ideal* of Adeline as the 'perfect angel'. In 1875 Leeper returned to Melbourne and began to write directly to her, seeking unequivocal support in winning over her reluctant father.[66] His close friend, Reverend George Wildig, captures the essence of the developing relationship:

> My dear Sandy, you have created a phantom and pursued it all your life long, not in loving a good woman, but in giving the reign to an exorbitant fancy, and letting your idea of AA take the place of reality ...
>
> Adeline Allen is a very respected, well-intentioned young woman, perhaps pretty, probably accomplished, and endowed with quite the ordinary amount of sense ... AA is not half or a quarter as sentimental as you—that is plain, and your flights of rodomontade give her pain, annoyance and discomfort.[67]

Adeline's responses to the avalanche of letters from Alexander demonstrate how readily she adopted the role of soother, comforter and provider of emotional support and advice that she would maintain throughout their marriage: 'Your letter this morning only made me long inexpressibly to soothe & cheer you. I hardly understand what hypochondria means'; '[d]on't add to your troubles & perplexities by making new ones'; 'never mind all your faults and shortcomings. I daresay I have quite as many though I do not think so much about them. Put away all those unhappy thoughts—they are not good for you or for me either. I will not let your morbidness affect me.'[68]

---

65   Alexander Leeper's 1870 diary: 4 April 1870, ALP, T5, box 35; Poynter, *Doubts and Certainties*, p. 30.
66   Poynter, *Doubts and Certainties*, pp. 36–39.
67   Rev. George Wildig to Alexander Leeper, 28 February 1876; Poynter, *Doubts and Certainties*, p. 78.
68   Adeline Allen to Alexander Leeper, 16 July 1879 (telegram), 26 July 1869, 4 December 1879, ALP, T1, box 22/44; Poynter, *Doubts and Certainties*, pp. 93, 94, 98.

For all his romantic idealism, Alexander Leeper was conscious of the everyday economic realities and practicalities of marriage. As he put it to Adeline, 'I sometimes think I scarcely explained to you fully enough what sort of thing it is to be married to a man of small means':

> If you turn out the clever wise little housekeeper that I expect you to be, I shall be much better off. I do want you, however, to begin to pay attention to <u>small</u> sums of money; for it is in small sums that incomes go chiefly & will you also begin to practise keeping accounts, that you may grow expert at it before we marry. Poor little victim. I know you will hate it … You said in your sweet foolish way last Friday week that you thought 'saving to be such fun' my dear innocent Adeline, you little know—It is very unpleasant.
>
> But what I want you to think of is this. You must realise what is the meaning of a 'small income'. They are simple words enough; yet truly dear I doubt if you quite know what they mean. In your own home, a want is no sooner felt than it is supplied …[69]

Moreover, when Adeline writes that her life had not been a particularly 'useful' one and that she welcomed marriage as a means of fulfilling her predestined role as wife and mother, Alexander responds in a manner that confirms his sister's worst fears, which is that he would make his new wife 'attend on you too much'.[70]

> You must find comfort in thinking how faithfully I have worked and waited for you, and also how greatly your power and usefulness will in all probability be increased in your new life. It is said often that a man is never <u>a complete</u> man until he has married. But it might be said even more truly, I think of a woman, that until she marries, she has not discovered the hundredth part of the possibilities of her own nature, that she does not know what life and duty really mean.[71]

As a self-proclaimed 'man of small means', married to a daughter of a rich and influential Sydney family, Leeper lacked the power and authority over his wife that most men typically derived from their sole-breadwinner role. Adeline did not come to marriage with a dowry. Her father had feared that if she did, the money might be eaten up in Leeper's efforts to make the financially struggling Trinity College

---

69   Alexander Leeper to Adeline Allen, 5 July 1879, ALP, T1, box 22/44, envelope 33.
70   Diary of Adeline Allen, c. 29 September 1877 (Poynter, *Doubts and Certainties*, pp. 83–84); Freda Leeper to Alexander Leeper, 1879, ALP, T1, box 30/70; Poynter, *Doubts and Certainties*, p. 80.
71   Alexander Leeper to Adeline Allen, 5 July 1879, ALP, T1, box 22/44, envelope 44.

viable. Instead he provided her with an annual allowance of £200 that might be revoked at his discretion.[72] The money gave Adeline a degree of economic independence and made possible a range of personal comforts to which she had been accustomed. She controlled the allowance as a personal fund separate from family finances. In practice, Leeper had few qualms about asking Adeline for money and Adeline was generous in her support of the college.[73]

The allowance symbolises the central role the Allen family assumed in the evolution of the marriage. In his biography of Alexander Leeper, John Poynter observes shrewdly that the 'Warden's Lodge in Trinity often seemed a mere outpost of a family based in Sydney'.[74] It was an outpost from which Adeline frequently retreated. She spent much of the first decade of the marriage and the full-term of three of her four pregnancies with her family. Her absences from Trinity were responses to a paternal 'imperious … decree' that insisted the Sydney family home offered superior care to that available at Trinity College.[75] Adeline's ready compliance was perhaps a tad too quickly given to rule out an element of complicity. The cloistered and sometimes fractious nature of Leeper's life at Trinity College sat uneasily with her. Whatever the personal calculation, her prolonged absences, as Alexander's daily letters to Adeline testify, reduced him to the role of hapless supplicant: 'I have been living a bachelor life—I hate it'; 'Give my love to your heartless family, not one of whom bestows upon me a moment's thought'; 'I suppose by the time this reaches you, you will be a mother again'; 'I think [your mother] seems to think the baby is her own'; 'How strange it seems to have a child one has not yet seen'.[76] Scarcely a letter passes without a plaintive request for confirmation of her imminent return to Trinity College.

Paradoxically, the correspondence generated during the frequent and lengthy periods apart also provides more direct comment on the physical and sexual aspects of marriage than exists for any of the other couples. Most of what we learn comes from the pen of Alexander and

---

72   Poynter, *Doubts and Certainties*, pp. 120–21.
73   Adeline Leeper to Alexander Leeper, 25 January 1888, 3, 9, 13 February 1888, ALP, T1, box 22/51.
74   Poynter, *Doubts and Certainties*, p. 119.
75   Poynter, *Doubts and Certainties*, p. 119.
76   Alexander Leeper to Adeline Leeper, 5 March 1893, 19 July 1892, 19 March 1888, 9 August 1882, 24 April 1888, ALP, T1, box 22, box 23.

is best understood in the context of a personality that took much of its shape from a profound sense of religious guilt and a deeply ingrained hypochondria. The one fostered the perception that he possessed an excessively lustful personality, the other induced the fear that marriage would unleash passions that would, as current Victorian thinking suggested, prove physically destructive. His father had bluntly attributed the tortuous courtship of Adeline 'to the Great Victorian Sin of "self abuse"' and 'self-medication ... with oils': 'If that terrible habit had been given up to which you were so addicted your health would have been long ago restored. The quantity of <u>oil</u> you imbibed <u>increased aphrodisiac tendencies</u>, and so the flame of Onanism was fed!'[77] A recently married friend, Reverend George Wildig, advised him to '<u>get married as soon as you can</u>', and added the personal observation that 'Indulgence <u>once a night</u>' did not 'fatigue me one bit'. The 'difficulty of restraint' would disappear, he assured Leeper:

> [with] a loving and sensible wife ... keeping you from over-indulgence. The very first night of your married life you will be able to tell her ... that matrimony is weakening & she must help you to be reasonable ... regular lawful indulgence removes entirely all inclination to lustful thoughts and irregular desires ...[78]

Wildig's advice rested upon the conventional view that prevailed within the Anglican Church: the sexual relationship once sanctified by God within marriage transcended its physical dimension and assumed a spirituality that took individuals a step closer to 'selflessness'. It is in these terms that Leeper's letters to Adeline engage frequently with intimate aspects of their marriage: 'Dear, what a beautiful thing marriage is, and married love'; 'What a real glory it is to have the deep and passionate love of such a woman as you. May God make me worthy of it, and help me to sanctify myself ...'.[79] At times Leeper was moved to contemplate marriage as an eternal union:

> if you survive me, I shd like you to be happy, & I wd not have anything cause a cloud between you & any one who might be worthy of your love. I suppose in the face of such verses as 'they neither marry nor

---

77 Canon Leeper to Alexander Leeper, 18 and 19 November 1878, Poynter, *Doubts and Certainties*, p. 90.

78 George Wildig to Alexander Leeper, 28 September 1875, ALP, T5, box 38; Poynter, *Doubts and Certainties*, pp. 52–53.

79 Alexander Leeper to Adeline Leeper, 15 August 1889, 19 June 1891, ALP, T1, box 21d, box 23.

are given in marriage' one is not justified in dwelling on the thought of eternal union & yet I cannot help it. Selfish man that I am, I want you to be mine always. Is that the lower part of my nature that speaks? ... give your heart to God before you get hardened, like me, & teach the children to love God & to hate sin.[80]

There is a suggestion that Adeline did not fit the sexually repressed stereotype of the Victorian middle-class woman.[81] At the end of an evening's work in his study during one of their more lengthy separations, Leeper recreates a familiar intimate interlude:

If you had been at home you would have been up here before now. I am afraid you would have come in boldly without knocking and the chances are would have walked up to me and seated yourself on my knee and perhaps you would have kissed me ...[82]

If Adeline's absences from Trinity mitigated the worst fears of Alexander's family that he would require his wife to 'attend' on him too much, the realities of the couple's married life at Trinity fell short of their best hopes. Reviewing Leeper's retirement from Trinity College, John Poynter suggests that Leeper was 'surrounded by women who supported and deferred to him, as he had been virtually all his life'.[83] Adeline's willing embrace of a life of service to the needs of others—a capacity to withdraw to Sydney notwithstanding—exposed her to the full force of Leeper's obsessive and mercurial personality. That she did not at first appreciate his total absorption in the task of making Trinity College a truly academic institution is clear from her suggestion—made shortly before their marriage—that he might find a more congenial life by returning to teaching at Melbourne Grammar or entering the Church.[84] Trinity was his mission, not hers. By her own admission, she lacked any ambition outside family life: 'I am afraid I have led a very selfish life for a long time & have thought only of you & the children & my own happiness ... I have been content & have not looked out for opportunities that I might easily have found.'[85]

---

80 Alexander Leeper to Adeline Leeper, 15 August 1889, ALP, T1, box 21d.

81 Susan Magarey, *Passions of the First Wave Feminists*, University of New South Wales Press, Sydney, 2001, pp. 1–18.

82 Alexander Leeper to Adeline Leeper, 21 June 1891, ALP, T1, box 21d.

83 Poynter, *Doubts and Certainties*, p. 411.

84 Poynter, *Doubts and Certainties*, p. 96; Adeline Allen to Alexander Leeper, 8 September 1879, 10 September 1879, ALP, T1, box 22.

85 Adeline Leeper to Alexander Leeper, 21 July 1889, ALP, T1, box 23.

Her conception of family life was a broad one that embraced not only the interests and preoccupations of husband and children and the extended Allen family in Sydney, but also those of Alexander's ageing parents and unmarried sisters in Dublin. As the latter's circumstances became increasingly precarious in the late 1880s, Adeline contemplated bringing them to Melbourne.[86] When this proved too difficult to accomplish, she used her annual allowance to initiate a 'money scheme' that involved remittances to Alexander's parents and both sisters. It was an act that invoked surprise and familial gratitude well captured in Freda Leeper's response:

> the money scheme which I confess I only half believed in, seems an accomplished fact … I must thank you & Adeline, more especially her, on whose part it seems almost too great an act of generosity. I scarcely know whether it is right for you both to take so much from your children, but as I look on it principally for the benefit of my father and mother, I can say nothing against it …[87]

Above all else, Adeline's ready involvement in the predicaments of Alexander's parents and siblings points to a generosity of spirit and to her absorption in what might be called a colonial form of the long family, in which remittances to the old world played an important role.

Absorption in the fabric of family life and companionable self-sacrifice was thus central to Adeline's perception of her role within marriage. The fact that it was a shared perception is, ironically, perhaps most clearly evident in the prescription Alexander addressed on the eve of his marriage to Mary Moule, three years after Adeline's death:

> you know, dear Mary, that I want you to be my companion in everything—a real helpmate—not a nurse, not a drudge, not a manager, not a leading philanthropist, not a society celebrity, not a Champion of the Women's Cause (with a big C), but a sweet loving helpful equal comrade, friend, counsellor, wife and darling.[88]

---

86 Adeline Leeper to Alexander Leeper, 7 July 1889, 21 July 1889, ALP, T1, box 23.
87 Freda Leeper to Alexander Leeper, 23 August 1888, 7 July 1889, ALP, T1, box 21d, box 30.
88 Alexander Leeper to Mary Moule, 18 January 1897, ALP, T1, box 36; Poynter, *Doubts and Certainties*, p. 262.

Henry and Mary Alice Higgins: Private sanctuary—public pronouncement

Like John Macmillan Brown and Alexander Leeper, Henry Higgins married a colonial woman. Geelong born and raised, Mary Alice Morrison was part of the first Australian-born generation of the Morrison clan, a distinguished educational dynasty of Scottish migrants. Her Celtic sympathies became increasingly important to the evolution of a marriage that was built around a set of conventional, educated, middle-class understandings of gender roles and expectations. The sharply drawn separation between the domestic and public spheres of the couple's life together developed within a framework that differed in several ways from that of the other four marriages in this study: it matured within and in relation to both the patriarchal and matriarchal extended families; its establishment phase occurred without financial pressures that might serve to modify gender roles. These differences and the attitudes they encouraged were consolidated by the restriction of their family, on medical advice, to one child, and by Mary Alice's reaction to the increasingly public and often controversial nature of Henry's career. For Henry and Mary Alice Higgins home became a 'private sanctuary', and marriage a personal and emotional refuge.

The year-long European tour that followed their wedding was meticulously planned and pursued enthusiastically.[89] They returned to Melbourne in 1886 and, aided by two servants and a gardener, settled into a lifestyle of elegant simplicity that was relatively modest by the standards of the booming 1880s. The birth of their only child Mervyn, in October 1887, was a difficult one. Heeding medical advice that further pregnancies might prove dangerous, they refrained from having further children. In his biography of Henry, John Rickard speculates that from this point on, the Higgins's marriage was an entirely cerebral and emotional one.[90] Whatever the reality, there were other and more visible consequences. As we shall see when we examine the upbringing of Mervyn in Chapter 8, it led to intense emotional ties between the family of three. Conversely, it allowed a fuller development of Henry's role within the lives of his extended

---

89 Palmer, *Higgins: A Memoir*, p. 106.
90 Rickard, *H.B. Higgins*, pp. 66–67.

family. Through the lives of his parents, siblings, nieces and nephews, he created an 'intimate family life' from which, one of his nieces has written, he drew 'inspiration'.[91]

Henry Higgins and Mary Alice have left behind impressions rather than intimate details of their marriage. Where Julia Wilding, like most diarists, wrote with posterity in mind, Mary Alice sought to shut it out. She destroyed the letters Henry wrote to her every day he was on circuit as a judge.[92] They were part of a private life that she believed should remain so. She emerges from the comments of her nieces as a somewhat enigmatic figure, meticulous in her attention to the detail of household management, 'preternaturally tidy' and bound, as strongly as her husband, by a work ethic and self-discipline that was expressed in strict adherence to routine.[93] The intensity with which Mary Alice dominated the household 'frightened the Christ out of' one young niece.[94] Others were less easily intimidated and found charm, humour and strength of character in a purposeful demeanour. It is tempting to characterise her as a 'gatekeeper', a headmaster's daughter, maintaining order and decorum on the domestic front and protecting her husband from unwanted intrusions on his time. Viewed in this way, the Higgins marriage exhibits much that fits the stereotypical Victorian domestic ideal, in which Mary Alice as 'mistress of the household' fosters a private sanctuary, 'a haven from the heartless world', to which Henry could retreat and turn to his books and his family.[95]

Such a characterisation derives its form from Mary Alice's perspective. Pursued from the same vantage point, we can see, in the quest for order, decorum and sanctuary, a desire to avoid standing out conspicuously from the professional set to which they belonged. A naturally private person, she shunned the controversy and notoriety that accompanied her husband's increasing involvement in radical politics. In a letter written from London in 1914, Nettie Palmer describes her 'aunt's terror' at the prospect that Henry, who was 'going about and lunching with all sorts of radicals—Sidney Webb and such like' might 'speak

---

91   Palmer, *Higgins: A Memoir*, pp. 181, 232.
92   Rickard, *H.B. Higgins*, plate 20 caption, pp. 60, 270–71, 310–11.
93   Nancy Adams, *Family Frescoes*, F.W. Cheshire, Melbourne, 1966, p. 52; Marnie Masson's interview with John Rickard 1974, Rickard, *H.B. Higgins*, p. 128.
94   Rickard, *H.B. Higgins*, p. 60.
95   Palmer, *Higgins: A Memoir*, pp. 181, 232, 266.

out too loud about his political friends'.[96] She was unsettled by the discomfort Henry's public pronouncements engendered within the Morrison clan. It is difficult—in the absence of the correspondence that might have opened a window on the subject—to determine the extent to which the companionate nature of the marriage embraced engagement with the concerns of Henry's public life. It seems likely that Mary Alice loyally listened and supported and stuck even more resolutely to her role as gatekeeper, guardian and mother. As her niece Nettie Palmer would later put it, 'she found complete self-expression through her work in the home and for her family'.[97]

To view the Higgins's marriage as a conventional middle-class union, in which the domestic and public spheres remained rigidly separate in a manner that preserved gender roles, is to ignore the senses in which the marriage is also defined by its relations with the extended Higgins family. Doona and Killenna stood nearby each other in Malvern as reminders of an Irish past and symbols of a continuing and resilient family solidarity. Henry's success in the public sphere ensured that he remained 'de facto' head of household of the Malvern branch of the extended family. It was in this role that he and Mary Alice came face to face with the changing nature of middle-class female expectations and, to a lesser extent, those of working-class women. We may best glimpse their private exposure to these changes in the life experiences of Henry's sister Georgina Higgins. Commonly known as Ina, she was some 10 years his junior and until recently as securely hidden from history as Mary Alice, in ways which confirm the marginalisation of unmarried, middle-class women at the end of the nineteenth century.

In a study that traces the 'waves' of feminism that shaped the Australian women's movement across three generations of the Higgins family, Deborah Jordan provides a context that sharpens our appreciation of the dilemmas that confronted Ina and those like her.[98] With her younger sister Anna, Ina was amongst the first intake at the Presbyterian Ladies' College, when it opened near Melbourne's

---

96 Nettie Palmer to her mother, quoted by Rickard, *H.B. Higgins*, p. 126.
97 Palmer, *Higgins: A Memoir*, p. 8. Palmer said this of Henry's mother and it applied just as much to his wife.
98 Deborah Jordan, '"Women's Time": Ina Higgins, Nettie Palmer and Aileen Palmer', *Victorian Historical Journal*, vol. 79. no. 2, November 2008, pp. 296–312.

Fitzroy Gardens in 1875.[99] The less academically inclined of the sisters, she nevertheless went on to qualify as one of the first female landscape designers in Australia and practised intermittently.[100] She appears in a received family narrative that survives in the recollection of great niece Helen Palmer, as 'the classic unmarried stay-at-home, whose career was interrupted in order to look after the grandmother'.[101] The sketchy historical record of her life suggests other interpretations. Effectively a single woman dependent, as were others at Killenna, upon her breadwinner brother, Ina also participated in a range of collective activities that defined the middle-class women's movement of late nineteenth- and early twentieth-century Melbourne. She signed the 1891 petition for the enfranchisement of women, became secretary to the United Council for Women and, in 1899, was one of two women elected to a Board of Advice within the municipality of Malvern. She was a member of the provisional committee that established the Richmond Club for Working Girls in 1896 to help their 'less fortunate sisters'. Inspired by the example of the Collingwood Working Girls' Improvement and Recreation Club and aware of the need to avoid the stigma associated with middle-class charity, the committee sought 'cultivated, genial young women' to assist them to provide opportunities for sociability, learning and recreation that might enrich lives and engender a sense of togetherness.[102]

These excursions into public prominence might, as Deborah Jordan suggests, describe an emerging first-wave feminist.[103] They also illustrate the range of middle-class female perspectives present within the extended Higgins family. It is a diversity framed within generational and personal contexts. Anne Higgins, as ageing matriarch,

---

99   M. O. Reid, *The Ladies Who Came to Stay: A Study of the Education of Girls of the Presbyterian Ladies College, Melbourne, 1875–1960*, Council of the College, Melbourne, 1960, pp. 51, 105, 248–49; Kathleen Fitzgerald, *PLC Melbourne: The First Century, 1875–1975*, Presbyterian Ladies College, Burwood, Victoria, 1975.

100   A. P. Wizenreid, *Green Grows Our Garden: A Centenary History of Horticultural Education at Burnley*, Hyland House, Melbourne, 1991, pp. 25–30; Ina Higgins, 'Women and Horticulture', in Frances Fraser and Nettie Palmer (eds), *Centenary Gift Book*, Robertson & Mullens for The Women's Centenary Council, Melbourne, 1934, pp. 134–36.

101   H. Palmer, 'Foreword', Introduction to the proposed reprint of Nettie Palmer's *Henry Bournes Higgins*, c. 1979, cited in Jordan, '"Women's Time"', p. 308.

102   Melbourne *Argus*, 5 June 1896, p. 6. Ina Higgins was also a member of the Women's Political Association, the Women's Peace Army and a women's farm at Mordiallic that provided employment for women and distributed its produce to the unemployed and struggling working class families.

103   Jordan, '"Women's Time"', p. 297.

saw little need for women's suffrage.[104] Ina and Mary Alice, of broadly similar age, took different stands. Ina, as an unmarried young woman, secure within the extended Higgins family and keen to apply her undoubted talents in the world of work, saw the suffrage as essential to the widening of opportunities for women and as a step along the road to full female citizenship. For Mary Alice, content within her role as wife and mother, the suffrage was an admirable cause, but not a pressing one.

Historians have found paradox in the fact that Ina's brother Henry, as President of the Industrial Conciliation and Arbitration Court, defined a gendered wage system that limited women's industrial citizenship.[105] If the paradox was recognised within the Higgins households at Killenna and Doona, it was less keenly felt and merged readily with shared perceptions of the family as the basis for social betterment. The public pronouncements and judgements that form the core of Henry Higgins's judicial career say a great deal about the importance he attached to marriage and the family. Indeed, as John Rickard observes, by 'insisting that the basic wage acknowledge the worker's right to marriage and children, Higgins explicitly incorporated the institution of the family in the theory of wage regulation'.[106] His celebrated Harvester Judgement of 1907 wryly assumed marriage to be 'the usual fate of adults', and set a minimum male wage at a level thought sufficient to support a family of 'about' five (a male breadwinner, economically dependent wife and three children) in a condition of 'frugal comfort'.[107] His subsequent decisions in the Fruit-Pickers' case (1912) and the Archer case (1919), in which he set minimum wages for women in the fruit-picking and clothing industries at lower rates than those for male employees made his gendered conception of industrial citizenship explicit.[108]

---

104 Jordan, '"Women's Time"', p. 299; Jordan, *Search for an Aesthetic*, pp. 20–21.

105 Jordan, '"Women's Time"', pp. 300–1, 309–10; Mark Hearn, 'Securing the Man: Narratives of Gender', pp. 1–24, cited by Jordan.

106 Rickard, *H.B. Higgins*, p. 175.

107 Rickard, *H.B. Higgins*, pp. 61, 172–76.

108 Mark Hearn, 'Making Liberal Citizens: Justice Higgins and his Witnesses', *Labour History*, no. 93, November 2007, pp. 57–72; Joe Isaac and Stuart Macintyre (eds), *The New Province for Law and Order: One Hundred Years of Australian Industrial Conciliation and Arbitration*, Cambridge University Press, Cambridge, New York and Victoria, 2004, pp. 207–8, 220–22; Magarey, *Passions of the First Wave Feminists*, pp. 132–37.

Historians have set their discussion of these momentous decisions in a variety of contexts. Some, as Frank Bongiorno points out, see the 1907 definition of family as a recognition of the declining size of families in Australia and the wider Western world towards the end of the nineteenth century.[109] Susan Magarey, for example, writes that while it was not Higgins's intention, his ruling 'could have been understood as an incitement to family planning and contraception'.[110] For Marilyn Lake, Higgins's Harvester Judgement was the embodiment of the victory of the women's movement's domestic ideal in a sex war, beginning in the 1890s, against the forces of the unrestrained 'masculinism' of the lone, nomadic bushman celebrated in the pages of the Sydney *Bulletin*.[111] Desley Deacon sees Higgins's family wage as consistent with the 'rationalist, paternalistic masculinism' of government officials, who, in the early twentieth century, sought to create an efficient society regularised by the new 'normalising' methodology of professional experts.[112] Central to most interpretations is the notion that by enshrining the principle of the family wage in law Higgins envisaged the establishment of a social compact between male breadwinners and the state. In return for a state-guaranteed standard of living that conferred greater rights of self-governance and citizenship, the male breadwinner was expected to be a prudent, sober, thrifty, temperate, self-improving, responsible, home-loving family man and respectful husband.[113]

However we locate Higgins's wage pronouncements, and whatever historical significance we attach to them, it is not possible to treat them in isolation from his personal and generational understandings of marriage and family. Notions of gender and work were, as Erik Olssen has written in another context, 'woven into the very tissue of people's deepest emotions'.[114] The poverty of the Dublin families and the burdens borne by the wives and mothers within them that

---

109 Frank Bongiorno, *The Sex Lives of Australians: A History*, Black Inc., Melbourne, 2012, pp. 62–63.
110 Magarey, *Passions*, p. 137.
111 Lake, 'Feminism Contests the 1890s', in *Debutante Nation*, pp. 2–14; Bongiorno, *The Sex Lives of Australians*, pp. 63–64; Hearn, 'Making Liberal Citizens', pp. 58–59, 66–67.
112 Desley Deacon, 'Reorganising the Masculinist Context', in Magarey et al. (eds), *Debutante Nation*, pp. 56, 58; Hearn, 'Making Liberal Citizens', pp. 60, 62–64, 70.
113 Bongiorno, *The Sex Lives of Australians*, p. 63; Hearn, 'Making Liberal Citizens', pp. 58–59, 66–67; Lake, 'Feminism Contests the 1890s', pp. 12–14.
114 Erik Olssen, 'Working Gender, Gendering Work: Occupational Change and Continuity in Southern Dunedin 1890–1939', in Brookes et al. (eds), *Sites of Gender*, p. 64.

Higgins witnessed as a young man, while he distributed religious tracts in the slums, were firmly etched in his mind. So, too, was the memory of his own mother's struggles to cope with the demands of seven children within the genteel poverty of a Wesleyan household in the aftermath of the famine.[115] He remained acutely conscious, as his niece Nettie Palmer has written, that his mother 'stinted herself and overworked continually' to ensure that her children did not know want or hunger.[116] Migration and establishing the family in Melbourne drew Henry, as eldest son, more and more into the role of de facto head of household and cemented a strong emotional bonding between them.

What family experience suggested, theoretical opinion endorsed. In essence, building on the views of the major enlightenment thinkers and the writings of John Stuart Mill, Higgins sought to protect married women from the burdens and degradations of paid employment, which he believed diminished a civilised society, and at the same time provide a buffer against poverty. He brought to the role of industrial arbiter the belief that 'the main impulse in the movement for better wages comes from the wonderful family instinct, the desire of parents to build up sound, sane, and well-nourished children'.[117] His view of the family unit as a fulcrum for social progress and individual fulfilment is made clear in *A New Province for Law and Order*:

> Give them relief from their materialistic anxiety; give them reasonable certainty that their essential material needs will be met by honest work, and you release infinite stores of human energy for higher efforts, for nobler ideals, when 'Body gets its sop, and holds its noise, and leaves soul free a little'.[118]

His recognition of what he called the 'problem of female labour', and his choice to set a basic wage for women that was equal to that of men only where men and women were carrying out the same work, has been variously characterised by historians. Rickard warned against 'applying the standards of today to decisions made in 1907–1912'.[119] Hearn has dismissed the implication that Higgins 'simply reflected

---

115 Palmer, *Higgins: A Memoir*, pp. 8, 22, 42.
116 Palmer, *Higgins: A Memoir*, p. 22.
117 Rickard, *H.B. Higgins*, p. 176.
118 Henry Bournes Higgins, *A New Province For Law & Order*, Constable & Company, London and Sydney, 1922, p. 38.
119 Rickard, *H.B. Higgins*, p. 177.

community values and standards' and 'imposed' a 'gendered liberal governance'.[120] Whether or not that was out of line with community opinion, it was a view that was perfectly consistent with the views on gender roles within marriage and family that prevailed at Killenna and Doona.

Frederick and Julia Wilding: Marriage and the ideal family

Julia and Frederick Wilding's marriage lasted for over 50 years, ending in 1936, when they were parted by death. On the face of it, their marriage was based upon a division of labour that reflected middle-class social norms. Within this apparent conventionality, they built a companionate marriage around an idealised conception of the family. Put simply, as 'joint heads of household' they sought to create an environment in which individual talent might flourish. The path to this end required, as they saw it, a marriage in which prevailing gender roles were not so much challenged as modified in rational ways that shrugged off the stereotypical Victorian romantic ideal with its concomitant truncating of individual potential. Their companionate marriage was thus shaped within understandings of society that were both idealistic and pragmatic.

The picture that emerges of the Wildings' marriage is gleaned from sources generated, for the most part, by Julia. Before her departure for New Zealand she had written articles for the *Hereford Times* about marriage, childrearing and the women's movement. As a wife and mother she created a detailed record of family life in the pages of household management diaries, events diaries, visitor books and the life events diaries she kept for each of her five surviving children. Julia was also keeper of correspondence and archivist of the public record of family activities. While she rarely comments directly upon her own marriage, it is possible to construct, from what she has left us, the texture of married life within the Wilding household. The fact that the processes and thinking involved in raising children are the

---

120 Hearn, 'Making Liberal Citizens', pp. 65, 59.

most thoroughly documented element of their lives reflects the focus of their marriage. Furthermore, it also makes it possible to gain an understanding of Frederick as father and husband.

Marriage and migration were for the Wildings inextricably linked. Details surrounding their engagement are sketchy, though it was likely to have been a lengthy one, given middle-class beliefs about the necessity of securing a firm economic basis for a comfortable life and the appropriate education of children prior to marriage. Julia argued in an article on 'Marriage' in the *Hereford Times* that:

> While the intrusion of sordid or worldly motives in the contemplation of marriage is justly regarded as despicable and wrong, so also are the contractions of such unions, when the means are not within reach of living comfortably and properly bringing up and educating a family, recognised as not only weak but also wicked.[121]

The only direct comments we have from Frederick about his impending marriage were expressed in the formal and conventional terms in which public farewells were conducted. 'Bound up with my fate in the long expedition which I am about to take', he told a gathering of Hereford Liberals on the eve of his wedding day, 'is the happiness of one who is dearer to me than I know how to express ... Tomorrow I know will be the happiest [day of my life].'

If we leap forward 18 years, we glimpse 44-year-old Julia, soon after the birth her sixth child, reflecting ecstatically upon her role as wife and mother. In a note to herself that she sealed in an envelope to be opened on her 70th birthday she wrote:

> Oh the joy of love and the joy of Life when one has love, full and brimming over. Is it possible to imagine greater happiness than the joy and love of motherhood, interwoven with, and inseparable from the love of husband and father? Here I am sitting at our bedroom window with our darling new baby Edwyn in his cot close by, ten days old, and the fruit trees in full blossom outside, the sun shining, and the breath and scent of spring coming in at the open window,— and I feel almost *too* happy. Our other darlings will be in soon,—my wise and beloved Gladys, who is already a comfort and a help to me,— my sturdy old Anthony, who although rather self-willed and difficult sometimes now, will I know grow up into a noble man—Franky wum,

---

121 Julia Anthony, 'Marriage', *HT*, 7 November 1874, p. 18.

still my little sunbeam,—and last but not least my sweet loving little Cora. How I love and worship them all, and how the love of them makes the world all bright and radiant. God grant my love of them may not make me selfish and lead me to think—not too much of them, that could not be—but not enough of others ... The future however lies in the laps of the Gods, and I will not go forward and anticipate disappointment, but make the most of my present happiness. My one prayer though is that my darlings, Gladys and Cora, may some day meet good true men, who will make them good husbands. A woman has not lived who does not know what it is to be a happy wife and mother.[122]

Her sense of personal fulfilment within domestic and family life embraced a conception of women's place in society that prized freedom of choice: marriage and motherhood should ideally be one pathway among the many that should be available to all women.

Julia Wilding's article on marriage was, as noted, one of a series of articles she wrote for the *Hereford Times* during the 1870s on the position of women in society. It drew heavily upon John Stuart Mill's *The Subjection of Women* (1869), described recently by Barbara Caine as 'one of the most searing and critical pictures of marriage to emerge in the nineteenth century'.[123] Julia, however, constructed her article around what she described as, 'Mill's beautiful passage on the ideal of marriage':

What marriage may be in the case of two persons of cultivated faculties, identical in opinions and purposes, between whom there exists that best kind of equality, similarity of powers and capacities with reciprocal superiority in them—so that each can enjoy the luxury of looking up to the other, and can have alternately the pleasure of leading and of being led in the path of development—I will not attempt to describe ... this only, is the ideal of marriage.[124]

122 Note by Julia Wilding, 8 October 1897, Cora Wilding Papers, Macmillan Brown Library, University of Canterbury, MB 183, Family and Personal Correspondence, box 4.1.
123 Barbara Caine, *English Feminism 1780–1980*, Oxford University Press, Oxford, 1997, p. 104.
124 John Stuart Mill, *The Subjection of Women* (1869), in Alice S. Rossi (ed.), John Stuart Mill and Harriet Taylor Mill: *Essays on Sex Equality (with an introductory essay by Alice S. Rossi)*, University of Chicago Press, Chicago and London, 1970, p. 235, quoted by Julia Anthony, 'Marriage'.

As she saw it, the institution of marriage amongst the middle classes was currently imprisoned within two older ideals: 'the ivy twining round the oak—the beautiful and helpless woman supported by the intellectually and physically strong man—or again the pattern housewife, who only appears to a studious husband in the light of a pleasant companion to while away his leisure moments'.[125] Abandoning these older ideals was necessary, because, she told her readers, quoting Mill: 'The moral regeneration of mankind will only really commence, when the most fundamental of the social relations is placed under the rule of equal justice, and when human beings learn to cultivate their strongest sympathy with an equal in rights and in cultivation.'[126]

Evolution towards the new ideal was already, she believed, taking place, but needed to be given a nudge. Education for women that matched that available to men held the key. It would pave the way for the removal of the legal disabilities that allowed the will of tyrannical husbands to prevail within marriage. Better education would also allow more women to become 'helpmates to men in the highest sense' and diminish the number of wives whose narrow domestic interests frequently dragged their better-educated husband down, so that he became 'a purely domestic man, with no interests or ambition beyond his own hearth and calling'.[127] Thus, by cultivating the full potential of women, the ideal marriage that Julia envisaged provided a means of improving individuals and the communities to which they belonged: 'the world might be a little better, its aims and rule of life a little higher, if this picture of marriage were universally accepted as the ideal one, and if people would strive to mould their aspirations after some such example'.[128] To those who may have struggled to accept such a shift in the place of women within marriage, she offered the reassurance that the 'call[ing] into play of not only the physical and emotional, but also the intellectual and higher faculties of our nature' would result 'not in the destruction, but the ennobling and exalting of all that is best and most sacred in the marriage tie'.[129]

---

125 Julia Anthony, 'Marriage'.
126 John Stuart Mill, *The Subjection of Women*, in Rossi (ed.), *Essays on Sex Equality*, p. 236; Julia Anthony, 'Marriage'.
127 Julia Anthony, 'Marriage'.
128 Julia Anthony, 'Marriage'.
129 Julia Anthony, 'Marriage'.

The young Julia's public comments on marriage make fleeting mention of the 'physical bonds of marriage' and tread warily around the issues raised by John Stuart Mill's unconventional union with Harriet Taylor.[130] The pair had married in 1852 after a 20-year-long intimate intellectual and spiritual relationship, while Taylor remained with her husband John Taylor. Mill's autobiography, published in 1873, depicts his marriage with Harriet and their prior relationship as an ideal one—a purely cerebral and spiritual union, in which baser animal instincts had been overcome. Most historians accept that it was a sexless union. The Mills, it seems, would hardly have found this goal difficult to achieve: John Stuart Mill's friend and biographer Alexander Bain was of the opinion that 'in the so-called sensual feelings, he was below average'; Harriet Taylor viewed the early years of her marriage to John Taylor as ones of sexual slavery, and, after the birth of their third child, insisted that she and Taylor abstain permanently.[131] Mill came to view the average marriage as a form of enslavement of women, sexual and otherwise. On the eve of his marriage to Harriet Taylor, he therefore renounced in writing all legal rights over Harriet Taylor that marriage would bestow upon him as her husband, and proceeded, in the eyes of his contemporaries, to allow Harriet to dominate him.[132] Phyllis Rose, in *Parallel Lives* (1984), suggests that Mill's behaviour towards his wife was a form of atonement for the collective crimes of a patriarchal society against women.[133] It is unclear if Julia shared Mill's vision of an ideal marriage as a non-sexual relationship. Her conventional public reticence on the subject did not mean, as we shall see later, that the marriage partnership she envisaged skirted the issue of sexual equality.

Similarly, within her *Hereford Times* articles, she does not address in any detail the issue of whether married women, and particularly mothers, should take paid employment. In general she followed Mill's arguments; she does not, however, seem to have fully shared his conviction that adding paid employment to a married woman's duties in the home was a form of cruelty, a distraction from her maternal role

---

130 Julia Anthony, 'Marriage'.
131 Phyllis Rose, *Parallel Lives: Five Victorian Marriages*, Alfred A. Knopf, New York, 1984, pp. 123, 109–11.
132 Rose, *Parallel Lives*, pp. 119–20.
133 Rose, *Parallel Lives*, pp. 135–37, 140.

within the family and devoid of any compensating benefit.[134] Her views on contemporary calls for legislation to prevent mothers working were derived instead from her elder brother Charles Anthony's *The Social and Political Dependence of Women*.[135] Published in 1867, before Mill's essay on marriage and heavily dependent upon the less cautious Harriet Taylor Mill's essay on the *Enfranchisement of Women*, it argued that legislation was both undesirable, in that it would restrict personal choice, and unnecessary, insofar as 'natural laws' would deal with any individual instances of incompatibility between women's paid employment and their responsibilities as mothers.[136]

Thus it was that the Wildings left Britain with a set of idealistic expectations of marriage, tied to Mill's conception of the family. As they envisaged their new domestic world, it would become 'a school of sympathy in equality, of living together in love, without power on one side or obedience on the other'.[137] In a variety of ways the migratory experience and the need to build anew facilitated, indeed demanded, more active partnership within marriage. The process of establishing themselves on their small farmlet on the outskirts of urban Christchurch took place within a context that facilitated a sharing of responsibility and placed a premium upon the useful rather than the decorative wife. 'His and her' spheres were blurred and power and authority more evenly distributed between them than either would have experienced in Hereford. The process undoubtedly derived some of its dynamic from the fact that Julia brought a remittance from her father to the first few years of the marriage. As a productive unit, Fownhope, with its vegetable garden, orchard, hens, dairy cows and horses, met the needs of the household and generated income. In its daily operation Julia found abundant opportunities to make herself

---

134 John Stuart Mill, *Subjection of Women*, in Rossi (ed.), *Essays on Sex Equality*, pp. 178–79; Rossi, 'Sentiment and Intellect: The Story of John Stuart Mill and Harriet Taylor Mill' (introductory essay), in Rossi (ed.), *Essays on Sex Equality*, p. 23; Caine, *English Feminism*, pp. 105–6.
135 Charles Anthony, jnr., *Social and Political Dependence*.
136 Julia Anthony, 'Suffrage', *HT*, 15 February 1873.
137 John Stuart Mill, *Subjection of Women*, in Rossi (ed.), *Essays On Sex Equality*, p. 175.

useful—tending to the hens and selling their eggs, working in the orchard and churning butter.[138] The farmlet was a site, moreover, where she and Frederick frequently worked alongside each other.

If necessity and colonial circumstance played a part in shaping the partnership that flourished in this domestic environment, developing a professional career determined a broadly traditional division of household labour. Julia was never to take on paid employment away from the home, while Frederick's legal career took him into the public domain, and the separation of his study from the rest of the household tended to reinforce the division.[139] Yet he wore the role of breadwinner lightly. Matters of household management were left to Julia, and the meticulous and methodical recording of financial details, household budgeting and domestic routines indicate that she took her responsibilities seriously, and that, in the prosecution of them, she became an unchallenged joint–head of household. Indeed the quiet sense of satisfaction evident in her discussion of them suggests that the role satisfied her quest to feel and be useful.

It is, as we shall see in the chapters that follow, in the nurturing of their children that Julia and Frederick's marriage most clearly exhibits its idealism. Their approach was grounded in John Stuart Mill's assertion that 'what is now called the nature of women is an eminently artificial thing'—a social construction—and that women could be men's equals in ability and accomplishment.[140] But they would cease to be 'decorative and dependent creatures' only when 'little girls were brought up in exactly the same fashion as little boys'.[141] The dictum carried with it the implication that within the family greater paternal involvement in the education of children would be a necessary precondition of change. It was an implication that the Wildings embraced. They jointly

---

138 This is an oblique reference to English middle-class migrant Jane Maria Atkinson's comment that in her new colonial New Zealand home, where servants were in short supply, she took delight in performing household chores, as it made her feel useful for the first time in her life. See Frances Porter, *Born to New Zealand: A Biography of Jane Maria Atkinson*, Allen & Unwin and Port Nicholson Press, Wellington, 1989, pp. 61–63. See also Raewyn Dalziel's classic article, 'The Colonial Helpmeet: Women's Role and the Vote in Nineteeth-Century New Zealand', *NZJH*, vol. 11, no. 2, 1977, pp. 112–23.

139 Tosh, *A Man's Place*, pp. 16–17, 21, 60, 182.

140 John Stuart Mill, *Subjection of Women*, in Rossi (ed.), *Essays on Sex Equality*, p. 148.

141 Rose, *Parallel Lives*, p. 136; Rossi, 'Sentiment and Intellect', in *Essays On Sex Equality*, pp. 59–60; John Stuart Mill, *Subjection of Women*, in Rossi (ed.), *Essays On Sex Quality*, pp. 141, 154–55, 148, 168, 181, 182, 190, 202, 218–23.

endeavoured to give their sons and daughters similar upbringings, including a general education that would encourage individual talent and inculcate the values of useful citizenship. This, they believed, would provide one of the many building blocks needed to promote social cohesion and progress.

The introduction to this chapter suggested that the understandings which supported the marriages discussed might be placed somewhere in the gap between the thinking of John Ruskin and John Stuart Mill. Each of the five couples envisaged marriage in ways that reflected a variety of idealistic positions. All imagined a future that could be made better by educated families and which cast aside male dominance. Each couple believed they had constructed a form of liberal partnership within their marriage. Whatever their specific nature, with only the one exception, they conformed to the conventional marriage partnership that was built around a male breadwinner. Helen Connon and John Macmillan Brown's attempt for some six years to sustain a marriage within a relationship that embraced occupational equality stands apart from the others. Whatever the individual and idiosyncratic elements of the difficulties they faced, the ultimate failure of their experiment underlines the dilemmas faced by middle-class men and women who attempted to break with the conventions of their day.

6

Educating Daughters: The Christchurch Girls

The next two chapters explore the extent to which four professional families (two in Christchurch, two in Melbourne) provided childhood environments for their daughters that embraced the objectives of the women's movement for educational equality and the broadening of opportunities for young women. University degrees and the pursuit of careers became central to conceptions of the 'New Woman' that emerged in the last decades of the nineteenth century. The family studies are presented in an order that proceeds from an uncompromising endorsement of the 'new', through purposeful commitment to change, to a hesitancy about discarding traditional attitudes to women's place in society. The location and style in which the girls were educated—whether, more traditionally, within the home by parents and governesses, or at private schools and later at university—may have varied, yet the precise mix of ideas, circumstance and family dynamics at work within each example can nonetheless be shown to rest upon a common desire to provide an education for girls that cast aside 'mere accomplishments'. The two New Zealand families (the Macmillan Browns and the Wildings) are the frontrunners and the Melbourne families (the Leepers and the Massons) the comparative laggards. Whether this was in part indicative of significant differences in the social contexts of Melbourne and Christchurch is a matter pursued elsewhere.[1] At this point, it is perhaps sufficient to observe

---

1   Chambers, *Lessons for Ladies*, pp. 95, 105–6.

that those at the forefront of the push for change in Christchurch believed themselves to occupy a time and place of special opportunity, and that historians subsequently have endorsed this sense of historical moment. The following chapter on the Christchurch girls makes considerable use of the relatively rich primary sources available to reveal the intense nature of the mother–daughter relationships that develop within each family.

The Macmillan Brown Girls: A prison of expectations?

Millicent and Viola Macmillan Brown spent most of their childhood and young adulthood within the comparatively sheltered environment of the family home. Theirs was an upbringing shot through with apparent contradictions. Despite both of her parents being prominent figures in New Zealand's public education system, Millicent did not attend a school until she was 12, and then only briefly, and Viola's education occurred similarly, for the most part, within the confines of the family.[2] Although both John and Helen Macmillan Brown endorsed the image of the strong, independent career woman, they proved in some ways to be overprotective parents. Furthermore, while a school-based education for girls was regarded by many as progressive, the Macmillan Browns favoured a sheltered home-based education for their daughters, isolated from the pressure of competition with their peers. Parenthood allowed the couple to put their beliefs about the desirability of individual tuition and relative freedom in early childhood into practice. Public examinations at the culmination of Millicent and Viola's education would test the success of their educational theories.

The site of this educational experiment, the Macmillan Browns' family home, Holmbank, was a relatively plainly designed eight-roomed wooden structure, set within five acres of garden, and woodland running down to a stream and boathouse. Rustic in appearance, the property contained cows, hens, pigs and horses,

---

2   According to New Zealand census figures, in 1881 4,143 girls were taught at home, out of a total population of 62,356 girls aged 5 to 15. The corresponding figures for 1896 are 3,596 out of 84,881. See 'Attendance at Schools—Increase 1871–1896 and Proportion to Population (5–15) Years', Table VIII, *Census, April 1896—Education of the People*, p. 268.

as well as a large vegetable garden and a small dairy. The interior of the house, more functional and comfortable than fashionable in style, presented a cultured appearance, with books spilling out of John Macmillan Brown's library to line the walls of the staircase and hallway, paintings of Italian scenes adorning the walls and ceramic tiles depicting Shakespearian plays framing a fireplace.[3] The running of the household and property was in the hands of at least two live-in servants: a general domestic/cook and a nursemaid or governess as the age of the children dictated, and a gardener and odd-jobs man who came to the house daily.[4]

As the previous chapter suggests, any assessment of the education of the Macmillan Brown daughters needs to acknowledge the unique features of their parents' marriage and the process of idealisation, which had already begun to attach itself to Helen Connon before her children were born. John Macmillan Brown was plainly the dominant influence in Helen Connon's rise to academic prominence. He personally smoothed the way for her admission to university study, nurtured the university career that culminated in her becoming the first woman to earn an MA with first-class honours in the British Empire, assisted her passage to the principalship at Christchurch Girls' High School and championed her as a reforming headmistress. Indeed, it could be said that the idealisation of Helen Connon as a path breaker owes much to his persistent advocacy. Inevitably, their marriage was celebrated as embodying the new ideal—a professional, working couple. The template for the education of Millicent and Viola had been fashioned. They would be raised in the image of their mother. University degrees beckoned from the day they were born.

It would be possible to see in the Macmillan Brown household a replication of the family life pattern prevalent within the upper-middle-class British society.[5] As a professional couple, neither Helen nor John involved themselves in the domestic labour of the family home. John worked at his hobby of gardening for an hour every

---

3   Grossmann, *Life of Helen Macmillan Brown*, pp. 47–48; Macmillan Brown, *Memoirs*, p. 181; Baxter, *Memoirs*, pp. 16–17; Lovell-Smith, *Easily the Best*, pp. 60–61.

4   Baxter, *Memoirs*, pp. 16–17, 24; Macmillan Brown, *Memoirs*, pp. 180–82; Lovell-Smith, *Easily the Best*, p. 61; 'Diary of Millicent Amiel Brown from 8 Jan. 1888 [to 6 September 1889]', JMBP, A11/13.

5   Gathorne-Hardy, *The Rise and Fall of the British Nanny*, pp. 64–70; Lovell-Smith, *Easily the Best*, pp. 65–66, 84.

morning before work; Helen supervised her servants and, while her early childhood experiences equipped her with domestic skills, she rarely worked alongside them. In her *Memoirs*, Millicent remembers the novelty of her mother once mowing the lawn and watching her on another occasion as she skimmed cream off milk in the dairy.[6] Difficulties in finding servants, as in 1902 after the family returned from a two-year period in Europe, left mother and daughter no option but to run the household themselves at times.[7] For the most part, however, the Macmillan Browns' daily domestic needs were taken care of by others. Millicent could thus justly claim later that she did nothing for herself while growing up.[8] Such an environment involved a considerable degree of separation of children from parents in their daily lives. In this it bore some resemblance to domestic practices prevalent within upper middle-class British society.[9] Equally, it may be seen as reflecting the intensity of both parents' academic careers, set out in the previous chapter, which ensured that there was no separation of work and home. Holmbank was a place of work and study, and this was to have significant consequences for the functioning of the household and the childhood of Millicent and Viola.

Nothing captures the philosophy upon which the academic reproduction of their daughters was based better than Grossmann's recollection of a conversation with Helen Connon, before she was married, on the place of accomplishments in a young girl's education:

> She once said to me with girlish warmth that she thought it vulgar and foolish for girls to learn accomplishments when they had only a miserable stock of general knowledge; it was like putting on jewellery over a ragged dress. Scholarship came first with her; the knowledge of languages, science, history, mathematics, and the rest might follow.[10]

---

6   Macmillan Brown, *Memoirs*, p. 186; Viola Helen Notariello's introduction to Macmillan Brown, *Memoirs*, p.xxvi; Baxter, *Memoirs*, p. 17.

7   Mrs Robert Craig to 'My Dear Sister' (Helen Macmillan Brown), 8 May 1902, JMBP, A19/7; Pata to Helen Macmillan Brown, 25 April [1902], JMBP, A19/10. On problems finding servants in New Zealand, see, for example, Charlotte Macdonald, 'Strangers at the Hearth: The Eclipse of Domestic Service in New Zealand Homes c 1830s–1940s', in Barbara Brookes (ed.), *At Home in New Zealand: History, Houses, People*, Bridget Williams Books, Wellington, 2000, pp. 41–56.

8   Lovell-Smith interview with Patricia Lawson, 5 March 2001, Lovell-Smith, *Easily the Best*, p. 84.

9   Lovell-Smith, *Easily the Best*, pp. 65–66, 84. Millicent and Viola Macmillan Brown did not have their meals with their parents.

10   Grossmann, *Life of Helen Macmillan Brown*, p. 35.

The danger that this firmly held and rigorously pursued educational philosophy might become a 'prison of expectations' within the family setting was an obvious and real one.[11] John Macmillan Brown's views on the role of the family in education are set out in *Modern Education* (1908). He describes the 'colonial family' as 'a helmless ship' that was 'often lax and unorganised' and as having a deleterious effect upon the 'character and career' of the nation's children. The home, he believed, needed to be 're-organise[d]' on a 'more deliberate and intelligent basis'.[12] The childhoods constructed at Holmbank for Millicent and Viola provided exemplars of the dictum. During the day the household operated as something of a microcosm of a girls' school, supervised by the principal/mother, and staffed by a governess and other educational experts as required. Until John Macmillan Brown returned from his 16-hour days at Canterbury College, it was also a female sanctuary.[13] As we shall see, however, his educational views provided the overarching framework within which the childhoods of Millicent and Viola unfolded.

The dominating presence of John Macmillan Brown at Holmbank is best illustrated by the regular Sunday morning breakfasts that he hosted for male students. Less social occasions than a further teaching and mentoring opportunity, which he saw as his duty to provide, they often developed into intense academic and philosophical discussions. Indeed, Sundays typically brought a steady stream of visitors to Holmbank, mainly Macmillan Brown's friends, fellow educationalists and men at the forefront of public and civic affairs.[14] At these times, his energetic and egocentric personality dominated all others, and the contrast of father and mother in the household was at its sharpest. In the introduction to her father's *Memoirs* (1974), Millicent described the gatherings as 'rather a strain'.[15] Whatever impact these comings and goings and the associated discussion had upon the young Millicent and Viola at the time and later, they stand as a reminder of where the controlling influence lay at Holmbank.

---

11   The phrase 'prison of expectations' comes from Mintz, *A Prison of Expectations*.

12   Macmillan Brown, *Modern Education*, pp. 8–9.

13   Macmillan Brown, *Memoirs*, p. 112.

14   Macmillan Brown, *Memoirs*, pp. 183–84; Viola Helen Notariello's introduction to Macmillan Brown's *Memoirs*, pp. xxviii–xxix.

15   Millicent Baxter's introduction to Macmillan Brown's *Memoirs*, pp. xviii–xix.

For the first six years of Millicent Macmillan Brown's life, both parents were largely absent from the home during the day, and she was left in the care and instruction of others. Yet they retained complete intellectual control of her upbringing, designing a program for her that they left others to implement. Millicent was born on 8 January 1888, during the Christchurch Girls' High School summer break. Three weeks later her mother Helen resumed her full-time position as principal of the school, a post she retained until 1894.[16] Our knowledge of the childcare arrangements for Millicent's infancy rests upon a single diary of uncertain authorship, which records the first 20 months of her life.[17] Close scrutiny of the handwriting, however, suggests that it was most likely Helen who kept the diary, and that in doing so she employed the third person as a literary device, so as to provide a more scientific tone to her observations.[18] Whoever the diarist was, the entries are plainly the work of a person of intelligence and literary ability, well versed in the developmental stages of infancy. It is abundantly clear from the diary that the overall control of Millicent's care was not relinquished by her parents to the nursing staff to whom she was entrusted; Helen remained firmly and actively in the director's seat. Indeed, in the supervision of her daughter's infant care, as inferred by her biographers, she seems to have adopted the same thoroughness and insistence upon 'absolute control' that she demanded as principal of Christchurch Girls' High School.[19]

The diary entries reflect the trend towards the scientific observation of infants and children stimulated by the example of evolutionist Charles Darwin and educationalists in nineteenth-century Britain and

---

16   Baxter, *Memoirs*, p. 16. Edith Grossmann claims that Millicent was named after a philosophic journal that her parents were reading in the period before her birth, Grossmann, *Life of Helen Macmillan Brown*, p. 48.

17   'Diary of Millicent Amiel Brown', JMBP.

18   Lovell-Smith, *Easily the Best*, pp. 63–64, concluded that neither Helen nor her sister Maria Connon, who was living at Holmbank at the time, could have written the diary as they were both referred to in the third person and were largely absent from the household during weekdays. Yet the handwriting seems to be that of Helen Macmillan Brown, and the diary entries at times bear the tone of a second-hand witness reporting on the events of the day. For example the entry for 20 February 1888: [Millicent] 'Is reported to have smiled a great deal today & to have clapped her hands.'

19   Grossmann, *Life of Helen Macmillan Brown*, pp. 38, 48–50; Lovell-Smith, *Easily the Best*, pp. 53, 66, 88–91.

Europe.[20] Though mainly brief, irregular and often retrospective, they record Millicent's physical, intellectual and social development and offer glimpses of the intensity of the interaction between Helen and individual caregivers. Millicent's physical care is left to her nurse. Helen is said to have bathed her once.[21] John Macmillan Brown emerges as a rather impatient father, who was irritated by the practical details of infant care and shielded from it as much as possible: 'the baby's father was rather annoyed at being kept a very few minutes outside Stranges whilst three bonnets were being selected to be sent home for the baby's approval';[22] 'her father has gone to the Senate today & we are going to try to do a great deal of Baby's sewing when he is away'.[23]

The involvement of both parents becomes increasingly apparent in entries that deal with the more explicitly cerebral aspects of Millicent's infant development.

> Baby has been progressing satisfactorily during the last few days— she says 'Agu' very often now. Five days ago we played the piano to see how it affected her—its effect was most marked—she smiled & went on cooing to herself nearly all the time & a melancholy air made her melancholy—the same thing has happened every time we tried her ...

> Baby for a long time has known nearly everything said to her.— For the last six weeks she has been able to say rhymes repeating them after they are said to her, for last two months has been able to say her letters after us.[24]

As Millicent moves into her second year and her motor and verbal skills develop, so her engagement with her father increases: 'She now for the last two months runs out of the library when her dada comes home from "leckshure" & helps him to take off his "coatee" then she pulls off his boots tugging at the tags & expecting the "tockings"

---

20 Tosh, *A Man's Place*, p. 43; Paul Mussen, John Conger and Jerome Kagan, *Child Development and Personality*, 4th edn, Harper Row Publishers, New York, 1974, p. 4; Elizabeth Gaskell, *My Diary: The Early Years of My Daughter Marianne (1835–38)*, Clement Shorter, London, 1923; Harriet Blodgett (ed.), *The Englishwoman's Diary: An Anthology*, Fourth Estate, London, 1992, pp. 315–16; Alison MacKinnon, *The New Women: Adelaide's Early Women Graduates*, Wakefield Press, Netley, South Adelaide, 1986, pp. 99–113; Selleck, *Finding Home*, p. 11.
21 Diary of Millicent Amiel Brown, 18 February 1888.
22 Diary of Millicent Amiel Brown, 18 February 1888; Lovell-Smith, *Easily the Best*, pp. 63–64.
23 Diary of Millicent Amiel Brown, 29 February 1888.
24 Diary of Millicent Amiel Brown, 29 February 1888, 6 September 1888.

to come off too.'[25] Significantly, the last entry in the diary provides an assessment of Millicent's intellectual development and indicates increasing parental scrutiny:

> During her second year she has not been so placid as in her 1st year. She has developed great liveliness and restlessness but she has always been very good … She speaks most articulately—the only sound she avoids are f & v & r at the beginning of words though she does not mind f & v in the middle of words—too she does not care for though she uses it sometimes … She has never had any childish ailments & is very strong & healthy—she is very fair with a very delicate though healthy complexion … she is still out nearly all day & generally has two sleeps a day inside in her perambulator. Her food at present is Nestle milk & bread, sago, porridge … She is very fond of having 'penkill' (pencil) & of 'yiting' (writing) …[26]

Millicent had passed from infancy to childhood and her care now moved even more firmly into the hands of her parents. From this point, we must reconstruct her childhood from more disparate sources. The dominant voice in the surviving testimony, as it is for the family history more generally, is John Macmillan Brown. As a public intellectual at the forefront of educational debate, his views of education shaped the form and substance of Millicent and later Viola's education. To balance his accounts, we rely upon fragments of family correspondence and the published reminiscences of family and friends. In sum, these sources provide some assessment of what may be seen as an attempt to put a set of educational precepts into practice. With these caveats in mind, we can identify three major stages in Millicent's educational development: from infancy until the age of eight; a second phase that ends with the death of her mother in 1903, when Millicent was 15 years of age; and a final phase that is dominated by preparation for university study.

In the first of these stages, marking the passage from infancy to childhood, we see the Macmillan Browns give full rein to their educational idealism. It was a time of free or semi-directed play in the home environment, in which formal teaching was minimised and adult involvement confined to the superintending of activities that fired the imagination. The key to success in education during this early phase

---

25 Diary of Millicent Amiel Brown, 6 September 1888.
26 Diary of Millicent Amiel Brown, 6 September 1888.

was, in Macmillan Brown's view, 'ever-changing variety' and 'never-failing cheerfulness'. This methodology included providing suitable toys, stimulating manual dexterity by encouraging the cutting of paper patterns, and promoting physical activities, such as skipping and dance to develop rhythm and balance. The greatest adult involvement, and clearly the most valued by the Macmillan Browns, was the reading of imaginative stories to Millicent. It was in this area that John Macmillan Brown made his most significant contribution to Millicent's childhood. He was to read her traditional children's stories, 'especially fairy stories', and invented his own fantastic tales, believing the use of the imagination to be critical to the mental and moral development of the young.[27] In Millicent, he found a responsive listener and mimic: 'I used to tell stories to myself all the time.'[28]

The idealised childhood that the Macmillan Browns sought to provide for Millicent depended ultimately upon their ability to arrange and oversee the daily care they entrusted to others. It also depended upon the availability of highly educated governesses.[29] In this, as in much else, the Macmillan Browns reveal attitudes to the family and to children that were a mixture of traditional and modern. They saw the family and the home (in its ideal state) as providing the most secure and desirable environment for the nurturing of the young and chose not to enrol Millicent in kindergartens available in the city.[30] They also accepted that the care and early development of the very young was best provided by women. As John Macmillan Brown put it, women possessed a 'rich equipment of emotions and instincts' that sensitised them to the needs of children.[31] And when the Macmillan Browns sought caregivers for Millicent, they drew upon the small group of young women endeavouring to make their way through to university. Helen had taught them at Christchurch Girls' High School and had

---

27 Macmillan Brown, *Modern Education*, pp. 24, 23–28; Grossmann, *Life of Helen Macmillan Brown*, pp. 48–50.

28 Baxter, *Memoirs*, p. 18; Violet Helen Notariello's introduction to Macmillan Brown's *Memoirs*, pp. xxvi–xxvii.

29 According to Coral Chambers, *Lessons for Ladies*, p. 73, one in six women teaching in New Zealand in 1891 was a governess.

30 The Macmillan Brown's educational philosophy was influenced in part by Rousseau's romantic idea of the child and the need for a secluded 'playground for children beyond the reach of the adult world', and Friedrich Fröbel's Kindergarten system. They shared the developing nineteenth-century respect for the individuality and the spontaneity of the child. See Tosh, *A Man's Place*, pp. 29, 39–42, 86–87, 91–92.

31 Macmillan Brown, *Modern Education*, p. 23.

involved herself closely in easing their passage into higher education. Janet Prosser, who became Millicent's governess in 1894, was taught by Helen from 1882 and won a junior university scholarship in 1888. Gertrude Boulton, whom Helen first knew as a neighbour in Avonside, was another former pupil and university student to act as governess at Holmbank. When the Macmillan Browns visited England and Europe in 1892, it was Helen's sister, Maria Connon, a 23-year-old Canterbury College student, who ran the household, took responsibility for Millicent's development and organised tutors in areas where she felt her training was inadequate. Maria's education had been closely moulded by Helen, and it is difficult to imagine that Millicent would have noticed any change in the routines and practices that prevailed at Holmbank. Organised spontaneity was in the hands of a family of professionals determined to provide the ideal childhood.

In 1894, 37-year-old Helen Connon retired from Christchurch Girls' High School, plagued by chronic insomnia. Did she become the headmistress of the household? There can be no doubt that her greater presence in the home coincides with a major shift in Millicent's childhood experience. Six years of age and judged by her parents as being ready for more formal lessons, her day now made room for the inculcation of routines expected to carry through to adulthood. It began with an early morning walk with her mother and was followed by two hours of tuition from Helen in French, spelling, Latin and, initially, music. A governess, Janet Prosser, taught her 'other subjects', including science.[32] Thoughts of sending Millicent to school had been rejected. In her mother's professional opinion two hours concentrated time at home with her was the equivalent of five in a classroom.[33] It is difficult to judge the nature of this mother–teacher–daughter education. Lovell-Smith suggests that Helen was more of a teacher than a mother to her daughters. Millicent and Viola later remarked upon the rather remote and intellectual persona of their mother during their childhoods. At the time, the situation would perhaps have appeared normal to them, for their sheltered upbringing provided few glimpses of alternative modes of mothering. Helen's pedagogical opposition to rote learning and preference for encouraging independent thought

---

32   Baxter, *Memoirs*, p. 24; Millicent Macmillan Brown to John Macmillan Brown ('Dear Daddie'), 7 July 1899, JMBP, A2/36.
33   Baxter, *Memoirs*, p. 24; Grossmann, *Life of Helen Macmillan Brown*, pp. 36, 50–52.

in children seems to have struck a responsive chord with Millicent.[34] Moreover, she took pains to ensure that after the intensity of the morning's lessons, those in the afternoon were less strenuous and devoted to subjects thought less demanding. Foremost among them were the reading of good literature, art and crafts, and music.

As a first and, until she was nine years of age, only child, Millicent's early life passed amongst adults. It was often a solitary one. As educationalists, both parents were aware of her need for interaction with children of a similar age, and they took steps to provide opportunities that would stimulate her social development. To encourage Millicent to enjoy the outdoors within the rambling five acres of Holmbank, they invited the children of university and teaching colleagues to their home in the hope that they might 'be her playmates'.[35] In 1893, for example, when Millicent was five years of age, the Dendy girls, Vera and Margaret, the daughters of a newly appointed biology lecturer at Canterbury College, became her first close friends. Their arrival stands out like a beacon in the life of a lonely young girl. Millicent, later to describe it as 'the great event of my childhood', led the two younger girls into 'endless scrapes', careering around gardens naked, clambering in the same state into 'a greenhouse tank' and climbing trees, 'including the forbidden one over the ... river'.[36] Helen encouraged the friendships by taking the girls to the seaside at New Brighton, where they could paddle in the sea, and treated them to currant buns.[37]

As a day out for the girls, these excursions underline the domestic, female and sheltered context of Millicent's childhood. The addition of Robin Bevan-Brown, the son of Christchurch Boys' High's headmaster, to the play group did little if anything to alter the nature of Millicent's interaction with other children. As Millicent acknowledges in her *Memoirs*, she was the 'dominating' force within the group of

---

34   Helen Macmillan Brown to John Macmillan Brown, 14 November 1900, JMBP, A3/91; Millicent Macmillan Brown to John Macmillan Brown, 17 November 1900, JMBP, A3/90; Lovell-Smith, *Easily the Best*, pp. 48–51.

35   Macmillan Brown, *Memoirs*, p. 190.

36   Baxter, *Memoirs*, pp. 18–19; Brian J. Smith, 'Dendy, Arthur (1865–1925)', *ADB*, vol. 8, 1981, pp. 279–80. Arthur Dendy was a Manchester-born and educated zoologist, who took up an appointment as demonstrator and assistant lecturer in Biology at the University of Melbourne in 1888. In 1893 he moved to New Zealand with his wife and children where he was professor of Biology at Canterbury College, Christchurch, until 1903. The Dendy family lived in the Cashmere Hills above Christchurch where the Macmillan Browns also had a cottage.

37   Baxter, *Memoirs*, pp. 19–20.

young friends. This was largely a reflection of her greater age, but there may have been an unconscious tendency for her to assume, in her own little world, the controlling persona of her parents and become a veritable headmistress of the playground. Moreover, the deliberateness with which the Macmillan Browns pursued their educational ideals—whether in school, university or within their own family—left little time for engagement in the more popular community activities that might have provided Millicent with a greater range of social interaction with others. Team games were shunned in favour of less competitive physical activities like walking which were able to be experienced individually or as a family group and were capable of being combined with explorations of the natural environment. The emphasis throughout was on providing a sheltered and mentally stimulating domestic setting, in which the seeds of future academic success could be sown.

The second phase of Millicent's education can be seen as coinciding with her father's retirement from Canterbury College in March 1896, as he struggled with eye-strain and was troubled by insomnia. Thereafter, John Macmillan Brown became an increasingly peripatetic scholar, public intellectual and prolific author. The change of circumstance was to put considerable pressure upon the parents' desire to continue to educate Millicent themselves and led to Millicent's first experiences of formal schooling outside the family home. It took place not in New Zealand, but in Britain, on the Continent and later in Australia and came with a degree of parental reluctance. The nine months that followed Macmillan Brown's retirement were spent by the family in Britain and Europe, and throughout this time Millicent's educational regime was a more relaxed one. Concentrated sessions with her mother were rarer, much time was devoted to family activities and learning occasions were limited to those associated with visiting historic buildings and places. While Macmillan Brown's suggestion that he intended to 'cultivate idleness' on the trip 'Home' was a flippant one, this period of Millicent's childhood stands out as one in which there was as much fun as work.[38] The trio learnt to cycle, spent time picnicking, walking, hiking, and visiting friends and family.[39]

---

38 'Canterbury College Farewell to Professor Brown', *Lyttelton Times*, 16 March 1896, p. 2.
39 Grossmann, *Life of Helen Macmillan Brown*, pp. 60–68; Macmillan Brown, *Memoirs*, pp. 189–94; Baxter, *Memoirs*, pp. 21–23; Millicent Baxter's introduction to Macmillan Brown's *Memoirs*, pp. xvi–xviii.

Four years passed before Millicent, now 12 years of age, attended a school. The family had grown in November 1897 with the birth of Viola, and in early 1900 all four, accompanied by governess Gertrude Boulton, set off again for Europe, principally to seek treatment for John Macmillan Brown at a Wiesbaden eye clinic. After settling their daughters in a London boarding house near Crystal Palace, Helen and John Macmillan Brown embarked upon a European tour late in May 1900. During their absence for some four months, Millicent attended a girls' day school, the pedigree of which had been carefully vetted and was run by a sister of an academic colleague, A. P. W. Thomas, Professor of Biology at the University of Auckland.[40] A further period of formal schooling occurred while her father underwent treatment at Wiesbaden, and Millicent, her mother, sister and governess lived at a boarding establishment in Montreux near Lake Geneva. The original intention was that the stay at Montreux should be devoted to an immersion in the French language. With characteristic thoroughness, Helen Macmillan Brown sought out a suitable woman to provide private tuition for them all at their apartment. To encourage her daughters' listening skills, she took them to church (the Eglise Libre) to hear the sermons delivered in French. Indeed, it was primarily as part of this quest for immersion in French language and culture that Millicent was enrolled in a local high school for girls.[41]

The letters that passed on an almost daily basis between John and Helen Macmillan Brown during this period reveal the closeness with which she monitored Millicent's schooling.[42] Helen wrote that the 'fees are wonderfully low, because I suppose it is a State affair—they

---

40   Macmillan Brown, *Memoirs*, p. 194; Baxter, *Memoirs*, p. 27; Keith Sinclair, *A History of the University of Auckland, 1883–1983*, University of Auckland/Oxford University Press, Auckland, 1983, p. 22. The school that Millicent attended in London was part of the Girls' High School Day Company group. Before the trip, Helen considered sending Millicent to Cheltenham Girls' School, but thought better of it after studying the school prospectus and receiving a report from friends who had visited the school on her behalf. Helen judged the school's atmosphere to be too religious and not relaxed enough for Millicent. (Helen Macmillan Brown to John Macmillan Brown, 6 June 1899, JMBP, A2/6.) Millicent writes that up until this point her 'education, by conventional standards, had been very spotty. For English, history, geography I was in the class normal for my years. For arithmetic and French, in both of which I was poor, I went down a class. For Latin I went up amongst girls of fifteen and sixteen who seemed to me practically grown up.' Baxter, *Memoirs*, p. 26.
41   Helen Macmillan Brown to John Macmillan Brown: 5 November 1900, JMBP, A3/67; 6 November 1900, JMBP, A3/87; 18 November 1900, JMBP, A3/89; 25 November 1900, JMBP, A3/66; 2 December 1900, JMBP, A3/89; 11 December 1900, JMBP, A3/30.
42   Between approximately 4 November 1900 and 20 December 1900.

are only 15 francs a quarter & 10 francs entry fee for the first term'. She approved the manner in which the school, with its 11 masters and 6 mistresses and only 130 pupils, maintained a desirably small class size. Nonetheless, before enrolling her daughter, she interviewed the school's director and Millicent's prospective teacher. She specified the hours Millicent would attend and took full advantage of the degree of individual choice the school allowed in the subjects to be studied, deciding that her daughter would 'take all—except religion & sewing & singing'. She paid particular attention to the learning environment that the school provided, praising its 'beautiful corridors and large well ventilated rooms' and noted that the children's individual desks could be 'lowered or raised to suit the pupils'. Above all else she was attracted by a level of state and municipal involvement that encouraged greater female participation in education by maintaining low fees.[43]

The monitoring of Millicent's schooling at Montreux was as persistent as it was insistent. The novelty of the situation required adjustment and was stressful for mother and daughter. Millicent was at first reluctant to go to school: she 'says she would not mind so much if I would not insist on her wearing her spectacles at school—perhaps if she wears them at home reading that would be enough for they are no good to her when looking at the blackboard'.[44] And Helen soon began to revise her first assessment: 'In spite of their splendid building, &c I don't think the school is as good as it might be.'[45] At the heart of her concerns was a pedagogical opposition to rote learning:

> Her mistress seems to be very old fashioned and nearly all the lessons are supposed to be learned by heart ... Geography, History, Reading— they say it to her in turn on the platform while the rest look on or play. I told Millicent she need not do more than read the lessons over carefully & tell the mistress she would write an account in her own words of the lesson set. I don't think more could be expected of her than that. But what a stupid way to teach.[46]

Convinced that Millicent was 'just wasting her time learning nothing' and that the director was not 'of much account' and unaware of what was 'going on', Helen kept Millicent at home for three days

---

43   Helen Macmillan Brown to John Macmillan Brown, 6 November 1900, JMBP, A3/87.
44   Helen Macmillan Brown to John Macmillan Brown, 5 November 1900, JMBP, A3/67.
45   Helen Macmillan Brown to John Macmillan Brown, 14 November 1900, JMBP, A3/91.
46   Helen Macmillan Brown to John Macmillan Brown, 14 November 1900, JMBP, A3/91.

and threatened to remove her from the school until she was put into a higher class with less rote learning. (Millicent was also evidently pale, tired and unable to eat breakfast before going off to school each day).[47] That the incident loomed large in the concerns of mother and daughter is evident in a letter from Millicent to her father:

> On Monday I shall go to a higher class. Mummie went to the Director and he said there would be less learning by heart and he said also that the Mistress was very nice. There will be a master for Geographie so I will not always hear the same voice.[48]

The change of class was accompanied by even greater parental intervention. Millicent would in future have just 12 to 14 hours of lessons per week and would cease arithmetic. Thereafter each day, Helen would proceed to the school carrying with her 'the remainder of [Millicent's] breakfast ... & some biscuits & chocolate drinks' for refreshment, and mother and daughter would take 'an hour's walk up the hills'. The changes appear broadly to satisfy both mother and daughter. There 'seem[ed] to be no rote learning' and while there was 'still room for improvement', Helen was satisfied with Millicent's general physical well-being.[49] Nonetheless, she continued to make her presence felt at the school, insisting, for example, that her daughter's desk be moved closer to the teacher.[50]

Helen's attentive mothering was infused with a determination to provide her daughter with opportunities that would enable her to realise the desired feminine ideal. It placed considerable importance upon health and fitness and achieving a proper balance between them and academic studies. In Millicent's case, these concerns took on an anxiousness associated with the fact that, at the time of the trip to Europe, she was on the cusp of adolescence and Helen's own health was compromised by chronic insomnia and several miscarriages. Indeed, Helen plainly thought that her daughter was neither physically nor mentally robust and needed 'a great deal of looking after'.[51] She encouraged her with 'little presents' and constantly urged

---

47   Helen Macmillan Brown to John Macmillan Brown: 17 November 1900, JMBP, A3/88; 22 November 1900, JMBP, A3/91; 19 December 1900, JMBP, A3/92.
48   Millicent Macmillan Brown to Macmillan Brown, 17 November 1900, JMBP, A3/88.
49   Helen Macmillan Brown to John Macmillan Brown, 20 November 1900, JMBP, A3/14.
50   Helen Macmillan Brown to John Macmillan Brown, 19 November 1900, JMBP, A3/92.
51   Helen Macmillan Brown to John Macmillan Brown: 8 December 1900, JMBP, A3/24; 25 November 1900, JMBP, A3/66.

that she conserve her energy. On one occasion, believing her daughter to be particularly tired after gym class, she insisted there be less arm swinging, though Millicent took no notice.[52] Each day she would accompany Millicent to school for her first class at 8.00 am, take her for a walk an hour later (during arithmetic class) and return in the afternoon to take another walk, after history and before a French literature class beginning at 4.30 pm. On another occasion she rebuffed Millicent's desire 'to go to more classes', because 'she must have plenty of time to walk, especially when the bright weather comes'.[53]

Health, exercise and education remained the dominant concerns of the time at Montreux. Few distractions were permitted. Sightseeing and entertainments, such as musical concerts, were rarely permitted to disrupt the family routine; they were judged to be luxuries and expenditure upon them was dispensed frugally. There was little time within this essentially spartan regimen for social engagements outside the family group; attempts to keep abreast of the issues of the day and visits to the *Kursaal* to read the *Daily Telegraph* and the *Times* were abandoned.[54]

The return to Christchurch and to the routines of Holmbank, in January 1902, were to be severely challenged by problems held by contemporaries to be part of colonial circumstance. Edith Grossmann argued that, in contrast to the New Zealand situation, in 'an old country a married woman may more easily continue in her profession, and everywhere it is possible for those who are childless, or for those who have such excellent servants and other agents that they can confine themselves to supervising'.[55] Whatever the argument's general applicability, the reality at Holmbank when the Macmillan Browns returned was that domestic help was hard to find and Millicent and her mother had no choice but to step into the breach. After briefly considering sending her daughter to Christchurch Girls' High School, Helen resolutely persisted with lessons at Holmbank. Millicent seems to have enjoyed the novel experience of housework, but her

---

52   Helen Macmillan Brown to John Macmillan Brown: 29 November 1900, JMBP, A3/3; 30 November 1900, JMBP, A3/4.
53   Helen Macmillan Brown to John Macmillan Brown, [6] December 1900, JMBP, A3/21.
54   Helen Macmillan Brown to John Macmillan Brown: 19 November 1900, JMBP, A3/13; 22 November 1900, JMBP, A3/11; 25 November 1900, JMBP, A3/66; 13 December 1900, JMBP, A3/36; 14 December 1900, JMBP, A3/38; 16 December 1900, JMBP, A3/42.
55   Grossmann, *Life of Helen Macmillan Brown*, pp. 53–54.

mother's anxieties about its impact on the more serious business of education were shared by her Sydney-based sister and sister-in-law: 'How unfortunate you have been with your household help. It's all very well for a little while to have everything to do—but a little spell goes a long way ... Glad you are able to carry on Millicent's study at home. The trouble will be those domestic interruptions ...'; 'Fancy you & Millicent bustling round & doing all the work'.[56]

Throughout 1902 Helen's health deteriorated, and in her search for a cure for her worsening insomnia, she spent large periods of time living in the family's hillside property in Cashmere and the new seaside Sumner cottage, away from her daughters and husband.[57] A miscarriage suffered in Montreux in early 1901 seems to have sapped her strength and vitality. Her sudden death in February 1903 at the age of 46, possibly from diphtheria, had a devastating impact on the family.[58] The changes that followed in the education of Millicent and Viola were, nonetheless, ones of form rather than substance. John Macmillan Brown had been as much its architect as Helen and, in the months that followed her death, the prevailing regimen was applied with even greater intensity. Millicent was now preparing for her first public examinations—the New Zealand university junior scholarship and the Sydney senior scholarship—and her recollection of the substitution of father for mother as teacher is unambiguous:

> There began a bad period of about four months. I look back on it now with considerable sympathy for my father. I had none then, only resentment, and I think even hatred. Very much upset by the death of his wife and left alone to bring up a teenaged and a five-year-old

---

56   Mrs Robert Craig [Bessie Brown] to Helen Macmillan Brown, 8 May 1902, JMBP, A19/7; Pata [Maria Craig née Connon] to Helen Macmillan Brown, 25 April – May 1902, JMBP, A19/10.

57   John Macmillan Brown had these homes built for Helen in the hope that the hill and seaside air and environment would cure her insomnia.

58   Some doubt surrounds the cause of Helen Macmillan Brown's death on 22 February 1903 in Rotorua during a family holiday. Her death certificate officially attributes the cause of death to diphtheria, gangrene of the fauces (or back of the throat), and cardiac failure. John Macmillan Brown believed that his wife had contracted diphtheria during the sea voyage to Rotorua. Grossmann, however, notes that Helen did not display all of the major symptoms of the disease. Millicent, similarly, did not believe that her mother had diphtheria, later speculating that her death was more likely related to the miscarriage in 1901, after which family and friends noted a marked and inexplicable deterioration in Helen's overall health. There is a hint of medical misadventure. Lovell-Smith attributes Helen's death to a combination of causes: chronic and inexplicable insomnia, the miscarriage suffered in 1901 and diphtheria. See Grossmann, *Life of Helen Macmillan Brown*, pp. 84–88; Macmillan Brown, *Memoirs*, pp. 213–14; Baxter, *Memoirs*, pp. 27–29; Lovell-Smith, *Easily the Best*, pp. 105–6, 111–14.

daughter, he became exceedingly irritable and was unable to control his temper. Coaching me for the Junior Scholarship and the Sydney Senior, he naturally let it out on me. I wasn't the brilliant student he had expected me to be. I don't think I ever came anywhere near his expectation of me. I don't know that I was particularly stupid. I was, I think, just ordinary average, and I had too much to do. I toiled through French, German, Latin, English, Greek and Roman history and Modern history 1790-1815 ... Those four months were just pure hell, and I don't suppose they were much better for him ... Certainly at that time I saw no way out.[59]

Nor was there much relief when a teacher from Christchurch Girls' High was employed as a mathematics tutor. Her complaints that Millicent had insufficient time to do work for her were rebuffed and Millicent recalls sitting up all Friday night preparing for her Saturday morning mathematics session.[60]

Millicent's ultimate failure in the examinations did not deter Macmillan Brown from his desire that she should proceed to university. But it did lead him to abandon his attempt to educate his daughter at Holmbank. In February 1905, the 17-year-old Millicent was sent to her aunt in Sydney and enrolled at the Presbyterian Ladies' College in Croydon. It was her longest continuous experience of school life, and Millicent was later to record 'extreme unalloyed delight' at her ultimate success in the matriculation exam.[61] Her father's voice remained the determining one throughout her subsequent university years and his pocket the paying one. All were spent outside New Zealand. They began in 1906 at the University of Sydney, where she completed a degree in Latin, French and German in 1908, continued at Newnham College, Cambridge, where in 1912 she gained a second in the tripos, and ended abruptly with the outbreak of World War One in Germany, where she had begun PhD studies in Old French at Halle University.[62] In her retrospective assessment of this period of her life, Millicent recalls her university experience as enjoyable, devoid of any sense of purpose or seriousness and marked by achievements that reflected

---

59 Baxter, *Memoirs*, pp. 29–30.
60 Baxter, *Memoirs*, pp. 30–31.
61 Baxter, *Memoirs*, p. 31.
62 By 1906, John Macmillan Brown had fallen out with some of his former Canterbury College colleagues, Millicent's prospective teachers, and decided that it would be in Millicent's best interests to attend another university.

effort expended.[63] Whatever its accuracy, it is an assessment that cannot obscure the reality that her education represents a full realisation of a feminine scholarly ideal formulated and pursued by Helen and John Macmillan Brown with unswerving determination. Yet, ultimately, the experiment was rescued by her attendance at a secondary school and at a distance from her father.

Millicent's childhood and education provided something of a template for her younger sister Viola. It did so within changing family circumstances. She was born in 1897 after both parents had retired, and her childhood was to be predominantly that of a motherless daughter with an older and frequently absent father. A governess, Gertrude Boulton, looked after her from birth, accompanying the family on a European sojourn in 1900, when Viola was two years old. After the death of Helen in 1903, when Viola was five, Gertrude assumed the maternal role. She was assisted by Millicent and occasionally the girls' aunts. Viola describes her experiences after her mother died as following a 'quiet pattern according to my father's theories. I had my lessons with Gertrude ... in the garden whenever possible, and, except for arithmetic (which I would not have chosen) I was free to choose what I wanted to learn—Spanish history, astronomy, botany, Romany and Sanscrit.' Her 'chief relationship' with her father was in the evenings when he told her stories and selected 'simple stories in French which he got me to read aloud to him to help me learn'.[64]

There is some evidence that Macmillan Brown was less prescriptive in the management of his younger daughter's childhood. In his *Memoirs*, he describes Viola as a 'beautiful little replica' of her mother and observes that, after Helen's death, he 'seemed to go back again into the simplicity and receptiveness of childhood ... and Viola's happiness made me happy'.[65] Millicent later judged her father to have had a better relationship with Viola than with her.[66] Macmillan Brown was, indeed, often to be more accommodating in his treatment of his younger daughter. When she was 14 years of age, he gave into her pestering and allowed her to attend a school so that she could

---

63   Baxter, *Memoirs*, pp. 31–45; Baxter's introduction to Macmillan Brown's *Memoirs*, p. xxv.
64   Notariello's introduction to Macmillan Brown's *Memoirs*, p. xxvii.
65   Macmillan Brown, *Memoirs*, pp. 214–15.
66   Baxter, *Memoirs*, p. 29. See also Griffith, *Out of the Shadows*, pp. 53, 129.

'be like the other children'.[67] Yet such concessions occurred within a framework that had changed little, if at all, from that which shaped Millicent's education. After Viola had matriculated in 1914 at age 17, her father resumed full control of her education, deciding that she would spend a year at home preparing for university. Her older sister Millicent, recently returned to the family from Germany, taught her French, German, Latin and Roman history during the day, and her father taught her Greek (traditionally a subject taught only to boys), middle English and essay writing in the evenings.[68]

In her university studies Viola was to turn away from the path followed by her mother and sister, enrolling at the Canterbury College School of Art. Art sat ambiguously within the range of disciplines the Macmillan Browns believed could increase women's participation in the civic community. It was something to be cultivated like other accomplishments, but after the serious scholarly disciplines had been mastered. Seen in this context, Viola's passage through art school and subsequent periods of study in Sydney and London supported by her father suggests willingness to compromise when faced with talent and enthusiasm.[69] However we interpret Macmillan Brown's actions, they empowered an independent-minded daughter. As one of a small cluster of predominantly progressive young women artists calling themselves 'The Group', some of whom saw themselves as challenging the 'Victorian atmosphere' and 'collective conservatism of the Canterbury Society of Arts', Viola became part of a flourishing

---

67   Notariello's introduction, p. xxvii. The Rangi Ruru Girls' School Register, perhaps mistakenly, records both Millicent and Viola Macmillan Brown's attendance at the private Presbyterian girls' school in Christchurch from 1904. There is no other evidence of Millicent having attended the school.
68   Notariello's introduction, pp. xxvii–xxviii.
69   Notariello's introduction, pp. xxviii, xxx. Viola Macmillan Brown attended Julian Ashton's School of Art in Sydney for a period c. 1919, and studied painting in London and Europe in the 1920s.

local female artistic community.[70] It was a choice made possible by remaining her father's helpmate and companion until his death in 1935.

The Wilding Girls: *'Mens sana in corpore sano'*

The process of educating the Wilding girls and their brothers was recorded by their mother Julia in the separate diaries that she kept for each of her children from their births until death—theirs or her own.[71] The detail and regularity of the entries stand as a marked contrast to the infant diary of Millicent Macmillan Brown kept (probably) by her mother for just 20 months. Indeed, the diaries of the Wilding children's lives reveal a mother consistently much closer and more directly involved in her children's developmental processes. The difference has a generational and philosophical dimension. Julia's thinking about children had occurred in Hereford, had been deeply influenced by her own family's interpretation of the writing of John Stuart Mill and was honed by her own experience. As a first generation, university-trained professional endeavouring to combine a career with motherhood at a time when the availability of domestic help was often limited, Helen's approach to motherhood relied upon her professional judgement and involvement, but there was less chance to chart and record its detail.

---

70   Margaret Lewis, *Ngaio Marsh: A Life*, Bridget Williams Books, Wellington, 1991, p. 31; Neil Roberts, *Concise History of Art in Canterbury, 1850–2000*, Robert McDougall Art Gallery, Christchurch, 2000, p. 39. The Group included Evelyn Polson, Margaret Anderson, Edith Wall, Ngaio Marsh, Cora Wilding, Rhona Haszard, William Montgomery and W. S. Baverstock. There was, amongst the various members of the group, and likewise subsequently amongst art historians, some disagreement about the extent of their 'radicalism' as artists. See Lewis, *Ngaio Marsh*, pp. 30–31; Janet Paul and Neil Roberts, *Evelyn Page: Seven Decades*, Robert McDougall Art Gallery with Allen and Unwin, Christchurch and Wellington, 1986, pp. 69–74, 24; Julie King, *Olivia Spencer Bower: Making Her Own Discoveries*, Canterbury University Press, Christchurch, 2015, pp. 83, 85. Also: Julie A. Catchpole, 'The Group', MA thesis, University of Canterbury, 1984; Nadia Gush, 'The Beauty of Health: Cora Wilding and the Sunlight League', *NZJH*, vol. 43, no. 1, 2009, pp. 1–17; Nadia Joanne Gush, 'Cultural Fields of the Canterbury Plains: Women and Cultural Citizenship in Canterbury c 1890–1940', PhD thesis, Victoria University of Wellington, 2007.
71   Life Events Diary of Gladys Wilding (GWLED) kept by Julia Wilding, (3 vols): vol. 1: November 1881 – 1 November 1885, vol. 2: 28 November 1885 – 13 May 1896 , vol. 3: 1 May 1896 – 24 November 1905, WFP, box 14/64-66/1-3; Life Events Diary of Anthony Wilding (AFWLED) kept by Julia Wilding, (2 vols): vol. 1: 1883–1889, vol. 2: 1889–1915, WFP, box 20/92-93/1-2; Life Events Diary of Cora Wilding (CWLED) kept by Julia Wilding, 1 vol.: 15 November 1888 – 4 April 1931, WFP, box 35/162/1. Life Events Diaries of Frank Wilding and Edwyn Wilding are kept in private hands.

Julia Wilding embraces the maternal role as a full-time profession of supreme importance and social significance, and one which she was prepared to give priority over all else. She employed nursemaids when her children were young, but as the Life Events Diaries show, they were clearly cast in the role of assistants to Julia in the physical care of the children. Young girls with little education, the nursemaids were instructed carefully, supervised closely and permitted little initiative. They often worked in Julia's presence and accompanied her when she took her large and growing family on outings to help care for the children.

The Life Events Diaries work on several different levels. They provide a repository of memories for a clearly doting mother and a record of factual information about the physical development and health of the children, with heights, weights and details of illnesses recorded systematically at the back of each child's diary. The accompanying commentary frequently takes on an almost scientific tone, as Julia attempts detached and analytical critiques of emerging personalities and all-round development, as well as the dynamics of family life. It is also often confessional in nature, revealing expectations and anxieties of an intensely committed mother. While the diaries are Julia's creation, they were in a sense not exclusively private in nature. The individual children were aware of their existence and sometimes shown entries, and, as we have seen, the records were destined to pass into their hands.[72] It is perhaps this intention that encourages Julia to record and acknowledge the extent to which the Wilding family experiment was built around a much fuller paternal participation than has been held to be the contemporary norm.

At the philosophical heart of their family experiment, and, in the recall of the children, given frequent airing by their mother throughout their childhood, was the Latin maxim, 'Mens sana in copore sano'. The balanced cultivation of mind and body was pursued with such determination that it became something synonymous, if not with the pursuit of excellence, then at least with a high level of competency. In practice, this meant the study by all children, without gender differentiation, of a broad range of subjects: mathematics, the sciences,

---

72   See, for example, CWLED: 10 March 1895, 19 June 1895, 1 February 1896; Harriet Blodgett, *Centuries of Female Days*, pp. 37, 63, 65, 66, 82; Judy Simons, *Diaries and Journals of Literary Women from Fanny Burney to Virginia Woolf*, Houndmills, Basingstoke, Hampshire, 1990, p. 6.

history, languages and the arts. The specific and individual talents that emerged were then nurtured to their fullest expression. It was a demanding philosophy, which required a great deal of effort on both the part of the parents and the children. Yet it encompassed a belief in the value of play as well as work. Indeed, it was the melding of fun and seriousness, social duty and individual fulfilment that gave the Wilding experiment more chance of achieving the balance they espoused.

In Gladys, their first child to survive infancy, nature and nurture proved comfortable companions. From the day of her birth, 1 November 1881, the Wildings watched anxiously for signs of intelligence and strove to create a stimulating environment. Throughout her infancy they read books and sang nursery rhymes to her, played music, provided age-appropriate toys and experiences and played with and talked to her constantly. At 18 months Gladys was, her mother declared, 'immensely intelligent and quick now, & understands everything'.[73] Quick to detect in Gladys's behaviour an interest in reading and counting, Julia introduced formal lessons into her day, including teaching her the alphabet. By the time Gladys was three years and three months old, Julia announced that she could:

> point out & name any letter of the alphabet in a book. I have tried to do it as an amusement, & should not have attempted if she did not like it, but every day, of herself, she asks me to do the letters with her. She only knows the capital letters yet, & to-day she was looking through a book & noticed all the dots over the i's, & she asks me 'what all those little black balls were for'.[74]

The detailed and perceptive observation underlines the intensity of Julia's involvement and it continued unabated. We learn:

> Gladdie can also count up to 20 now, & in playing with the shells she is learning just the elementary rules of addition, subtraction & multiplication. She is extremely fond of doing all these things, & is certainly a very intelligent child, & has a wonderfully good memory.[75]

---

73 GWLED, 1 May 1883.
74 GWLED, 1 February 1885.
75 GWLED, 1 February 1885.

Four months later Gladys was 'getting on splendidly with her little things with me, & can quite read now. She is remarkably quick and intelligent & such a darling to teach, so observant, & interested in everything'.[76] By Christmas 1885, however, signs of waning interest were noted and strategies devised to rekindle it. A break from lessons was judged necessary: 'she has not been so good at them just lately, & I think she will begin again better perhaps'.[77] The comment appears relaxed enough but Julia's subsequent actions reveal how quickly her daughter's apparent loss of enthusiasm was interpreted as challenging the mother's fundamental belief in the necessity for hard work and self-discipline in the quest for self-improvement. Developing the talent of her daughter was the civic duty of the parent.

The response was a carefully constructed and conscientiously administered system of rewards and prizes. Gladys was to have 'a good or bad mark every day after her lessons, & when she has 40 good marks, she is to have a little book or prize'.[78] Julia remained unyielding and uncompromising in the face of Gladys's obvious distress; simply noting that she 'cries & is very unhappy'—when awarded a bad mark.[79] The seriousness of her intent becomes further apparent on 27 March 1886:

> Gladys got her first prize today,—a scrap book. I give her a good or bad mark every day after lessons, & she was to have a prize when she had 40 good ones. Today she got her 48th good mark, as she had 8 bad ones & had to get the extra 8 good ones to counterbalance them & make up the 40 good. Woman was so delighted with her prize, & got Fanny to make her some paste at once, so as to begin pasting pictures in. She has been cutting pictures out that I give her, for a long while past.[80]

The assistance of family and friends was enlisted in support of the new regime: 'Her father & Mr Lewis have both promised Gladys that they will give her a prize if she gets 40 good marks without a single bad one. She is most anxious about it, & she has already about 20 good marks,—without a bad one.'[81] The relentlessness with which the

---

76 GWLED, 3 June 1885.
77 GWLED, 25 December 1885.
78 GWLED, 28 December 1885.
79 GWLED, 10 January 1886.
80 GWLED, 27 March 1886.
81 GWLED, 12 July 1886.

regime is pursued suggests a desire to inculcate competitiveness, and a striving for excellence as a basis for precocious achievement. In its rationalist approach, it also bore some resemblance to the education of her hero John Stuart Mill by his father and Jeremy Bentham.[82]

During the subsequent months the Life Events Diary abounds in detailed and anxious comment: 'Gladys can really read very well now, but I have not taught her spelling yet at all & from one or two questions I have sometimes asked her, I don't think she has any idea of it.'[83] While she was thought 'remarkably quick' and a 'very affectionate darling little woman' who 'likes to try at everything', she did 'not always quite like being shown the way'.[84] Increasingly, though, there are signs that Gladys was beginning to measure up. When '4 $\frac{3}{4}$'-year-old Gladys's first letter to the 'Children's Corner' of the *Christchurch Weekly Press* was published, Julia noted proudly that she was the youngest child to have done so and that the next youngest to 'appear' was seven. Gladys, we are told, 'composed & wrote it all herself, the only help I gave her being to tell her how to spell the words'.[85] But the concession that Gladys was 'immensely fond' of producing 'real letters all written in capitals' was coupled with the observation that she did 'not much like her copy book lessons' and had been told by her mother that she would 'never write properly until she can make small letters too'.[86]

A subsequent letter written shortly after Gladys turned five met with greater maternal approval:

Dear Mr Editor,

… Nearly every morning we go and help Emma to feed the fowls, and sometimes I give the grain. The rest of the morning I play with my brother Anthony and with our puppy dog, named Toby, and for an hour I do lessons with my mother. I do music treble clef, reading, sums and time table up to five times, & copy book, & in the afternoon I go for a walk with our nurse, & sometimes I go for a walk with my mother, and other times I go in the carriage to town. This morning

---

82   Bruce Mazlish, *James and John Stuart Mill: Father and Son in the Nineteenth Century*, Hutchinson, London, 1975, pp. 169–75.

83   GWLED, 12 July 1886.

84   GWLED, 12 July 1886.

85   GWLED, 18 September 1886.

86   GWLED, 9 October 1886.

I picked strawberries with my father. I have got a little brother named Anthony, and he came too and helped, and sometimes he pinches me and hurts me. I get up at a quarter-past seven in the morning and have a cold bath, and on Friday nights I have a warm bath. I go to bed at half-past six at night. On Thursday nights I have cocoa for tea, and sometimes I have breakfast with my mother and father.

Gladys Wilding
Five Years Old[87]

It was not, of course, the full story, but the letter does capture something of the routine and regularity of Gladys's earliest years and the intensity of Julia's involvement in her daughter's education.

As their daughter approached her sixth birthday, the Wildings reassessed their approach to her education. Gladys now had three siblings (Anthony, Frank and Cora), and Julia had involved herself just as determinedly in their day-to-day education. It was nonetheless with reluctance that she began to consider placing Gladys in the care of a professional teacher: 'I am sorry to give up though, but it is an experiment we can but try', and one she hoped would bring 'increased stimulus and interest'.[88] The transition from having lessons with her mother and younger brother, Anthony, in the enclosed veranda-schoolroom at Fownhope took place in the summer of 1888, when they both began attending Miss Tabart's small, private school based in the home of a neighbouring family, the Andrew Andersons.[89] With at most 12 other pupils—boys and girls of varying ages—Julia believed Gladys was ensured a relatively high degree of individual attention.

The change did not signal any lessening of Julia's involvement in the day-to-day progress of her daughter's education. Julia determined Gladys's course of study and visited the school frequently, checking on both Miss Tabart's teaching and Gladys's progress. Examination marks and end of term school reports were scrutinised closely. Miss Tabart's

---

87   *Christchurch Weekly Press*, 14 December 1886; GWLED, 6 January 1886.

88   GWLED, 7 January 1888, 30 January 1888.

89   Andrew Anderson and his family lived in Wilson's Road, Opawa, close to Fownhope; his children Mabel, Gladys and Frederick were classmates of Gladys and Anthony in Miss Tabart's school (GWED, 1 November 1893). Andrew Anderson and his brother, John, ran the city's leading engineering and construction company, J. & A. Andersons, a family business founded in 1857 by their Scottish father, John Anderson (1820–1897), who was also a local politician. See Gordon Ogilvie, *The Port Hills of Christchurch*, Reed, Auckland, 1991, pp. 125–28, 131; P. G. Lowe, 'Anderson, John (1820–1897)', *DNZB*, vol. 1, pp. 4–5.

observation that she had 'never seen such a clever child' was recorded and elaborated by an ever-attentive Julia: 'She certainly is marvellously quick at learning and grasping things.'[90] During school holidays she seized the chance to resume her teaching role. For her part, Gladys managed the transition from home to school with such apparent ease that her mother gradually extended the range of subjects she studied until, by 1891, it included Latin, botany, elementary science, writing, arithmetic, composition, literature, geography and drawing.

It was the closeness of Julia's involvement with her daughter's education that ushered in a decisive shift of emphasis. When Gladys had difficulty shrugging off a lingering cold at the end of May 1892, Julia reacted by arranging for her daughter to spend two terms at Miss Mannering's private school for girls in Sumner, a seaside suburb favoured by the middle classes for its healthy climate.[91] A weekly boarder, she returned home at the weekends, and Julia was able to monitor closely both her health and the impact the change was having upon her daughter's education. From the outset Gladys's intellectual ability was judged far in advance of her age group, and when Miss Mannering expressed the opinion that 'she ought to be doing more' and subsequently increased the level of difficulty in her work, Julia welcomed the move.[92] There were five other girls at the school, ranging in age from 11 to 16, and we learn that Gladys outperformed them all in the examinations for scripture history, geography, science, grammar rules, Roman history, dates, mythology, grammar, Australian geography, English history and spelling. As an educational experiment, as the Life Events Diary shows, the time at Sumner was judged a spectacular success.

Indeed, a bemused and slightly uncomfortable Julia recorded the enthusiasm the stimulus of competition seemed to generate in her daughter. Gladys now threw herself into her lessons with apparently boundless energy and approached her examinations without fear. The eagerness drew the maternal observation that her daughter was 'certainly very ambitious and anxious to get on' and a concern that balance had been lost: 'The only fear is that she may overdo' her

---

90   GWLED, 12 May 1889.
91   GWLED, 15 May 1892 – 15 December 1892.
92   GWLED, 25 September 1892.

lessons 'a little'.[93] Gladys left the school at the end of the last term for 1892, taking with her a book she had been awarded as a prize: 'Mrs Mannering told her she was very pleased, & considered that she had made very good progress in everything.'[94] Across the summer of 1892–93 the blossoming of Gladys's intellectual aptitudes was assessed, and the form of her future education came increasingly to resemble that which Julia had herself experienced in Hereford.

We can now observe greater confidence in Julia's handling of her daughter's education. She had successfully ushered her daughter through the years of early childhood and now began to take a pleasure in a precociously talented and biddable daughter entering a stage of her education that she remembered with pleasure from her own childhood. Julia's preference was for Gladys to return to Fownhope and be taught by a 'daily governess' and a range of specialist tutors. Such a formula would undoubtedly have given greater opportunity for maternal supervision and involvement. For 1893, a compromise was reached: Gladys attended Miss Tabart's school for the mornings and in the afternoons attended private lessons with specialist tutors in drawing, Euclid and algebra, the latter subject being one she excelled at and in which, Julia pointed out, few girls received instruction. In 1894 attempts to secure a suitable governess were abandoned and, with some misgivings on Julia's part, Gladys was enrolled as a 'day scholar' at William and Drusilla Wilson's Cranmer House School for girls and boys, in Cranmer Square: 'we are going to try this, & I do hope it will successful'.[95] A medium-sized school with approximately 70 pupils, run by the English-born and professionally trained teachers William Wilson, formerly head of the Normal School and Teacher's Training College lecturer, and his wife Drusilla, who had worked at a teacher training institution in Brighton, England, it catered for the children of professional families seeking higher education for their sons and increasingly their daughters.[96] Julia was impressed that, while the

---

93 GWLED, 15 July 1892, 25 September 1892.
94 GWLED, 15 December 1892.
95 GWLED, 25 March 1894.
96 David Wilson, 'Wilson's School, 1892–1908 and Wirihana School 1909–1927', ms, CMDRC, folder 1130; 'Information about Wilson's School in Cranmer Square 1892–1927' (Wilson, William and Drusilla), CMDRC, ARC 1900.527. Drusilla Wilson was a student of John Macmillan Brown at Canterbury College in 1892 and was also on the founding committee of the Canterbury Women's Institute, a feminist organisation established in Christchurch in 1892. Lovell-Smith, *Easily the Best*, p. 72.

boys and girls were taught in separate classes, the curriculum was the same, apart from some additional subjects for the girls, and included Latin.

In this environment Gladys continued to blossom academically. We hear little of Julia's reaction to the traditionally female subjects of singing, drawing, needlework and French, taught to the girls by Drusilla Wilson. But there was no doubting Julia's views upon her daughter's response to her academic work: she 'simply loves her lessons' and was 'quite devoted' to William Wilson.[97] Performance matched perception. After coming 'second of the whole school' at the end of 1894, 13-year-old Gladys was, with Julia's enthusiastic encouragement, 'withdrawn from ordinary classes in order to pursue her special course of study for matriculation'.[98] She approached the examinations with her by now customary fervour and confidence, earning within the Wilding family the nickname 'No. 46', her candidate number.[99] With an 'average of nearly 70 per cent' in English, Latin, French, geography, arithmetic, algebra and Euclid, she passed all subjects. It was her first experience of a national examination, and the success fuelled both mother and daughter's eagerness for comparison and competitive streaks. To satisfy their desire to 'find out <u>how</u> she passed, & her percentage of marks', the family worked through their contacts within the university community.[100]

Gladys clearly stood on the cusp of an academic future. Significantly, Julia sought the advice and reassurance of her brother and scholar, Edwyn, to whom she sent Gladys's matriculation exam papers. His response was both reassuring and unsettling. He 'strongly advises us to let her go on for her degree', noted Julia, adding that he had sent her the London University entrance papers for comparison with the University of New Zealand equivalents.[101] We do not learn whether Edwyn suggested that Gladys might study at London University, where it was already possible for a woman to graduate. Nor is there any evidence that Julia and Frederick considered the possibility. The appeal to Edwyn was more a matter of maternal pride than an

---

97   GWLED, 4 April 1894, 11 July 1894.
98   GWLED, 19 December 1894, 10 March 1895; letter to Frederick Wilding from William Wilson, principal of Cranmer House School, 2 May 1895.
99   GWLED, 2 November 1895, 10 December 1895 – 18 December 1895.
100   GWLED, 18 December 1895 – 31 January 1896, 8 March 1896.
101   GWLED, 8 March 1896, 26 September 1896.

indicator of any colonial insecurity. In any event, there was much to do. The 14-year-old Gladys was deemed too young to sit the junior university scholarship examination, success in which would confer a degree of financial independence as well as academic prestige. Consequently, between 1896 and 1898 she effectively assumed the lifestyle of a university student. She spent two to three days each week at Cranmer House School, where she received individual tuition from William Wilson. The rest of the time she studied at home, and her educational program was once more carefully crafted by her mother.

Gladys's days at Fownhope resembled those experienced by her mother some 40 years previously in Hereford. There were lessons in music, elocution and dancing with specialist tutors. And, just as her brothers had done at the Elms, Julia designed a reading program built around the works of the nineteenth-century intellectuals and theorists who had shaped her own thinking: Charles Darwin, John Stuart Mill and John Ruskin. To them she added Macaulay's multi-volumed *History of England*, with its confident depiction of British history as a progressive march towards a more liberal society, and the more recent additions to the growing body of evolutionary and rationalist thought, most notably S. Laing's *Human Origins* (1892). Such study was integrated with work being done at Cranmer School, where Gladys was preparing essays on the South African question and the Spanish-American War. The feminist strand in Julia's thinking was evident also in the inclusion of the *Recollections of Mary Somerville* (1780–1872), in which her daughter Martha chronicled her pioneering work as a woman scientist.[102]

The attempt to win a scholarship was invested with a degree of feminist significance. Gladys had spent the great majority of her schooling alongside boys, and she had plainly not been intimidated intellectually by their presence. At the beginning of 1898 Julia observed that Gladys had 'set her heart on not only winning a scholarship but also

---

102 A reading list constructed by Julia Wilding for Gladys Wilding was placed at back of GWLED vol. 2. It also included Camille Flammarian's *Popular Astronomy*, Buckle's *History of Civilisation, The Rise and Decline of Rationalism*, 'Grieg's works', 'S. Laing's works' and Martha Somerville, *Personal Recollections, From Early Life to Old Age, of Mary Somerville*, Roberts Brothers, Boston, 1874. Samuel Laing (1812–1897), British railway administrator, liberal politician and popular science writer offered an optimistic view of the 'progressive modernity'. His works included *Modern Science and Modern Thought* (1885), *Problems of the Future and Essays*, Chapman and Hall, London, 1889, and *A Modern Zoroastrian*, Chapman and Hall, London, 1892.

coming out at the head of the list, a position which, so far, no girl has attained'.[103] She permitted herself to wonder whether Gladys 'could get anything like' the previous year's top score achieved by a boy.[104] In the event, 17-year-old Gladys came sixth on the credit list, and her failure to win one of the 14 junior scholarships awarded in 1898 was therefore doubly disappointing. It was Gladys's first experience of academic disappointment, and, given the closeness with which mother and daughter had been involved in the preparation for it, the failure deeply affected both of them. Julia was at first philosophical: 'I think we really ought to be satisfied as girlie is only just seventeen, & so many go in two or even three times. The boy M. Blair of Nelson who heads the scholarship list, was 8th on the credit list last year.'[105] She was not too surprised, but plainly dubious, when Gladys announced that she would sit the examination again at the end of 1899, despite the pair's intention to travel 'Home' that year to visit friends and family: 'I don't see how she can possibly gain one, as she will not be able to work very much while we are in England.'[106]

Doubt was soon replaced by determination. The combined resources of mother and daughter, aided by Julia's elder brother, the Oxford-educated mathematician and scholar, Edwyn, turned the trip 'Home' into an opportunity to mount a serious effort to secure the scholarship. Once the Wildings were established within the family network in Hereford, Edwyn, as Julia put it, took Gladys 'in hand with her mathematics'—the subject in which her mark was lowest in the previous year's examination—and devoted several hours each day to the task. A master from Hereford Cathedral School, one of her father's old schools, was engaged to provide daily Latin lessons. After spending at least three hours each day in study, Gladys returned to New Zealand three weeks before the scholarship examinations. Once back in Christchurch, Julia arranged for daily Latin lessons with some last-minute coaching by her former teacher, William Wilson, at Fownhope.[107]

---

103 GWLED, 3 February 1898.
104 GWLED, 3 February 1898.
105 GWLED, 3 February 1899.
106 GWLED, 3 February 1899.
107 GWLED, 15 May 1899, 25 November 1899.

As an example of maternal, familial and personal commitment and cooperation, Gladys's preparation for the scholarship examination plainly rivals, if not surpasses, the effort and attention evident in the education of the Macmillan Brown girls. It was to bear fruit. Placed sixth on the scholarship list, she was one of only two Christchurch girls to be successful. The reactions of mother and daughter capture the high standards they set themselves. Gladys was 'very happy' but confessed that, as Julia reports, 'she cannot be perfectly satisfied, as she did not head the list,—her great ambition'. Declaring herself '<u>quite</u> satisfied', Julia suggests that had Gladys been 'working steadily all this year, she would probably have come out on top'.[108] In Hereford, Charles and Edwyn celebrated their niece's success in the family-owned and operated *Hereford Times*, emphasising that she was the 'highest girl' on the list and giving public support to Julia's private view that with a less disrupted year Gladys would have topped the list. Looking to the future, they predicted a 'distinguished university career' for their talented niece.[109]

If there was one thing that distinguished Julia Wilding's attitude to the education of her children, it was an insistence that life possessed a cultural dimension and that the appreciation of music should be foremost in the education of all children. Looking back upon her life in 1924, she explained her attachment to music in passionate terms:

> All fine music is uplifting. Love of humanity, striving after better things, high ideals of life, to me are all embodied or expressed in Beethoven's Symphonies, Mendelssohn's concerted music etc, etc. Yes, music is a joy,—sacred, ennobling, soothing, stimulating, and it means more to me than anything in the world, except <u>Love</u>, in its widest sense.[110]

In general, she had previously explained her views on the place of fine arts more prosaically. Music, singing, acting, drawing and painting possessed a potential to enrich life for the individual and community alike. They were disciplines whose mastery required effort and persistence—attributes she believed to be commendable social values. As a talented, European-trained pianist who had performed publicly, she poured scorn on the notion that piano playing was

---

108 GWLED, 25 January 1900.
109 Cutting from *HT*, pasted into GWLED, (vol. 3), next to entry for 29 June 1900.
110 Julia Wilding, 'Note', January 1924, WFP, box 12/61/142.

a feminine accomplishment and a mere adornment to drawing-room entertainment. Rather it was a discipline in which progress and skill were to a degree measurable by formal examination and performance. As such, it was appropriate for serious study by both girls and boys.

Julia gave all her children music lessons and strove to share her love of music with them, but it was Gladys who was judged the most musically gifted, and the full weight of maternal expectation was exerted in an effort to develop her latent talent. Julia had first detected that Gladys 'had a good ear' when her daughter was two-and-a-half and began teaching her to read music, and the following year to play the piano: 'her little fingers do not go very well at present, but she is proud of beginning to "play" as she calls it, & I think will get on'.[111] She continued to give Gladys daily music lessons after the girl began attending Miss Tabart's school and also expected Miss Tabart to oversee half an hour's practice each day, providing a table of 'exactly what is to be practised'.[112] By the age of seven, Gladys had begun playing duets with her mother at public concerts for charities, with much praise bestowed upon the pair to Julia's delight.[113] Exactly how Gladys felt about it is unclear. There is, however, a suggestion in Julia's diary entries that an element of coercion was sometimes necessary. Gladys's interest level waxed and waned, at times 'going to the piano herself' and on other occasions preferring theoretical exercises to playing.[114]

Nonetheless, the generally biddable Gladys continued her piano lessons and achieved a standard that encouraged her mother's ambitions. In 1893 she employed a piano tutor to teach Gladys twice a week in the hope that the change might prove more stimulating. To an extent, the ploy succeeded, and at the end of the year Gladys made her first public performance in a concert arranged for young performers.[115] Between 1894 and 1897 Gladys studied for and passed her junior, second and third-year music examinations conducted by Canterbury College. In the latter year, both mother and daughter began to take accompaniment lessons with a private tutor. Indeed Julia's reluctance to let the more academic studies squeeze the piano from her daughter's life held firm until the winter of her matriculation year. Music lessons

---

111 GWLED, 22 January 1884, 25 January 1887.
112 GWLED, 25 January 1892.
113 GWLED, 7 June 1889, 15 October 1889, 7 October 1890, 3 December 1891.
114 GWLED, 8 March 1890, 1 July 1892.
115 GWLED, 5 February 1893, 30 May 1893, 3 October 1893.

were also abandoned during her preparation for the scholarship examination. There remained a strong maternal pressure upon Gladys to practise by herself.[116] With a touch of sadness, Julia acknowledged that the demands of university studies would not leave time for the piano, and marked a waste of talent.[117]

The centrality of music in Julia's life and her sustained effort to nurture whatever musical talent she discerned in her daughter did not prevent her from providing all her children with the opportunity to explore the arts more generally. Indeed, in sharp contrast to Helen Connon's injunction that cast the arts aside until the academic heights had been conquered, Julia Wilding embraced them as an essential part of a balanced education. As an active member of the musical community, she and Frederick were part of the city's cultural community and able to take such opportunities as it provided to enhance the educational opportunities of their children. From the middle-class young girls attending morning classes at the Canterbury College of Art they chose a Miss Stoddart, one of four sisters who enrolled at the college when it was established in 1882, to instruct Gladys in the rudiments of drawing and painting.[118] It was also from within this embryonic cultural milieu that they sought out opportunities for Gladys (and all their children) to develop such confidence as might be gained from exposure to the performance arts, most notably dance and recital classes.[119] Such training, it was hoped, would provide the composure that would allow them in time to take a leading part in community life.

The importance of Julia Wilding's role in the education of Gladys is undeniable, but it is equally clear that the part played by her father provides evidence of greater involvement than the stereotype of the remote and rigid patriarch allows. Indeed, highly educated nineteenth- and early twentieth-century women such as Julia operated with, and at times skilfully exploited, the support and encouragement of fathers, brothers and husbands of liberal, progressive persuasion. Frederick

---

116 GWLED, 31 July 1895, 3 February 1898.
117 GWLED, 15 November 1901.
118 This was possibly Margaret Stoddart (1865–1934), who became known for her flower paintings and was the most successful artist of the sisters. New Zealand artist Evelyn Page writes of Stoddart giving private art lessons: Paul and Roberts, *Evelyn Page*, pp. 24–25.
119 GWLED, 24 July 1894: Gladys and Anthony begin attending monthly public performance classes, where they had to recite poetry, play a piece of music, sing, act or deliver a speech. Dance lessons began for them both on 30 May 1891.

Wilding was the dominant male influence in his daughters' childhoods. His part in the discussions between husband and wife that provided the backdrop to the decisions that shaped the education of Gladys remains shadowy, compressed in the 'we have decided' entries by Julia in the Life Events Diaries.[120] Nonetheless his was an encouraging and involved presence. He read Gladys stories, took an interest in her activities, helped her with her French and music and offered comments on her essays.[121] What is abundantly clear, however, is that his role in securing the health and physical fitness of his children was paramount and constitutes an integral part of the education of all the Wilding children.

His boyish enthusiasm for games, which captured the attention of his children and lingered long in their childhood memories, rested, as we have seen, upon a belief in their role in providing the necessary balance between the needs of mind and body. It converged neatly with Julia's belief that girls and young women should assert their right to cultivate their physical strength and endurance and lead energetic lives. It led naturally to an almost spartan household regime of cold baths, fresh air and plain food. His belief in the efficacy of games led him to create what might be seen as a child-centred home at Fownhope, resplendent with tennis courts, croquet green, cricket pitch and swimming baths. There was room for bicycles, roller skates and go-carts, and boisterous play saw the Wilding children careering around the neighbourhood. It is perhaps not too fanciful to see this environment as helping to instil competitiveness that recognised few, if any, gender boundaries.[122]

The Wildings' family environment provided greater scope for social engagement with a more varied section of society than the comparatively cloistered Macmillan Brown household. Throughout the childhoods of Gladys and her siblings, Fownhope was the setting for countless social afternoons of tennis, music and food, as Julia and Frederick entertained international sporting teams, Antarctic explorers, musicians, politicians and community leaders.[123]

---

120 For some examples, see GWLED, 18 August 1888, 27 May 1892; and AFWLED, 29 May 1895.
121 For some examples, see GWLED, 1 September 1889, 6 June 1894.
122 Cora Wilding, 'Notes and Information on the Life of Julia Wilding', WFP; Gladys, Anthony and Cora Wilding's Life Events Diaries, passim.
123 Events Diaries kept by Julia Wilding, 2 vols: 1879–1908, 1909–1942, WFP, box 11/54-55; Fownhope Visitor's Book: 1911–1945, 1975, WFP, box 11A/56c/56c. See also LED.

The relative informality of the occasions provided space for children and the opportunity for them to develop social awareness. It is perhaps a measure of Frederick's involvement in his children's lives that he quickly became the main attraction at the regular children's parties held at Fownhope for as many as 70 girls and boys. As a veritable master of games, he entertained the children with fireballs and organised every imaginable running race: sack, egg and spoon, and three-legged, as well as the conventional variety. By precept and example he hoped to stimulate participation, and as his children grew older he encouraged them to organise their own mixed tennis tournaments and children-only dances at the family home. Above all else, Frederick's enthusiasm for games for all was deeply infused with a desire to cultivate excellence amongst those with sporting talent. This aspect of his involvement with his children became more evident in the education of his son Anthony. In Gladys's upbringing we can see Frederick's sporting enthusiasms as providing the balance so much prized by a mother in theory, but in practice almost compromised in a quest for musical and scholarly excellence.

In 1900 Gladys confidently embarked upon an arts degree at Canterbury College. An objective she had anticipated since her teens, it rested upon the firm foundations of a carefully constructed education, and was made more secure by the pioneering generation of women graduates, whose success encouraged emulation and eroded opposition. Gladys had grown to maturity in a household where feminist goals had been quietly pursued and university study was viewed as a right won by merit alone. She was comfortable within an institution that had by 1900 seen more than 100 women graduates pass through its gates and appears to have rejected suggestions that the ancient universities of 'Home' might have more to offer.[124] Cambridge and Oxford might be attractive destinations for the sons of the colonial middle class, but, as Julia and Gladys were well aware, they were reluctant to confer degrees upon women. London University, as her uncle Edwyn had pointed out, had been doing so since 1880. Whatever its attractions, the congenial and familiar environment of Canterbury College was embraced with enthusiasm.

---

124 Gardner, *Colonial Cap and Gown*, p. 106; Gardner, 'Formative Years', p. 157; Matthews, *In Their Own Right*, pp. 88–89.

Like the great majority of female students, Gladys pursued an arts degree built around English and French. Distinctions and prizes followed: the University of New Zealand Bowen Prize (1902) for her essay on the Indian Mutiny, the French Exhibition (1902), the University of New Zealand senior scholarship for French and English (1903). A BA degree with first-class honours in French and second-class honours in English was conferred in 1903 and an MA, with first-class honours in French and English languages and literature, in 1904. Throughout Gladys's studies her parents' level of interest changed little though circumstances led to a gradual increase in their involvement. Towards the end of her first university year she was struck by a debilitating and unexplained back problem that forced her to reduce her attendance at lectures, relinquish her junior scholarship and work mostly at home. Her greater presence at Fownhope encouraged both mother and father to engage more frequently with the progress of her studies. Both parents read her essays, discussed marker's comments and offered encouragement. Frederick was so impressed with his daughter's essay on the Indian Mutiny that he had it published.[125] It was with scarcely contained maternal pride after Gladys's graduation in June 1904 that Julia Wilding acknowledged the realisation of a family endeavour: 'we are so very pleased … She has got all she wanted & worked for now, & it is a splendid winding up to her university career'.[126]

In terms of her mother's professed objectives, talent had been nurtured and rewarded; Gladys had become an educated, cultured individual and was ready to make a useful contribution to society. The possibility of knowing the precise form this might take was tragically denied by Gladys's sudden death on 19 October 1905, aged 23. A week after she gained her master's degree from Canterbury College, she had sailed for Europe as she had long planned. The decision was loaded with educational purpose. Gladys wanted the chance to try out her foreign language skills and Julia provided, as she was to do for all her children who travelled abroad, a list of books to be read and museums and art galleries to visit. In late October 1904, however, Gladys was diagnosed with spinal tuberculosis. During the months in England spent lying flat on her back waiting to recover, she became increasingly anxious

---

125 Gladys J. Wilding, *The Indian Mutiny of 1857: Its Causes and Results* (New Zealand University Bowen Essay 1901), Lyttelton Times Co., Christchurch, 1902; GWLED, 25 February 1902.
126 GWLED, 17 February 1904, 24 June 1904.

to 'feel capable of earning a little myself'.[127] For several months she worked steadily editing and indexing the manuscript of *Two Years in the Antarctic* written by Albert Armitage, a friend and member of the 1901–4 British national Antarctic expedition.[128] The experience stimulated her interest in the natural sciences and led her to contemplate writing a book on New Zealand flora and fauna as well as enrolling for a science degree upon her return to Christchurch.[129] Nature and nurture had produced an industrious and enthusiastic scholar seemingly about to make herself useful.

In the second Wilding daughter nature and nurture often proved uncomfortable companions. How to solve the problem of Cora was a constant preoccupation for both parents, and adjustments were made within the parameters of the educational framework that continued to shape their daughters' education, in order to accommodate a different set of talents. The fourth child in the Wilding family, born in 1888, Cora was seven years Gladys's junior and for her first nine years the youngest member of the family. Within this increasingly busy household, the less biddable Cora emerges, at least in the judgement of her parents, as an excitable and energetic girl: intelligent, strong willed, quick tempered and ill-disciplined. By the time she was three years old Cora was declared by her mother to be 'the most difficult to manage of all the children', though Julia expressed the hope that she would 'get better as she grows older'.[130] What followed was a process of experimentation in which Julia and Frederick sought to harness such talents as they detected. In essence, the education of Cora involved greater use of professional teachers away from Fownhope as a day student and as a boarder at some distance from Christchurch.

The process began in September 1892 at Miss March's private kindergarten in Opawa near Fownhope, and it continued there until 1897.[131] We learn something of what Cora did and how Miss March

---

127 Letter from Gladys Wilding to Julia Wilding, 11 March 1905, WFP, box 17/82/104.

128 Albert Borlase Armitage, *Two Years in the Antarctic: Being a Narrative of the British National Antarctic Expedition*, Edward Arnold, London, 1905. A captain in the British Navy, Scottish Albert Armitage (1864–1943) was Robert Falcon Scott's navigator and second-in-command on the *Discovery* expedition to Antarctica (1901–4). Along with other members of the expedition, Armitage attended tennis parties at Fownhope when their ship docked in Lyttelton in 1901.

129 Letters from Gladys Wilding to Julia Wilding, 11 March 1905, 5 June 1905, WFP, box 17/82/104, box 17/83/115.

130 CWLED, 28 January 1892.

131 CWLED, 20 September 1892 – December 1897.

assessed her progress from a surviving report: 'reading (attentive), writing (improving slowly), arithmetic (good), drawing (painstaking) and occupations (rather untidy)'. We learn also that while Cora was late 16 times and absent five times, her general conduct was thought 'attentive and good'.[132] During the school holidays, it was elder sister Gladys, and not her mother, who continued the general daily lessons.[133] Julia persisted with singing and piano tuition for some 18 months before observing that Cora's 'little temper shows here too sometimes, & I think she would make better progress with a stranger than with me'.[134] By 1897 the music lessons had also been passed to Miss March. Progress was 'very slow' and Julia was disappointed: 'She does not like it all, & will not practise at home as she ought.'[135]

In February 1898 the 10-year-old was sent to Mr Wilson's school, as had Gladys and her brothers. The decision was made with some trepidation, and her doubts issued in an outpouring of maternal anxiety:

> Cora is a very difficult little woman to manage. She is passionate & very naughty & rude sometimes, but she has very strong feelings & very high spirits & is exceedingly affectionate. She needs a lot of patience in dealing with her, & I often feel that I have not half enough. She really is very trying & I cannot help being cross sometimes when I know I ought only to be <u>very</u> patient. Cora's is one of those dispositions which can be made or marred according to the way she is managed, & I often feel that I am deficient in the patience and forbearance which I am sure ought to be the foundation of managing her.[136]

Wilson's Cranmer House School proved to be a short-term solution; Julia subsequently planned a trip 'Home' with Gladys for the following year and decided it would be best for Cora to stay at a boarding school in her absence. Consequently, in 1899 Cora was sent to Mrs Torlesse's school in Rangiora, 32 kilometres from Christchurch, where in an all-girls' class she was taught Latin, 'Kindergarten' (reading, writing and arithmetic) and drawing. On Julia's return to Christchurch in November 1899, she noted an improvement in Cora's manners as a

---

132 'Kindergarten I Report for Third Term, 1892. Cora Wilding' (Miss March's kindergarten, Opawa), CWLED.

133 For an example, see CWLED, 31 July 1895.

134 CWLED, 28 February 1896.

135 CWLED, 24 September 1898.

136 CWLED, 14 February 1898.

result of the boarding experience, though her concerns seemingly lingered.[137] The search for a solution to the problem of Cora's education began in earnest the following year with an attempt to educate Cora and her special friend, Ruth Anderson, at Fownhope with a 'daily governess'. Julia was soon to confess that while Miss Smythe was 'very nice with Cora' she was 'hardly strict enough'.[138] Behind these worries lurked the realisation that her daughter did not make enough effort. Such a thought was a troubling one since industry was fundamental to a good and useful life:

> Cora is <u>certainly</u> not very fond of her work, & is not an industrious girlie. I was talking to Miss Smythe about her, & she thinks that she would make much more progress if she took a real interest in her work, but at present Cora does not seem to have a pronounced taste for anything ... Cora is the most impulsive, maddest girlie possible, but <u>so </u>affectionate & loving.[139]

The conclusion that boarding school might be the answer to the perceived problem of Cora was nonetheless resisted for now. Instead, in 1901 Cora was enrolled at Christchurch Girls' High School, something of a nursery for Canterbury College students, with a reputation for academic achievement, hard work and strong female role models.[140]

Cora struggled in the new environment, where she had 'impositions' or detention nearly every day. The ever vigilant Julia was satisfied that Cora was made to work a great deal harder and had much more homework, though she insisted that she was put in a lower class. Her emergence as a talented athlete and tennis player was similarly read as a sign of greater endeavour. Yet before the verdict of the teachers appeared in their end of year school report for 1902—a report that showed Cora had come second in three subjects (algebra, Euclid and English literature) and third in 'mathematics total'—Julia reported:

---

137 CWLED, 21 January 1899, 1 February 1899, 5 February 1899, 26 February 1899, 15 November 1899, 21 December 1899.

138 CWLED, 10 February 1900, 28 February 1900, 9 March 1900.

139 CWLED, 3 June 1900.

140 CWLED, 31 January 1900. For information about Christchurch Girls' High School see Peddie, *Christchurch Girls' High School*; Lovell-Smith, *Easily the Best*, pp. 31, 41–54, 66–67, 71–75; Grossmann, *Life of Helen Macmillan Brown*, pp. 44–45; Gardner, *Colonial Cap and Gown*, pp. 97–98.

> We have just decided to send Cora to Nelson College [in the Tasman district] next year. We think the discipline & going away from home for a while, will be good for her & we have heard that it is such a good school & such a nice set of girls there. Cora is herself delighted at the thought of going.[141]

As much as anything, the decision reveals a mother's determination to explore to the full all possibilities of nurturing whatever innate talent her daughter possessed. There are hints also that it was a decision shaped in part by the desire to provide an opportunity for Cora away from the shadow of her high achieving older sister, now distinguishing herself at Canterbury College.

Nelson College for Girls was staffed by university graduates and disciples of Helen and John Macmillan Brown, and prided itself upon getting girls through matriculation exams. By Julia's assessment Cora was 'getting on famously' there.[142] In her academic studies she topped her class in arithmetic and geography and was second in Euclid and, despite expressing reservations that she was not 'altogether competent', was placed on the school magazine committee.[143] On the playing fields she had been appointed captain of the Boarders' hockey team in 1904, judged its best back and all-round player, and she also won prizes in swimming and played water polo. Despite the promising progress, in September 1904 Julia wrote that 'Cora is not going in for Matriculation after all this year'.[144] The decision embodied a recognition by Julia that an academic future of the kind envisaged for Gladys was simply not appropriate for her younger daughter. It was followed by the construction of an equally thorough educational program built around an emerging artistic talent. After much consultation within the artistic community, lessons in drawing and painting were arranged, both at Fownhope and in the city. At Julia's insistence Cora attended classes, as a cultural student, in French and English literature at Canterbury College.[145] In September 1905 Julia was to acknowledge that nature

---

141 CWLED, 26 September 1902. For Cora Wilding's experiences at Christchurch Girls' High School, see also entries in her Life Events Diary for 1901: 9 February, 16 March, 30 April, 19 May, 14 June, 29 October, 8 December; 1902: 20 February, 22 May, 21 October, 22 November.
142 CWLED, 19 July 1904. On Nelson College for Girls, see, for example, Chambers, *Lessons for Ladies*, pp. 153–54.
143 CWLED, 11 May 1903, 4 July 1904.
144 CWLED, 17 September 1904.
145 CWLED, 9 February 1905.

and nurture had at last reached equilibrium: 'I think Cora is getting on with her painting and drawing … & is more persevering at it I think than anything else.'[146]

In its recognition of persistence, the observation looks backwards to a decade or more of familial encouragement and points the way to an approved future for her daughter. Within a month, Gladys had tragically died, and, while accompanying her parents on a pilgrimage to visit their daughter's grave in Eastbourne, Cora took the opportunity to have art lessons in London. On return to New Zealand she studied at the Christchurch School of Art, between 1907 and 1911. There followed two years in England and Europe studying painting, funded by her father. At the end of 1913, aged 24, she gave her first exhibition in Christchurch. That same year her parents had a studio built for her on the family property at Fownhope and began providing her with an allowance of £100 per year.

Several broad conclusions may be drawn from the education of the Wilding and Macmillan Brown daughters: the process occurred within mother–daughter relationships of unusual attention; within each family we may identify an adaptability and flexibility, as each couple recognise and adjust to the personality of their children; fathers played supportive and sometimes crucial roles. Julia Wilding's meticulous and demanding involvement in the education of her first daughter, Gladys, possessed elements of the unrelenting rationalism characteristic of her hero John Stuart Mill's own education, and normally associated with Benthamite utilitarianism. Moderated by a quest for balance and cultural awareness, the apparent rigidities of this approach were also softened by a personality grounded in a psychological and emotional understanding of individual needs. As university graduate and headmistress, Helen Macmillan Brown's relationship with her daughters was expressed in ways that later seemed to them to be aloof and distant. She sought to create for her young daughters a learning program tailored to their individual needs and did so within a sheltered family environment. Her tragic early death prevents us from fully assessing the adjustments that are clearly evident within the Wilding family as both parents respond to the quite different challenges presented by their second daughter.

---

146 CWLED, 10 September 1905.

7

Educating Daughters:
The Melbourne Girls

The daughters of University of Melbourne academics Alexander Leeper and his colleague Orme Masson lived with their families in provided residences within or adjacent to the grounds of the university. Their families were the least wealthy of those in this study and the most urban. In the Leeper household, the education of Katha and Kitty, Valentine and Molly was a shared enterprise based on mutual agreement between their parents, though Alexander was always the dominant influence. In the Masson household the maternal influence was the strongest force shaping the instruction of Flora Marjorie (Marnie) and Elsie. Three of the four Leeper girls undertook university degrees at the University of Melbourne; the Masson girls did not attend university formally, though Elsie underwent professional training as a nurse during World War One. The thinking that lay behind the type of educational experience received by these six girls captures something of the complex array of attitudes held by men and women towards the relatively new phenomenon of the female university graduate and the professional woman during the last decades of the nineteenth century and the early twentieth century.

The debate that developed about the appropriate social role for daughters of the new professional classes was, as we shall see, embedded in discussions of gender and class. Support for equal educational opportunities was not always accompanied by support for women's rights to complete political, legal and social equality.

Orme Masson supported the suffrage movement and favoured university education for women; his wife did not. Alexander Leeper championed women's right to university education, supported women's entry into the medical profession and agitated in favour of the ordination of women in the Church. He was slow, however, to accept women's suffrage, until women had proven their capabilities in World War One.[1]

The Leeper Girls: Kitty and Katha, Valentine and Molly

'A fair Home of religion and learning.'[2] Alexander Leeper used this phrase to characterise the type of environment he wished to provide for female university students at Trinity Women's Hostel. It could just as easily have described the family environments he created with both of his wives: Adeline Allen Leeper, 1853–1893 (mother of Kitty, born 1881, and Katha, born 1882), and Mary Moule Leeper, whom he married in 1897 (mother of Valentine, born 1900, and Beatrice 'Molly', born 1901). Within these marriages, Leeper's wives took on important but largely subordinate roles in shaping the content and form of their daughters' education. Any differences in the educational experiences of Kitty and Katha, Valentine and Molly largely stemmed from changes in the availability of secondary education for girls in Melbourne. When Kitty and Katha were at secondary school age, the Presbyterian, Methodist and Catholic churches offered such an education, but the Anglicans did not. Leeper was, as Marjorie Theobald points out, a 'key figure' in making good this deficiency by persuading the Anglican Church to purchase Merton Hall, a private girls' school, in 1903.[3] Lyndsay Gardiner discusses the role of Leeper in these developments within the context of the provision of accommodation for women

---

1   In relation to Alexander Leeper's views on women's rights see Lyndsay Gardiner, *Janet Clarke Hall*, pp. 1–6; Poynter, *Doubts and Certainties*, pp. 133, 136, 241, 337, 409–10, 428.

2   Alexander Leeper to Lillian Alexander, 4, 30 August 1888, Trinity College Council Minutes, 1883-1961 and Janet Clarke Hall Archives, cited by Gardiner, *Janet Clarke Hall*, p. 8.

3   Theobald, *Knowing Women*, p. 79. Merton Hall was established in 1893 by a former principal of the Trinity Hostel, Emily Hensley, after a falling out with Leeper. In 1898 it was purchased by Leeper's friend, W. E. Morris, for two of his daughters, Mary and Edith, to run. The school, at Leeper's suggestion, came under the provisional supervision of an Anglican Church council in 1900 and was purchased by the Church in 1903. See Poynter, *Doubts and Certainties*, p. 302.

at the University of Melbourne.[4] Whatever Leeper's role, for him personally, the establishment of such an Anglican church–run school opened up the prospect of a school-based education for Valentine and Molly, the daughters of his second marriage.[5]

Eldest daughters Katha and Kitty's education may be briefly summarised: tuition at home until their mid-teens, two years studying at a girls' secondary school in London, followed by a return to Melbourne, where they undertook arts degrees. It was carried out in a manner that replicated their mother's own education. Daily tuition from a governess was supplemented with teaching by their parents, and specialist tutors were engaged for music and dance lessons. This pattern continued beyond their mother Adeline's death in 1893 and ended with their father's remarriage in 1897. They were then escorted to London by their maternal aunt, Ida, and uncle, Boyce, with whom they lived while they studied for two years at a private girls' secondary school. This arrangement had been settled with Adeline as she faced imminent death from cancer. The decision reflected the Allen family's persistent and at times insistent role in the education of their granddaughters and nieces; it was based on a realistic assessment of family circumstance and probably not one that would have been considered had Adeline lived. The lack of an Anglican girls' school equivalent to Melbourne Grammar for boys, which Katha and Kitty's younger brothers attended from the age of seven and eight, might have been a decisive consideration, however. Given his steadfast Anglicanism, Leeper would have found it difficult, if not intolerable, to send his girls to schools of other denominations.[6]

Anglicanism and Trinity College dominate the upbringing of Katha and Kitty. Their childhoods were spent within the principal's residence, a three-storey, sandstone, 'Late-Gothic'-style building in the grounds adjoining the University of Melbourne.[7] Near Tin Alley, with its entrance and driveway facing onto Sydney Road (later Royal

---

4   Gardiner, *Janet Clarke Hall*, pp. 1–69.
5   Rosslyn McCarthy and Marjorie Theobald (eds), *Melbourne Girls' Grammar School: Centenary Essays, 1893–1993*, Hyland House, Melbourne, 1993, pp. 38, 57.
6   See Poynter, *Doubts and Certainties*, pp. 260–62, 265, 279–81; Alexander Leeper to Mary Moule, 31 December 1896, ALP, T1, box 21d; Alexander Leeper's diary for 1897: 10 April 1897, ALP, T5, box 38; Alexander Leeper to Boyce Allen, 28 August 1898, ALP, T1, box 30/68; Boyce Allen to Alexander Leeper, 11 October 1898, ALP, T1, box 30/68.
7   Poynter, *Doubts and Certainties*, p. 64.

Parade), the building consisted of 19 rooms; the three largest served the Trinity College students as dining room, library and chapel and were entered by a separate entrance from that of the Leeper's family home.[8] The size of the residence facilitated, to all appearances, some separation of parents from children, and of work from family life, thus replicating, in some degree, the patterns of upper-class family life in Britain. Alexander Leeper's study was located on the third floor— visiting students were announced to Leeper by a maid via a hose which stretched from the ground floor to the top level.[9] His wife's quarters occupied the second floor; two nurseries and a schoolroom were on the first floor.

In the day-to-day lives of the two girls, these apparent lines of demarcation blurred. The nature of the children's relationship with their mother meant that they had no qualms about entering her domain uninvited and frequently did so.[10] The family attended daily morning services in the chapel with the Trinity College students.[11] Meals were brought to the Leeper family from the college kitchen and the college porter also served the Leepers. A live-in maid, nurse and governess completed the Leepers' array of domestic help. Adeline did not engage in domestic work and was not involved in the basic day-to-day physical care of her children, though she tended conscientiously to them when they were ill.[12] Absolved from the constraints of domesticity, the Leeper family created a home that was, even more so than the household of the Macmillan Browns, a site of learning.

Within this confined setting, Alexander Leeper's personality and educational philosophy dominated. In the judgement of his biographer John Poynter, Leeper was scholarly and charming, possessed a lively sense of fun, but was also intense and emotionally demanding in his relations with his family.[13] His world-view centred

---

8   Poynter, *Doubts and Certainties*, p. 78.

9   Poynter, *Doubts and Certainties*, pp. 322–33.

10   For examples, see Adeline Leeper's letters from Trinity College, Melbourne, to Alexander Leeper in Britain: 12 August 1889, 30 June 1889, 5 July 1889, 19 July 1889, ALP, T1, box 23, envelope 52, 53.

11   The Trinity College students dubbed the tall, thin figure of Alexander Leeper 'Bones', while his children were affectionately called 'the Ossicles'. Poynter, *Doubts and Certainties*, p. 282.

12   For examples, see Adeline Leeper's letters from Trinity College, Melbourne, to Alexander Leeper, Britain: 30 June 1889, 5 July 1889, 23 August 1889, 29 August 1889, ALP, T1, box 23, envelope 52, 53.

13   Poynter, *Doubts and Certainties*, pp. 232–33.

upon a devout Anglicanism, a deep reverence for the values and literature of the classical world, but also a deeply ingrained belief in women's intellectual equality and their right to the same educational opportunities as men. They were beliefs formed in the Ireland of his youth. His mother was a strong, unusually well-educated woman, and his scholarly elder sister, Jeannie, frequently made him aware of her deeply held sense of grievance that she had been denied the education received by her brothers.[14] Consequently, Leeper supported the entry of women into degree courses at the University of Melbourne, and established the first women's residential university college in the southern hemisphere at Trinity College, in order to ensure that female university students could enjoy the educational advantages available to men. He later became involved, as noted, in the establishment and running of Melbourne Church of England Girls' School.[15]

Like John Macmillan Brown, Leeper greatly admired the writer George Eliot. He turned to her when seeking to sketch out his ideal of the educated woman. Was it not a 'staggering fact', he asked in a lecture on 'University Women':

> to those who hold that higher education tends to unfit women for domestic duties that Marian Evans during the years that she was proving herself an accomplished housekeeper, and organiser of charitable movements in her parish, was also mastering Latin, Greek, German, Italian and Hebrew, and was absorbing the multifarious knowledge with which her books overflow.[16]

If Eliot stands here as a rejoinder to those who saw the educated woman as a danger to the home and family, the classics assume the role of lodestar. For Leeper, immersion in classical studies would lead inevitably to an appreciation of the foundation of the liberal democratic ideal and 'would furnish the community with its best leaders and thinkers'.[17] In this belief, at least at the theoretical level, he drew no gender distinction. The Hellenic belief in the ultimate perfectibility

---

14 Gardiner, *Janet Clarke Hall*, p. 2; Poynter, *Doubts and Certainties*, pp. 14, 80, 131–32.

15 Poynter, *Doubts and Certainties*, pp. 131–50, 202–23; Gardiner, *Janet Clarke Hall*, pp. 1–69; Theobald, *Knowing Women*, pp. 75–80.

16 Lecture delivered by Alexander Leeper, 'University Women', cited by Poynter, *Doubts and Certainties*, p. 327.

17 Alexander Leeper, A *Plea for the Study of the Classics*; Marion Poynter, *Nobody's Valentine: Letters in the Life of Valentine Alexa Leeper, 1900–2001*, Miegunyah Press with Trinity College, University of Melbourne, Melbourne, 2008, pp. 19–20.

of humanity became in the Leeper household the basis for a moral injunction for Alexander's daughters: to cultivate industriousness and make strenuous efforts in all things.

More than any of the other girls in this study, Katha and Kitty grew up in a household steeped in the poetry, literature and values of the ancient classical world. As youngsters they listened to their father's stories drawn from the myths and legends of Greece and Rome and attended the Greek plays he produced at Trinity College. Kitty, in particular, became an enthusiastic student of the classical world and, at the age of 12, asked to be taught Latin by her father.[18] Some months before, Leeper announced simply in his diary that he had that day given his wife and daughters 'a little preliminary lesson in Greek grammar'.[19] The brevity of the statement should not obscure its wider import. Greek was a subject traditionally thought too difficult for girls. In nineteenth- and early twentieth-century Britain, knowledge of Greek was regarded as a marker of scholarly and gentlemanly status, and this belief was well established in colonial Australia. Since it was a compulsory component of an arts degree at the University of Melbourne, it followed that Greek was embedded in the curriculum of the city's private boys' schools.[20] Leeper's diary entry may thus be read as indicating the path that he felt his daughters' education should take.[21] Kitty was perhaps a more willing participant in the lessons than Katha. Writing to her father from her mother's family in Sydney, 12-year-old Kitty was 'very very glad to be coming back to Trinity. I want to begin Latin and Greek as soon as ever I get there ... .'[22] In confirming her sister's enthusiasm, Katha complains that she had sat down to her Latin at Kitty's insistence, 'although the Georgics and Medea always make me dead with sleep, which shows I can't have much love for Classics'.[23]

---

18   Kitty Leeper to Alexander Leeper, 10 September 1893, Poynter, *Doubts and Certainties*, p. 231.
19   Alexander Leeper's diary for 1893: 4 January 1893, ALP, box 38.
20   Greek ceased to be compulsory for entry to the University of Melbourne in 1913. See Poynter, *Doubts and Certainties*, pp. 355–56.
21   As an optional component of the arts degree in New Zealand universities, Greek was often avoided by the early generation of women students who lacked the preparation for it. Gladys Wilding chose not to study the subject. Mathematics and Latin were, however, compulsory subjects in the BA course at the University of New Zealand until 1911 and 1917 respectively.
22   Kitty Leeper to Alexander Leeper, 10 September 1893, Poynter, *Doubts and Certainties*, p. 231.
23   Katha Leeper to Alexander Leeper, 2 February 1899, ALP, T2, box 21d; Poynter, *Doubts and Certainties*, p. 281.

Leeper's biographer depicts him as a man permanently locked in a struggle with his conscience between Hellenism's 'sweetness and light', a belief in the presence of 'noble and divine' elements in humans, and Hebraism's deep sense of the presence of sin.[24] Whether his children absorbed this sense of moral struggle from their highly religious upbringing is unclear, but there can be no doubt that Leeper demanded a high level of moral accountability from them. Religious instruction was an important part of their education and religious observance part of their daily life. They attended morning prayers in the Trinity College chapel with the students from Monday to Saturday and St Mary's Church service on a Sunday morning, before going to a Sunday school class conducted by their mother.

Leeper's role as the definer of a strict and demanding moral code, fixed within an orthodox Anglican framework and buttressed by certainties derived from the classical world, is an important dimension of his influence in his daughters' upbringing. It is not, however, the only one. Despite a busy professional life, his active involvement in their education reached beyond teaching them Latin and Greek. Signs of intellectual development prompted delight and were followed by efforts to extend and encourage. When Kitty 'wrote a sonnet on Faith in wonderfully short time after [he] showed her the structure from Matthew Arnold's Sonnets', he recorded the event excitedly in his diary.[25] He was enthused similarly when 'Thea [Kitty] wrote a beautiful little poem "Day and Night" in irregular metre' and judged it 'Very full of promise'.[26] He helped her prepare poems for recitation at the Daffodil Club, which she attended regularly on Saturdays, and watched plays that she produced and inveigled friends and siblings to act out.[27] On occasions he acted alongside them in performances of scenes from Shakespeare's plays, produced for the family's entertainment.[28] He also made outings to the theatre and musical concerts a feature of family life. Indeed, these demonstrations of paternal involvement

---

24   The phrase 'sweetness and light' comes from Matthew Arnold's essay, *Culture and Anarchy*, (1869). For Alexander Leeper's views on classical values and studies see, for example, Poynter, *Doubts and Certainties*, pp. 1–6, 355–58, 418, 429–30.

25   Poynter, *Doubts and Certainties*, p. 233, fn 28 29 October 1895, 8 March 1896; Alexander Leeper's diary for 1895: 29 October 1895, diary for 1896: 8 March 1896, ALP, box 38.

26   Alexander Leeper's diary for 1892: 7 February 1892, ALP, box 38.

27   See, for example, Alexander Leeper's diary for 1892: 4 June, 25 July, 20 August, 10 September, ALP, box 38.

28   Poynter, *Doubts and Certainties*, p. 261.

reveal a capacity to be charmed by his daughters in ways that seem to be less evident, as we shall see in Chapter 8, in his relations with his sons.[29]

There can be little doubt that the Leeper household was a patriarchal one. And within its recorded remnants, we glean a less complete picture of the maternal influence. Educated, refined and musically talented, Adeline shared her husband's belief in the importance of a classical liberal education for her daughters. On a practical level, it was she who engaged the governess and watched over her work, and organised the children's attendance at music, dance, French and gymnastic class lessons outside the family home. Above all else, she encouraged and fed the girls' voracious reading habits. Her birthday and Christmas presents to them were 'principally books', on one occasion 'about 9 or 10'.[30] She showed little inclination to measure and record the stages of her daughters' intellectual development, as Julia Wilding had done so meticulously. Such comments as we may glean are made most commonly in letters to her husband during times when they are apart and, more rarely, in a personal diary. In both these Adeline strikes a note of affectionate bemusement and pride in the different enthusiasms and achievements of her two girls. Katha's mania for sums and Kitty's for spelling and poetry draw special mention:

> Katha has spent a great part of the day doing sums—I never saw anything so funny as her craze for sums. She is always begging people to set her addition & subtraction sums and when she can get no [one else she] plods through Kitty's not very intelligible rows of figures & when I went up to kiss her in bed this evening she was sitting up ... doing an addition sum that she had persuaded Mary [maid] to set up for her. Kitty says 'how can Katha like those horrid things'—& I am amused too—she is evidently going to be mathematical.[31]

---

29   Poynter, *Doubts and Certainties*, pp. 232–33, 324, shows how Leeper 'doted' on Kitty and Katha.

30   Adeline Leeper to Alexander Leeper, 3 July 1889, 9 July 1889, 21 July 1889, ALP, T1, box 23, envelopes 52–53.

31   Adeline Leeper to Alexander Leeper, 30 June 1889, ALP, box 23/52.

In another letter Adeline told her husband that eight-year-old Kitty had been spelling words out loud on a tram, to the general amusement of the passengers.[32] She recorded in her diary, with amusement and amazement, that Kitty 'wrote a lovely little poem' while waiting 'to be allowed to go & help scramble eggs!!'.[33]

As well as being an attentive mother, Adeline was also a powerful and demonstrative role model. She continued after marriage to dedicate much of her time to self-improvement. She read widely and frequently studied literary and religious texts with her husband.[34] Shakespeare and George Eliot were constant companions, and Adeline's German was with some persistence good enough to translate German texts into English for easier discussion, or, as in the case of some admired German prayers, for spiritual enhancement. She studied, for example, various literary works based around the classic German legendary figure of Faust, a dissatisfied intellectual who bargains with the devil, as well as the novel by German playwright and novelist Gustav Freytag, *Soll und Haben* (*Debit and Credit*), published in 1855, which championed the German middle classes.[35] That she spent much time perfecting her German language skills and approached the task of self-improvement earnestly is abundantly clear.[36] After attending an 'at home' that turned out to be a 'dull affair', she 'worked hard at German all this evening to make up' for the wasted time.[37] In the quest for personal betterment she was also prepared to give convention a nudge:

> I am going to have some singing lessons from Herr Hasting & begin tomorrow. I hope I shall like him & that he will teach well & be strict & very particular. I cannot bear those ordinary society teachers who don't like to find fault too often—I am not going to tell anyone about it but you (Ida of course knows & I daresay has told mother) for it looks rather ridiculous for such an ancient matron as I am now with four children too![38]

---

32 Adeline Leeper to Alexander Leeper, 11 July 1889, ALP, box 23/52.

33 Adeline Leeper's diary for 1892: 2 February 1892, ALP, T5, box 38.

34 For example, see Alexander Leeper's diary for 1892: 3 July 1892: 'AML read the first chapter of Hatch's lectures to me', 20 August 1892: 'Read *Paradise Lost* c AML in the drawing room', ALP, box 38; Adeline Leeper to Alexander Leeper, 21 June 1889: 'I have been reading a book that I want to talk to you about. But I want to tell you everything that interests me', ALP, box 23/52.

35 Adeline Leeper to Alexander Leeper, 14 July 1889, ALP, box 23/52.

36 Adeline Leeper to Alexander Leeper, 14 June 1889, 21 June 1889, 14 July 1889, 4 August 1889, 29 September 1889, 6 October 1889, ALP, box 23/52.

37 Adeline Leeper to Alexander Leeper, 4 August 1889, ALP, box 23/52.

38 Adeline Leeper to Alexander Leeper, 28 July 1889, ALP, box 23/58.

Adeline recognised the tension between this desire for self-improvement and her role as a mother: 'I am trying to work at German but don't get much chance [on these] damp foggy days. The children cannot go out & I do not like to leave them too much in the nursery.'[39] Her preference was, as she wrote to her husband, to make her children happy and their demands on her time were willingly and cheerfully borne.[40] The terms of her relationship with her children were less demanding than that between the girls and their father. There was also a more balanced approach to their education. She sanctioned complete holidays from lessons for her daughters, when she judged it necessary, reporting to her husband on one such occasion that the girls were 'jubilant over it'.[41]

The fact that she set high standards for her daughters is also evident from her letters to Alexander: 'I enclose a very badly written letter from Kitty—don't show it to anyone. She can do & write so much better, dear careless little thing but she scuttled it off in two minutes.'[42] Her attitude to Katha and Kitty's music lessons similarly reveal strictness and high expectations.

> [Katha] is at the moment practising away very industriously. She is such a good child about her music much better than dear flighty Kitty who hates overcoming difficulties & wants everything to come by inspiration. She would never practise properly if we did not look after her—however they are both getting on very well and can play a great many tunes.[43]

Adeline also sought and admired strictness in those engaged to teach her daughters. She approved a particular teacher of dance precisely because he was 'strict', and liked to attend the dance classes with her children so that she could observe and later reinforce the lessons: 'Unless I go with the children I cannot know what they are to practise for next time.'[44] When the teacher scolded the entire class for 'not practising properly', Adeline took it as personal affront to her

---

39   Adeline Leeper to Alexander Leeper, 14 July 1889, ALP, box 23/58.
40   Adeline Leeper to Alexander Leeper, 30 June 1889, 5 July 1889, 10 July 1889, 21 July 1889, 26 July 1889, 4 August 1889, ALP, box 23/58.
41   Adeline Leeper to Alexander Leeper, 10 July 1889, ALP, box 23/58.
42   Adeline Leeper to Alexander Leeper, 16 August 1889, ALP, box 23/58.
43   Adeline Leeper to Alexander Leeper, 14 July 1889, ALP, box 23/58.
44   Adeline Leeper to Alexander Leeper, 4 August 1889, ALP, box 23/58.

mothering skills, resolving 'to make my two practise up well for the next lesson. They have brought home their poles & blocks for their heads & I am determined that they shall do better next time.'[45]

The strictness and maternal oversight extended to social relationships. Her reluctance to allow her daughters to enrol at the private school Merton Hall was grounded as much in her unwillingness to countenance her daughters travelling across the city to South Yarra as it was in her husband's insistence upon a definitively Anglican school. Her keenness to accompany her daughters to dance classes grew in part from a desire to act as a type of social gatekeeper for them. From a wealthy legal and political Sydney family (of convict origin), she found lack of education and social refinement distasteful.[46] After attending a fund-raising meeting in Melbourne with the mayor and town clerk, she told Alexander that 'the want of education in the one and the prosiness of the other is almost unbearable'.[47] Her daughters' social circle consisted largely of other university professors' children living within the university grounds. At times, the social acceptability of some of them was sharply questioned. After holding a party for Katha's birthday, attended by 10 children from university families, Adeline declared she had seldom seen children so 'ugly and common' as those belonging to the Cambridge-educated mathematician Professor Edward Nanson.[48] Similarly, she judged the Australian-born children of the Yorkshire Methodist Professor Sugden, Principal of Queens College, to be 'warm-hearted but certainly not refined with terrible accents'.[49] For these reasons, she was reluctant at first to allow her daughters to attend dance lessons along with the Nansons and Sugdens, but relented because her girls 'like[d] the strange children'.[50]

Adeline's death in 1893 of cancer and their father's remarriage in 1897, when Kitty and Katha were 16 and 14 years of age, had dramatic consequences. The reconstitution of family life that followed was

---

45   Adeline Leeper to Alexander Leeper, 17 August 1889, ALP, box 23/58.

46   Poynter, *Doubts and Certainties*, p. 27.

47   Adeline Leeper to Alexander Leeper, 26 July 1889, ALP, box 23.

48   Adeline Leeper to Alexander Leeper, 21 July 1889, ALP, box 23; Selleck, *The Shop*, pp. 141–42.

49   Adeline Leeper to Alexander Leeper, 21 July 1889, ALP, box 23; Selleck, *The Shop*, pp. 239–41.

50   Adeline Leeper to Alexander Leeper, 26 July 1889, ALP, box 23. Penny Russell, 'A Wish of Distinction', ch. 1–2, examines women's role in upholding class distinctions and social standards of femininity in Melbourne for an earlier period.

shaped within the wider context of the extended Leeper–Allen families. Adeline's death had been preceded by a lengthy illness. She approved a decision that should Leeper remarry, the girls would complete their schooling in London and live with their mother's unmarried younger sister Ida, brother Boyce and his family. Above all else, this would allow them to continue their studies. Leeper could but reluctantly assent. These were, as Janet McCalman has written, 'terrible years in Victoria' and hard economic times brought 'a recognition of necessity'.[51] Adeline had brought an allowance to their marriage, and this had been used to fund the children's education.[52] But it was also a decision that grew naturally from a marriage in which the maternal extended family had played a significant role. During sicknesses and pregnancies, at times when Alexander was absent from Melbourne and for holidays, the Allen family home in Sydney had become an accepted part of childhood. Similarly, Ida had spent considerable periods of time helping her sister Adeline at Trinity College during Leeper's lengthy absences overseas pursuing college business. Her constant presence in the Leeper household after Adeline's death and as a companion on the journey to England and at the home of her brother Boyce Allen in London represented another continuity in the lives of the two girls.[53]

Precisely what impact this experience was to have on Kitty and Katha psychologically and emotionally remains unclear, but here we may briefly summarise the external markers of this transition from childhood to adulthood at the completion of schooling. During their two years in England (1897–99), both girls sat the Oxford and Cambridge Joint Board Higher Certificate Exam, though Kitty did not pass. They returned to Melbourne in November 1899 as planned, although Kitty had continued to express a desire to attend Oxford University.[54] Back at Trinity College, after coaching from their father,

---

51 Janet McCalman, *Journeyings: The Biography of a Middle-Class Generation 1920–1990*, Melbourne University Press, Carlton, Victoria, 1993, p. 55, citing Brian Fitzpatrick, *The Australian People, 1788–1945*, Melbourne University Press, Carlton, Victoria, 1951, pp. 217–18.

52 Poynter, *Doubts and Certainties*, pp. 120, 230–31, 234–35, 238–39, 261, 280.

53 See Davidoff, *Thicker than Water*, pp. 153–57, for a discussion about interdependence between unmarried, married siblings and their spouses.

54 Poynter, *Doubts and Certainties*, pp. 280–81; Alexander Leeper to Boyce Allen, 28 August 1898; Boyce Allen to Alexander Leeper, 11 October 1898, ALP, T1, box 30/68; Kitty Leeper to Alexander Leeper, 2 February 1899, ALP, T1, box 21d; Katha Leeper to Alexander Leeper, 6 April 1899, ALP, T1, box 21d; Rex Leeper's diary for 1899. Kitty and Katha Leeper left Australia on 10 April 1897 and returned in late November 1899.

both sat and passed the University of Melbourne matriculation exams in 1900. The following year, Kitty began an arts degree and Katha enrolled in the university's music conservatorium, having won an Exhibition in performance. In the blended family they now entered, new roles needed to be negotiated; without Adeline's presence, Leeper struggled to adjust to daughters, now 20 and 19 years of age, used to greater independence than he remembered. He was shocked, for example, at Katha's behaviour at university dances they attended, when she allowed particular men to dominate her dance card, and at her habit of staying out until 2.00 am after attending such dances. After initial success at university, sharing an exhibition in 1902, and having two songs she had written published the same year, Katha failed her course in 1904. Stimulated by her experiences in amateur theatricals, Kitty wanted to abandon university studies and become an actress, but, despite failing her course in 1902, continued at her father's behest and graduated in 1905.[55]

Throughout these years of awkward transition, the maternal extended family offered other possibilities. The Allen family had sailed back to Australia with the two girls and took up residence again in Sydney. Their Sydney home continued, as it had in their childhoods, to be regarded by Katha and Kitty to be as much a part of the family they belonged to as Trinity College.[56] Both girls spent a great deal of time singly and together with the Allens, and it is tempting to see them as a greater influence in these transition years than that now able to be exerted from within the blended Leeper family. Like the Boyce Allens, Katha and Kitty were increasingly leaning towards Anglo-Catholicism and away from the Anglicanism they had imbibed from their father.[57] In 1906 Katha (24) and Kitty (25) followed their maternal family to London, where their uncle Boyce Allen had now settled permanently, representing the legal firm Allen, Allen & Hensley. Ostensibly their trip was to continue their studies—Katha music in Berlin, Kitty to improve her German and pursue her literary interests.[58] Their lives would be lived out in the old world, not the new.

---

55 Poynter, *Doubts and Certainties*, pp. 283, 297, 322–25; Alexander Leeper's diary for 1902: 30 July 1902, 1 August 1902, ALP, box 37.
56 Poynter in *Doubts and Certainties*, p. 324, notes that when visiting the Allen household in 1905 Alexander Leeper had commented that 'family affection in this house almost takes the place of religion'.
57 Poynter, *Doubts and Certainties*, p. 281.
58 Poynter, *Doubts and Certainties*, p. 325.

What, if any, differences existed in the education of Alexander Leeper's twentieth-century daughters? Valentine Alexa was born in 1900 and Beatrice Mary (Molly) in 1901 to his second wife Melburnian Mary Moule, the mature-aged and not previously married daughter of the late Frederick Gore Moule, a partner of a prominent legal firm. Mary was, like Adeline, a scholarly and cultivated member of what John Poynter has described as the 'narrow world of Melbourne society'. At 37 years of age, she moved comfortably within that society, more comfortably than Sydney-sider Adeline ever had. Well-versed in the philanthropic activities of the city, she fitted quickly into a life at Trinity College.[59] By the turn of the century, governesses were hard to find, and Mary assumed the mantle of teacher of both daughters, relinquishing the responsibility only when she and Alexander visited England in 1908. From that point, until mid-1912, the two girls were taught within their home by Miss Cornwall, the sister of the college registrar. In its form and content there was little divergence here from the educational experience of their half-sisters, Katha and Kitty. Just as he had done a decade before, Leeper taught them Greek and Latin and read them stories from the Odyssey. When the girls reached secondary-school age, they were enrolled at Melbourne Church of England Girls' Grammar School. It had by then been receiving students for nearly a decade.[60] Leeper had played a major role in the purchase of the school by the Church and taken his place on the inaugural school council; he remained on its governing body until his death in 1934. Mary, thought to have possessed advanced views on women's education, shared her husband's enthusiasm for such a school and was to take her turn on the school council in 1915, while the girls were students. They helped create a school that would provide an educational pathway to university within an Anglican environment.[61]

In retrospect, and measured against the norms of time and circumstance, we can see in the childhood education and subsequent lives of Valentine and Molly Leeper the reproduction of two strains of late nineteenth-century middle-class thinking about women's place in society and in the family. Both were provided with an education

---

59   Poynter, *Doubts and Certainties*, pp. 246–65. Poynter's comment about the narrowness of Melbourne society is on p. 264.
60   Marion Poynter, *Nobody's Valentine*, pp. 19–29.
61   Theobald, p. 79; Marion Poynter, *Nobody's Valentine*, pp. 25–28; Poynter, *Doubts and Certainties*, pp. 383, 411.

thought progressive and modern by contemporaries. Described as possessing a keen intellect, Valentine took her place amongst the small group of young women who progressed through to an academic degree, winning a senior state scholarship to university and completing a BA at the University of Melbourne in 1921. As the eldest daughter of ageing parents, expectations and loyalties combined in ways familiar to her generation.[62] Financial constraints experienced by the family after Leeper's retirement in 1918 meant that they could not employ domestic servants, administrative assistants or carers. Parental expectations and Valentine's sense of duty to others, combined with her mother's failing eyesight and her father's physical ailments, meant that Valentine and her sister shouldered the burden of household work. At times Valentine's domestic duties had interfered with her university studies and affected her marks; such demands suggested a future which would continue to be held within the family environment that had shaped her.

Valentine became her father's secretary in 1922 and, along with her sister Molly, carer for both her ailing parents until their deaths— Leeper's in 1934 and Mary's in 1952. Soon after her mother's death, Valentine, aged 53, began a career as a teacher to supplement the sisters' small inheritance. In Molly's case, the circumstances of time, place and gender can be seen in a future that was to mimic that of her mother: unlike Valentine she did not proceed to university after leaving Melbourne Church of England Girls' Grammar School but became immediately immersed in domestic chores and joined her mother in philanthropic and civic activities.[63]

These were constrained choices, limited by family obligations and financial difficulties, and ones that seemed to embrace the norms of the day rather than the liberating notions implicit in the idea of the 'new woman' that point more to independent careers.[64] They were an indication, perhaps, that over 40 years after the University of Melbourne's first female students graduated, the pursuit of higher education and paid employment in the professions by middle-class

---

62 Carol Dyhouse, *Feminism and the Family in England 1880–1939*, pp. 25–27, 30–36.
63 Marion Poynter, *Nobody's Valentine*, pp. 28–42, and passim; Poynter, *Doubts and Certainties*, pp. 411, 430.
64 Kay Whitehead, 'The Spinster Teacher in Australia from the 1870s to the 1960s', *History of Education Review*, vol. 36, no. 1, 2007, pp. 1–17.

females still required significant emotional and financial support from their families. It also suggests the degree of difficulty involved in following pathways that were less than traditional for women.

This is not to imply that philanthropic and civic activities were somehow lesser than academic and professional ones. Valentine and Molly certainly did not see it this way. Moreover, such an interpretation would fly in the face of the importance that the Leeper family attached to familial and social duty, as well as adult lives of activism and social involvement that speak of civic commitment. Through Valentine's letter-writing to newspapers and influential public figures, and her involvement in a number of organisations, including the local League of Nations and the Victorian Aboriginal Group, she became a 'fearless champion of social justice'.[65] Molly worked for the Victoria League and the English Speaking Union, and, like Valentine, belonged to a range of organisations, including the Classical Association and the Australian Institute of International Affairs. The childhoods examined in this study suggest that the educated and cultured middle-class young women of the late nineteenth and early twentieth centuries were at one and the same time constrained by circumstances and liberated by the childhoods that had shaped them.

Marnie and Elsie Masson: 'The last of the Mohicans'.[66]

Like the Leeper girls, Marnie and Elsie Masson were born and raised within the vicinity of the University of Melbourne. Unlike them, neither pursued a degree there. Explaining why this was so takes us to the heart of contemporary debates amongst upper middle-class families about two interrelated questions: what social role might their daughters be expected to play and what form of education would this role require? Throughout the childhoods of Marnie and Elsie, we observe Orme and Mary Masson answering these questions within the privacy of family in increasingly different ways. Their answers might be characterised as mirroring the public struggle between

---

65   Marion Poynter, *Nobody's Valentine*, front jacket cover, passim; Poynter, *Doubts and Certainties*, pp. 411, 430.
66   Marnie Masson, Heronswood Log Book, 27 February 1906, Flora Marjorie (Marnie) Bassett Papers, UMA, 7/26/13, Rickard, *H. B. Higgins*, p. 207.

those who envisaged greater involvement by women in the public and professional spheres, and those who preferred middle-class women to devote their energies to charitable and philanthropic activities. It has become common to label these arguments progressive and traditional, and to link the former with the campaign for providing women with the same educational opportunities as men. Such a characterisation does less than justice to the subtleties within the conservative argument, which seems at first glance to require little change in the education of young women, yet which was, as discussed below, sometimes infused with an ambition to contribute to social progress and looked as much forward for its rationale as it sought legitimacy in the past.

The childhoods of Flora Marjorie Masson (Marnie, born 1889) and Elsie Masson (born 1890) have been viewed, from the perspective of adulthood, as ones of thwarted or delayed realisation of potential. That characterisation was endorsed in Len Weickhardt's *Masson of Melbourne*, in which the author accepts that it was Mary Masson's beliefs regarding girls' education and the social role of upper-middle-class women that 'denied' her daughters a formal university education.[67] That Orme and Mary developed conflicting views on the subject is clear: Orme supported women's right to equal educational opportunities, his wife wished to qualify her support. The fact that her qualification was to involve a denial of opportunity is also clear. It was Mary who prescribed that Marnie and Elsie's education should be one of tuition at home with a governess, followed by travel in Europe, finished by a stint of formal education at Melbourne's Church of England Girls' Grammar School and attendance at university lectures in French as cultural students only.[68] What is not so clear is how and why she came to hold this viewpoint, and how it came to be that her views prevailed.

On the face of it, the position adopted by Mary Masson regarding her daughters' education seems at odds with her own Scottish experience and her parents' beliefs. Born and raised in Aberdeen, she was a governess-educated, cultivated young woman with considerable

---

67   Weickhardt, *Masson of Melbourne*, p. 72. Weickhardt bases this analysis on an interview with Marnie Masson, n.d., and uses the word 'denied'. See DOMFP, box 6/10/1; Marnie Bassett, 'Notes', Marnie Bassett papers, 7/26/13. Selleck, *Finding Home*, concurs (see pp. 82–84, 98–99).
68   Weickhardt, *Masson of Melbourne*, pp. 72–74; Marnie Bassett, 'Notes', Marnie Bassett papers, 7/26/13; Selleck, *The Shop*, p. 651.

musical talents, and sat in on classes at the University of Aberdeen.[69] The university had extended its local exams to girls in 1880 and opened its courses to women in 1883, but it was a further nine years before women were admitted to degrees in Scotland. Both male sides of the family were prominent in the Scottish medical profession. Mary's uncle James Struthers, a Leith medical practitioner, had facilitated women medical students' entry to Leith Hospital. Her father Sir John Struthers (1823–1899), anatomist and Professor of Anatomy at the University of Aberdeen from the 1860s, was the lone authority supporting Miss Garrett Anderson in her unsuccessful attempt to obtain medical admission when he had been a lecturer at Surgeon's Hall, Edinburgh.[70]

Mary's mother, Lady Christina Alexander Struthers was an unusually well-educated woman for her times, taught by her mother, a former governess, and by her father, a country medical practitioner in Wooler, Scotland. In the 1860s she was an active member of the women's movement in Aberdeen. An outspoken advocate of higher education for women, she was a foundation member of the Aberdeen Ladies' Educational Association, launched in 1877 to provide a program of lectures delivered especially to women by university professors. She came to the realisation, however, that such classes were dominated by leisured women, who, because of their social class and gender, were ill-prepared for serious study. Lady Struthers consequently campaigned for a 'systematic' and 'continuous' teaching of girls and women.[71] She also believed it was important for women to gain university degrees: 'We must have attainment stamped and certified by the granting of degrees. [We are] training the future educators of the community.'[72] Whether Lady Struthers was referring to the more middling class of girls who would have to earn a living or included upper middle-class girls and women in her vision is unclear.

---

69   Marnie Bassett, 'Notes', Marnie Bassett papers, 7/26/13. Mary Struthers Masson was born in 1862.
70   *In Memoriam: James Struthers, M. D. of Leith*, Oliver and Boyd, Edinburgh (n.d.) (pamphlet), DOMFP, box 7/10/3, John Struthers, *Memoir of Dr. Alexander Wooler* (published pamphlet, n.d.), DOMFP, box 7/10/3.
71   Jenny Young, 'Mary Struther's Family Tree', ms, 1973, 'Mamma's Forebears', ms, n.d. or author given, 'Lady Struthers' (Obituary), *Journal of Education*, September 1907, pp. 602, 604, DOMFP, box 7/10/3.
72   'Lady Struthers' (Obituary), DOMFP, box 7/10/3.

Measured against these family attitudes, the position adopted by Mary Masson towards the education of her own daughters in Melbourne is a complex and seemingly ambiguous one. That it was not one based on any notion of women's innate inferiority, or an acceptance of a subordinate position, is abundantly clear from the influence she was able to assert within the family (most notably, in the education of her daughters) and in the more public roles she played. She was largely responsible for bringing university wives into the social life of the institution; hitherto, they had been all but excluded. As a founding member of the Lyceum Club established in Melbourne in 1912, she insisted that membership be awarded to women solely on the basis of individual merit, rather than that of their husbands or fathers.[73] Along with her husband, she supported the efforts of Helen Sexton, one of the first female medical students at the university.[74] Together with Mary Moule Leeper, she helped Lucy Archer, a widowed gentlewoman fallen on hard times, to obtain the principalship of Trinity College Hostel for Women (1906–18) despite her lack of formal university qualifications.[75]

For Mary Masson the issue of appropriate education for girls seems to hinge upon issues of class and gender. She drew a distinction between the 'gentlewoman' and 'the new woman', and the woman who needed to be educated in order to earn a living and the woman who did not. There were other dualities in her thinking: the value of working to support oneself and one's family as set against the worthiness of voluntary, unpaid work for the betterment of the community and society; the value of the pursuit of higher learning for its own sake, as opposed to the pursuit of formal qualifications. It is within this framework of ideas that Mary Masson's educational philosophy was given practical expression in the management of her daughters' educations. Put in its simplest terms, her answer to the question of what role should her daughters play in the Melbourne of the early twentieth century was unambiguous: as upper middle-class

---

73 Weickhardt, *Masson of Melbourne*, pp.74–75; Marnie Bassett, 'Once upon a Time', Address to the Lyceum Club, 21 November 1972, Marnie Bassett Papers, 7/26/13. See also Marnie Bassett to Elsie Malinowski, 6 December 1921, p. 5, DOMFP, box 5/5/2; Selleck, *The Shop*, pp. 524, 669; Joan M. Gillison, *A History of the Lyceum Club*, Melbourne Lyceum Club, Melbourne, 1975, pp. 26–28.
74 Weickhardt, *Masson of Melbourne*, pp. 39, 177. See also Helen Sexton to Mary Masson, 1 November 1935, DOMFP, box 5/6/2.
75 Weickhardt, *Masson of Melbourne*, p. 75; Gillison, *A History of the Lyceum Club*, pp. 32–33; Gardiner, *Janet Clarke Hall*, pp. 56–59.

and privileged girls, they should busy themselves alongside her in a life of philanthropy and good works until their marriage. It followed naturally from this answer that her daughters should be educated in ways that best prepared them for this social purpose. A university degree was unnecessary and interpreted by Mary as an exercise in selfish individualism, when pursued by young women who did not need to fashion a career. Furthermore, on a deeper psychological level, to encourage her daughters to pursue a lifestyle different from her own would possibly have been seen by Mary as undermining the validity of her own activities.

Mary Masson's strongly held views met muted opposition from her husband. Like Mary, Orme came from a family of highly educated, path-breaking women sympathetic to the objectives of the women's movement. Soon after his arrival at the University of Melbourne in 1887, he supported the successful attempt to have women admitted to Melbourne's medical school, the only course still denying women entry at the university. He subsequently gave much assistance to one of the first female medical students, Helen Sexton.[76] He is reported to have announced to his class at the time: 'Gentlemen, the ladies have come to stay.'[77] His support for women students was couched in terms that made clear that he expected their arrival to occur decently and with order. He saw Bella Lavender (née Guerin), Melbourne University's first woman MA graduate (1885), as someone who 'flaunts her MA degree', had a 'craving for notoriety' and was not a suitable role model for his 'impressionable daughter', Elsie.[78] Despite caveats he placed on his support for women within the university, his preference was that his daughters should take advantage of the opportunities that lay before them at the University of Melbourne. That he deferred to Mary flowed naturally from his more supporting than active role in the education of his daughters.

---

76 Weickhardt, *Masson of Melbourne*, pp. 39, 146, 177.

77 Selleck, *The Shop*, p. 650.

78 The first two quotes are direct ones from Orme Masson written in a letter from Melbourne to daughter Marnie Masson, England from Melbourne, 24 June 1917, DOMFP, box 6/9/1; the last quote is from Selleck, *The Shop*, pp. 651–55. Julia Margaret (Bella) Lavender née Guerin (b. 1858), the daughter of Irish-Catholic parents, became in 1883 the first female graduate of an Australian university when she graduated with a BA from the University of Melbourne in 1883. She went on to become a teacher, writer, suffragist, rationalist, anti-conscription campaigner and social feminist, and was briefly married in 1909 to George Lavender. See Selleck, *The Shop*, pp. 264–65. It was perhaps Lavender's involvement in the anti-conscription campaign that most upset Orme Masson.

Unlike their older brother Irvine, who attended Melbourne Church of England Boys' Grammar School, Marnie and Elsie Masson were for the most part taught at home by a 'daily governess' (usually a University of Melbourne graduate). Presumably for reasons of economy as well as social contact, they shared their lessons with the daughters of the biology professor Walter Baldwin Spencer, who had arrived at the University of Melbourne from Lancashire with his wife in January 1887.[79] The two families became close friends.[80] Mary Masson, who preferred a sheltered environment for her daughters, was uncomfortable with the Carlton in which the university stood, recalled later by Marnie as a 'down-at-heel area with a pub at every corner—a Dickensian squalor with drunken men reeling from pub to pub doors at any time of day'.[81] She rejected the idea that Marnie and Elsie travel across town to attend Melbourne Girls' Grammar School, though both girls would have welcomed the opportunity to make more friends outside their small university community.[82]

Marnie Masson later characterised her childhood education years and those of her sister as out of step with the times. She and Elsie were, as she put it, the 'last of the Mohicans'.[83] Home-based tuition from governesses was certainly becoming less and less common. As Ann Larson demonstrates, between 1871 and 1891 the percentage of Melbourne girls being educated at home (a category wider than that of governess) had fallen from 16 to 7 per cent.[84] Their education was as traditional in content and form as it was in its locale: dancing and music lessons (Marnie was a talented violinist) and drawing sat alongside the study of languages: French, German and Italian, English grammar and literature, history, geography, biology and mathematics.

The childhoods of Marnie and Elsie were, conversely, less driven by parental agendas than was apparent in the Wilding, Macmillan Brown or Leeper families. Here, we neither see a mother pouring her energies and anxieties into life events diaries that track all progress

---

79   Selleck, *The Shop*, pp. 287–89; D. J. Mulvaney, 'Spencer, Walter Baldwin (1860–1929)', *ADB*, vol. 12, 1990, pp. 33–36.

80   Weickhardt, *Masson of Melbourne*, p. 51.

81   Weickhardt, *Masson of Melbourne*, p. 35, quoting Marnie Masson, 'Once upon a Time', Address to the Lyceum Club, Melbourne, 21 November 1972, p. 24.

82   Weickhardt, *Masson of Melbourne*, p. 51.

83   Rickard, *H.B. Higgins*, p. 207.

84   Larson, *Growing Up in Melbourne*, p. 77.

towards a desired goal, as Julia Wilding did, nor is there any attempt for mother to become teacher, as in the case of Helen Connon; nor do we see a father as demanding as John Macmillan Brown or as impelled by enthusiasms as Frederick Wilding. What we observe is a mother keeping a watchful and careful eye over the education of her daughters, while maintaining a space between herself and them, and an attentive father absorbed in university affairs and prepared to leave the education of his daughters in the hands of his wife. Insofar as this was a conscious choice, it was one that reaffirmed a gendered approach to the education of the Masson children; as we shall see, a different pattern is evident in the education of their only son. It is possible also to interpret Mary Masson's approach to the education of her daughters as being an expression of a nostalgic yearning for Scotland. It took many years for her to adjust to life in colonial Melbourne, and it may have been a comfort to her to mould her daughters' education as close to that of her own as she could.[85]

The cloistered, gendered and traditional elements of the education of the Masson girls were vividly recalled by Marnie. This account accords with her view as a 17-year-old on the eve of the sojourn in Europe that would complete her education, and was recaptured just as vividly in verse. The occasion that prompted the reflection was both typical and special. Elder brother Irvine's friendship with Mervyn Higgins at Melbourne Boys' Grammar had led to invitations for both Masson girls to stay at Heronswood, Dromana, the country home of Henry Higgins. There, as Marnie recalls, they became part of the self-named 'Heronswood Push', a group that brought together the teenage children from the three middle-class, professional Melbourne families that constitute this study and a cluster of their contemporaries: Mervyn Higgins; Rex Leeper; Irvine, Marnie and Elsie Masson; Esmond Lillies;

---

85   Mary Masson's 'sense of loneliness in a still alien setting was to persist for years, until expanded interests took an affectionate grip on her being. She could not agree in later life with another expatriate wife that the happiest years of a woman's life were those when her children were young. "No", she said, "those years can be very lonely."' (Weickhardt, *Masson of Melbourne*, p. 36, quoting Marnie Bassett's address to the Lyceum Club, 'Once upon a Time', pp. 39–40.) In 1916 Masson unsuccessfully applied for the principalship of Edinburgh University (Weickhardt, pp. 85–86) and remarked to Lady Ramsay that 'in a few years we hope to go home for good' (Weickhardt, p. 129). By 1921 they had changed their minds and decided that it would be 'miserable living at Home' (Marnie Masson to Elsie Malinowski, 6 December 1921, DOMFP, box 5/5/2).

Robert Bage; and Hester and Nancy Mitchell, daughters of barrister Edward Mitchell and granddaughters of Dr Alexander Mitchell, Headmaster of Scotch College (1857–1903).[86]

At the close of 1906, the Heronswood Push was about to disband. Mervyn Higgins was bound for Oxford, and the Masson girls were joining their mother on a European tour early the following year. In the Heronswood log book Marnie recorded her thoughts:

One more day at Heronswood
One more day in which to view
The dark outstanding pines against
The water's shimmering blue.
One more day to gather fruits
That in the orchard valley grow
To rest upon the terrace top
Where the flowers blow.
After this we separate
Each will follow his own way
Boys to Varsities to work
And the girls to play.
But however wise they grow
With Engineering, Science, Arts
Or Civil work, dear Heronswood
Will never leave their hearts.
The girls will travel half the world
And many famous places see
But still the charms of Heronswood
Will fresh as ever be.[87]

---

86   Rickard, *H.B. Higgins*, pp. 206–7; Heronswood Log Book 1903–1916, Marnie Bassett Papers, 7/26/13; Nancy Adams, *Family Frescoes*, p. 52; E. M. Finlay, 'Mitchell, Agnes Eliza Fraser (1890–1968), *ADB*, vol. 10, 1986, pp. 528–30; E. L. French, 'Morrison, Alexander (1829–1903), *ADB*, vol. 5, 1974, pp. 295–97. Edward Frederick Robert Bage (born 17 April 1888), also a pupil at Melbourne Boys' Grammar, was the son of a chemist and junior partner in Felton, Grimwade & Co., and brother of Frederika Bage, University of Melbourne science graduate (BSc, 1905; MSc, 1907) and later biology demonstrator at the university (1907–12) and biology lecturer at the University of Queensland (1913–46). Robert Bage undertook a degree in civil engineering at the University of Melbourne, graduating in 1910. He was part of the Mawson Antarctic expedition in 1910–13 and died at Gallipoli in May 1915. See Jacqueline Bell, 'Bage, Anna Fredericka (Freda) (1883–1970)', *ADB*, vol. 7, Melbourne University Press, Carlton, Victoria, 1979, pp. 131–32. Esmond Lillies was also a pupil at Melbourne Boys' Grammar.
87   Poem by Marnie Masson, 1906, written in the Heronswood Log Book, 27 February 1906, Marnie Bassett Papers, 7/26/13, quoted by Rickard, *H.B. Higgins*, pp. 206–7.

And so 'to play'. The 17-year-old Marnie and 16-year-old sister Elsie spent most of 1907 travelling through England and the Continent, sightseeing in Scotland and studying languages, architecture and art informally in Germany and Italy. Their education was 'finished' with a period of formal schooling at Melbourne Girls' Grammar School. Elsie thrived on the experience. Marnie, tired and rundown, lasted only 12 weeks. Both succeeded in passing the matriculation exams that paved the way for university study—Elsie between 1907 and 1908 at Melbourne Girls' Grammar, and Marnie previously, in 1905, under the guidance of a governess. In deference to their mother's reservations, neither proceeded to formal university study but as 'cultural' students they attended 'French Part I' lectures at the University of Melbourne.[88]

As two educated and cultured young women, Marnie and Elsie now faced the transition from childhood to adulthood. The pathway each followed illustrates the confining and liberating aspects of their education and social position. Denied by maternal decree and family loyalty from pursuing a university education, Marnie took shorthand and typing lessons with the hope of finding employment in Sydney before 'secretly' and 'very reluctantly' abandoning her plans when her father, now president of the Professorial Board, offered her the position of secretary to the board.[89] Encouraged by the Professor of History, Ernest Scott, of Melbourne University, she attended his lectures (c. 1909–15) despite her mother's views. An article she subsequently wrote on the foundation of Melbourne University for the *University Review* revealed, as Ann Blainey has observed, an 'unusual historical aptitude', and she was subsequently invited to give five lectures to third-year history students on French colonial policy in the Pacific.[90] In 1915 she was awarded a government research scholarship to undertake research on 'the Scottish Political Exiles to Australia

88   Marnie Bassett, 'Cooling Streams', a Catalyst Paper, 10 November 1969, pp. 22–24, Marnie Bassett Papers, 7/26/13; Marnie Bassett, 'Notes', 8 February 1974, Marnie Bassett Papers, 7/26/13; Marnie Bassett to Weickhardt, DOMFP, box 6/10/1; Weickhardt, *Masson of Melbourne*, pp. 72–73.
89   Marnie Bassett, 'Notes', quoted by Weickhardt, *Masson of Melbourne*, pp. 72–73.
90   Weickhardt, pp. 72, 76; Ann Blainey, 'Bassett, Lady Flora Marjorie (Marnie) (1889–1980)', *ADB*, vol. 13, Melbourne University Press, Carlton, Victoria, 1993, pp. 127–28; *University of Melbourne Review* 1913.

1793–1794'. The research was disrupted by the war during which she worked in secretarial and administrative positions in Australia and London arranged by her father. Married in Melbourne in 1923, she raised three children before returning to history. Between 1940 and 1969, she published five histories and received honorary LLD degrees from Monash University and the University of Melbourne in 1968 and 1974 respectively.[91]

After returning from Europe at the end of 1907, Elsie Masson spent several years at her mother's side as companion and assistant. At the age of 21 she moved to Darwin as tutor and companion to the daughter of the former professor of veterinary pathology at the University of Melbourne, John Anderson Gilruth, who had been appointed Administrator of the Northern Territory. The letters that she wrote home from Darwin formed the basis of a book published in 1915, *An Untamed Territory: The Northern Territory of Australia*.[92] Returning to Melbourne on the outbreak of World War One, Elsie trained as a nurse at the Royal Melbourne Hospital from September 1914 until February 1919. She married the Austrian anthropologist Bronislaw Malinowski, against her parents' wishes, on 6 March 1919, and, in 1920, the pair sailed for England, where Bronio had been appointed to a post at the London School of Economics. Motherhood and illness dominated her later life. She died in Natters, northern Italy, in September 1935 aged 45.[93]

These two thumbnail sketches of life between schooling and marriage suggest, as Marnie's telling phrase 'the last of the Mohicans' does, something of the tension that existed within the lives of young women equipped by education and social position to fashion independent careers, yet in other ways constrained by family and custom. Marnie and Elsie were not so much students at the gates clamouring to get in

---

91 Weickhardt, *Masson of Melbourne*, pp. 75–76, 90–93, 98–105, 127, 191; Marnie Masson, 'Letters Home' (typescript), 6 December 1916 – 18 November 1918, DOMFP, box 3/2/1, pp. 1–11, 70–74, 179–83, 143, 216, 378–80, 389, 450, 558, 566–67; Blainey, 'Bassett, Lady Flora Marjorie (Marnie)', pp. 127–28.

92 Elsie Masson, *An Untamed Territory: The Northern Territory of Australia*, Macmillan, London, 1915.

93 Weickhardt, *Masson of Melbourne*, pp, 73, 75, 92–93, 99–100, 102–5, 131, 133, 146–47, 167–68, 170, 175–77; Selleck, *The Shop*, pp. 565, 590, 650–51; Wayne (ed.), *The Story of a Marriage*.

as raised within the cloistered walls of academe. Neither were they confined by the accomplishments that defined a different education for girls nor free from the constraints of maternal expectation. In their individual negotiation of different pathways through these tensions, they demonstrate both the continuities and the changes that shaped their lives.[94]

---

94   Elsie Locke, *Student at the Gates*, Whitcoulls, Christchurch, 1981; Elizabeth Plumridge, 'Labour in Christchurch: Community and Consciousness, 1914–1919', MA thesis, University of Canterbury, 1979.

8

Boys

The previous chapters on educating girls attempted to show the intensity with which parents approached the academic side of their daughters' upbringing at a time when the role of women in society was at the forefront of public debate. To the extent that the family and the home were the critical site of a gradual shift in middle-class attitudes to the education and upbringing of daughters, there were consequential adjustments within the lives of their brothers. The childhoods of middle-class boys have received less attention than those of their sisters, but they were just as much the product of an unsettled age, in which gender relations and definitions of masculinity and femininity were in a state of flux: 'The "New Man" was as likely to be found in the home in his leisure time as the "New Woman" was outside of it.'[1] The childhoods of the five boys discussed in this chapter—Anthony Wilding, Allen and Rex Leeper, Irvine Masson and Mervyn Higgins— occurred at a time that has been characterised by historians as beset by gender wars; in their wake masculinity became firmly lodged in the domestic realm, as 'patriarch' gave way to 'family man' cast in the role of breadwinner, father and husband. The quest for this more domesticated man was nowhere pursued more assiduously than in the homes of colonial middle-class professional families. It was a pursuit that began in the suburbs of colonial cities such as Melbourne and Christchurch, was concluded in British universities and drew upon the resources of the extended family in both the new world and the old.

---

1   Brookes et al. (eds), *Sites of Gender*, p. 3.

The colonial family environments in which the childhoods of the five boys of this study occurred differ in significant ways from those of the old-world environments that have shaped the historiography. The middle-class suburban homes of the four Melbourne boys were well-connected by inner city transport systems that allowed them to become day-boys rather than boarders throughout their schooling. The location of the Wilding home on the fringe of Christchurch likewise offered no obstacles in the way of parents who wished to have their children grow up in a domestic setting. The early, formative years of all five boys were not unlike those of most upper middle-class English boys; however, they were not dominated by the exclusively masculine environment of public schools, which minimised the feminising influence of the home. Whatever the precise nature of each family environment, it was the home and not a school community that became the most important and enduring influence in the boys' lives. Nowhere was the family's influence more evident than in the definition of gender roles and expectations. The extent of a gender-differentiated approach to educating sons and daughters can be measured more easily within families where brother and sister are close in age. Sisters and mothers will accordingly loom larger in this chapter than boys and fathers did in the section on educating daughters. The separate and collective female influence was particularly, but not exclusively, felt in the years before formal education away from the home began. If the process of expanding opportunities for daughters was sometimes prescriptive, the expectations that defined boy's lives were equally confining and heavily constrained by the demands of family endogamy.

As was customary for this period, the boys in this study were educated at home alongside their sisters until approximately the age of eight, either by their mother or by a governess. Then, unlike their sisters at the same age (with the exception of Gladys Wilding), they were sent to school. The Melbourne boys attended Melbourne Church of England Grammar School in South Yarra. Established in 1849 and described as one of 'six great public schools' in Melbourne, it catered for the sons of Melbourne's wealthiest and most influential citizens.[2] The school's city location meant that it was regarded as more of a day-school than

---

2   Bob Bessant, *Schooling in the Colony and State of Victoria*, Centre for Comparative and International Studies in Education, School of Education, La Trobe University, 1983, p. 48.

a boarding establishment, and boarders were always a minority.[3] It was as day-boys that Allen and Rex Leeper, Mervyn Higgins and Irvine Masson travelled by tram to South Yarra in a manner that was considered unsafe for their sisters. For Anthony Wilding the journey to the centre of Christchurch was a shorter one, which he undertook with his older sister to attend a privately owned and run non-denominational establishment.

Historians have characterised Melbourne Grammar's attempt to develop the 'trappings of an English public school tradition of leadership and identity' as being thwarted by parental indifference to the authority of headmasters and moderated by a quest for an innovative curriculum and scholastic achievement.[4] During the 1890s, as the four Melbourne boys of this study entered the school gates, the balance between academic and moral training may have shifted in ways that strengthened the emphasis upon character building. Macintyre and McCalman have suggested that this shift may have its roots in the economic crisis that revealed the hollowness of Melbourne's boom-time excesses and made middle-class parents more receptive to the moral elements of the public school educational program.[5] Certainly, George Blanch (1899–1914), whose years as headmaster coincided with the school years of all four boys, promoted academic rigour and drill with equal fervour.[6] By contrast, the small private institution which Wilding attended was resolutely academic in its pursuits. His early exposure to the character-building philosophies of the English public school came from his father, an old boy of Shrewsbury School, and was expressed most persistently in his espousal of athleticism.

Whatever influence their formal schooling exerted in the lives of the five boys, the school took second billing to the home. The greater time spent by boys in the domestic environment offered opportunities for mothers to expand their influence in the lives of their sons. Precisely how this was understood by the five mothers in this study is difficult

---

3   Weston Bate and Helen Penrose, *Challenging Traditions: A History of Melbourne Grammar*, Arcadia, Melbourne, 2000, pp.35, 30.

4   Bate and Penrose, *Challenging Traditions*, pp. 3, 32, 34–35, 39.

5   Stuart Macintyre, *History for the Homeless: Kathleen Fitzpatrick's Vocation and Ours*, Department of History, University of Melbourne, Melbourne, 1995, pp. 2–3; Janet McCalman, *Solid Bluestone Foundations and Rising Damp: The Fortunes of the Melbourne Middle Class, 1890–1990*, Department of History, University of Melbourne, Melbourne, 1994, p. 3; Crotty, *Making the Australian Male*, pp. 47–48.

6   Bate and Penrose, *Challenging Traditions*, pp. 99, 113, 116.

to gauge. The most explicit comment was provided by Julia Wilding. Before her marriage and departure for New Zealand, she expressed her views in the pages of the *Hereford Times*. Her article on 'Early Influences' in children's lives argued that the English practice of sending sons to boarding school from around the age of 12 gave heightened significance to their earlier and formative experiences within the home. The daily example of an egalitarian or at least companionate marriage could, she believed, influence the boys' views about marriage and gender relations. Similarly, the nature of their relationships with their sisters would lay the foundation for their attitudes to and expectations of women. As she saw it, instilling a proper appreciation of male and female potential was to be the work of both parents. It would be best accomplished by teaching sons and daughters together, and in their youngest years, within the home.[7]

No other mother addresses this issue explicitly. Without the reference point of the English public school that framed Julia Wilding's thinking, the colonial girls—Helen Macmillan Brown, Adeline Leeper and Mary Alice Higgins—approached the issue from within the everyday realities of their families. As the mother of two girls, Helen Macmillan Brown's concerns focused on providing a range of playmates for her daughters that included young boys.[8] Adeline Leeper's tragic death when her eldest son was six prevents us from fully understanding her attitudes. We see a mother who plays a supporting role in her husband's enthusiastic and demanding involvement in the intellectual development of all four children, in ways that cut through gender differences. Mary Alice Higgins saw the socialising of her son and only child primarily in terms of providing suitable companions. She found them at first in the extended Higgins family and later in the network of family friends that included Marnie and Elsie Masson and the Leeper boys.[9] Mary Masson's involvement in the education of her son was predicated upon the conventional assumptions of her class: a mother's role in the education of a son was to be a dominant one during a boy's early childhood, when he might be taught alongside his sisters, and then defer to school and husband, as the serious business of shaping a career began.

---

7   Julia Anthony, 'Early Influences', *HT*, 9 December 1876; John Stuart Mill, *Subjection*, in Rossi (ed.), *Essays*, pp. 218–20.
8   Baxter, *Memoirs*, p. 20.
9   Rickard, *H.B. Higgins*, pp. 206–7.

The precise nature of a father's influence within the family during the early years of a boy's life is difficult to disentangle from family life. Nevertheless, the activist roles of Alexander Leeper and Frederick Wilding emerge with unmistakeable clarity. The intense religiosity of the Trinity College household over which Alexander Leeper presided dominated his relationship with his sons. The defining event in their childhoods was the death of their mother Adeline in 1893, when they were five and six years old respectively. Adeline's death augmented the role of the extended maternal family, so that the two boys remained at Trinity College in the care of their father and their mother's sister, Ida.[10] The separation from their older sisters, who lived periodically with Adeline's brother Boyce and his family in Sydney and later in Britain, had the effect of increasing the paternal influence in their lives.

Alexander held great expectations of all his children, and there were subtle and gendered differences in his attitudes to them. These differences derived from an idealistic attitude to women, a preoccupation with sin and, above all, a reluctant recognition that sons rather than daughters would live their lives in the public sphere. From the first flowed a tendency to indulge the whims of his daughters and an acceptance that his 'guardian angel[s]', as he dubbed them, would act as the 'moral guardian[s]' of a domestic haven.[11] Conversely, his notions of human failure were attached almost exclusively to men and necessitated earnest attention to the spiritual elements of a young boy's education from an early age. Accordingly, from the age of seven or eight, his sons were required to write summaries of Sunday sermons, which Leeper dutifully corrected and assessed by awarding marks out of 10.[12] Through this deliberate and meticulously observed attention to the religious education of his sons, Alexander Leeper was laying a moral foundation that would provide the framework for the Christian and scholarly lives he envisaged for them.

Frederick Wilding's involvement in the early years of his first-born son Anthony was different in form, but was nonetheless grounded in a concern to provide a basis for the inculcation of a set of secular moral values. As we observed when discussing the education

---

10   Davidoff, *Thicker than Water*, pp. 168–69.
11   Alexander Leeper to Mary Moule Leeper, 31 August 1900, ALP, T6, box 36; Poynter, *Doubts and Certainties*, p. 324.
12   Allen Wigram Leeper, 'Book of Sermons', 23 October 1898, ALP, T6, box 29.

of his sister Gladys, the idealism that underlay Julia and Frederick Wilding's marriage placed children at the centre of their lives. It is possible to identify a number of broad strands in their thinking: a concern to maintain direct involvement in the upbringing of their children; a determination to minimise gender differences in their children's childhoods; a desire to provide an upbringing that balanced intellectual and physical development; and, above all, the inculcation of a set of secular values that prized social usefulness. Our understanding of the way these threads were woven together in Anthony's childhood depends—as did our understanding of the childhood of his sister—heavily upon the detailed life events diaries, in which Julia recorded with surprising frankness the successes and failures of parenthood.[13] It is in this context that we can discern distinctive elements of Frederick Wilding's involvement in his son's development.

Anthony Wilding was the second of the Wilding children and two years younger than his sister Gladys. The age difference simplified the organisation of their early joint education at Fownhope by their mother, or by 'Miss Tabart' in a small group of children at the home of a neighbour. Moreover, Gladys's precocious ability to learn quickly and her enthusiastic response to her mother's every encouragement allowed her to transform the role of big sister into something of a 'mothering' one. This relationship was actively encouraged by their parents, as they shaped Anthony's education. It lay behind their decision to ignore the boys' schools expanding in Christchurch to cater for the sons of the growing number of middle-class professionals and enrol brother and sister in a small private school run by a married couple in the centre of the city.[14] Girls and boys were taught separately; the courses of study were broadly similar, academic in emphasis, and provided a secular and family ethos that appealed to the Wildings.

Parental idealism is rarely inexhaustible, and the young Anthony Wilding's temperament stretched that of his parents' to its limits. Less malleable and cooperative than his sister, he was slow to develop an interest in learning to read, barely tolerated efforts to engage him in activities arranged for him and frequently responded with irrational

---

13   Anthony Wilding's 'Life Events Diary', vol. 1: 31 October 1883 – 26 February 1899, vol. 2: 15 November 1899 – 9 May 1915, WFP, box 20/92-93/1-2.
14   AFWLED, vol. 1, 29 May 1893.

outbursts.[15] Direct confrontation of this kind struck at the very heart of the rational and harmonious childhood that both parents had envisaged and Julia struggled to find a response:

> Anthony is such a little pickle, and is always up to some kind of mischief. His spirits are so high sometimes that he does not know how to give them sufficient vent, & all sorts of mischievous tricks are the result. We do not like curbing the little man too much, but he has to be punished sometimes. His will is so strong, & when he has made up his mind to do anything he is quite violent & so resolute, when he is not allowed to have his own way, that I am obliged sometimes to lock him in a little cupboard place we have. I find it brings him to reason more than anything else, & of course I only keep him there a few minutes. He will be a difficult boy to manage, & I am sure that with him, much will depend on the way he is treated and brought up. How earnestly I hope that we may manage him in the right way.[16]

In the analysis of the problems of disciplining a fractious son that Julia committed to her diaries, we glimpse an earnest mother in touch with expert opinion on childrearing and struggling to bring theory and practice into harmony:

> I am sure that the proper way to manage him is to lead him through his affections, & to lead not force him. But it is much easier to have theories as to how to treat children than it is to carry them out, & lead one's children wisely & well as one ought.[17]

This was to become a recurrent refrain. A year later she acknowledged the same dilemma:

> he has tremendous animal spirits, & I am afraid we sometimes curb him when we ought really only to direct his energies into a proper channel. I am quite sure that more than half the naughtiness of children is simply through not giving them something to interest & occupy them.[18]

---

15   AFWLED, vol. 1, 26 July 1888, 20 August 1885, 25 December 1885, 26 May 1886, 5 September 1887, 23 December 1887, 1 February 1888.
16   AFWLED, vol. 1, 28 January 1888.
17   AFWLED, vol. 1, 28 April 1888.
18   AFWLED, vol. 1, 12 September 1889.

In April 1891, her patience finally ran out:

> Last Sunday I gave Anthony his first beating. He is very disobedient
> sometimes, & if I scold or slap him, he gets worse & is very rude
> & even violent to me, so I thought it was really very necessary to take
> strong measures. I have an old riding whip of mine, & when he was
> rude & disobedient on Sunday (I had warned him some days before),
> I got it & gave him a good beating with it on the calves of his legs.
> He struggled and tried to kick for some time, but finally I mastered
> him & made him cry & he was quiet afterwards.[19]

Believing it 'did him the world of good', she hoped that the whip
would be 'very rarely' used in the future. But a month later she
acknowledged another beating and observed: 'I have found Anthony
much more obedient since I have taken to use the whip with him
myself. I have only had to use it twice ... it is not good to curb children
too much.'[20] Julia's discomfort at administering physical punishment
reflected, in part, a shift away from corporal discipline within the
home during the nineteenth century.[21]

If Julia bore the brunt of dealing with the young Anthony's behavioural
problems, the solution came from Frederick and in ways that illustrate
the active role he played in the early childhood years of his son.
His involvement was woven into the fabric of family life at Fownhope.
At its centre was a thoroughgoing commitment to the realisation
of a sporting playground in the spacious ground on the fringe of
suburban Christchurch. The opportunities for physical play included
a swimming pool, tennis courts, a croquet green and a cricket pitch.
There were trees to climb, a pony to ride and nearby hills to roam.
Over all this Frederick Wilding presided as an enthusiastic domestic or
family sports master. It was in this role that he engaged most directly
with his children. It would be wrong to see this as little more than
a high-spirited father indulging his love of games with his children.
Here he developed an affectionate understanding of their individual
temperaments. As someone who had imbibed deeply the central tenets
of the English games cult that saw the playground as an uncovered
classroom, he subscribed fully to the belief that games could develop

---

19   AFWLED, vol. 1, 15 April 1891.
20   AFWLED, vol. 1, 20 May 1891.
21   Tosh, *A Man's Place*, pp. 91–92.

important social and behavioural skills.[22] Frederick, rather than Julia, first realised that the uncovered classroom had greater appeal for the young Anthony than the covered one.

The discovery that games and physical activity were useful as behavioural tools for an obstreperous child was an unlikely basis upon which to build an enduring and creative relationship between father and son. It ultimately produced an international tennis champion, but its immediate relevance lies in its evolution within a familial context. The experience of games was one shared by all the Wilding children, and it is difficult to discern any gender differentiation. As a social setting for community Sunday tennis afternoons that brought friends and their children to Fownhope, the childhood experience of sport was devoid of the masculinity that characterised its more public form. Moreover, the family nature of the sporting relationship was not disrupted or overlain by the demands of a games master. Rather, as early childhood gave way to adolescence, the nature of the father–son sporting relationship took on a different and more intimate form, in which the terms 'emulation' and 'mentor' take precedence. As an active and prominent participant in shaping the city's sporting world—most notably in cricket and tennis—Frederick Wilding effectively shaped his son's induction into competitive club sport.[23] The transition from domestic to competitive sport proceeded gradually and with an enthusiasm on Frederick's part that spoke as much of sporting companion as it did of an overzealous father. On cricket field and tennis court they developed a father–son sporting partnership that captured the imagination of the sporting community. While significant in sporting terms, the relationship between Frederick and Anthony Wilding is grounded in a conception of family that embraced an active and engaged fatherhood.

The role fathers played in the early childhood of their sons expanded noticeably throughout their adolescence, as the world of work beckoned. In his study of British middle-class fathers, John Tosh

---

22 Frederick Wilding, 'Holidays', 8 August 1896, WFP, box 41/1; Anthony F. Wilding, *On the Court and Off*, Methuen & Co., London, 1912, p. 89; L. and S. Richardson, *Anthony Wilding*, pp. 195, 199.

23 Hall, 'Wilding, Frederick', *DNZB*, vol. 2, pp. 576–77; Appleby, *Canterbury Cricket: 100 Greats*; Daniel Reese, *Was It All Cricket?*, Allen & Unwin, Christchurch, 1948, pp. 25–26; T. W. Reese, *New Zealand Cricket 1841–1914*, p. 326; D. O. and P. W. Neely, *The Summer Game*, p. 31.

argues that ensuring the success of their sons was a critical component in the middle-class father's sense of self-worth and essential to the maintenance of gentlemanly status. As uneasy and insecure members of this section of British society, the five fathers of this study subscribed, implicitly or explicitly, to the view that they stood a better chance of meeting this expectation in the colonies. Their efforts to realise these aims produced a remarkable degree of occupational continuity: the two legal families groomed lawyers, the academic families produced scholars, whose interests reflected the intellectual preoccupations of the father. It would be wrong, however, to see in this process a diminution of the role of the mother in a son's upbringing. Rather, the importance of a son's education was recognised in a shared belief that the full resources of the family should be committed to ensuring a son's professional future. The importance attached to ensuring a son's future career manifested itself in different ways in the lives of mothers and sisters. Moreover, since the road to a professional career led each of the five boys to a British university, it was a process that reached back to their old world extended families in ways that underline the persistence of the family link within the ranks of the first generation professional class.

The education of their sons was thus pursued with the same seriousness of intent that was evident, for the most part, in the education of their daughters. Academic progress was carefully monitored. That less than full commitment could bring firm and decisive intervention by them is clearly evident in the education of Anthony Wilding. The decision to send him to a small private school rather than the city's larger boys' schools was based upon the recognition that his academic talents would require careful and persistent nurturing.[24] His failure, in 1900, to pass the matriculation examination required to enter university brought swift action from his parents, who had presumed he would naturally and inevitably take a law degree and join his father in the family practice.[25] A private tutor was engaged and required to produce regular written reports. The format was firm and the routine demanded strict adherence:

---

24   AFWLED, vol. 1, 25 September 1893, 29 May 1895.
25   AFWLED, vol. 2, 30 January 1901.

Anthony began lessons with Mr Smith to-day. He is to go to him every morning from 8.30 to 9.30 & then he goes to his Father's office where he has a room to himself to work in. He works till 12, then comes home to lunch, & then works again from 2 to 4. We hope he will really work well this year.[26]

Educational attainment was clearly regarded as an inescapable social obligation and the discipline required for success interpreted as an indicator of moral worth and potential usefulness.

It was when schooldays were over, however, that the parental role assumed its most directive form. Unlike their sisters, the boys took degrees at a British university—Oxford, Cambridge, London or Edinburgh—after a period of undergraduate study at Melbourne University or Canterbury College.[27] The gender difference was not so much founded in a belief in the educational superiority of the old world institutions, as upon a perception that the experience would stamp a British imprint on their sons that they would carry into the very British public world of professional advancement, in which their careers would inevitably take shape. Within this general perception, it is possible to find a mix of motives at work. There are hints in the observations of Henry Higgins and Alexander Leeper that sending their sons to Oxford was an opportunity to lay unfulfilled ambitions to rest: a university education was beyond the resources of the Higgins family when Henry was a young man, and Alexander Leeper had not completed his degree at Oxford.[28] Julia Wilding took the view that immersion in old world culture was desirable and best achieved at Cambridge. It was a view that her husband did not initially share. As he saw it, their son's propensity for putting sport ahead of study might be better monitored if he studied at Canterbury College and continued to live at Fownhope. He surrendered this position, however, after his wife enlisted the support of her brother, a Hereford gentleman scholar.[29]

---

26 AFWLED, vol. 2, 4 February 1901.
27 Millicent Macmillan Brown was the only female in this study to attend a British university. After gaining a BA degree from the University of Sydney, she studied at Piele Hall, Cambridge University, between 1909 and 1912, but was not awarded a degree, as was customary for women at the time. See Millicent Baxter, *Memoirs*, pp. 35–42.
28 Rickard, *H.B. Higgins*, pp. 207–8; Autobiography of Henry Bournes Higgins (ms), p. 30, HBHP; Poynter, *Doubts and Certainties*, p. 44.
29 AFWLED, vol. 2, 11 March 1902.

Whatever the rationale behind the individual family decisions, the phenomenon of the first-generation, colonial-born son at a British university created a peculiarly colonial version of the transnational family. The phenomenon demonstrates how middle-class British/colonial families constructed frameworks that advanced their collective social position and underwrote their Britishness. An education at one of the ancient universities was costly. All the boys of this group remained financially dependent upon their families throughout their university study; only Irvine Masson and Rex Leeper held scholarships. Each depended upon an annual allowance remitted by their parents—£200–250 for Anthony Wilding, £300–350 for Mervyn Higgins.[30] The households of extended British family—aunts, uncles and cousins—offered a way of lessening the expense during university holidays and, in varying degrees, represented a source of advice and assistance. It was from within the context of this wider family that Anthony Wilding was introduced during his long summer vacations to the myriad tennis tournaments that made up the English tennis circuit. Here also he experienced the less formal world of Hereford cricket.[31] In short, for Wilding as for other colonial students, the family eased the transition into English life.

The English family was often to play an important and direct role in determining courses taken, monitoring academic progress and spending habits. Indeed, the watchful eye of the family may have at times seemed ever present in the lives of the colonial boys. In this respect Wilding's experience offers the strongest example. His mother's brothers, Charles and Edwyn Anthony, scholarly proprietors and editors of the *Hereford Times*, took an almost paternal interest in the education of their colonial nephew. Edwyn, an Oxford graduate and qualified, though non-practising barrister, provided sensible and perceptive advice to his sister:

---

30   AFW to JW, 6 October 1902, WFP, box 20/95/13; Mervyn Higgins's Letters to his Parents: Oxford and War, letterbook (typescript), 18 October 1907, HBHP, series 2, box 6, pp. 77, 105. The Leeper boys were largely dependent upon disbursements from Adeline Allen Leeper's estate. It is unclear how much Irvine Masson received annually or if his parents provided him with an allowance in addition to his scholarship payments.

31   For example, AFW TO JW, 3 January 1903, 12 April 1903, July 1903, 26 December 1903, 30 December 1903, WFP, box 21/97-99/22,29,39,40, box 22/100/57.

I think you are wise not to urge too much about books. 'Tony' has plenty of intelligence—all men with unusual energy and a strong will must almost of necessity have—and he will probably settle down into an excellent lawyer. But he is not what you would call a 'bookish' man. Therefore I should not urge him further in that direction than to let him know that you wish him to keep abreast with his examinations, that is to say, that at every stage of the course he should be about where the majority of men are, who do not seek particular distinction but who take their degrees about the usual time.[32]

The complex interweaving of maternal and paternal elements of the Leeper family produced, during their years at Oxford, a tussle for paternal authority over the boys between their father and their mother's brother, Boyce Allen.[33] Following Adeline's death, Boyce become administrator of an allowance from her estate. After taking up more or less permanent residence in Oxford, where he established a legal practice, he gradually assumed the role of mentor in the lives of his nephews. Transnational conflict ensued as Alexander Leeper advised his son, Rex, to read modern languages and Boyce counselled modern history. The rights and wrongs of the exchanges between them aside, the earnestness that pervades Boyce's summary of the issues testifies to the importance each man attached to the educational choices before the family:

> The main thing is that the Modern Language School means simply a most minute study of one modern language—oral, written, prescribed authors history of the language including early authors, history of the literature including criticism, style and political and social history to some extent, and further a special subject. All this has reference to one language only. Now which is best for Rex—this or the Modern History School? I incline to the latter as a better education generally, bringing him more into contact with leading men at Oxford and probably, so far as we can see, a better equipment for life and for a profession. If he took Modern Language only, he would be confined to the Taylorian for his teaching and would scarcely come into contact with the distinctive Oxford teaching at all. Further as a preparation for the Student Interpretership Exam he has in mind, it would be useless. For all these reason his New College tutor advises History. Rex also strongly favours it.[34]

---

32 Edwyn Anthony to JW, 9 July 1904, Hereford, WFP, box 30/141/575.
33 For examples see correspondence from Boyce Allen to Alexander Leeper 1898–1919, ALP, T1, box 30; Davidoff, *Thicker than Water*, pp. 167–69.
34 Boyce Allen to Alexander Leeper, 25 October 1909, ALP, box 21d.

Boyce's hand in these discussions was by far the stronger one. Along with his brother, he administered Adeline's estate and controlled the disbursement of funds to the boys throughout their university years. He was a thrifty, censorious and sometimes tactless custodian of the family fortune:

> There is no doubt, my dear Alex, that both the boys came to England with utterly mistaken ideas as to their Oxford life—as to what success at Oxford meant in the way of effort—and as to the possibilities of travel open to them as compared with their leisure and their small means ... to be frank, I do think you gave mistaken advice to both the boys. I think a lot of valuable money has been wasted ... both boys came to Oxford with absurd ideas ...[35]

His presence in Oxford gave him the opportunity to play an active role in the progress of Allen Leeper's studies. In the correspondence between Boyce and Alexander we can see the different sets of values that shaped their advice. Where Alexander encouraged a thoroughgoing immersion in European language and culture, Boyce thought in more narrowly vocational and pragmatic ways:

> I only gradually found out what was in Allen's mind, how much he had spent during the time you were in England, how much he was spending during his first year at Oxford, how completely the mania for travelling was filling his mind—and how likely this dissipation of interest was to wreck the hopes you and we all had formed for him. When I did realise this (it was about last May) I came down on Allen with all my might. I must have walked him up and down our garden for an hour one Sunday afternoon, showing him the utter folly of all he had in his mind. I also interviewed his tutor (J. A. Smith) a hardheaded Scotchman and a first rate man and was convinced by my talking with him of the necessity of my pulling up Allen as I had done.[36]

Of all the boys, Mervyn Higgins benefited least from the comforts of an extended family nearby. His father's Irish family were in no position to offer much in the way of support. Perhaps for this reason, he sailed for England accompanied by his mother and her sister Hilda Morrison.[37] Just as they had previously eased Mervyn's transition

---

35   Boyce Allen to Alexander Leeper, 25 October 1909, ALP, box 21d.
36   Boyce Allen to Alexander Leeper, 25 October 1909, ALP, box 21d.
37   Mervyn Higgins to Henry Bournes Higgins, 21 August 1906, letterbook, pp. 12–14, HBHP.

from home to the masculine environment of Ormond College, in which he had lived while briefly attending the University of Melbourne, together mother and aunt took over sorting out the details of his domestic arrangements at Oxford. As Mervyn reported to his father in Melbourne, after inspecting the rooms allotted him at Balliol, his mother had a 'sort of overmantle fixed up' and was arranging for some 'very ugly red chairs' to be recovered. She purchased a bicycle so that he could get about Oxford, 'a Humber—three speed gear and freewheel'.[38] After a European sojourn she returned to Oxford, spending several weeks attending to the needs of her son as she saw them, before sailing home to Australia.

The dependency on parents and family that came with university training deepened an already strongly rooted sense of obligation. At the most basic level, this required regular correspondence with parents and maintaining regular contact with the extended British family. The letter home to Mother became an important ritual in the life of the colonial student and it is tempting to see it as increasing the maternal influence in a boy's life. Among the letters home also sits what we might call the letter of account. Addressed mostly to a father, although sometimes preceded by an apologetic letter to a mother, it reported expenses incurred and academic progress made. It was, for example, to his mother that Anthony Wilding first reported in 1903 that he had failed his law examinations and was 'really frightfully sorry for you both'. He had 'been very silly foolish etc not to have worked very hard' and admitted to wasting 'very many whole days of work' on the sports field. With an ingenuity common to the genre, he argued that his year could be assessed 'a different way'; he was in 'perfect health', had experienced a 'splendid life', had been 'improved a lot' by it and had not 'learnt any vices smoking etc'. He ended his analysis with the claim that during the course of the year he had 'learnt the value of money & have found out what a very long way a little will go'.[39]

38 Mervyn Higgins to Henry Bournes Higgins, 6 September 1906, 8 October 1906, letterbook, pp. 21, 8, HBHP.
39 AFW to JW, 7 December 1903, WFP, box 22/100/55.

There is a similar mixture of contrition and defensiveness in Mervyn Higgins's explanation of his decision to abandon the 'Greats'—so much a part of his father's expectation—and proceed immediately with the more specialist law degree:

> have given up Greats, and am now reading Law. It was not a sudden impulse or done because I was anxious to shirk collections or anything of the sort ... I can only say that, though you may not think it, I have got some determination and ambition, and I hope, as much pluck and grit as most people. I think I shall like Law ...[40]

The decision registered Mervyn's realisation that the attractions of the River Isis, where he was by 1908 already making a name for himself as captain of the Balliol boats, far outweighed those of the library.[41] For some time afterwards, there was a pronounced sensitivity to any questioning of his study habits: he had only gone to the Oxford-Cambridge rugby match in London and attended a Colonial Club dinner because it was vacation time, he told his father.[42]

Such tensions about acceptable progress as developed between fathers and sons reflected the strong sense of family enterprise that underlay the quest for professional qualification. Fundamental to the quest was the understanding that sons would follow in the footsteps of fathers. The expectation is seen at its clearest in the legal families. That Mervyn Higgins and Anthony Wilding would join their father's practice was deeply rooted in the expectation of all parents, and as both begin to immerse themselves in their legal studies, the process of induction begins to show in letters to their fathers. Mervyn Higgins began to take a keen interest in his father's Arbitration Court cases. He eagerly awaited the outcome of the Harvester ruling with the intention of discussing it with his Oxford tutor and integrating the material into his weekly essays.[43] Anthony Wilding's engagement with the niceties of the law was less convincing and quickly overtaken by detailed accounts of his cricketing and tennis successes. The process by which he ultimately drifted away from law and embraced a mercantile career is embedded in his emergence as an international tennis player and

---

40   Mervyn Higgins to Henry Bournes Higgins, letterbook, 24 January 1908, p. 87, HBHP; Rickard, *H.B. Higgins*, p. 208.
41   Rickard, *H.B. Higgins*, pp. 208–9.
42   Mervyn Higgins to Henry Higgins, 21 February 1908, letterbook, p. 92, HBHP.
43   For example, Mervyn Higgins to Henry Bournes Higgins, 26 December 1907, letterbook, 5 August 1908 (p. 105), 20 August 1908, pp. 105–6, HBHP.

was the occasion of much family soul-searching. Julia admitted she did not like the idea nearly as much as the thought of Anthony as a barrister.[44]

Within the two academic families of this study—the Massons and the Leepers—the process of inducting sons into the occupational world of the father took place in ways that reflected the centrality of each father's academic preoccupations in their domestic lives. Both Rex and Allen Leeper made their way to Oxford—Allen to Balliol and Rex to New College—as Australasian exemplars of the Christian gentleman-scholar. Mervyn Higgins best captured the widespread expectation which prevailed amongst friends and acquaintances, as Allen was about to arrive at Oxford, that he would win academic prizes there:

> I am glad Allen Leeper is coming to Balliol, but I do not think he will be able to do so very much pothunting as you call it. A great many of the boys coming up from the Public Schools know as much Classics as he does, I should think, and there are not many pots to hunt at any rate at Balliol.[45]

The expectation and fervour with which the Leeper boys entered Oxford to pursue the nineteenth-century-scholar ideal was, as we have seen, viewed sceptically by Boyce Allen. His ambitions for the boys were commonly expressed in a more mundane concern about 'small means' and the need to improve the financial prospects of his nephews. Allen Leeper did not live in Balliol College, instead finding less expensive lodgings near his uncle's home.

The secular rationalism in which the relationship of Orme Masson and his son Irvine matured was no less idealistic than the religiosity that was the cornerstone of Alexander Leeper's influence upon his two sons. Of Irvine Masson it could be said that nature and nurture combined to produce in the son an academic clone of the father. From Melbourne Grammar, Irvine had proceeded to Melbourne University, completing a BSc with first-class honours in chemistry in 1907, while his father was still professor there. After briefly studying medicine, he returned to chemistry and won an 1851 Exhibition scholarship that took him first to the University of Edinburgh and then University College, London, in 1911. There he worked alongside

---

44   AFWLED, vol. 2, 20 May 1909.
45   Mervyn Higgins to Henry Bournes Higgins, 17 April 1908, letterbook, pp. 96–98, HBHP.

Sir William Ramsay, recipient of the Nobel Prize for Chemistry (1904) and, as Len Weickhardt acutely observes, became his 'last personal assistant, a splendid alpha and omega of family chemical genius, as his father at Bristol some thirty years before had been the first of an illustrious line'. Whereas his father had migrated to fulfil his research ambitions, Irvine's academic career flourished in the more science-friendly environment that developed in Britain during the years after World War One. In 1924, some 38 years after his father was appointed to the Chair of Chemistry in Melbourne, Irvine became Professor of Chemistry at the University of Durham, England.[46]

In this university phase of the boys' lives, sibling relationships assumed their mature or adult form. As children who had received the bulk of their early education at home, and as day-boys rather than boarders throughout their school years, their relationships with siblings underwent little of the dilution by peer group pressures held to be characteristic of the English public schoolboy.[47] Indeed, the pattern of their suburban, middle-class childhoods embraced what historians have identified as a central preoccupation of the middle-class Victorian home—the fostering of 'sibling solidarity'.[48] Paradoxically, the separation of siblings brought about by a brother's period of study at a British university allows us to see the nature of this relationship more clearly; at times it brought a consolidation rather than a disruption of sibling relationships.

Perhaps the best illustration of this trend is the relationship between Gladys and Anthony Wilding. We can see in their early upbringing the classic pairing that has been identified by historians as growing between children close in age.[49] Less than two years separated them and much of their education had proceeded in tandem as part of a conscious effort to promote better gender understanding within the family. After graduating MA (Honours) from Canterbury College in June 1904, Gladys had joined her younger brother in England as part of a grand tour of Europe and America. By then, Anthony was in his third year at Trinity College, Cambridge. The reciprocal nature of their relationship is revealed as they negotiated their experience of the old world from within the extended family and network of friends

---

46   Weickhardt, *Masson of Melbourne*, pp. 57–58, 72, 91, 99, 106, 130–32.
47   Tosh, *A Man's Place*, pp. 117–21; Mintz, *Prison of Expectations*, pp. 147–50.
48   Mintz, *Prison*, p. 148.
49   Caine, *Bombay to Bloomsbury*, p. 204.

and acquaintances of their mother. The terms of sibling solidarity quickly resumed the forms they had exhibited throughout their childhood. Gladys slipped into a role somewhere between mother and helpmeet, cajoling her brother for perceived laxness in behaviour and appearance and performing the functions of secretary or personal assistant, keeping track of social engagements and obligations to family and friends. She dutifully attended most of her brother's tennis tournaments, until doctors' orders confined her to bed rest, and wrote a number of articles that appeared in sporting magazines under his name.[50]

Gladys's regular letters to their parents assumed the tone of a progress report on a joint family venture. Her assessment of her younger brother's approach to his university studies is earnest and objective. He and his friends knew and read nothing that was not concerned with sport; a little more attention to his books was needed, but she remained confident her brother would complete his degree.[51] In a homily that might pass as a paraphrase of the family attitude to learning and the law, she urged her brother not to 'enshroud himself in the intricacies of law, but to let as much light of the literae humaniores as possible fall upon him [and] resolutely aim at obtaining some of the culture that is possessed by the well-educated and well-read Englishman'. By so doing, she reasoned, he would 'be able to take his place confidently among the leaders in any branch of life' and 'carry more weight both in his profession and in any society'.[52] In short, Gladys's relationship with her brother developed around a desire to ensure that social obligations were met in ways that conformed to middle-class notions of gentlemanly behaviour.

The reciprocity within the relationship was clear and exhibited in customary ways. During September and October 1904 Anthony assumed the role of male travelling companion, partnered Gladys at social functions and arranged an array of introductions to suitable friends. On occasions brotherly concern was expressed in acts of surprising thoughtfulness. Worried that Gladys's colonial clothes

---

50   AFW to JW, July 1905, WFP, box 23/107/108; GW to JW, 4 September 1904, 7 September 1904, 13 September 1904, 17 September 1904, 14 October 1904, 26 October 1904, 23 June 1905, 27 July 1905, 31 July 1905, WFP, box 17/81/85,86,90,91, box 18/83/117,120; Davidoff, *Thicker than Water*, pp. 108–32.

51   GW to Frederick Wilding, 26 October 1904, GW to JW: 4 September 1904, 14 October 1904, 9 November 1904, WFP, box 17/80-81/85,90,91.

52   GW to JW, 23 June 1905, WFP, box 18/83/117.

would stand out amongst the more fashionable English styles, he arranged for a female friend to take Gladys on a shopping expedition in the quest for something more suitable. He later organised her medical care in Shoreham and Eastbourne and visited her frequently while she was laid up, confidently expecting her full recovery. The relationship was clearly strengthened and enriched by the extended family context in which it predominantly occurred. We may see it as part of the gradual induction of a young man into the code of gentlemanly expectation that enveloped middle-class family life.

If Anthony Wilding's relationship with his sister revealed reciprocity and a mutual concern for each other that rested upon familial expectations, it also offers a context in which to gauge his attitude to the changing role of women in society. The clearest indication of this can be gleaned from his caricature of women university students, in which he contrasted the posturing of the stereotypical 'Oxford Girl' with his sister's quiet, studious demeanour:

> 'Trixy' [Marshall] is an Oxford girl, don't you know & quite gets on my nerves at times. Gladys can get a degree & all that sort of thing & be a girl without saying what a fine lot the female students of Canterbury College are. Miss Trixy tries to use varsity language & talk 'exactly' as if she had been a man up there. Talks about brekkers, coffees, freshers, blues etc etc & wears an Oxford Blue hat band ... You would think the St.Hilda, Lady Margaret Halls etc etc were 'Oxford' & the Colleges Christchurch etc sort of afterthoughts. If she knew how little we take notice of Girton & Newnham ... she would be rather surprised. It is really rather a condescension on the part of the University to allow the existence of these Colleges. Why should a pack of uninteresting (noble exceptions of course) females on practically nothing be allowed to come 'up', & enjoy the privileges of all our advantages in the shape of lectures etc when we have to pay about £300 per annum & value our degree as much on the social advantage it has given us as on the knowledge acquired. Don't for a minute misunderstand me. If Oxford & Cambridge were the only places in the world that gave degrees to women, then by all means let them all come. But when there are literally hundreds of other universities giving equally good degrees ... why, I want to know, can't they keep away from just Oxford & Cambridge & let us maintain our old & historical distinction of being 'the' two universities of the world for men ... That girls ought to have

occupations & get degrees there is no doubt whatever & I thoroughly <u>believe</u> in it but I don't like them treading on our grass which we buy so dearly & enjoy so much.[53]

In their original context—a letter to his mother—these views were undoubtedly intended to provoke a reaction in the Wilding household.

Exaggeration and hyperbole aside, it was a characterisation that sought to protect privileges held as part of 'the world of men' and did so in ways that reflected some of the ambiguity that was present in the attitude of middle-class professional families to the education of their sons and daughters. As a generation that sought change in the education of their daughters, they faced decisions in the education of their sons that reflected the conventions of the past. Sending their sons to ancient universities and daughters to colonial ones (or dismissing a university education as inappropriate, as in the case of the Masson girls) represents a gendered compromise that satisfied a desire for change and met the middle-class expectation that measured a family's worth in the careers of its sons. The desire to round out the colonial adolescence of their sons with an exposure to the cultural richness that history had bestowed upon Britain might in parody be seen as turning the ancient universities into veritable finishing schools that eased a son's passage from adolescence to manhood.

That would be a harsh parody and one that would not do justice to the earnest and optimistic hopes that infused the parents' efforts to provide their sons with an education they valued. Henry Higgins's desire that his son Mervyn should begin his days at Oxford 'working towards the Greats' rested upon a belief that studying the 'literae humaniores' at Oxford was 'the most interesting and valuable course in the world'.[54] That view was most strongly espoused by Alexander Leeper and prompted, as we have seen, a sometimes vituperative exchange with his brother-in-law, Boyce Allen, about the course of study the Leeper boys should pursue at Oxford. Julia Wilding had despatched Anthony to Cambridge with a list of approved authors and texts and an injunction to immerse himself in the great works of English literature. Frederick Wilding rejected claims that the ancient universities should embrace practical utility and specialisation, in measured and unmistakable terms:

---

53 AFW to JW, 22 May 1905, WFP, box 23/105/101.
54 Rickard, *H.B. Higgins*, p. 208; Autobiography of Henry Bournes Higgins (ms), p. 30, HBHP.

> The object of University training is to teach men how to learn, to give them a knowledge of mankind and mental gymnastics, so that they shall go out into the world equipped not with an apparatus of special knowledge, but with a catholicity of mind and a texture of character which shall enable them to cope successfully with the difficulties of life, and I think the old system is quite as likely to make men as any reformed system which would always carry with it drawbacks which are well-known to every thinker and obvious to anyone who knows Oxford and Cambridge ...[55]

Only Alexander Leeper harboured any feeling of disappointment with the reality of British university education. His conception of a university embraced Wilding's 'texture of character' but entertained the hope that scholarship might flourish within its cloisters. He was to find little to satisfy his pious hope in the judgment of his son Allen: 'Oxford is certainly a most memorably unique and inspiring system of education, and it would be impossible to devise a better, I think, for turning out a gentleman. If this be the ideal of a university then nothing equals it.' But 'absolutely no research' was carried on there and, while it might be an 'an ideal university for a ruling class', it offered, in Allen Leeper's view, little encouragement to scholars.[56] It is perhaps pertinent here that Irvine Masson, the only scientist amongst the five boys, took his degree at University College, London, where a stronger research culture had developed.

As idealised by their parents, colonial sons would return to their antipodean surroundings ready to acquire the material means to provide for a wife and family in a manner befitting an educated gentleman. Marriage thus became the final step in a passage to manhood for the sons of the colonial middle class. The most potent influence on the journey was the family.[57] It began, as John Tosh suggests it did for British middle-class boys, in a situation of 'domestic dependence' and would end in 'domestic authority' within marriage.[58] Yet for the colonial boys of their generation and class, the step was complicated by the question of where that domestic life might best be lived. The very extended families that had made their university

---

55   Frederick Wilding, 'Mr. Wilding Interviewed In New Zealand. His Views on English Politics, Society and Sport', *Lyttelton Times*, *Press*, 27 November 1907, WFP, box 41/1.
56   Allen Leeper to Alexander Leeper, 26 May 1911, ALP, T1, box 30; Poynter, *Doubts and Certainties*, p. 341.
57   Tosh, *A Man's Place*, pp. 108–9.
58   Tosh, *A Man's Place*, p. 122.

years possible and eased their passage into British middle-class society now made it possible for them to weigh the relative merits of the two worlds in which they moved.

The obligation to return home was most keenly felt within the legal families. Frederick Wilding, who, before his departure from Hereford in 1879, had railed against the dynastic framework of the English legal community, could by the early years of the twentieth century envisage Anthony assisting him in creating one of his own. For Henry Higgins, the prospect of Mervyn, his only child, joining him within the legal profession, as John Rickard makes clear, reflected the abiding hope of a father that was ultimately fulfilled by a dutiful and responsive son.[59] The likelihood of a return to Australia by the sons of academic fathers was more unpredictable. The most likely areas of employment—the universities or the public service—offered little scope to dynastic ambition. Alexander Leeper's hopes that Rex and Allen would carve out scholarly futures necessarily embraced the prospect that his sons might find the old world more responsive to their talents than Australia. In Orme and Irvine Masson, talent and disposition were most nearly replicated—the question of returning home was no less fondly desired but more likely to be dictated by the vagaries of university requirements than parental influence or preference.[60]

Whatever the hopes and expectations that were invested in the education of the five boys, only Mervyn Higgins and Anthony Wilding returned home to take up the occupation their parents desired. For Wilding the return was brief. In 1908 he settled back into the Opawa home of his parents and negotiated the qualifying exams that would allow him to join his father's legal practice. In 1910, however, he sailed for Britain determined to win the Wimbledon Championship. He did not return and during the years before the outbreak of World War One, as he established himself as the international tennis star of the age, his attitude to an eventual return to New Zealand was ambiguous. There was nothing ambiguous in Allen Leeper's estimate of the prospects facing both he and his brother, Rex: 'there would be little use in our returning to Australia as there

---

59   Rickard, *H.B. Higgins*, pp. 207–10.
60   The bunching of 'age cohorts' pointed to by Davison in *Marvellous Melbourne*, pp. 2–3, 13 and passim, made the problem of finding employment in Melbourne a more general one. A marriage boom among the children of the gold-rush generation in the 1880s led to a spike in the birth rate around the time that the Leepers, Higgins and Masson boys were born.

is incomparably more scope for <u>our particular line of work</u> here'.[61] Moreover, their experience of Oxford, 'so much in the centre of action and thought' and free of 'the prejudiced, unreasoning and petty politics of Melbourne, and eternal talk of sport' had produced a desire to stay in the old world: 'I don't want at all to return to Australia.'[62] Irvine Masson, as we have seen earlier, quickly found his place in the research friendly environment that developed in Britain during and after World War One.

Nothing better reveals the familial context in which the colonial boys lived their post university lives better than their choice of marriage partner. Rex Leeper and Irvine Masson found wives within the cousinages of their respective families. Davidoff argues that while 'work … and travel' exposed people to a wider range of acquaintances beyond their family circle, 'for many this only served to enhance the central significance of familial identification'.[63] Rex Leeper, after anguished exchanges within the family, married his first cousin, Primrose Allen, daughter of his uncle, Boyce.[64] At the time of marriage in 1917 Rex was 29 and Primrose 27. For Irvine Masson, courtship unfolded within the framework of the Masson family's Edinburgh circle of friends, drawn from the city's educated elite. His marriage before World War One to Flora, daughter of Helen (Nell) Masson, his father's younger sister, who had married George Lovell Gulland, a notable Scottish haematologist, took place with less anguish within the very family context in which his parents had been married almost 30 years before. The only courtship and marriage to move out of the family circle was that of Allen Leeper. His scholarly talents and linguistic aptitudes had won him a position in the Foreign Office, and it was in this context that he met, courted and married Janet Hamilton, the niece of Sir Ian Hamilton, fresh from the controversy that surrounded his handling of the Gallipoli campaign.[65]

61   Allen Leeper to Alexander Leeper, 30 September 1910, Poynter, *Doubts and Certainties*, p. 339.
62   Allen Leeper to Alexander Leeper, 23 August 1911, Poynter, *Doubts and Certainties*, p. 339.
63   Davidoff, *Thicker than Water*, pp. 131, 185–94; Tosh, *A Man's Place*, p. 109.
64   Rex Leeper to Alexander Leeper, 2 June 1914, 9 June 1914, 20 June 1914, 15 September 1914, 6 October 1914, ALP, T1, box 30.
65   Poynter, *Doubts and Certainties*, pp. 416, 430.

Both Anthony Wilding and Mervyn Higgins died in World War One and were denied the chance to complete the final stage of the journey to manhood signified by marriage. At the time of his death Wilding was 31 and Mervyn Higgins 29 years of age. In different ways, each had fulfilled family expectations of them. Wilding's sporting achievements, universally hailed as embodying the athletic ideal of his age, represented to his parents the full development of talent they sought to develop. The completion of a degree at Cambridge spoke of the balanced development of body and mind they had espoused. His quest for a wife had been a fraught one. Sporting fame transformed the range of his social contacts, but did little to enhance his status as a suitor within middle-class society. His abandonment of the law and entry into the commercial world in 1910—a departure from the script envisaged by his parents—was motivated in large part by the desire to accumulate money and improve his standing in the marriage market.[66]

The younger Mervyn Higgins's situation was more straightforward. While at Oxford, he had discussed with his father ways of establishing a legal career and laying the foundation for subsequent marriage. There was an initial hesitancy in his reaction to Henry's suggestion that he become his associate:

> do you think yourself that it would be a good thing for me to take? I should like it for filial and financial reasons but would it be of any value to me when I start on my own? I shall be about 24 when I come out perhaps 25, and as I shall in any case have to sit in a chair or wait for a year or two, it seems as if I should be practically wasting a year or two ...[67]

But after his return to Melbourne in February 1912, he gladly accepted the position and his life took very much the shape he had envisaged it might. He served a year as his father's associate and began to lay the foundation for a career at the Bar. Just as he had always done, he took his place at Doona, the family home in Melbourne, and Heronswood, their country residence at Dromana. His final step from childhood to manhood was to be achieved in war, not in marriage.

---

66   AFWLED, vol. 2, 20 May 1909; L. and S. Richardson, *Anthony Wilding*, pp. 197–98, 269, 274–75; Myers, *Captain Anthony Wilding*, p. 200.
67   Mervyn Higgins to Henry Bournes Higgins, 15 April 1909, letterbook, p. 129, HBHP.

The childhoods of this small cluster of colonial boys and their individual passage towards manhood reveal the dreams and dilemmas of a generation of middle-class professional families. Their collective desire to create dutiful and educated sons who might assume significant and useful roles in colonial society, as part of a reconstructed family that softened the sharp gender differences of a past age, was central to their world view. In attempting to realise their ideal, they were confronted by consequences and wider circumstances they had never seriously contemplated. They had provided their sons with educations that made it possible for them to slot into the British professional community. As a generation their dreams for their sons and hopes for the future were to turn to disillusion as war transformed the world and shattered lives.

Conclusion

Family Experiments concentrates upon the experience of five middle-class professional families, whose individual and collective experiences, in Melbourne and Christchurch, constitute a small strand in the fabric of Australasian family and social history. It is a strand, however, which for a brief period at the end of the nineteenth century exercised considerable influence upon the wider understandings of family that were beginning to emerge throughout Australasia.

The years between 1880 and 1914 were transitional ones in the history of the middle-class family in Britain and Australasia. Changes in the legal position of women within marriage, greater access to higher education and, in New Zealand and Australia, the extension of the franchise to women were achievements that owed much to middle-class advocacy. Within Britain's aspirant professional generation that came to maturity in the 1870s, support for these reforms came to be seen as touchstones of progressive thought. They could be pursued as ends in themselves or form the basis of a wider set of expectations. We see these expectations take their most idealised form in the writing of Julia Wilding in the years before her marriage and departure for New Zealand. Put simply, she regarded the individual family as the fulcrum of social progress. The domestic world thus became a potentially transformative one, in which children and the full realisation of their individual talents became the focus of a family life whose objective was the cultivated and socially useful citizen. This is not to imply that this high-minded idealisation of the family is indicative of the shared aspirations of the generation of middle-class professionals represented in the five families of this study. Rather, it is employed here as a fixed point against which we may attempt to characterise how a group of professional families sought to negotiate the circumstances of time and place to give effect to a range of aspirations within their colonial families.

The liberalism of the Wildings was that of England's provincial professional middle class. It was grounded in a strongly moral stand opposing what it believed to be a decadent and moribund aristocracy, against which it posited its own social usefulness and industry. For many, like Julia and Frederick Wilding, proclaiming liberal principles became a form of secular evangelism. In the mid-1870s, disenchantment with liberalism's immediate English prospects bred a gospel of hope, in which the British settler societies became potential sites for social betterment. Viewed in this way, migration came to be couched in optimistic and experimental terms; experimental in the sense that for the Wildings and families like them a return to the known world of family and friends, whatever its frustrations, remained a safety valve. The sense of family experiment varies in proportion to the security of middle-class status; some could afford the luxury of experiment more than others. For Orme and Mary Masson, the risk of failure was mitigated by the strength of their 'long' Scottish families and the relative security offered by the university framework in which migration occurred. Neither the resources of his Scottish family nor academic credentials that fell short of his best hopes provided John Macmillan Brown with much scope for experiment, and it was 10 years after his arrival in New Zealand and at the age of 38 that he married.

The migrations and motivations of Henry Higgins and Alexander Leeper are grounded in Irish circumstances. They invoke family in ways that speak to issues of individual and collective survival within a deeply religious framework. Nothing better exemplifies this context than Henry Higgins's sea voyage to Australia with his mother and his younger siblings. It marks off Henry's Irish childhood from his Australian adulthood and his emergence as the de facto male head of household in ways that defined his subsequent relationship with his mother and siblings and prefigured the role he later adopted within his extended Australian family. Whereas Higgins's understanding of family was already shedding the Methodism of his parents, religion remained a central dynamic for Alexander Leeper. He made his way to Australia as an envoy of his concerned parents, in the quest for his prodigal elder brother, who had departed hastily for Australia in 1866. Alexander's subsequent return to Ireland and the ultimately more considered decision to emigrate and marry in Australia were constructed within the terms of Anglican religiosity in which his family was steeped. The marriage he envisaged would be one which would take its shape within a spiritual haven maintained by an idealised and saintly wife, in which reciprocal obligations and loyalties protected individuals from the vicissitudes of life.

By any assessment, the families observed here must be judged significant contributors to the colonial societies they joined. The broad features of their individual stories suggest rapid acceptance within an emerging middle-class elite and steadily improving financial circumstances. Residences within or adjacent to the University of Melbourne shielded the Leepers and the Massons from the economic pressures of the housing market and provided an impeccable middle-class address. For them, as for John Macmillan Brown, acceptance within the colonial middle-class elite was determined by their roles within the emergent colonial university. Unqualified respect for the intellectual was rarely a feature of colonial life, but as the first generation of a recognisable British institution, they found ready acceptance within a small educated elite of Melbourne and Christchurch. For John Macmillan Brown, this rapidly acquired status and acceptance was marked in the public acclamation of his marriage to Helen Connon, the Headmistress of Christchurch Girls' High School. If status came more readily than wealth for academic families, the two marched in unison in the lives of the legal families.

Status was not simply a matter of occupation or wealth. The establishment of the Wilding family indeed suggests that there were other pathways to acceptance within colonial society that lay outside these crude determinants. Just as the universities conferred instant status upon their earliest generations of British professors, so did the fledgling sporting and cultural fraternities offer opportunities for talented enthusiasts such as Frederick and Julia Wilding to emerge as prominent figures within an urban middle-class circle with the time and money to pursue leisure activities. Within a decade of their arrival Frederick's talents as cricketer, tennis player, sports administrator and games advocate had made him arguably the city's best-known sporting figure and certainly its most enthusiastic supporter. Talent as a performance pianist allowed Julia Wilding to carve out a significant role within the city's musical community. Their range of activity drew them into a cluster of overlapping interest groups and secured their place within the city's social elite.

It is fashionable to describe the integration of migrant British families into settler societies in terms that invoke the idea of networking. Such a description implies a greater degree of deliberation and forethought than is perhaps justified. Clearly, however, as a fragment of the British professional class establishing itself throughout the Empire, the five families of this study encountered few impediments as they made their way in colonial society. Of the 18-year-old Henry Higgins alone could it be said that the ethnic and religious connections available to him on arrival proved of limited value. Such networks as aided his passage into the established middle class emerged within the framework of his academic study. It is there, for example, that he began to understand the nature of colonial liberalism alongside his fellow student Alfred Deakin. He later turned to Deakin for advice before entering politics, and it was Deakin who appointed him to the Commonwealth Arbitration Court in 1906. The Masson and Leeper families negotiated their linkages with middle-class society from the university environment they shared. Perhaps the most distinctive feature of the social relationships of the three Melbourne families was its interconnectedness. Nowhere is this better represented than by the 'Heronswood Push', a self-conscious imitation of working-class city gangs, in which the teenage Masson, Leeper and Higgins children entertained themselves in mildly bohemian ways. The 'Push' links between the three families flowed through to the old world university years at Oxford, where Mervyn Higgins and Allen Leeper were at Balliol College, and Rex Leeper in New College, and at the University of Edinburgh where Irvine Masson studied.

There is similarity and difference in the ways the two Christchurch families slotted into the small but expanding enclave of educated British professionals beginning to assert an influence in civic affairs. Their occupations alone gave them entry to the clubs and organisations that were defining the city's cultural and political life. Talent and enthusiasms provided the basis for communities of interests that brought together clusters of like-minded individuals and families. In this context the Wildings and the Macmillan Browns found common cause in the campaign for higher education for girls and the enfranchisement of women. Here, too, the city's brand of liberalism was taking root. Its chief definer was William Pember Reeves, a young lawyer and journalist, who as neighbour, friend and fellow cricketer inducted the Wildings into the more interventionist aspects of colonial liberalism. When Reeves called the big landowners 'social pests', he spoke in terms that sat comfortably within the liberal lexicon of provincial liberalism that the Wildings brought with them from Hereford.[1]

These public manifestations of private family lives indicate something of the nature of the marriage relationships that supported them. The understandings that underpinned the five marriages shared the fundamental premise that as members of an educated and professional elite which proclaimed its meritocratic nature they were morally obliged to give effect to its values within their families. Beyond this, the marriages demonstrate the changes and the continuities evident within the thinking of a generation of middle-class professional families exerting their influence within colonial society. The idealisation of the family as the fulcrum of social progress gave immense authority within the marriage relationship to Julia Wilding. Since the ideal family rested equally upon greater paternal involvement in elements of domestic life, most notably the upbringing of children, it also shaped a marriage that realised in large part the ideal union of partnership to which they aspired. The marriage of Adeline and Alexander Leeper derived its ethical dimension from deeply ingrained religious beliefs and an idealisation of women as veritable 'angels in the house' that both gave authority within the marriage and defined the limits of that authority.

The marriage of Helen Connon and John Macmillan Brown embodies a form of idealisation that had both a public and private dimension. Celebrated in public by contemporaries as a marriage of an independent career-woman and feminist, its private manifestation confronted a dilemma that lay at the heart of late nineteenth-century familial feminism: how did the independent woman fulfil the 'double duty', as Benjamin Jowett had put it, inherent in the dual roles of motherhood and profession? The tragic resolution that ensued, with its tale of failing health, disillusion and early death, prompted speculation by Connon's biographer, Edith Searle Grossmann, that the Australasian societies that had granted women the vote and facilitated their pursuit of higher education lacked the servant class that, she believed, smoothed the path of their British sisters.

1   Sinclair, *William Pember Reeves*, pp. 136–37.

The marriages of Henry and Mary Alice Higgins, and Orme and Mary Masson were secure in their material foundations. A chair in chemistry at the University of Melbourne was judged sufficient testimony of Orme Masson's capacity to reproduce the middle-class domestic circumstances that Mary's Scottish family deemed essential. An established legal career and a house in Malvern met Henry Higgins's self-imposed preconditions for marriage. In meeting middle-class norms, both couples were accepting the broad conventions in which they had been nurtured and which were widely shared within their professional communities. The evolution of each marriage exhibited patterns that now seem familiar, but which derived their individual character in the negotiation of the circumstances of time and place. For Henry and Mary Higgins marriage derived much of its character from a mutual and intense absorption in the needs of an only child, an enduring and intimate relationship with Henry's extended Irish-Australian family and in the creation of a domestic and private shelter from a public life that was often controversial. The institutional setting of the Masson household provided a buffer between the public and the private spheres, created an essentially inward-looking domestic environment and, for Mary Masson, exacerbated the unsettling effects of migration. Within this environment the Masson marriage exhibits the conventional outward forms that prevailed amongst a professional society structured around a mistress of the household supporting a professionally occupied husband.

Middle-class families were at the heart of the campaign to open up higher education to women. A central concern of this study has been to examine the attention the professional classes gave to the education of their daughters and to explore what, if any, adjustments in the nature of family life this entailed. Put simply, if there is any strand of thinking in which the group of families observed in *Family Experiments* were united, it was in the pursuit of an education for their daughters that reached beyond that commonly available to them. In the Wilding family, it was a pursuit that gained its direction from an intense identification of a mother in her daughter's education, and its roots in a commitment to realising social progress through the usefulness of the individual. For the Macmillan Browns, the intensity of parental involvement in the education of their two daughters can be traced directly to the middle-class feminist aspirations with which their marriage had been associated and owes as much to the father as it does to the mother. Parental roles in the education of the Leeper girls exhibit an even stronger fatherly involvement and one which, while concerned to shape a more academic program of learning for his daughters, was pursued without quite the moral intensity that marked his interaction with his sons. Only in the Masson family did the pursuit of an academic education for daughters stop short of university degrees. The decision was a maternal one grounded in the belief that the middle-class woman possessed a duty of service, which led not to the professional possibilities that lurked in the shadows of university study, but to committees of philanthropic or charitable activity.

Thus a belief in improving the education of daughters did not indicate a shared vision of the ends to which such education might be put. Julia Wilding understood that the 'new woman' she worked so diligently to bring to fruition was to be educated in ways which enabled her to become a socially useful individual. Beyond this ethical injunction there lay an ambiguity, if not of purpose, then about possibilities. Education would, she believed, open up the prospect of a career. Equally, it would enlarge the circle of cultivated and educated women who might contribute to general social progress from within marriage and the family. This pluralisation of the civilised individual, as Raymond Williams has termed it, stopped short of engaging with what became the common dilemma of the small group of young educated middle-class women of her daughters' generation: what to do with an advanced education in the humanities?[2] The dilemma is perhaps most acutely registered by Marnie Masson in verses she wrote at the Dromana country home of Henry and Mary Higgins in the summer of 1906, as the 'Heronswood Push' left their schooldays behind them: 'Boys to Varsities to work / And the girls to play.'[3] If a university degree offered greater prospects, it may well be that the very middle-class families that were able to obtain such a qualification might also have aroused expectations that were not readily realised.

In the education of their daughters, the middle-class families of this study pursued idealistic objectives whose consequences they could scarcely have foreseen. In the education of their sons, there is more

2   Raymond Williams, 'The Bloomsbury Fraction', in Raymond Williams, *Problems in Materialism and Culture: Selected Essays*, Verso and NLB, London, 1980, pp. 165–68.
3   Marnie Bassett, 'Heronswood Log Book', Marnie Bassett Papers, UMA, 7/26/13.

that conforms to norms prevalent within the antipodean professional middle class. The ambiguity and uncertainty that surrounded the quest for higher education for daughters gives way to persistent and clear-sighted objectives to maintain the newly created colonial family. Most obviously present within the legal families where meritocracy could be overridden more readily by a desire for dynastic continuity, the tendency towards occupational reproduction is evident in all families. The uniformity of objective is matched by a common form: a colonial education that mimicked the traditional education of the British public school, but was experienced as day-boys from suburban households and moderated by the influence of family. Within this framework there was space for parents with philosophical or educational axes to grind to exert considerably more influence than any headmaster or school. In the Wilding household this space was filled by a mother who sought to realise in her first-born son her understandings of a cultured gentleman, and by a father who believed the British love of sport held the key to a balanced life. Alexander Leeper's piety and scholarly enthusiasm for the world of classical antiquity impressed itself deeply upon his sons. A domestic environment in which test tubes were close at hand did more to stimulate Irvine Masson's interest in scientific enquiry than Melbourne Grammar's narrow science curriculum. For Mervyn Higgins, the status of an only child created an extremely close identification with his parents that brought with it a sense of obligation and, to some degree, a desire to emulate.

Recent British historical writing on masculinities sees a 'contradiction between the greater priority attached to manliness for boys and the greater role of mothers in teaching it'.[4] This cluster of professional families would not have recognised any contradiction. The new *concept* of manliness that began to be registered within boys' schools throughout Australasia in the late nineteenth and early twentieth centuries, in the 1890s made little impact within families whose educational ideals had been formulated in mid-Victorian Britain before their departure for the new world. The realisation of the civilised individual, in which a balance was struck between the cultivation of body and mind, best captures this thinking, and is given clearest expression within the Wilding family. The problem of what to do with

---

4   John Tosh, *Manliness and Masculinities in Nineteenth-Century Britain: Essays on Gender, Family and Empire*, Person Longman, London, 2005, p. 137.

sons was not to be found in the definition of the roles of mothers and fathers within the family but in finding a place for them in a colonial society that provided a narrow range of employment opportunities. This was a dilemma that had also shaped the fathers' own careers.

James Belich places the migrant professional classes of the late nineteenth century at the centre of what he calls 'the recolonisation process', in which New Zealand's colonial status was reaffirmed culturally.[5] Within his interpretation, sending sons 'Home' for their university education becomes a touchstone of colonialism. This study suggests another interpretation. The education of sons also reveals the degree to which these first-generation members of the Australasian professional middle class summoned the resources of the extended British family and its networks to confront the very real problem of what to do with their sons. The question was as troubling as that posed by their educated daughters. A legal practice might become a family enterprise without recourse to an old world university, but the avenues for professional advancement were more restricted. Thus, university study at 'Home' made sense at a number of levels: with the assistance of family it was realisable; a British degree undoubtedly carried weight throughout the settler societies; reliance upon British relatives might encourage a greater sense of familial identification; it would provide an incentive, if one was needed, to make a family trip 'Home'. Among the least remarked features of the phenomenon, immersion in the life of the extended British parent family produced, as we have seen, marriage within the cousinage.

Historians have had more difficulty reconciling themselves to the ambiguities they detect in the lives of the middle-class professional households than is evident in the lived lives of the families observed in this study. Their generation has been described as a transitional one that redefined the family and women's role within it, but stopped short of confronting the structural and social changes needed to endow full citizenship. Theirs was also a generation that possessed an enduring faith in education to create the basis of a more civilised society. Whatever individual emphases they brought to this idealistic and optimistic philosophy, faith in the transformative possibilities of education and a belief in the family as the handmaiden of a progressive

---

5   Belich, *Paradise Reforged*, pp.29-30, 53-86.

society were its fundamental tenets. Together, these two strands in their thinking were in tune with the liberalism of their age. Nowhere is this given clearer expression than in the concept of the family wage enunciated in 1907 by Henry Higgins, the most politically radical of their number. If the Harvester Judgement can be seen as constituting a high point of familial liberalism, the outbreak of war in August 1914 marked, for this generation of middle-class professionals, the end of their optimistic expectation of social progress. Dream had become disillusion: replenishing the constructive impulses that had shaped their family experiments was a task for the future.

Bibliography

The bibliography is arranged under the following headings:

Primary Sources

A. Official Publications
B. Family Papers and Other Archival Collections
C. Contemporary Newspapers and Periodicals
D. Contemporary Books, Pamphlets and Articles

Secondary Sources

E. Books
F. Articles
G. Manuscripts
H. Unpublished University Theses and Research Essays

Primary Sources

A. Official Publications

Appendices to the Journals of the House of Representatives, 1880–1920.

New Zealand Census, 1887–1916.

New Zealand Official Year Book, 1915.

Victorian Census, 1884, 1891, 1901.

Victorian Year Book, 1895–1898.

Wise's Post Office Directories, c.1880–1914.

B. Family Papers and other Archival Collections

Bassett, Flora Marjorie (Marnie), Papers, University of Melbourne Archives, 1980.0079.

Brown, John Macmillan, Papers, Macmillan Brown Library (MBL), University of Canterbury (UC), Christchurch, MB 118.

Canterbury Lawn Tennis Club/Association Minute Books, 1881–1902, Canterbury Museum Documentary Research Centre (CMDRC), Christchurch, ARC.1996.33.

Gardner, W. J., Papers, MBL, UC, Christchurch, MB 107.

Higgins, Henry Bournes, Papers, National Library of Australia, Canberra, MS 1057.

Higgins, Henry, Stonnington History Centre Catalogue, Melbourne, MP 353, MP 12540.

Leeper, Alexander, Papers, Trinity College Archives, University of Melbourne. (*Refer to the Trinity College Archivist regarding the possible reorganisation of this collection.)

Masson, David Orme, Family Papers, University of Melbourne Archives, 1980.0080 (80/80; 106/54).

Wilding, Cora, Papers, MBL, UC, MB 183.

Wilding, Family Papers, CMDRC, Christchurch, ARC.1989.124.

C. Contemporary Newspapers and Periodicals

Age 1880–1914.

Argus 1880–1914.

Australasian 1880–1914.

Canterbury Times 1880–1914.

Hereford Mercury and Independent 1870–79.

Hereford Times 1832–80.

Lyttelton Times 1880–1914.

D. Contemporary Books, Pamphlets and Articles

Anthony, Charles, jnr., *Duty and Privilege*, National Press Agency, London, 1886.

——, *Popular Sovereignty*, Longmans, Green and Co., London, 1880.

——, *The Social and Political Dependence of Women*, Longmans, Green and Co., London, 1867.

Anthony, Charles, snr., *Hereford Times Prospectus*, Hereford Times (*HT*), 1 May 1832.

Anthony, Julia, 'Early Influences', *HT*, 9 December 1876.

——, 'Education', *HT*, c. 1875.

——, 'John Stuart Mill', *HT*, 17 May 1873.

——, 'The Love of Nature', *HT*, 6 May 1876.

——, 'Marriage', *HT*, 7 November 1874.

——, 'Peace and War', *HT*, 8 November 1873.

——, 'The Power of Realisation', *HT*, 6 March 1875.

——, 'Scepticism v Orthodoxy', *HT*, c. 1874.

——, 'Scientific Investigation', *HT*, 9 August 1873.

——, 'Theory and Practice', *HT*, 5 August 1876.

——, 'The Tyranny of Custom', *HT*, 6 December 1873.

——. 'Women's Suffrage', *HT*, 15 February 1873.

——, 'Women: Two Conflicting Tendencies', *HT*, 14 October 1876.

——, 'Utilitarianism, *HT*, 14 November 1876.

Armitage, Albert Borlase, *Two Years in the Antarctic: Being a Narrative of the British National Antarctic Expedition*, Edward Arnold, London, 1905.

Arnold, Matthew, *Culture and Anarchy: An Essay in Politics and Social Criticism* [1869], John Murray, London, 1923.

Barff, H. E., *A Short Historical Account of the University of Sydney*, Angus and Robertson, Sydney, 1902.

Barrie, James, *An Edinburgh Eleven: Pencil Portraits from College Life*, Office of the British Weekly, London, 1889.

Beeton, Isabella, *Mrs Beeton's Book of Household Management*, S. O. Beeton, London, 1861.

Brown, John Macmillan, 'Advice to Teachers: Professor Brown's Address', *Lyttelton Times*, 25 March 1889.

——, 'Early Days and Early Students', *Lyttelton Times*, 12 May 1923.

——, *Julius Caesar: A Study*, Whitcombe & Tombs, Christchurch, 1894.

——, *Limanora, the Island of Progress*, Putnam, New York, 1903.

——, *Modern Education: Its Defects and their Remedies*, Lyttelton Times Company, Christchurch, 1908.

——, 'Professor Brown's Opening Address', *Press*, 12 May 1878.

——, *Rialloro*, Putnam, New York, 1901.

——, *Student Life and the Fallacies that Oftenest Beset It: An Inaugural Address Delivered at Canterbury College Dialectic Society at the Commencement of its Session, 1881*, The Canterbury College Dialectic Society with Tombs and Co., Christchurch.

——, 'Woman and University Education', Wilding Memorial Lectures, Lecture II, Canterbury College, Christchurch, 1926.

Butler, Samuel, *The Way of All Flesh*, Grant Richards, London, 1903.

Canterbury College Jubilee, *Lyttelton Times*, 12 May 1923 (*Press* Supplement).

Carlyle, Thomas, *Sartor Resartus* [1836], Chapman and Hall, London, 1858.

Collier, James, Introduction to D. Collins, *An Account of the English Colony in New South Wales*, Whitcombe & Tombs, Christchurch, 1910.

——, Introduction to E.G. Wakefield, *A View of the Art of Colonization*, Clarendon Press, Oxford, 1914.

——, *The Pastoral Age in Australasia*, Whitcombe & Tombs, London, 1911.

Darwin, Francis (ed.), *The Life and Letters of Charles Darwin, including an autobiographical chapter*, John Murray, London, 1887.

Gaskell, Elizabeth, *My Diary: The Early Years of My Daughter Marianne* [1835–38], privately printed by Clement Shorter, London, 1923.

Grossmann, Edith Searle, *The Heart of the Bush*, Sands and Co., London, 1910.

——, *In Revolt*, Eden, Remington, London, 1893.

——, *Life of Helen Macmillan Brown: The First Woman to Graduate with Honours in a British University*, Whitcombe and Tombs, Christchurch, 1905.

Higgins, Henry Bournes, *A New Province for Law & Order*, Constable & Company, London, 1922.

Leeper, Alexander, *Fourteen Satires of Juvenal, translated into English*, Macmillan, London, 1912.

——, *A Plea for the Study of the Classics. Inaugural Lecture Delivered Before the Classical Association of Victoria, 22nd April, 1913*, Melville and Mullen, Melbourne, 1913.

Leeper, Alexander (with H. A. Strong), *A Guide to Classical Reading, Intended for the Use of Australian Students*, George Robertson, Melbourne, 1880.

——, *Juvenal: Thirteen Satires, translated into English, after the Latin text of J.E.B. Mayor*, Macmillan, London, 1882.

Littlebury's Directory and Gazetteer of Herefordshire 1876–1877.

Masson, David Mather, *Life of John Milton*, (7 vols), Macmillan & Co., London, 1859–94.

——, *Recent British Philosophy*, Macmillan, Cambridge, London, 1887.

Masson, Elsie, *An Untamed Territory: The Northern Territory of Australia*, Macmillan, London, 1915.

Masson, Rosaline (ed.), *Three Centuries of English Poetry*, Macmillan, London, 1876.

Mill, Harriet Taylor, 'Enfranchisement of Women', *Westminster Review*, London, July 1851.

Mill, John Stuart, *Autobiography* [1873], Shields, Currin V. (ed.), Liberal Arts Press, New York, 1957.

——, *On Liberty*, John W. Parker & Son, London, 1859.

——, *On Representative Government*, Parker, Son & Bourn, London, 1861.

——, *The Subjection of Women*, Longmans, London, 1868.

——, *Utilitarianism*, Parker, Son and Bourn, London, 1863.

Myers, A. Wallis, *Captain Anthony Wilding*, Hodder and Stoughton, London, 1916.

Redmond, G. McLeod, *Geelong College: History, Register and Records*, Sands & McDougall, Melbourne, 1911.

Reeves, Maud Pember, *Round About A Pound A Week* [1913], Virago, London, 1999.

Reeves, William Pember, *State Experiments in Australia and New Zealand* [1902], Macmillan, Melbourne, 1969.

Ruskin, John, *Sesame and Lilies* [1865], Ward, Lock and Co., London, 1911.

——, *Unto This Last*, Collins Clear-Type Press, London, 1862.

Sheppard, Kate, 'A Noble Bohemianism', *White Ribbon*, February 1897.

Somerville, Martha, *Personal Recollections from Early Life to Old Age, of Mary Somerville*, Roberts Brothers, Boston, 1874.

Spencer, Herbert, *Descriptive Sociology, or Groups of Sociological Facts, parts 1–8*, classified and abstracted by David Duncan, Richard Schepping, and James Collier, Williams and Norgate, London, 1873–81.

Trollope, Anthony, *The Way We Live Now*, Chatto and Windus, London, 1875.

Wilding, Anthony F., *On the Court and Off*, Methuen & Co., London, 1912.

Wilding, Gladys J., *The Indian Mutiny of 1857: Its Causes and Results* (New Zealand University Bowen Essay 1901), Lyttelton Times Co., Christchurch, 1902.

Wilding, Frederick, 'Jottings of a Voyage to the Antipodes', *HT*, 22 November 1879.

——, 'Life in New Zealand', *HT*, 22 May 1879.

——, 'Life in New Zealand', *HT*, 29 November 1879.

——, 'Life in New Zealand', *HT*, 27 December 1879.

——, 'Life in New Zealand', *HT*, 17 July 1880.

——, 'Life in New Zealand', *HT*, 22 May 1880.

Secondary Sources

E. Books

Adams, Nancy, *Family Frescoes*, F. W. Cheshire, Melbourne, 1966.

Akenson, Donald Harman, *Half the World from Home: Perspectives on the Irish in New Zealand 1860–1950*, Victoria University Press, Wellington, 1990.

Allen, Judith A., *Rose Scott: Vision and Revision in Feminism*, Oxford University Press, Melbourne, 1994.

Annan, Noel, *The Dons: Mentors, Eccentrics and Geniuses*, HarperCollins, London, 1999.

Anstruther, Ian, *Coventry Patmore's Angel: A Study of Coventry Patmore, His Wife Emily and the Angel in the House*, Haggerston Press, London, 1992.

Appleby, Matthew, *Canterbury Cricket: 100 Greats*, Reed, Auckland, 2002.

Austin, A. G. (ed.), *The Webbs' Australian Diary 1898*, Sir Isaac Pitman & Son, Melbourne, 1965.

Ballantyne, Tony, *Webs of Empire: Locating New Zealand's Colonial Past*, Bridget Williams Books, Wellington, New Zealand, 2012.

Barnes, Felicity, *New Zealand's London: A Colony and its Metropolis*, Auckland University Press, Auckland, 2012.

Barrett, Bernard, *The Inner Suburbs: The Evolution of an Industrial Area*, Melbourne University Press, Melbourne, 1971.

Barrowman, Rachel, *Victoria University of Wellington 1899–1999: A History*, Victoria University Press, Wellington, 1999.

Bassett, Marnie, *Henry Fyshe Gisborne; and Once upon a Time*, Royal Historical Society of Victoria, South Melbourne, 1985.

——, *The Hentys: An Australian Colonial Tapestry*, Oxford University Press, London, 1954.

Bate, Weston and Penrose, Helen, *Challenging Traditions: A History of Melbourne Grammar*, Arcadia, Melbourne, 2000.

Baxter, Millicent, *The Memoirs of Millicent Baxter*, Cape Catley, Whatamongo Bay, Queen Charlotte Sound, New Zealand, 1981.

Beaglehole, J. C., *The University of New Zealand: An Historical Study*, New Zealand Council for Educational Research, Wellington, 1937.

Belich, James, *Making Peoples: A History of the New Zealanders: From Polynesian Settlement to the End of the Nineteenth Century*, Penguin, Auckland, 1996.

——, *Paradise Reforged: A History of the New Zealanders from the 1880s to the Year 2000*, Penguin, Auckland, 2001.

——, *Replenishing the Earth: The Settler Revolution and the Rise of the Anglo-world, 1783–1939*, Oxford University Press, Oxford, 2009.

Bell, Duncan, *The Idea of Greater Britain: Empire and the Future of World Order, 1860–1900*, Princeton University Press, Princeton, 2007.

Bessant, Bob, *Schooling in the Colony and State of Victoria*, Centre for Comparative and International Studies in Education, School of Education, La Trobe University, 1983.

Biagini, Eugenio F. (ed.), *Citizenship and Community: Liberals, Radicals and Collective Identities in the British Isles, 1865–1931*, Cambridge University Press, Cambridge, 1996.

Blainey, Geoffrey, *A Centenary History of the University of Melbourne*, Melbourne University Press, Carlton, Victoria, 1957.

Blainey, G., Morrissey, James and Hulme, S. E. K., *Wesley College: The First Hundred Years*, The President and Council Wesley College in association with Robertson and Mullins, Melbourne, 1967.

Blodgett, Harriet, *Centuries of Female Days: Englishwomen's Private Diaries*, Sutton, Gloucester, 1989.

Blodgett, Harriet (ed.), *The Englishwoman's Diary: An Anthology*, Fourth Estate, London, 1992.

Bongiorno, Frank, *The Sex Lives of Australians: A History*, Black Inc., Melbourne, 2012.

Booth, Alison, *How to Make It as a Woman: Collective Biographical History from Victoria to the Present*, University of Chicago Press, Chicago and London, 2004.

Borrie, W. D., *The European Peopling of Australasia: A Demographic History 1788–1988*, Demography Program, Research School of Social Sciences, The Australian National University, Canberra, 1994.

Brasch, Charles, *Indirections: A Memoir 1909–1947*, Oxford University Press, Wellington, 1980.

Breward, Ian, *History of Australian Churches*, Allen & Unwin, St Leonards, NSW, 1993.

Brookes, Barbara, *A History of New Zealand Women*, Bridget Williams Books, Wellington, 2016.

Brookes, Barbara (ed.), *At Home in New Zealand: History, Houses, People*, Bridget Williams Books, Wellington, 2000.

Brookes, Barbara, Cooper, Annabel and Law, Robin (eds), *Sites of Gender: Women, Men and Modernity in Southern Dunedin, 1890–1939*, Auckland University Press, Auckland, 2003.

Brookes, Barbara, Macdonald, Charlotte and Tennant, Margaret (eds), *Women in History 2: Essays on Women in New Zealand*, Bridget Williams Books, Wellington, 1992.

Brown, John Macmillan, *The Memoirs of John Macmillan Brown*, Whitcombe and Tombs, University of Canterbury, Christchurch, 1974.

Buckner, Phillip and Francis, R. Douglas (eds), *Rediscovering the British World*, University of Calgary Press, Calgary, 2005.

Bunkle, Phillida and Hughes, Beryl (eds), *Women in New Zealand Society*, George Allen & Unwin, Sydney, 1980.

Butchers, A. G., *A Centennial History of Education in Canterbury*, Centennial Committee of the Canterbury Education Board, Christchurch, 1950.

Bygott, Ursula and Cable, K. J., *Pioneer Women Graduates of the University of Sydney 1881–1921*, Sydney University Monographs, no. 1, University of Sydney, Sydney, 1985.

Byrnes, Giselle (ed.), *The New Oxford History of New Zealand*, Oxford University Press, Melbourne, 2009.

Caine, Barbara, *Bombay to Bloomsbury: A Biography of the Strachey Family*, Oxford University Press, Oxford 2006.

——, *Destined to be Wives: The Sisters of Beatrice Webb*, Clarendon Press, Oxford and New York, 1986.

——, *English Feminism 1780–1980*, Oxford University Press, Oxford, 1997.

——, *Victorian Feminists*, Oxford University Press, New York and Oxford, 1992.

Cannadine, David, *Class in Britain,* Penguin, London, 2000.

Capaldi, Nicholas, *John Stuart Mill: A Biography,* Cambridge University Press, New York, 2004.

Chambers, Coral, *Lessons for Ladies: A Social History of Girls' Education in Australasia, 1870–1900*, Hale and Iremonger, Sydney, 1986.

Chandos, John, *Boys Together: English Public Schools 1800–1964*, Hutchinson, London, 1984.

Clerehan, Neil, *Historic Houses of Australia*, Australian Council of National Trusts, Cassell Australia, North Melbourne, Victoria, 1974.

Cohen, Deborah, *Family Secrets: Shame and Privacy in Modern Britain*, Oxford University Press, New York, 2013.

Collini, Stefan, *Public Moralists: Public Thought and Intellectual Life in Britain, 1850–1930*, Clarendon Press, Oxford, and Oxford University Press, New York, 1991.

Connell, R. W., *Gender and Power: Society, the Person, and Sexual Politics*, Stanford University Press, Stanford, 1987.

——, *Masculinities*, Allen & Unwin, Sydney, 1995.

Cookson, John and Dunstall, Graeme (eds), *Southern Capital Christchurch: Towards a City Biography 1859–2000*, Canterbury University Press, Christchurch, 2000.

Cooper, Annabel, Paterson, Lachy and Wanhalla, Angela (eds), *The Lives of Colonial Objects*, Otago University Press, Dunedin, 2015.

Cooper, Frederick, *Colonialism in Question: Theory, Knowledge, History,* University of California Press, Berkeley, 2005.

Coveney, Peter, *The Image of Childhood: The Individual and Society: A Study of the Theme in English Literature*, Penguin Books, Middlesex, 1967.

Crotty, Martin, *Making the Australian Male: Middle-Class Masculinity, 1870–1920*, Melbourne University Press, Carlton South, Victoria, 2001.

Cumming, Ian and Cumming, Alan, *History of State Education in New Zealand 1840–1975*, Pitman, Wellington, 1978.

Dale, Leigh, *The English Men: Professing Literature in Australian Universities*, Association for the Study of Australian Literature, Canberra, 1997.

Daley, Caroline, *Girls & Women, Men & Boys: Gender in Taradale 1886–1930*, University of Auckland Press, Auckland, 1999.

Daley, Caroline and Montgomerie, Deborah (eds), *The Gendered Kiwi*, Auckland University Press, Auckland, 1999.

Daley, Caroline and Nolan, Melanie (eds), *Suffrage and Beyond: International Feminist Perspectives,* Auckland University Press, Auckland, and Pluto Press, Annandale, 1994.

Darian-Smith, Kate, Grimshaw, Patricia and Macintyre, Stuart (eds), *Britishness Abroad: Transnational Movements and Imperial Cultures*, Melbourne University Press, Melbourne, 2007.

Davidoff, Leonore, *The Best Circles. Women and Society in Victorian England*, Rowan & Littlefield, Totawa, New Jersey, 1973.

——, *Thicker than Water: Siblings and their Relations, 1780–1920*, Oxford University Press, Oxford, 2012.

Davidoff, Leonore and Hall, Catherine, *Family Fortunes: Men and Women of the English Middle Class, 1750–1850*, Hutchinson, London, 1987.

——, *Family Fortunes: Men and Women of the English Middle Class, 1750–1850*, revised edn, Routledge, London, 2002.

Davie, George, *The Democratic Intellect: Scotland and her Universities in the nineteenth century*, Edinburgh University Press, Edinburgh, 1981.

Davison, Graeme, *The Rise and Fall of Marvellous Melbourne* [1978], Melbourne University Press, Carlton, Victoria, 2004.

Davison, G., Hirst, John and Macintyre, Stuart (eds), *Oxford Companion to Australian History*, Oxford University Press, Melbourne, 2001.

de Courcy, Anne, *The Viceroy's Daughter: The Lives of the Curzon Sisters*, Weidenfield & Nicholson, London, 2000.

de Serville, Paul, *Pounds and Pedigrees: The Upper Class in Victoria, 1850–80*, Oxford University Press, Melbourne, 1991.

de Symons Honey, J. R., *Tom Brown's Universe: The Development of the Victorian Public School*, Millington, London, 1977.

Deacon, Desley, *Managing Gender: The State, the New Middle Class and Women Workers 1830–1930*, Oxford University Press, Melbourne, 1989.

Deans, John, *Pioneers on Port Cooper Plains: The Deans Family of Riccarton and Homebush*, Simpson and Williams, Christchurch, 1964.

Denoon, Donald, Mein-Smith, Philippa with Wyndham, Marivic, *A History of Australia, New Zealand and the Pacific*, Blackwell, Oxford, 2000.

Devine, Thomas, *The Scottish Nation: A History 1700–2000*, Allen Lane and Penguin Press, London, 1999.

Drummond, Alison (ed.), *Married and Gone to New Zealand: Being Extracts from the Writings of Women Pioneers*, Paul's Book Arcade, Oxford University Press, Hamilton and London, 1960.

Duman, Daniel, *The English and Colonial Bars in the Nineteenth Century*, Croom Helm, London, 1983.

Duncan, W. G. K. and Leonard, Roger Ashley, *The University of Adelaide, 1874–1974*, Rigby, Adelaide, 1974.

Dunn, W. H., *James Anthony Froude: A Biography, vol. 1: 1818–1856*, Clarendon Press, Oxford, 1961.

Durack, Mary, *Kings in Grass Castles*, Lloyd O'Neil, Melbourne, 1974.

Dyhouse, Carol, *Feminism and the Family in England 1880–1939*, Basil Blackwell, Oxford, 1989.

Eagle, Chester, *Play Together, Dark Blue Twenty*, McPhee Gribble, Melbourne, 1986.

Edmond, Rod, *Migrations: Journeys in Time and Place*, Bridget Williams Books, Wellington, 2013.

Eldred-Grigg, Stevan, *A Southern Gentry: New Zealanders Who Inherited the Earth*, Reed, Wellington, 1980.

Elenio, Paul, *Centrecourt: A Century of New Zealand Tennis, 1886–1996*, New Zealand Lawn Tennis Association, Wellington, 1986.

Ellis, Amanda, *Rebels and Conservatives: Dorothy & William Wordsworth & their Circle*, Bloomington, Indiana University Press, 1967.

Else, Ann, *Women Together: A History of Women's Organisations in New Zealand*, Historical Branch, Department of Internal Affairs and Daphne Brasell Associates Press, Wellington, 1993.

Fairburn, Miles, *The Ideal Society and Its Enemies: The Foundations of Modern New Zealand Society, 1850–1900*, Auckland University Press, Auckland, 1989.

Finn, Jeremy, *Educating for the Profession: Law at Canterbury*, Canterbury University Press, Christchurch, 2010.

Fitzgerald, Kathleen, *PLC Melbourne: The First Century, 1875–1975*, Presbyterian Ladies' College, Burwood, Victoria, 1975.

Fitzpatrick, Brian, *The Australian People, 1788–1945*, Melbourne University Press, Carlton, Victoria, 1946.

Fitzpatrick, David, *Oceans of Consolation: Personal Accounts of Irish Migration to Australia*, Melbourne University Press, Carlton, Victoria, 1995.

Flanders, Judith, *A Circle of Sisters: Alice-Kipling, Georgiana Burne-Jones, Agnes Poynter and Louisa Baldwin*, Viking, London, 2001.

Fletcher, Brian H., *The Place of Anglicanism in Australia: Church, Society and Nation*, Broughton Publishing, Mulgrave, Victoria, 2008.

Fletcher, Sheila, *Victorian Girls: Lord Lyttelton's Daughters*, Hambledon Press, London, 2004.

Ford, Boris (ed.), *The Penguin Guide to English Literature: From Dickens to Hardy*, Penguin, Middlesex, 1966.

Forsyth, Hannah, *A History of the Modern Australian University*, NewSouth Publishing, Sydney, 2014.

Foster, Stephen, *A Private Empire*, Pier 9 (Murdoch Books), Millers Point, NSW, 2010.

Fox, James, *Five Sisters: The Langhornes of Virginia*, Simon & Schuster, New York, 2001.

Fraser, Frances and Palmer, Nettie (eds), *Centenary Gift Book*, Robertson and Mullens, Melbourne, 1934.

Fraser, Lyndon, *A Distant Shore: Irish Migration and New Zealand Settlement*, University of Otago Press, Dunedin, 2000.

——, *Castles of Gold: A History of New Zealand's West Coast Irish*, Otago University Press, Otago, 2007.

Fraser, Lyndon and McCarthy, Angela, *Far from Home: The English in New Zealand*, Otago University Press, Dunedin, 2012.

Fraser, Lyndon and Pickles, Katie (eds), *Shifting Centres: Women and Migration in New Zealand History*, University of Otago Press, Dunedin, 2002.

Frost, Lionel, *The New Urban Frontier: Urbanisation and City Building in Australasia and the American West*, New South Wales University Press, Kensington, 1991.

Fry, Margot, *Tom's Letters: The Private World of Thomas King, Victorian Gentleman*, Victoria University Press, Wellington, 2001.

Fry, Ruth, *It's Different for Daughters: A History of the Curriculum for Girls in New Zealand Schools, 1900–1975*, New Zealand Council for Educational Research, Wellington, 1985.

——, *Maud and Amber: A New Zealand Mother and Daughter and the Women's Cause, 1865–1981*, Canterbury University Press, Christchurch, 1992.

Garden, Don, *Victoria: A History*, Thomas Nelson Australia, Melbourne, 1985.

Gardiner, Lyndsay, *Janet Clarke Hall 1886–1986*, Hyland House, Melbourne, 1986.

Gardner, W. J., *The Amuri: A County History*, Amuri County Council, Culverden, 1956.

——, *Colonial Cap and Gown: Studies in the Mid-Victorian Universities of Australasia*, University of Canterbury, Christchurch, 1979.

——, *The Farmer Politician in New Zealand History*, Massey Memorial Lecture 1970, Massey University Occasional Publication No. 3, Palmerston North, 1970.

Gardner, W. J. (ed.), *A History of Canterbury, Volume II*, Whitcombe & Tombs, Christchurch, 1971.

Gardner, W. J., Beardsley, E. T. and Carter, T. E., *A History of the University of Canterbury 1873–1973*, University of Canterbury, Christchurch, 1973.

Garrett, Eilidh, Reid, Alice, Schurer, Kevin and Szreter, Simon, *Changing Family Size in England and Wales: Place, Class and Demography 1891–1911*, Cambridge University Press, Cambridge, 2001.

Gathorne-Hardy, Jonathan, *The Public School Phenomenon, 597–1977*, Hodder and Stoughton, London, 1977.

——, *The Rise and Fall of the British Nanny*, Arrow Books, London, 1974.

Gillett, Paula, *Musical Women in England, 1870–1914: 'Encroaching on All Man's Privileges'*, St. Martin's Press, New York, 2000.

Gillison, Joan M., *A History of the Lyceum Club Melbourne*, Lyceum Club, Melbourne, 1975.

Glynn, Sean, *Urbanisation in Australian History, 1788–1900*, Nelson, Melbourne, 1970.

Grant, James, *Episcopally Led and Synodically Governed: Anglicans in Victoria, 1803–1997*, Australian Scholarly Publishing, North Melbourne, 2010.

——, *Old St Paul's: The Story of St Paul's Church, Melbourne, and Its Congregation, 1850–1891*, Melbourne, c.2000.

——, *Perspective of a Century: A Volume for the Centenary of Trinity College, Melbourne 1872–1972*, Council of Trinity College, Melbourne, 1972.

Griffith, Penny, *Out of the Shadows: The Life of Millicent Baxter* [October 2015], PenPublishing, Wellington, February 2016.

Grimshaw, Patricia, *Women's Suffrage in New Zealand*, Auckland University Press, Auckland, 1972.

Grimshaw, Patricia, McConville, Chris and McEwen, Ellen, *Families in Colonial Australia*, George Allen & Unwin, Sydney, 1985.

Gros, Frederic, *A Philosophy of Walking*, Verso Books, UK, 2014.

Hamer, David, *The New Zealand Liberals: The Years of Power, 1891–1912*, Auckland University Press, Auckland, 1988.

Harper, Melissa, *The Ways of the Bushwalker*, University of New South Wales Press, Sydney, 2007.

Hartz, Louis, *The Founding of New Societies*, Harcourt, Brace & World, New York, 1964.

Hergenhan, L. T. (ed.), *A Colonial City: High and Low Life, Selected Journalism of Marcus Clarke*, University of Queensland Press, St Lucia, 1972.

Hewitson, Jim, *Far Off in Sunlit Places: Stories of the Scots in Australia and New Zealand*, Melbourne University Press, Carlton, Victoria, and Canongate Books, Edinburgh, 1998.

Hickman, Katie, *Daughters of Britannia: The Lives & Times of Diplomatic Wives*, Flamingo, London, 2000.

Hight, James and Candy, Alice M. F., *A Short History of the Canterbury College (University of New Zealand): With a Register of Graduates and Associates of the College*, Whitcombe & Tombs, Auckland, 1927.

Higley, John, Deacon, Desley and Smart, Don, with Cushing, Robert G., Moore, Gwen and Pakulski, Jan, *Elites in Australia*, Routledge and K. Paul, London and Boston, 1979.

Hirst, John, *Sense and Nonsense in Australian History*, Black Inc. Agenda, Melbourne, 2005.

Hobsbawm, E. and Ranger, T., *The Invention of Tradition*, Cambridge University Press, Cambridge, 1983.

Holland, C. H. (ed.), *Trinity College Dublin and the Idea of a University*, Trinity College Dublin Press, Dublin, 1991.

Holm, Janet, *Nothing but Grass and Wind: The Rutherfords of Canterbury*, Hazard Press, Christchurch, 1992.

Holmes, Katie, *Spaces in her Day: Australian Women's Diaries of the 1920s and 1930s*, Allen and Unwin, Sydney, 1995.

Home, R. W. (ed.), *Australian Science in the Making*, Cambridge University Press, Cambridge, and Australian Academy of Science, Melbourne, 1988.

Hoppen, K. Theodore, *The Mid-Victorian Generation, 1846–1886*, Clarendon Press, Oxford, 1998.

Horne, Julia and Sherington, Geoffrey, *Sydney: The Making of a Public University*, Miegunyah Press, Melbourne, 2012.

Hughes, Kathryn, *The Short Life & Long Times of Mrs Beeton*, Harper Perennial, London, 2006.

Hutching, Megan, *Leading the Way: How New Zealand Women Won the Vote*, HarperCollins Publishers, Auckland, 2010.

Isaac, Joe and Macintyre, Stuart (eds), *The New Province for Law and Order: One Hundred Years of Australian Industrial Conciliation and Arbitration*, Cambridge University Press, Cambridge, New York and Victoria, 2004.

Jackson, H. R., *Churches & People in Australia and New Zealand 1860–1930*, Allen & Unwin, North Sydney, and Port Nicholson Press, Wellington, 1987.

Jalland, Pat, *Women, Marriage and Politics 1860–1914*, Oxford University Press, Oxford, New York, Melbourne, 1988.

Janssens, Angelique (ed.), *Gendering the Fertility Decline in the Western World*, Peter Lang, Bern, 2007.

Jasper, J. M., *The Social Movements Reader*, Blackwell, Oxford, 1968.

Johansen, Shawn, *Family Men: Middle-Class Fatherhood in Early Industrializing America*, Routledge, New York, 2001.

Johnson, Joseph, *The Royal Melbourne Golf Club: A Centenary History*, Royal Melbourne Golf Club, Black Rock, Victoria, 1991.

Jones, John, *Balliol College: A History, 1263–1939* [1988], 2nd edn, Oxford University Press, Oxford, 2005.

Jordan, Deborah, *Nettie Palmer: Search for an Aesthetic*, History Department, University of Melbourne, Carlton, Victoria, 1999.

Jupp, James, *The English in Australia*, Cambridge University Press, Cambridge, 2004.

Kaye, Bruce (ed.), *Anglicanism in Australia: A History*, Melbourne University Press, Carlton, Victoria, 2002.

Kelly, Paul, *The End of Certainty: Power, Politics and Business in Australia*, revised edn, Allen & Unwin, St Leonards, NSW, 1994.

Kelly, Paul, *The End of Certainty: The Story of the 1980s*, Allen & Unwin, St Leonards, NSW, 1992.

Kerr, Margaret, *Colonial Dynasty: The Chambers Family of South Australia*, Rigby, Adelaide, 1980.

King, Julie, *Olivia Spencer Bower: Making Her Own Discoveries*, Canterbury University Press, Christchurch, 2015.

Kociumbas, Jan, *Australian Childhood: A History*, Allen and Unwin, Sydney, 1997.

Koopman-Boyden, Peggy G. (ed.), *Families in New Zealand Society*, Methuen, Wellington, 1978.

Larson, Ann, *Growing Up in Melbourne: Family Life in the Late Nineteenth Century*, Demography Program, The Australian National University, Canberra, 1994.

Lemon, Andrew, *A Great Australian School: Wesley College Examined*, Helicon Press, Melbourne, 2004.

Levine, Philippa (ed.), *Gender and Empire: Reflections on the Nineteenth Century*, Oxford University Press, Oxford, 2004.

——, *Victorian Feminism 1850–1900*, Oxford University Press, Oxford, 1997.

Lewis, Jeremy, *Shades of Greene: One Generation of an English Family*, London, Jonathan Cape, 2010.

Lewis, Margaret, *Ngaio Marsh: A Life*, Bridget Williams Books, Wellington, 1991.

Light, Alison, *Common People: The History of an English Family* [2014], Penguin Books, UK, 2015.

Locke, Elsie, *Student at the Gates*, Whitcoulls, Christchurch, 1981.

Lovell, Mary S., *The Mitford Girls: The Biography of an Extraordinary Family*, London, Abacus, 2002.

Lovell-Smith, Margaret, *Easily the Best: The Life of Helen Connon, 1857–1903*, Canterbury University Press, Christchurch, 2004.

——, *Plain Living High Thinking: The Family Story of Jennie and Will Lovell-Smith*, Pedmore Press, Christchurch, 1995.

Lovell-Smith, Margaret (ed.), *The Woman Question: Writings by Women who Won the Vote*, New Women's Press, Auckland, 1992.

Lowerson, John, *Sport and the English Middle Classes 1870–1914*, Manchester University Press, Manchester, 1995.

Macdonald, Charlotte, *A Woman of Good Character: Single Women as Immigrant Settlers in Nineteenth-Century New Zealand*, Bridget Williams Books, Historical Branch, Department of Internal Affairs, Wellington, 1990.

Macintyre, Stuart, *A Colonial Liberalism: The Lost World of Three Visionaries*, Oxford University Press, Melbourne, 1991.

——, *History for the Homeless: Kathleen Fitzpatrick's Vocation and Ours*, Department of History, University of Melbourne, 1995.

——, *Ormond College Centenary Essays*, Melbourne University Press, Carlton, Victoria, 1984.

——, *Oxford History of Australia, Volume 4, 1901–1942: The Succeeding Age*, Oxford University Press, Melbourne, 1986.

Mackinnon, Alison, *The New Women: Adelaide's Early Women Graduates*, Wakefield Press, Adelaide, 1986.

MacLeod, Roy (ed.), *Commonwealth of Science: ANZAAS and the Scientific Enterprise in Australasia, 1888–1988*, Oxford University Press, Melbourne, 1988.

Magarey, Susan, *Passions of the First Wave of Feminists*, University of New South Wales Press, Sydney, 2001.

——, *Unbridling the Tongues of Women: A Biography of Catherine Helen Spence*, Hale & Iremonger, Sydney, 1985.

Magarey, Susan, Rowley, Sue and Sheridan, Susan (eds), *Debutante Nation: Feminism Contests the Nineties*, Allen & Unwin, Sydney, 1993.

Magee, Gary and Thompson, Andrew S., *Empire and Globalisation: Networks of People and Capital in the British World, c 1850–1914*, Cambridge University Press, Cambridge, 2010.

Magnusson, Magnus, *The Clacken and the State*, Collins, London, 1974.

Marsden, Gordon (ed.), *Victorian Values: Personalities and Perspectives in Nineteenth Century Society*, Longman, Essex, 1990.

Masson, Flora, *Victorians All*, Chambers, Edinburgh, 1931.

Masters, Brian, *The Dukes: The Origins, Enoblement and History of Twenty-Six Families*, Pimlico, London, 2001.

Matthews, Kay Morris, *In Their Own Right: Women and Higher Education in New Zealand Before 1945*, New Zealand Council of Educational Research, Wellington, 2008.

Mazlish, Bruce, *James and John Stuart Mill: Father and Son in the Nineteenth Century*, Hutchinson, London, 1975.

McAloon, Jim, *No Idle Rich: The Wealthy in Canterbury and Otago, 1840–1914*, University of Otago Press, Dunedin, 2002.

McCalman, Janet, *Journeyings: The Biography of a Middle-Class Generation 1920–1990*, Melbourne University Press, Carlton, Victoria, 1993.

——, *On the World of the Sixty-Nine Tram*, Melbourne University Press, Carlton, Victoria, 2006.

——, *Solid Bluestone Foundations and Rising Damp: The Fortunes of the Melbourne Middle Class, 1890–1990*, Department of History, University of Melbourne, Melbourne, 1994.

——, *Struggletown: Public and Private Life in Richmond 1900–1965*, Melbourne University Press, Carlton, Victoria, 1985.

McCarthy, Angela (ed.), *A Global Clan: Scottish Migrant Networks and Identities Since the Eighteenth Century*, Tauris Academic Studies, London and New York, 2006.

McCarthy, Rosslyn and Theobald, Marjorie R. (eds), *Melbourne Girls Grammar School Centenary Essays 1893–1993*, Hyland House, Melbourne, 1993.

McConnell, Lynn and Smith, Ian, *The Shell New Zealand Cricket Encyclopedia*, Moa Beckett, Auckland, 1993.

McCrone, Kathleen E., *Playing the Game: Sport and the Physical Emancipation of Women 1870–1914*, University of Kentucky Press, Kentucky, 1988.

McKinnon, Alison, *The New Women: Adelaide's Early Women Graduates*, Wakefield Press, Adelaide, 1986.

McLaren, Ian A., *Education in a Small Democracy: New Zealand*, Routledge & Kegan Paul, London, 1974.

McMurtry, Jo, *English Language, English Literature: the Creation of an Academic Discipline*, Archon Books, Hamden, Connecticut, 1985.

McNicholl, Ronald, *Number 36 Collins Street, Melbourne Club 1838–1988*, Allen & Unwin/Haynes in conjunction with the Melbourne Club, Sydney, 1988.

Mein Smith, Philippa, *A Concise History of New Zealand*, Cambridge University Press, Melbourne, 2005.

Mein Smith, Philippa, Hempenstall, Peter and Goldfinch, Shaun, *Remaking the Tasman World*, Canterbury University Press, Christchurch, 2008.

Mendelssohn, Joanna, *Letters and Liars: Norman Lindsay and the Lindsay Family*, Angus and Robertson, Pymble, 1996.

Mendelssohn, Joanna, *Lionel Lindsay: An Artist and His Family*, Chatto & Windus, London, 1988.

Middleton, Susan (ed.), *Women and Education in Aotearoa*, Allen & Unwin, Wellington, 1988.

Mill, John Stuart, *Autobiography* [1873], Currin V. Shields (ed.), Liberal Arts Press, New York, 1957.

Millen, Julia, *Colonial Tears and Sweat: The Working Class in Nineteenth Century*, A. H. Reed, Wellington, 1984.

Mintz, Steven, *A Prison of Expectations: The Family in Victorian Culture*, New York University Press, New York, 1983.

Modjeska, Drusilla, *Stravinsky's Lunch*, Picador, Sydney, 2001.

Moffat, Kirstine, *Piano Forte: Stories and Soundscapes from Colonial New Zealand*, Otago University Press, Dunedin, 2011.

Morrell, W. P., *The University of Otago: A Centennial History*, University of Otago Press, Dunedin, 1969.

Mosley, Charlotte (ed.), *The Mitfords: Letters Between Six Sisters*, Harper Perennial, London, 2008.

Moyal, Ann, *A Bright and Savage Land: Scientists in Colonial Australia*, Collins, Sydney, 1986.

Murdoch, Martha, *They Built for Tomorrow: The Story of the Blair Family*, Otago Daily Times Ltd, Dunedin, 1970.

Mussen, Paul H., Conger, John J. and Kagan, Jerome, *Child Development and Personality*, 4th edn, Harper Row Publishers, New York, 1974.

Neely, D. O. and Neely, P. W., *The Summer Game: The Illustrated History of New Zealand Cricket*, Moa Beckett, Auckland, 1994.

Neely, Don and Romanos, Joseph, *An Illustrated History of Lancaster Park*, Trio Books, Wellington, 2006.

Nelson, Claudia, *Invisible Men: Fatherhood in Victorian Periodicals, 1850–1910*, University of Georgia Press, Athens, 1996.

Niall, Brenda, *The Boyds: A Family Biography*, Miegunyah Press, Melbourne, 2002.

Nolan, Melanie, *Breadwinning: New Zealand Women and the State*, Canterbury University Press, Christchurch, 2000.

——, *Kin: A Collective Biography of a Working-Class New Zealand Family*, Canterbury University Press, Christchurch, 2005.

Notman, G. C. and Keith, B. R., *The Geelong College 1861–1961*, Geelong College Council and Old Geelong Collegians Assoc., Geelong, Victoria, 1961.

O'Farrell, Patrick, *The Irish in Australia 1788 to the Present*, University of New South Wales Press, Sydney, 2000.

Ogilvie, Gordon, *Pioneers of the Plains: The Deans of Canterbury*, Shoal Bay Press, Christchurch, 1996.

——, *The Port Hills of Christchurch*, [1978], Reed and Philip King Booksellers, Christchurch and Dunedin, 1991.

——, *The Shagroons' Palace: A History of the Christchurch Club, 1856–2006*, Henry Elworthy for the Christchurch Club, Christchurch, 2005.

Oldfield, Audrey, *Woman Suffrage in Australia: A Gift or a Struggle?*, Cambridge University Press, Cambridge and Melbourne, 1992.

Olssen, Erik, *A History of Otago*, John McIndoe, Dunedin, 1984.

Olssen, Erik, Griffen, Clyde and Jones, Frank, *An Accidental Utopia? Social Mobility and the Foundations of an Egalitarian Society, 1880–1940*, Otago University Press, Dunedin, 2011.

Openshaw, Roger and McKenzie, David (eds), *Reinterpreting the Educational Past: Essays in the History of New Zealand Education*, Council of Educational Research, Wellington, 1987.

Palmer, Nettie, *Henry Bournes Higgins: A Memoir*, George G. Harrap & Co. London, 1931.

Parkes, Susan M., *Kildare Place: The History of the Church of Ireland Training College 1811–1969*, CICE, Dublin, 1984.

Parnaby, Owen, *Queen's College, University of Melbourne: A Centenary History,* Melbourne University Press, Carlton, Victoria, 1990.

Passmore, John, *A Hundred Years of Philosophy*, Gerald Duckworth & Co. Ltd, London, 1957.

Patterson, Brad (ed.), *The Irish in New Zealand: Historical Contexts & Perspectives*, Stout Research Centre for New Zealand Studies, Victoria University of Wellington, Wellington, 2002.

——, *Ulster-New Zealand Migration and Cultural Transfers*, Four Courts Press, Dublin and Portland, 2006.

Patterson, Brad, Brooking, Tom, and McAloon, Jim with Lenihan, Rebecca and Bueltmann, Tanja, *Unpacking the Kists: The Scots in New Zealand,* Otago University Press, Dunedin, 2013.

Paul, Janet and Roberts, Neil, *Evelyn Page: Seven Decades*, Robert McDougall Art Gallery with Allen and Unwin, Christchurch and Wellington, 1986.

Peddie, Barbara, *Christchurch Girls' High School 1877–1977*, Christchurch High School Old Girls' Association, Christchurch, 1977.

Perkin, Harold, *The Rise of Professional Society: England since 1880*, Routledge, London and New York, 1989.

Peterson, M. Jeanne, *Family, Love and Work in the Lives of Victorian Gentlewomen*, Indiana University Press, Bloomington and Indianapolis, 1989.

Pickles, Katie, *Christchurch Ruptures*, Bridget Williams Books, Wellington, 2016.

Pietsch, Tamson, *Empire of Scholars: Universities, Networks and the British Academic World 1850–1939*, Manchester University Press, Manchester and New York, 2013.

Phillips, Jock, *A Man's Country? The Image of the Pakeha Male: A History*, Penguin, Auckland, 1987.

Phillips, Jock and Hearn, Terry, *Settlers: New Zealand Immigrants from England, Ireland and Scotland 1800–1945*, Auckland University Press, Auckland, 2008.

Pogue, Kate, *Shakepeare's Family*, Praeger, Westport, Connecticut, 2008.

Pool, Ian, Dharmalingam, Arunachalam and Sceats, Janet, *The New Zealand Family from 1840: A Demographic History,* Auckland University Press, Auckland, 2007.

Porter, Frances, *Born to New Zealand: A Biography of Jane Maria Atkinson*, Allen & Unwin and Port Nicholson Press, Wellington, 1989.

Porter, Frances and Macdonald, Charlotte (eds), *'My Hand Will Write What My Heart Dictates': The Unsettled Lives of Women in Nineteenth-Century New Zealand as Revealed to Sisters, Family and Friends*, Auckland University Press and Bridget Williams Books, Wellington, 1996.

Poynter, John, *Doubts and Certainties: A Life of Alexander Leeper*, Melbourne University Press, Carlton, Victoria, 1997.

Poynter, Marion, *Nobody's Valentine: Letters in the Life of Valentine Alexa Leeper, 1900–2001*, Miegunyah Press with Trinity College, University of Melbourne, Melbourne, 2008.

Pugh, Martin, *The Pankhursts: The History of One Radical Family*, Allen Lane, London, 2008.

Putnam, Robert D., *Bowling Alone: The Collapse and Revival of American Community*, Simon & Schuster, New York and London, 2000.

Reader, W. J., *Professional Men: The Rise of the Professional Classes in Nineteenth-Century England*, Weidenfeld and Nicolson, London, 1966.

Reese, Daniel, *Was It All Cricket?*, Allen & Unwin, Christchurch, 1948.

Reese, T. W., *New Zealand Cricket 1841–1914*, Whitcombe & Tombs, Christchurch, 1927.

Reid, M. O., *The Ladies Came to Stay: A Study of the Education of Girls at the Presbyterian Ladies' College*, Council of the College, Melbourne, 1960.

Rice, Geoffrey W. (ed.), *The Oxford History of New Zealand*, 2nd edn, Oxford University Press, Auckland, 1992.

Richards, Eric, *Britannia's Children: Emigration from England, Scotland, Wales and Ireland since 1600*, Hambledon, London, 2004.

Richardson, Len and Shelley, *Anthony Wilding: A Sporting Life*, Canterbury University Press, Christchurch, 2005.

Rickard, John, *Class and Politics*, The Australian National University Press, Canberra, 1976.

——, *A Family Romance: The Deakins at Home*, Melbourne University Press, Carlton South, Victoria, 1996.

——, *H.B. Higgins: The Rebel as Judge*, Allen & Unwin, Sydney, 1984.

Roberts, Neil, *A Concise History of Art in Canterbury, 1850–2000*, Robert McDougall Art Gallery, Christchurch, 2000.

Rose, Phyllis, *Parallel Lives: Five Victorian Marriages*, Alfred A. Knopf, New York, 1984.

Rossi, Alice S. (ed.), *Essays on Sex Equality: John Stuart Mill and Harriet Taylor Mill. Edited and with an Introductory Essay by Alice S. Rossi*, The University of Chicago Press, Chicago and London, 1972.

Rowse, Tim, *Nugget Coombs: A Reforming Life* [2002], 2nd edn, Cambridge University Press, Melbourne, 2005.

Russell, Penny, *Savage or Civilised? Manners in Colonial Australia*, University of New South Wales Press, Sydney, 2011.

——, *'A Wish of Distinction': Colonial Gentility and Femininity*, Melbourne University Press, Carlton, Victoria, 1994.

Ryan, Greg, *The Making of New Zealand Cricket 1832–1914*, Frank Cass, London, 2004.

Saunders, Kay and Evans, Raymond (eds), *Gender Relations in Australia: Domination and Negotiation*, Harcourt, Brace Jovanich, Sydney, 1992.

Scott, Ernest, *Historical Memoir of the Melbourne Club*, Specialty Press, Melbourne, 1936.

Selleck, R. J. W., *Finding Home: The Masson Family*, Australian Scholarly Publishing, Melbourne, 2013.

——, *The Shop: The University of Melbourne 1850–1939*, Melbourne University Press, Carlton, Victoria, 2003.

Sherington, Geoffrey, *Learning to Lead: A History of Girls' and Boys' Corporate Secondary Schools in Australia*, Allen & Unwin, Sydney, 1987.

Shuker, Roy, *The One Best System? A Revisionist History of State Schooling in New Zealand*, Dunmore Press, Palmerston North, 1987.

Simons, Judy, *Diaries and Journals of Literary Women from Fanny Burney to Virginia Woolf*, Houndmills, Basingstoke, Hampshire, 1990.

Sinclair, Keith, *A History of the University of Auckland, 1883–1983*, University of Auckland/Oxford University Press, Auckland, 1983.

——, *William Pember Reeves: New Zealand Fabian*, Clarendon Press, Oxford, 1965.

Slatter, Gordon, *Great Days at Lancaster Park*, Whitcombe & Tombs, Christchurch, 1974.

Smith, F. B., *Illness in Colonial Australia*, Australian Scholarly Publishing, Melbourne, 2011.

Solnit, Rebecca, *Wanderlust: A History of Walking*, Granta Books, UK, 2014.

Solomon, Barbara, *In the Company of Educated Women: A History of Women and Higher Education in America*, Yale University Press, New Haven, 1985.

Stanford, William and McDowell, Robert, *Mahaffy: A Biography of an Anglo-Irishman*, Routledge & Kegan Paul, London, 1971.

Stephen, Reginald (ed.), *The First Hundred Years: Notes on the History of the Church of England in Victoria*, Executive Committee of the Anglican Assembly, Melbourne, 1934.

Strongman, Thelma, *The Gardens of Canterbury: A History*, A.H. & A.W. Reed, Wellington, 1984.

Sturrock, Morna, *Bishop of Magnetic Power: James Moorhouse in Melbourne 1876–1886*, Australian Scholarly Publishing, Melbourne, 2005.

Sutton-Smith, Brian, *A History of Children's Play: The New Zealand Playground 1840–1950*, New Zealand Council of Educational Research, Wellington, 1982.

Szreter, Simon, *Fertility, Class and Gender in Britain 1860–1940*, Cambridge University Press, Cambridge, 1996.

Telfer, Kevin, *Peter Pan's First XI: The Extraordinary Story of J. M. Barrie's Cricket Team*, Sceptre, London, 2010.

Theobald, Marjorie, *Knowing Women: Origins of Women's Education in Nineteenth-Century Australia*, Cambridge University Press, Melbourne, 1996.

Thomas, Geoffrey, *The Moral Philosophy of T.H. Green*, Clarendon Press, Oxford and New York, 1988.

Thompson, E. P., *The Making of the English Working Class*, Penguin, Harmondsworth, Middlesex, England, 1968.

Thompson, F. M. L. (ed.), *The Cambridge Social History of Britain 1750–1950*, Vol. 2, Cambridge University Press, Cambridge, 1990.

Thomson, John M., *Distant Music: The Life and Times of Alfred Hill, 1870–1960*, Oxford University Press, Auckland, 1980.

——, *The Oxford History of New Zealand Music*, Oxford University Press, Auckland, 1991.

Todd, Jan, *Colonial Technology: Science and the Transfer of Innovation to Australia*, Cambridge University Press, Melbourne, 1995.

Todd, Selina, *The People: The Rise and Fall of the Working Class* [2014], John Murray, London, 2015.

Tolerton, Jane, *A Life of Ettie Rout*, Auckland, Penguin, 1992.

Tosh, John, *Manliness and Masculinities in Nineteenth-Century Britain: Essays On Gender, Family and Empire*, Pearson Longman, London, 2005.

——, *A Man's Place: Masculinity and the Middle-Class Home in Victorian England* [1999], Yale University Press, New Haven and London, 2007.

Toynbee, Claire, *Her Work and His: Family, Kin and Community in New Zealand 1900–1930*, Victoria University Press, Wellington, 1995.

Turner, Frank M., *The Greek Heritage in Victorian Britain*, Yale University Press, New Haven, Connecticut, 1981.

Vincent, A. and Plant, R., *Philosophy, Politics and Citizenship: The Life and Thought of British Idealists*, Blackwell, Oxford, 1984.

Wanhalla, Angela, *Matters of the Heart: A History of Interracial Marriage in New Zealand*, Auckland University Press, Auckland, 2013.

Wayne, Helena (ed.), *The Story of a Marriage: The letters of Bronislaw Malinowski and Elsie Masson, volume 1, 1916–1920*, Routledge, London and New York, 1995.

——, *The Story of a Marriage: The letters of Bronislaw Malinowski and Elsie Masson, volume 2, 1920–35*, Routledge, London and New York, 1995.

Weickhardt, Len, *Masson of Melbourne: The Life and Times of David Orme Masson: Professor of Chemistry, University of Melbourne, 1886–1923*, Royal Australian Chemical Institute, Parkville, Melbourne, 1989.

Wernick, Andrew, *Auguste Comte and the Religion of Humanity: The Post-Theistic Program of French Social Theory*, Cambridge University Press, New York, 2001.

Williams, Raymond, *Culture and Society 1870–1950*, Pelican, Harmondsworth, 1982.

——, *Problems in Materialism and Culture: Selected Essays*, Verso and NLB, London, 1980.

Wilson, A. N., *The Victorians*, Hutchinson, London, 2004.

Wineapple, Brenda, *Sister Brother: Gertrude & Leo Stein*, London, Bloomsbury, 1996.

Wizenreid, A. P., *Green Grows Our Garden: A Centenary History of Horticultural Education at Burnley*, Hyland House, Melbourne, 1991.

Young, Michael, *Malinowski: Odyssey of an Anthropologist 1884–1920*, Yale University Press, New Haven, 2004.

F. Articles

Aitken, Jo, 'Wives and Mothers First: The New Zealand Teachers' Marriage Bar and the Ideology of Domesticity 1920–40', *Women's Studies Journal*, vol. 12, no. 1, Autumn 1996, pp. 83–98.

Bridge, Carl and Fedorowich, Kent, 'Mapping the British World', *Journal of Imperial and Commonwealth History*, vol. 31, issue 2, (2003), pp. 1–15.

Brown, Nicholas, 'Born Modern: Antipodean Variations on a Theme', *The Historical Journal*, vol. 48, part 4, 2005, pp. 1139–54.

Cleall, Esme, Ishiguru, Laura and Manktelow, Emily J., 'Imperial Relations: Histories of Family in the British Empire', *Journal of Colonialism and Colonial History*, vol. 14, no. 1, Spring 2013.

Comacchio, Cynthia, '"The History of Us": Social Science, History, and the Relations of Family in Canada', *Labour/Le Travail: Journal of Canadian Labour Studies*, vol. 46, Fall 2000, pp. 167–220.

Culley, Margo, '"I Look at Me": Self as a Subject in the Diaries of American Women', *Women's Studies Quarterly*, vol. 17, parts 3 and 4, 1989, pp. 15–22.

Dalziel, Raewyn, 'The Colonial Helpmeet: Women's Role and the Vote in Nineteenth-Century New Zealand', *NZJH*, vol. 11, no. 2, October 1977, pp. 112–23.

Doust, Janet, 'Kinship and Accountability: The Diaries of a Pioneer Pastoralist Family, 1856 to 1898', *History Australia*, vol. 2, no. 1, November 2004, pp. 4.1–4.14.

Evans, Tanya, 'The Use of Memory and Material Culture in the History of the Family in Colonial Australia', *Journal of Australian Studies*, vol. 36, no. 2, 2012, pp. 207–28.

Fairburn, Miles, 'The Rural Myth and the Urban Frontier, 1870–1940', *NZJH*, vol. 9, no. 1, 1975, pp. 3–21.

Featherstone, Lisa and Smaal, Yorick, 'The Family in Australia', *Journal of Australian Studies*, vol. 37, no. 3, 2013, pp. 279–84.

Graham, Jeanine, 'Editorial Introduction', *NZJH*, vol. 40, no. 1, April 2006, pp. 1–6.

Graham, Jeanine, 'New Zealand', in Fass, Paula (ed.), *Encyclopedia of Children and Childhood in History and Society, vol. 2*, Macmillan Reference, New York, 2004, pp. 623–25.

Gush, Nadia, 'The Beauty of Health: Cora Wilding and the Sunlight League', *NZJH*, vol. 43, no. 1, 2009, pp. 1–17.

Hearn, Mark, 'Making Liberal Citizens: Justice Higgins and His Witnesses', *Labour History*, no. 93, November 2007, pp. 57–72.

Jasper, James M., 'The Emotions of Protest: Affective and Reactive Emotions in and Around Social Movements', *Sociological Forum*, vol. 13, no. 3, September 1998, pp. 397–424.

Jones, Diana K., 'Researching Groups of Lives: A Collective Biographical Perspective on the Protestant Ethic Debate', *Qualitative Research*, vol. 1, no. 3, 2001, pp. 325–46.

Jordan, Deborah, '"Women's Time", Ina Higgins, Nettie Palmer and Aileen Palmer', *Victorian Historical Journal*, vol. 79, no. 2, November 2008, pp. 296–313.

Leewen, Marco H. D. van and Maas, Ineke, 'Endogamy and Social Class in History: An Overview', *International Review of Social History*, 50, Supplement, 2005, pp. 1–23.

McAloon, Jim, 'Class in Colonial New Zealand, Towards a Historiographical Rehabilitation', *NZJH*, vol. 38, no. 1, 2004, pp. 3–21.

McGeorge, Colin, 'How Katy Did at School', *New Zealand Journal of Educational Studies*, vol. 2, no. 1, 1987, pp. 101–11.

North, Lorraine, 'Victorian Legacy', Perspective, *The Press*, 13 April 2011.

Papanek, Hanna, 'Men, Women and Work: Reflections on the Two-Person Career', *American Journal of Sociology*, vol. 78, part 4, 1973, pp. 852–72.

Pickles, Katie, 'A Natural Break from Our Colonial Past', Perspective, *Christchurch Press,* 8 April 2011, (A15).

Pickles, Katie, 'Colonial Counterparts: The First Academic Women in Anglo-Canada, New Zealand and Australia', *The Women's History Review*, vol. 10, no. 2, pp. 273–97.

Rothery, Mark, 'The Reproductive Behaviour of the English Landed Gentry in the Nineteenth and Early Twentieth Century', *Journal of British Studies*, vol. 8, no. 3, 2009, pp. 674–94.

Russell, Penny, 'Travelling Steerage: Class, Commerce, Religion and Family in Colonial Sydney', *Journal of Australian Studies*, vol. 38, no. 4, 2014, pp. 383–95.

Schouten, Erica, 'The "Encyclopaedic God-Professor": John Macmillan Brown and the Discipline of English in Colonial New Zealand', *Journal of English Literature*, vol. 23, part 1, 2005, pp. 109–23.

Seccombe, Wally, 'Starting to Stop: Working-Class Fertility Decline in Britain', *Past and Present*, no. 126, 1990, pp. 151–88.

Stone, Lawrence, 'Prosopography', *Daedalus*, vol. 100, no. 1, 1971, pp. 46–79.

Strange, Julie-Marie, 'Fatherhood, Providing, and Attachment in Late Victorian and Edwardian Working-Class Families', *The Historical Journal*, vol. 55, no. 4, 2012, pp. 1007–27.

Strick, James 'Darwinism and the Origin of Life: The Role of H. C. Bastian in the British Spontaneous Generation Debates, 1868–1873', *Journal of the History of Biology*, vol. 32, no. 1, 1999, pp. 51–92.

Whitehead, Kay, 'The Spinster Teacher in Australia from the 1870s to the 1960s', *History of Education Review*, vol. 36, no. 1, 2007, pp. 1–17.

Australian Dictionary of Biography (ADB) and *Dictionary of New Zealand Biography (DNZB)* Articles

Bell, Jacqueline, 'Bage, Anna Fredericka (Freda) (1883–1970)', *ADB*, vol. 7, Melbourne University Press, Carlton, Victoria, 1979, pp. 131–32.

Blainey, Ann, 'Bassett, Lady Flora Marjorie (Marnie) (1889–1980)', *ADB*, vol. 13, Melbourne University Press, Carlton, Victoria, 1993, pp. 127–28.

Earlam, Malcolm S., 'Craig, Robert Gordon (1870–1931)', *ADB*, vol. 8, Melbourne University Press, Carlton, Victoria, 1981, pp. 133–34.

Finlay, E. M., 'Mitchell, Agnes Eliza Fraser (1890–1968)', *ADB*, vol. 10, Melbourne University Press, Carlton, Victoria, 1986, pp. 528–30.

Francis, Charles, 'Stawell, Sir William Foster (1815–1889)', *ADB*, vol. 6, Melbourne University Press, Carlton, Victoria, 1976, pp. 174–77.

French, E. L., 'Morrison, Alexander (1829–1903)', *ADB*, vol. 5, Melbourne University Press, Carlton, Victoria, 1974, pp. 295–97.

Gill, Peter, 'Corrigan, James (1823–1871)', *ADB*, vol. 3, Melbourne University Press, Carlton, Victoria, 1969, pp. 464–65.

Hall, Fiona, 'Wilding, Frederick (1852–1945)', *DNZB*, vol. 2, pp. 576–577.

Hamer, David, 'Stout, Robert (1844–1930)', *DNZB, Volume Two, 1870–1900*, Bridget Williams Books and Department of Internal Affairs, Wellington, 1993, pp. 484–87.

Hunt, Lyall, 'Hackett, Sir John Winthrop Hackett (1848–1916)', *ADB*, vol. 9, Melbourne University Press, Carlton, Victoria, 1983, pp. 150–53.

Hutley, F. C., 'Cobbett, William Pitt (1853–1919)', *ADB*, vol. 8, 1981, pp. 40–41.

Keith, B. R., 'George Morrison (1830–1898)', *ADB*, vol. 5, 1974, p. 298.

La Nauze, J. A., 'Hearn, William Edward (1826–1888)', *ADB*, vol. 4, Melbourne University Press, Carlton, Victoria, 1972, pp. 371–72.

Lowe, P. G., 'Anderson, John (1820–1897)', *DNZB, Volume One, 1769–1869*, Allen & Unwin and Department of Internal Affairs, Wellington, 1990, pp. 4–5.

Maling, Peter B., 'Haast, Johann Franz Julius von (1822–1887)', *DNZB*, vol. 1, 1990, pp. 167–69.

McKay, K. J., 'Stawell, Florence Melian (1869–1936)', *ADB*, vol. 12, Melbourne University Press, Carlton, Victoria, 1990, pp. 55–56.

Mulvaney, D. J., ' Spencer, Walter Baldwin (1860–1929)', *ADB*, vol. 12, 1990, pp. 33–36.

Rickard, John, 'Higgins, Henry Bournes (1851–1929)', *ADB*, vol. 9, 1983, pp. 285–289.

Roberts, Heather, 'Grossmann, Edith Searle, (1863–1931)', *DNZB*, vol. 2, 1993, pp. 180–81.

Serle, Geoffrey, 'MacFarland, Sir John Henry, (1851–1935)', *ADB*, vol. 10, 1986, pp. 266–67.

Smith, Brian J., 'Dendy, Arthur (1865–1925)', *ADB*, vol. 8, 1981, pp. 279–80.

Thomson, John Mansfield, 'Hill, Alfred Francis (1870–1960)', *DNZB*, vol. 2, pp. 213–15.

Waterhouse, Jill, 'Collier, James (1846–1925)', *ADB*, vol. 8, 1981, pp. 69–70.

Weickhardt, L. W., 'Masson, Sir David Orme (1858–1937)', *ADB*, vol. 10, 1986, pp. 432–35.

Wykes, Olive, 'Morris, Edward Ellis (1843–1902)', *ADB*, vol. 5, 1974, pp. 293–94.

G. Manuscripts

Armstrong, John, 'The *Hereford Times* Desk: Its History and Associations', ms, 1982, HWRO BC97.

Bassett, Marnie, 'Cooling Streams: A Catalyst Paper', November 1969, Flora Marjorie Bassett Papers.

Bassett, Marnie, 'Once Upon a Time: Address to the Lyceum Club', 21 November 1972, Flora Majorie (Marnie) Bassett Papers.

Donnelly, A. T., 'The Late Mr. Frederick Wilding, K. C., Broadcast Tribute, Given from 3YA, Christchurch, on the 13 July, 1945', pp. 1–7, WFP.

Ross, Angus, 'The Macmillan Brown Lectures 1977: New Zealand to 1947 – The Slow Progress of the Favourite Child', typescript, Macmillan Brown Library, University of Canterbury, Christchurch.

Wilding, Frederick, 'Script of a radio broadcast given by Frederick Wilding about William Pember Reeves', 29 November 1937, WFP, 43/194/61 A.

Wilkinson, James R., 'Educational Reminiscences from 1866', Documentary Research Centre, Canterbury Museum, ARC1992.54.

Wilson, David, 'Wilson's School, 1892–1908 and Wirihana School 1909–1927' (Wilson, William and Drusilla ? 1929), ms, Documentary Research Centre, Canterbury Museum, ARC.1900.527, 1130.

H. Unpublished University Theses and Research Essays

Bones, Helen K., 'A Dual Exile: New Zealand and the Colonial Writing World, 1890–1945', PhD thesis, University of Canterbury, 2011.

Catchpole, Julie A., 'The Group', MA thesis, University of Canterbury, 1984.

Doolittle, Megan, '"Missing Fathers": Assembling a History of Fatherhood in Mid-Nineteenth Century England', PhD thesis, University of Essex, 1996.

Doust, Janet, 'English Migrants to Eastern Australia 1815–1860', PhD thesis, Australian National University, 2004.

Gush, Nadia Joanne, 'Cultural Fields of the Canterbury Plains: Women and Cultural Citizenship in Canterbury c 1890–1940', PhD thesis, Victoria University of Wellington, 2007.

Howe, Renate, 'The Wesleyan Church in Victoria, 1855–1901', MA thesis, University of Melbourne, 1965.

McLennan, N., 'From Home and Kindred: English Emigration to Australia 1860–1900', PhD thesis, ANU, 1998.

Pfeil, Helen, 'Raising Colonial Families: The Upper-Middle-Class in Eastern Australia, 1840–1900', PhD thesis, ANU, 2009.

Plumridge, Elizabeth, 'Labour in Christchurch: Community and Consciousness, 1914–1919', MA thesis, University of Canterbury, 1979.

Richardson, Shelley, '"Striving After Better Things": Julia Wilding and the Making of a "New Woman" and a "Noble Gentleman"', MA thesis, University of Canterbury, 1997.

Vincent, G. T., 'Sports and other signs of civilisation in Colonial Canterbury, 1850–1890', PhD thesis, University of Canterbury, 2002.

Woods, Megan, 'Behind Closed Doors: A Study in Elite Canterbury Masculinity 1856–1900', BA (Hons) essay, University of Canterbury, 1995.

Wyse, Stephanie Jessica, 'Gender, Wealth and Margins of Empire: Women's Economic Opportunity in New Zealand Cities, c.1890–1950', PhD thesis, King's College London, University of London, 2008.

Index

www.ingramcontent.com/pod-product-compliance
Lightning Source LLC
Chambersburg PA
CBHW040146270326
41929CB00025B/3387